LITERARY IMPRESS
MODERNIST AES...

Jesse Matz examines the writing of such modernists as Henry James, Joseph Conrad and Virginia Woolf, who used the word "impression" to describe what they wanted their fiction to present. Matz redefines literary Impressionism, focusing on the way that impressions destroy standard perceptual distinctions between thinking and sensing, believing and suspecting. He argues that these writers favored not immediate subjective sense, but rather a mode that would mediate perceptual distinctions. Just as impressions fall somewhere between thought and sense, Impressionist fiction occupies the middle ground between opposite ways of engaging with the world. Reconceiving Impressionist fiction in these terms, this wide-ranging study addresses the problems of perception and representation that occupied the great Modernist writers.

JESSE MATZ is Assistant Professor of English at Harvard University. He has published articles on Walter Pater, T. E. Hulme, E. M. Forster, and V. S. Naipaul.

LITERARY IMPRESSIONISM AND MODERNIST AESTHETICS

JESSE MATZ

Assistant Professor
Department of English and American Literature and Language
Harvard University

CAMBRIDGE
UNIVERSITY PRESS

CAMBRIDGE UNIVERSITY PRESS
Cambridge, New York, Melbourne, Madrid, Cape Town, Singapore, São Paulo

Cambridge University Press
The Edinburgh Building, Cambridge CB2 2RU, UK

Published in the United States of America by Cambridge University Press, New York

www.cambridge.org
Information on this title: www.cambridge.org/9780521803526

First published 2001
This digitally printed first paperback version 2006

A catalogue record for this publication is available from the British Library

Library of Congress Cataloguing in Publication data
Matz, Jesse.
Literary impressionism and modernist aesthetics / Jesse Matz.
p.   cm.
Includes bibliographical references (p.) and index.
ISBN 0 521 80352 7
1. English fiction – 20th century – History and criticism.
2. Impressionism in literature.
3. Proust, Marcel, 1871–1922. A la recherche du temps perdu.
4. English fiction – 19th century – History and criticism.
5. Modernism (Literature) – Great Britain.
6. Modernism (Literature) – France.
7. Aesthetics, Modern.   I. Title.
PR888.I57 M37 2001
820.9′11–dc21   2001025134

ISBN-13 978-0-521-80352-6 hardback
ISBN-10 0-521-80352-7 hardback

ISBN-13 978-0-521-03301-5 paperback
ISBN-10 0-521-03301-2 paperback

For Rose Marie Laster

Contents

Acknowledgments   *page*   viii

Introduction   Proust's deathless analogy   1

1   Impressions of modernity   12

2   Pater's homoerotic impression   53

3   The woman of genius   79
    "Call down Dolly"   79
    James and the woman of genius   85
    Hardy's defensive impression   120

4   The distant laborer   130
    Proust in Eulalie's bedroom   130
    Conrad's distant laborer   138
    Ford's peasant cabman   155

5   Woolf's phenomenological impression   174

6   Three Impressionist allegories   207

Conclusion   Mrs. Brown and Mrs. Bell   239

Notes   250
Index   275

Acknowledgments

I owe greatest thanks to two pairs of advisors: Paul Fry and Mark Wollaeger, who supervised my dissertation; and Phil Fisher and Helen Vendler, who gave me the advice necessary to turn the dissertation into a book. Paul Fry inspired everything good in the pages that follow here; indeed, every fruitful "seed" – to use Henry James's word for that from which suggestive ideas grow – turned up in the path of conversation with him. Mark Wollaeger taught me most of what I know about Modernism and gave me vital support and guidance even after moving halfway across the country. Philip Fisher was a great source of light, wisdom, and hope in the darker days of junior scholarship, as was Helen Vendler, whose bracing aptitudes and solicitudes helped me to decide how and why to work.

I want to thank those who read drafts of the book at various stages: Margaret Homans, David Southward, Rebecca Laroche, Patricia Klindienst, Alexander Welsh, Tyrus Miller, David Bromwich, Robert Kiely, Jed Esty, Doug Mao, Bianca Calabresi, Jim Carson, Shuchi Kapila, Jonathan Warren, Kevis Goodman, Daniel Albright, Sophia Padnos, and, especially, Ian Duncan, whose help was truly heroical.

I also want to thank those with whom I had helpful conversations: particularly, Lawrence Buell, who helped me plan strategies, and Lawrence Rainey, James Engell, Jonah Siegel, Tamar Katz, Tom Otten, Margery Sokoloff, Richard Dellamora, Bob Caserio,, Ruth Yeazell, Richard Brodhead, Matt Greenfield, Bill Jewett, Annabel Patterson, David Marshall, Marc Micale, and Fellows at the Whitney Humanities Center.

I had great technical help from Diane Jowdy, Carol Forney, Jay Boggis, Katherine O'Neil, Lara Heimert, and of course Ray Ryan, my wonderful editor at Cambridge, Rachel de Wachter, and Linda Woodward.

And then, finally, the money, and the family: without financial and institutional support from the Whitney Humanities Center, National Endowment for the Humanities, Harvard University, and the Huntington Library, I could never have had time to write; and without my parents, my brothers and my sister, and Jeff Bowman, I could never have had the resolve.

Introduction *Proust's deathless analogy*

"Fiction *is* an impression": so said Henry James, and many others, from Hardy to Woolf, from Pater to Conrad to Proust. But they did not mean that fiction should keep to the sketch, the fragment, the moment, the surface, the sense – that it should be "impressionistic." Such connotations come from painting, where impressions are momentary brushstrokes, or from philosophy, where impressions are primary sensations. The literary Impressionists meant that fiction should locate itself where we "have an impression": not in sense, nor in thought, but in the feeling that comes between; not in the moment that passes, nor in the decision that lasts, but in the intuition that lingers. If "fiction is an impression" it *mediates* opposite perceptual moments. It does not choose surfaces and fragments over depths and wholes but makes surfaces show depths, make fragments suggest wholes, and devotes itself to the undoing of such distinctions. To get in the impression not just sense perception but sense that is thought, appearances that are real, suspicions that are true and parts that are whole – this was the "total" aspiration of the Impressionist writer. The Impressionist writer sought perceptual totality, at a time in which fiction seemed perhaps best able to claim it. When the Impressionists took it up, fiction had proven its link to life and was ready to enter the realm of art. It had been fantastic and natural, had done social life on a massive scale and scaled itself down to individual psychologies. And to this breadth of interest it designated a perceptual correlate, making many agree, with James, that fiction is both most vital and most artful when it is an impression; with Conrad that an "impression conveyed through the senses" might join men's hearts with their worlds, and with Pater, Proust, and Woolf that fiction's Impressionism is even the key to success in *life*.

As an impression, however, fiction was nothing very certain, and so its "total" aspirations came with second thoughts. For its resolutions often seemed like compromises, collapses, or strange combinations. Joining sensation and thought might sensationalize thought or dematerialize sense, and depth of appearance might become depth of falsehood, or at least didactic description. Even worse, the ambiguity that undoes distinction might efface the moments of writing, and leave the Impressionist without a way to work.

What principally gives rise to these doubts about the impression's totality is the force of distinctions that militate against totality at another level. Perceptual moments are never simply or exclusively perceptual; rather, they come associated with sociocultural "moments" – with the distinctions of social life. The distinction between sensations and ideas (as Marxists dreaming of totalities have noted) corresponds to the distinction between classes, or (as feminists since Wollstonecraft have noted) to the distinction between women and men. If the impression promised totality, it did so against the will of distinctions dividing high from low, male from female, civilized from savage – distinctions at least as dear as the dream of perceptual unity.

How the impression entailed such social mixture, and with what result for Impressionism, is the subject of this book. Its first concern, to redefine Impressionism in literature in terms of the theory of the impression and its diverse mediations, leads to a second: to reckon with those collateral mediations that recast Impressionism into new social and political roles.

Taking the impression's double totality as a point of departure from which to revisit the problem of Impressionism in literature, this book intends, finally, to reconfigure Impressionism's cultural history. If Impressionism is a troubled theory of perceptual totality, it is important to the history of modernity, intervening (historically) between romantic unities and modernist fragmentation, and (conceptually) between utopianism and social critique. Such intervention makes it very different from mere pictorial embellishment, for it puts Impressionism in fiction's best possible place between the advent of modernity and its latest alienations.

Through his window at Balbec, the resort that sets the scene for Proust's *In a Budding Grove* (*À l'ombre des jeunes filles en fleurs*), young Marcel sees a changing picture. When he returns to his room to dress for dinner in the early days of the season, his window shows a sea sharply lined by daylight. As the days grow shorter, the sun shines more diffusely; the window highlights a violet sky and lets in light that runs livid reflections across the glass panels of the room's mahogany bookcases. To Marcel, these paneled reflections seem like old reliquary paintings dismantled and hung side by side in a modern gallery. Sometimes these separate paintings make a "Cloud Study," a set of pictures of the same sky caught in the different tones of different hours. Sometimes there is uniformity, as the sea fills the whole window, raised up by the sky's matching blue. A few weeks later, the sun sets even before Marcel returns to his room, so that the window shows only a band of red, or, a bit earlier, a sky like pink salmon over a sea of cold blue mullet. These various seascapes come one after another, but they also accumulate, so that throwing himself onto his bed at season's end Marcel finds himself surrounded on all sides by every possible picture of the sea.

After dinner downstairs, he sometimes drives drunk to the casino of a nearby hotel. Alcohol stretches his nerves and opens him wide to intense momentary sensations. Usually so introverted, he finds that drunkenness helps him to "[cling] body and soul to the scent of a woman at the next table, to the politeness of the waiters, to the contours of the waltz that the band was playing."[1] He becomes "glued to the sensation of the moment, with no extension beyond its limits, nor any object other than not to be separated from it" (II: 540). In this state – this state in which "everything is reduced to appearances and exists only as a function of our sublime self" (II: 540) – he forgets all other preoccupations, enthralled by the "extraordinary intensity" of immediate sensuous experience.

Is this literary Impressionism? So it seems: pictorial descriptions of shifting light and color, subjective accounts of sensuous experience, transmission of immediate and evanescent feelings – these are literary Impressionism's specialties. Impressionists, we say, convey intense momentary perceptions, pitching sensibility to heights sublime enough to reduce the world to apparition, but the power they thereby get to "make us *see*" does not show us much more than "reduced" appearances. Impressionists reproduce all the lush kaleidoscopic beauty of Marcel's motile seascape, but this amounts to little more than drunken sights and sounds. So Marcel's Balbec experiences seem Impressionist, in style and in limitation, insofar as Impressionism records unextended sensation and the passing picture.

But Proust himself has other names for Marcel's pictorial and sensuous experiences. Of his gluing to momentary sensations, Proust writes, "inebriation brings about for an hour or two a state of subjective idealism, pure phenomenalism" (II: 540). "Idealism" and "phenomenalism" are Proust's names for this clinging to pure appearances – reserving "Impressionism," it would seem, to name something else. In his account of the pictures that flood his room at Balbec, Proust recalls that he was too distracted to "receive any really profound impressions of beauty" (II: 524). "As often as not," he writes, "they were, indeed, only pictures [des images]." Only pictures, rather than profound impressions: it would be more accurate to call Marcel's experience here "pictorialist" – and once again let "Impressionist" stand for something else.

Marcel recalls that his phenomenalism lacks "extension." He tells us that his pictorialism lacks "connexion": he remembers the pictures at Balbec as "no more than a selection, made afresh every day, of paintings which were shown quite arbitrarily in the place in which I happened to be and without having any necessary connexion with that place" (II: 525). Here there is no "depth behind the colour of things," no extension beyond the phenomenal (II: 524). Proust distinguishes the arbitrary picture from the "profound impression" it fails to make.

What then, if not pictorial description or subjective sensuous report, is Impressionism?[2]

Impressionism is what occurs when Marcel (or the narrator) *does* receive "profound impressions" – moments that define the very form and focus of Proust's *recherche*.[3] Impressionism occurs, for example, in *Time Regained* when Marcel steps over uneven paving stones. He feels an obscure happiness, a pleasure at returning to a past time in Venice, something like the pleasure brought to him by the taste of the madeleine. Determined in this case, however, not to let the pleasure pass unknown, Marcel prolongs his staggering, hoping that tripping again will reproduce the pleasure, and indeed finds that it leads him onward toward a theory. "Seize me as I pass if you can, and try to solve the riddle of happiness which I set you" (VI: 256): what speaks here is the impression, and the answer to the riddle is Proust's theory of Impressionism.

When Marcel seizes the impression, he discovers lost sensations "waiting in their place," and finds that the pleasure of doing so somehow restores joy to life. But he does not know *why* this experience of two moments at once has "given [him] a joy which

was like a certainty and which sufficed, without any other proof, to
make death a matter of indifference" (vi: 257). He does what he can
to prolong the experience, and other impressions come: wiping his
mouth with a napkin returns him to Balbec; unfolding the napkin
unfolds "the plumage of an ocean green and blue like the tail of a
peacock" (vi: 259). Marcel finds himself enjoying "not merely these
colours but a whole instant of my life on whose summit they rested."
"Extensions" and "connections" now proliferate. What marks the
moment is its way of connecting two sensations – the two "unfold-
ings" – and its way consequently of sinking the present into the
depth of a lost "instant." Marcel only now truly enjoys Balbec. In
this enjoyment he gives a good definition of the impression. The
instant he now experiences is one "freed from what is necessarily
imperfect in external perception, pure and disembodied" (vi: 259). It
is not the kind of "external perception" that preoccupied him years
ago at Balbec, but some pure internal experience found in the
common abstract essence of two different moments; it is not
phenomenal or pictorial, but the internal essence that two pictures
or phenomena might have in common. It bridges varieties and
moments of experience.

    The impression is an experience freed from external imperfection,
attached to its true counterpart in another time and place, and, in
that connection, a paradise. Proust means "paradise" literally: the
impression brings immortality. An impression is an experience of a
present moment that is also an experience of a distant one, "so that
the past was made to encroach upon the present and I was made to
doubt whether I was in the one or the other" (vi: 262). The
impression is therefore "extra-temporal," it puts Marcel "outside
time," and gives him the power to "rediscover days that were long
past, the Time that was Lost." It is the "miracle of an analogy" that
dispels the threat of death. When an impression is in progress,
Marcel no longer worries about death, because the impression's
miraculous analogy finds something "common both to the past and
to the present" which "is much more essential than either of them"
and robs the word "death" of its "meaning" (vi: 263). Insofar as
cheating death is his goal, Proust owes his success to the impression's
deathless analogy.

    Impressionism is therefore not simply vivid pictures or intense
sensations, but Proust's larger aesthetic enterprise. Pictures and
sensations certainly participate in it, but as part of the larger process,

which exploits the impression's strange perceptual status to extend, connect, and analogize the moments that lead from pictures and sense to meaning. Impressions may begin in sense, but once the work of the whole *Recherche* is done, they fully cover the range of life from sense to the full apotheosis of mind and heart. As Proust finally defines it, "Only the impression, however trivial its material may seem to be, however faint its traces, is a criterion of truth and deserves for that reason to be apprehended by the mind, for the mind, if it succeeds in extracting this truth, can by the impression and by nothing else be brought to a state of greater perfection and given a pure joy" (VI: 275–76). In the case of the paving stones, the madeleine, and, by extension, countless other moments, an impression is that unit of experience that seems trivial, faint, or superficial, but is nevertheless a "criterion of truth" which, when well apprehended, perfects the mind and its pleasures.

Unlike other terms for aspects of perception and understanding, the impression has no location, but conveys perception and understanding from one point to the next, like a miraculous analogy among distinct perceptual moments. It is neither sensation nor idea; it combines present and past experience, connects the mind to the body, and, in such mediations, attains to immediate illumination more lastingly meaningful than the most timeless concept.

Proust was far from alone in trying for the impression's rhetorical dynamism. Many writers from Walter Pater to Virginia Woolf sought to "know one's own impression as it really is" and proceed onward from there to the best aesthetic judgment and to a life well lived.[4] They thought fiction was "in its broadest definition a personal, a direct impression of life."[5] Like Proust, these writers found in the impression a metaphor for perception through which to aspire to "greater perfection," if not "pure joy."

They also found any number of questions about the metaphor's rhetorical behavior and its practical implications: what, first of all, *is* an impression, if neither sensation nor idea? What exactly is its perceptual status? How is it received, and how transmitted in literary form? And what process intervenes, through which the writer "apprehends" it? It is one thing to aspire to perceptual totality; it is another to theorize it sufficiently to enable some real activity. The Impressionist writers always found that passage through theory to literary act a problem. Walter Pater, for example, may have seen the "single sharp impression" as life's quintessence, but he had no clear or consistent theory about it. It is "single" and "sharp," but then also something "dissipated" in groups, and "unstable, flickering, inconsistent" (*Renaissance* 187–88). It sometimes has the immediate materiality of a sensation and sometimes the removed discretion of an idea; it is sometimes a focus of Epicurean confidence in the adequacy of human perception, and sometimes a focus of skepticism. This uncertainty becomes definitive; diverse questions, rather than single answers, become key: where between sense and intellect does the impression happen? Does Impressionist experience flow and flicker, or does it strike sharply? Is the Impressionist's world one in which truth is available to perception, or one in which its depths are dark? Is Impressionist experience a matter of receptivity or discretion? Impressionists perpetually give different tentative answers to these questions and then dramatize the controversy that results. In this tendency, the Impressionist temperament worries itself into prominence and discovers the source of its ingenuity.

Notice what such ambiguity does in Proust's account of the larger process through which his *recherche* develops. He describes the impression's value: "For the truths which the intellect apprehends directly in the world of full and unimpeded light have something less profound, less necessary than those which life communicates to us against our will in an impression which is material because it enters us through the senses but yet has a spiritual meaning which it is possible for us to extract" (VI: 273). In this one sentence the impression does many different things. Proust explains its power to pertain, profoundly and necessarily (and with the "connexion" Marcel's pictorial experience lacks), to the real world, a power that comes through a combination of materiality, obscurity, and disruption of human agency. The impression commands attention, grabbing us before our thinking selves get in the way, and delivers life itself; from this sign of life we can extract the "spiritual" meaning that makes life worthwhile and makes art possible. But where and how does this spiritual meaning come in? It is the point of the *recherche* to answer this question, but what kind of answer does it give? Ambiguity surrounds the process through which the impression "enters through the senses," and then obtains to spiritual meaning. It is not clear why the intellect apprehends directly, in "unimpeded light," while impressions, better known for immediacy or superficiality, enter less directly and more deeply. The impression matters because it is not an idea – not a product of intellectualizing, and therefore more authentic – but also because it is not a sensation – not merely a visual image or sensuous phenomenon. It is not concrete, for it is not brute or basic, and entails generalization; it seems abstract, since it finds the common pattern of different instances; but then again it lacks the detachment of an abstraction. It is, in Proust's words, "real without being actual, ideal without being abstract" (vi: 264). It mediates these standard oppositions, but inconsistently, so that extracting meaning from an impression can only be an unpredictable and exhilarating occupation. Proust can commit himself to "this contemplation of the essence of things," but he must perpetually wonder "how, by what means, was I to do this?" (vi: 269).

The confusion has benefits, manifest in the charm of the para-doxes it produces. Something real but not actual, something ideal but not abstract, has always been fiction's dream. But the confusion also has its hazards; with the exhilaration comes doubt. Proust writes that a writer "goes astray" when "he has not the strength to force himself to make an impression pass through all the successive states that will culminate in its fixation, its expression" (vi: 278–79). Does *he* have the strength? If the impression's material or sensuous aspect requires vitality, will he have the strength to manage it? If the succeeding states are not clearly marked, can any amount of force guide the impression through? Such questions come up explicitly at the end of the *recherche*, as Proust wonders if he has waited too long to start writing. And such questions come up implicitly throughout the work as Proust wonders what perceptual acuities the impression requires. Should an impressionist have strong sensory receptivity, or deep "spiritual" capacities, or acute powers of intellectual extraction – or, if possible, all at once? Collapsing familiar distinctions, the impression demands new powers and new strengths of will.

Virginia Woolf, too, fears that she lacks the strength to force the impression through; Joseph Conrad at times equates such strength with savagery, which he would prefer (paradoxically) to disclaim. But we owe the best work by these and other writers to the impression's dubious demands. When Proust, for example, worries about his power at once to receive and to extract meaning from his impres-sions, he makes the plan that gives his work its famous scope. The conflicting demands of receptivity and judgment become functions of experience and retrospection: a former self first receives an impression, and a later self receives its later counterpart and does the work of retrospective analysis. In other words, the search for "lost time" itself answers the demand of Impressionism's "successive states" – as Proust spreads those states out over the broad temporal expanse of his work. In Woolf and Conrad such tactics must make us grateful for the Impressionist's uncertainty. In Woolf, it gives us a number of metafictional meditations on the process through which the writer of "modern fiction" confronts the stuff of "life itself." In Conrad, it gives us insight into the epistemological basis of the confrontation between the civilized and the savage.

First, the impression solves old aesthetic problems; then, the ambiguity of its solutions causes productive uncertainties, recreating old aesthetic problems in new forms. Proust reconfigures the old opposition between sense and intellect as a collaboration between past and present selves, and this self-division appears in the work of every literary Impressionist. And just as Proust makes Impressionist mediation the work of *collaborating* selves, his fellow Impressionists imagine some collaborative relationship, some juncture through which they can have *both* the impression's inspiring mediation *and* some safer division of perceptual categories. Most often, these collaborative relationships join types who best typify the elements of the impression's synthesis. The Impressionist writer tends to cast him- or herself in the role of the intellectual, abstract mind; for his or her counterpart – for the sensuous, concrete element – the Impressionist tends to draw on cultural stereotypes. He or she singles out someone whose social role makes that person a likely source of material vitality. For the "strength" necessary to launch the impression into its series of successive states, the Impressionist writer turns to women and the lower classes, engineering the impression's mediation through their greater apparent sensuous or nonintellectual receptivity. What Proust gains from his meeting of past and present selves, Ford Madox Ford gets from calling upon a peasant cabman, a figure whose impressionability is a figural boost to Ford's own Impressionist discretion. For Conrad, in the Preface to *The Nigger of the "Narcissus"*, this boost comes from a laborer working in the distance; for Woolf, it comes from "Mrs. Brown"; for James, it is a "woman of genius" who, in "The Art of Fiction," helps James explain how the literary impression runs its full perceptual range.

These figures personify the attempt to have the impression's unity while holding onto old distinctions. Impressionist collaboration is a strange compromise – a strange way to have things both ways – and,

like any such compromise, it leads to more trouble. But because of
the way it conforms to social cliché, this trouble becomes, like the
compromise in Proust, a spur to creativity. It gives Impressionist
fiction more generally some of its most compellingly self-conscious
plots and structures, as Impressionism becomes a focus of *allegorical*
revision. Henry James, for example, for whom the novel *is* an
impression, is unsure how to combine the receptivity and discretion
that impressions seem simultaneously to demand. So he tends to
make full experience a matter of collaboration between the intellectual connoisseur and the receptive "woman of genius." Dissatis-
fied with that collaboration, James gives it the revisionary attention
of plot; his collaborating selves become allegorical figures, as in *The
Portrait of a Lady* (1881), where the problem of marrying brilliant
female receptivity to exploitative male sophistication comes to a
crisis. That novel's bad marriage between Isabel Archer and Gilbert
Osmond becomes the allegorical version of Impressionist collaboration, through which James reconsiders his own aesthetic theory.
Similarly, Woolf revisits her Impressionism in *Mrs. Dalloway* (1925),
where Mrs. Brown becomes two different characters and gets the
revisionary treatment of feminism and elitism alike. In other writers
as well, Impressionism extends to allegorical revision, as each writer
lets the questions raised by the impression give structure to the
fictions it motivates.

Proust writes that each of us has within us an "inner book of
unknown symbols," a book that only we can read, and the translation of which is the only valid basis for art. This book gets its claim
to significance from the nature of its relation to reality: "This book,
more laborious to decipher than any other, is also the only one which
has been dictated to us by reality, the only one of which the
'impression' has been printed by reality itself" (VI: 275). In other
words, our deep inner experiences and perceptions are impressions
printed obscurely by reality; it takes enormous inner scrutiny to
decipher them; and our best books are those that decipher and
transmit these impressions in art. "Impression" appears here in
quotes because of a pun on printing: the best books are those that
reality itself prints, as if there were no interference between that
printing and what we see on the page. This of course is the dream of
the literary Impressionist – this production of a book which bypasses
all the interference that our perceptual categories place between
reality and writing. But if the impression inspires that dream it also

keeps it from coming true. For this impression starts to fail as soon as it starts to work: the impression printed by reality's press upon us is hard to decipher because it is alien to us. It prints in a foreign language. The immediate impression takes time to decipher, and so it is not effectively immediate; the immediacy comes only after the work of deciphering, only after some mediation occurs. Just short of paradox, this problem perfectly epitomizes the Impressionist book. Wanting immediately to record reality's impressions, the Impressionist book ends up featuring the limitations of our figures for aesthetic perception, and therefore becomes the record of its own undoing.

As the record of that record, this book returns to a familiar problem – the problem thinkers have sought to solve ever since the "aesthetic" emerged to mediate between human reason and alien nature, between the forms of thought and the content of the world. Moreover the problem is familiarly that of Modernism itself, which famously entails a bid for immediacy which ends up only featuring the by-products of its failure to get it. But if the problem is familiar, the impression's part in it is not. Why so many writers sought to render impressions, and how the effort continues that of early aesthetic and romantic theory; how the impression summed up early Modernism's aesthetic hopes, but could not bear the weight of its sociocultural expectations; how it gave way to Modernism properly, and determined so many of Modernism's plots and themes: these things remain to be explained. It remains to show the impression for the impresario it was.

CHAPTER I

Impressions of modernity

I "WHAT WAS LITERARY IMPRESSIONISM?"

"Impressionism," now the name for the most popular form of modern art, originally meant nothing. When Louis Leroy coined the term in his satirical review of Monet's *Impression: Soleil Levant* (1872), he knew it would sound absurd. "Impression" would connote transient, insubstantial, passive sensation; "ism" would imply some systematic, doctrinal, activist idea; the compound would make no sense, and its meaninglessness would neatly publicize Monet's defects. Leroy might have known, however, that the nonsense would not last. By the time of the first Impressionist exhibition, "sensation" had already become aesthetic doctrine, one that, together with the acceptance bred by familiarity, quickly effaced "Impressionism's" self-contradiction. Its absurdity was forgotten well before the century turned. The term became if anything too meaningful, and soon had to bear the very different refusal of the "post" that English art-criticism prefixed to it.[1]

When "Impressionism" is *literary*, however, its incoherence remains. Literature, it seems, means ideas, reflection, and judgment, and so it has no place for the merely perceptual impression. "Literary Impressionism" has therefore entered literary history only under suspicion. As a name for late nineteenth- and early twentieth-century subjective writing, it has enjoyed only uneasy legitimacy; for the most part, Leroy's sense of Impressionism's incongruity has prevailed. Impressionism has lost a place in literary history to the belief that literature and Impressionism rule each other out and that to admit their juncture would reduce literature's intelligence to mere sense.

So "Impressionist literature" still sounds like a contradiction in terms, despite the fact that it might have sounded *redundant* to many late nineteenth- and early twentieth-century writers and critics. To many Anglo-American writers, "impression" meant not non-literary sensation, but the very instance of aesthetic representation. The term is key to a series of pivotal statements of literary doctrine. It makes its first relevant appearance in Walter Pater's Preface to *Studies in the History of the Renaissance* (1873), which made the effort to "know one's impression as it really is" the key to aesthetic criticism.[2] It appears in Henry James's "The Art of Fiction" (1884), which influenced much twentieth-century fiction and criticism with the claim that "a novel is in its broadest definition a personal, direct impression of life."[3] Thomas Hardy agreed that "a novel is an impression"; Joseph Conrad made the impression central to his famous endeavor, described in his Preface to *The Nigger of the "Narcissus"*, to "make you *see*," and Virginia Woolf called modern fiction an effort to render the "myriad impressions" that fall upon the mind.[4] In these uses of the term – and in others by Vernon Lee, Oscar Wilde, Hamlin Garland, May Sinclair, T. E. Hulme, and Elizabeth Bowen[5] – the impression is by no means any merely sensuous, superficial, or insubstantial perception. As these writers invoke it, the impression is nothing less than a name for the aesthetic moment itself, a new sign for the old bridge between art and life. Like aesthetic experience, it pitches consciousness between sense and reason. Hardly a threat to literature's intelligence, it gives the literary mind new links to life.[6]

This impression has of course not gone undetected. Criticism has recognized it, and recognized the Impressionism it entails. Michael Levenson and H. Peter Stowell have urged us to see Impressionism as a turning-point momentous enough to be "the incipient moment of literary modernism,"[7] and together with Ian Watt, Fredric Jameson, Maria Elisabeth Kronegger, and John Carlos Rowe, have proven Impressionism fundamental and pervasive.[8] They describe an Impressionism that begins in the Empiricisms of Locke and Hume, finds early expression in romantic theories of the imagination, takes nominal inspiration from Impressionist painting, matures in Pater's epicurean sensibility and James's theory of consciousness, and reaches its apotheosis in fiction by James, Conrad, Ford, Stephen Crane, and Marcel Proust. To these writers, critics variously claim, Impressionism meant rendering life as it really seemed to individual subjective experience. It meant making fiction "plunge into consciousness" and fuse "the transcendent subjectivity of romanticism and the omniscient objectivity of

realism" toward a kind of utopian compensation for modern alienation.[9] Impressionism seeks generally to suggest atmosphere and
mood; it subordinates plot, fixes moments, fragments form, and
intensifies affective response; it fuses subject and object, finds truth in
appearances, and evokes the dynamic feeling – the "flow, energy,
vibrancy" – of life itself.[10] Comparing these powers to aspects of the
philosophies of William James, Henri Bergson, and Edmund
Husserl, critics have called Impressionism a literary phenomenology,
attributing to it the advent of modernism, the *nouveau roman*, and
ultimately the style we read most often today.

Even so, doubt about literary Impressionism persists, and most
often prevails, disenchanting even those critics charmed by the
impression's effects. The first essay to call attention to Impressionism
in literature, for example, stops well short of real endorsement:
Ferdinand Brunetière's "L'Impressionisme dans le roman" (1879)
concludes its appreciative account of Daudet's "impressionist" style
with regret that Daudet only presents "apparances," "la surface
ondoyante," and is therefore not "maître absolument de sa
plume."[11] Joseph Conrad, too, had two faces about the style so often
attributed to him. On December 1, 1897, he wrote Stephen Crane, to
praise Crane's writing: "Your method is fascinating. You are a
complete Impressionist. The illusions of life come out of your hand
without a flaw."[12] Four days later, Conrad wrote with tempered
enthusiasm to Edward Garnett that Crane was "*the only* impressionist
and *only* an impressionist" – his writing "concise, connected, never
very deep."[13] Ezra Pound was also of two minds, calling Ford Madox
Ford "the father or at least the shepherd of English Impressionist
writers," but then writing, "I do not mean that one should swallow
the Impressionist manner whole or without due discrimination," and
finally dismissing literary Impressionism out of hand: "Impressionism belongs in paint, it is of the eye."[14]

Such doubt grows as it approaches our contemporary moment. In
1968, a "Symposium in Literary Impressionism" found Impressionism everywhere, and yet effectively concluded with a recommen-
dation in favor of "dropping *impressionism* and *impressionist* . . . from
the literary vocabulary."[15] In 1990, Michael Fried treated "impressionism" in Conrad, Crane, and Norris despite the fact that Fried
remained "unpersuaded by the many attempts that have been made
to define that concept."[16] Putting Impressionism in scare-quotes,
Fried finds punctuational shorthand for the ambivalence that criti-

cism has felt since Brunetière – an ambivalence that has most recently compelled William Gass to recognize the questionable diversity of "Ford's Impressionisms."[17]

Current accounts of literary Impressionism continue to worry, with Louis Leroy, that the impression can constitute no *ism*, even as others claim it constitutes Modernism itself and much that came before and after. To the question, "what was literary Impressionism?" there has therefore been a range of answers. Some confidently equate Impressionism and Phenomenology; others less ambitiously give Impressionism an Empiricist basis, or more diffidently connect Impressionist writing to Impressionist painting, or skeptically observe the lack of fit between perceptual impressions and literary ideas. On some accounts, Impressionism was in literature what it was in painting – representation of intense and evanescent visual effects with emphasis on the ways that color and light subjectively appear. On other accounts, it was a Lockean belief that consciousness begins in sense, or a belated romantic theory of the imagination, or another name for Aestheticism. Some critics want to limit Impressionism to the pictorial effects of a handful of authors; to others, it identifies everything from Flaubert's narrative style to Virginia Woolf's visual effects to Sartre's moods of existential isolation, joining Positivism and Vitalism, blending the Epicureanism of Proust with the skepticism of Conrad, and making bedfellows of Pater and Chekhov. And this range of answers extends to two extreme refusals even to ask the question: some would not ask what literary Impressionism *was*, believing either that it still *is* the way literature is written or that it never really *was* a literary mode at all.[18]

Such lack of consensus – what one critic has called a "critical chaos" – might finally just prove "literary Impressionism" meaningless.[19] It might explain why our dictionaries of literary terms stress the word's "vagueness" and allow it only to stand for a "tendency."[20] But what if Impressionism's tendency toward definitional vagueness is itself definitive? What if we take seriously the possibility that Impressionism covers everyone from Locke to Sartre, and elicits everything from veneration to dismissal, because of the *range* of the *impression itself*?

What is an impression? In everyday parlance, it is a feeling, an inchoate sense of things, an untested belief at once tentative and convincing. When we speak of "having an impression" we refer to a hunch, an intuition, or a belief that is partial but comprehensive, a product at once of caprice and discretion; "taking impressions," as people used to do when traveling or looking at art, similarly means making incomplete or passive observations that nevertheless convince. Such impressions are superficial but have their own kind of depth, so that we trust *first* impressions more than many of the estimations that follow before judgment comes; we wait for an impression's correction, but expect its vindication. An impression is personal, but universal – subjective, but not therefore wholly idiosyncratic – and falls somewhere between analytic scrutiny and imaginative invention.

This in-betweenness is essential. An impression is never simply a feeling, a thought, or a sensation. It partakes, rather, of a mode of experience that is neither sensuous nor rational, neither felt nor thought, but somewhere in between. Belonging to none of these categories, an impression similarly belongs to no one theoretical way of thinking. In Empiricism, impression means sensation, but also perception, and feeling, and incipient idea; it connotes an initial printing, but also a subsequent traceless flux. In romanticism, an impression is "the highest form of fancy" but then also an empiricist fallacy, and in Impressionist painting it evokes both soft-focus and rigorous color-science.[21] The impression appears at once, in the 1890s, in empirical psychology (transmitted by physical mechanism) and aesthetic culture (the property of Wilde's "temperament exquisitely susceptible to beauty").[22] In the twentieth century, the impression is phenomenology's much-valued unit of primordial experience, but also what Irving Babbitt in 1906 called the essence of irresponsible criticism – the essence of what journalists now call the "impressionistic." Philosophically important, snubbed in journalism, the impression is nothing if not metamorphic. Gass has recently listed no fewer than ten definitions, and, implying endless interaction among them, recognized endless definitional variation.[23] Impressions are empirical, imaginative, and painterly; they are everything from visual to emotional to rational; and even within such categories and discourses, they connote both the imprint that lasts and the feeling that passes, error and insight, authenticity and irresponsibility.

Obviously, this account of what Meyer Schapiro calls the impression's "confusing richness" could go on and on.[24] The point here, however, is not to contribute to the "critical chaos", but to point out its source and value. The impression's variation confuses, but the confusion, blurring disciplinary distinctions, forms of judgment, and perceptual moments, has productive results. Lumping together empirical psychology and aestheticism, confusing the difference between thoughts and feelings, erasing the line between superficial appearances and deep knowledge, the impression brings art richer connections. It promises *mediation*, and thereby to release art into places it could not otherwise go. A proper definition of literary Impressionism needs to recognize the fact that good ambiguity has followed bad – to see Impressionism, in other words, as this positive power to undefine. Whereas other definitions have tried to go with a single interpretive scheme, or to distinguish among the impression's various meanings, an accurate definition will make the impression's variety itself definitive.

But such a definition must also recognize that the literary Impressionist never fully commits to the impression's definitive variety. To Pater, James, Woolf, and the rest, impressions play a crucial *mediatory* role, standing somewhere between sensations and ideas, and likewise undoing other basic oppositions. But such mediations happen only incompletely, haphazardly, and uncertainly. Whereas the Impressionist author sets out to implement that mediatory impression, he or she falls into uncertainty about its perceptual status – feeling a version of the same doubt through which Louis Leroy coined "Impressionism" in the first place. Exactly where does the impression fall between sensation and idea? Unsure, how does the literary artist prepare to receive and transmit it? What sensory capacities, or imaginative synthesis, or rational discretion, does the impression require? Might it render intellectual habits – and valued literary tradition – obsolete? Might it not after all entail a sensualist debasement of the writer's mind or require a sensitivity of which that mind may not be capable? Are the impression's mediatory feelings amenable to representation, or are they, because indeterminate, essentially ineffable? Are they atomic (fragmentary) or fluid (unified) – fleeting (as the plural form suggests) or deeply marked? Is mediation an occasion for epicurean delight, or skeptical regret, and does it happen in the service of a kind of empiricist realism, an idealist transcendence, or pragmatic experience? These questions, implicit everywhere the impression is invoked, call for further definitional variety. And they require *not* that we define Impressionism as an aesthetic that ranges from the empirical to the ideal, from the pictorial to the ethical, and the traditional to the iconoclastic, but rather that we see Impressionism as a problematic tendency to range

– to try for the impression's many mediations, to express confusion about them, and to produce writing on the basis of this ambivalence.

Accounts of Impressionism have, here and there, recognized the theoretical problem in question, but not making it *definitive*, they make it a source of further confusion.[25] In such accounts, the poles of uncertainty become the far-flung boundaries of Impressionism's aesthetic territory. Rather than treating uncertainty as a structural problem, most accounts treat it as a range of possibilities; they turn dilemmas into options. They define Impressionism, for example, as the result of everything from empiricist realism to a kind of symbolist idealism, rather than recognizing that above all it remains indecisive about these very ways of coming to conclusions about the impression's nature. What typifies this problem is a tendency, in the best accounts of literary Impressionism, to conflate Impressionism and the philosophical tradition of Phenomenology.[26] Phenomenology cements the impression's kind of mediation. It is the style of thinking in which old opposites – sensations and ideas, surfaces and depths, subject and object – finally come together, in a perceptual theory that can encompass such mediations. Claiming that Impressionism reaches this same full theorization, critics have been only half right: Impressionism does aspire to something like the phenomenological synthesis, but without phenomenology's inclination to define it clearly. The comparison therefore misleads by contriving a solution to what is essentially an unsolved problem. Then, other critics – such as Michael Fried – become "unpersuaded" that "Impressionism" means anything literary.

This critical confusion, then, must clear to reveal its source: the creative irresolution of the Impressionists themselves. For our current definitional chaos is but the latest result of the uncertainty that created some of the monuments of early Modernism. We will understand Impressionism when the impression is for us what it was for them: a mercurial *metaphor for perception*, one that inspires and endangers aesthetic effort. From M. H. Abrams to Jules Law, criticism has recognized the way in which "metaphors of mind" have unavoidably mixed the art of rhetoric with the science of theory. As Abrams notes, mental process is only "sometimes explicitly formulated." More often, writers "intimate" theory "by the structure of the metaphors" through which people figure the mind.[27] But such metaphors do therefore not merely supplement theory. Studying empiricist "reflection," Jules Law notes that Empiricism's rhetorical figures "have a more complicated story to tell about the itinerary of that intellectual tradition than we have yet recognized."[28] In other words, the tradition's rhetorical figures have largely determined the shape of intellectual history, actively giving structure to our sense of the very possibility of thought and perception. What Law says about "reflection" is true of "impression": if we see the impression as a rhetorical figure borne out of empiricist uncertainties, complicated in romantic ideology, exploited in theories of painting and psychology, and then borrowed for better and for worse by writers from Pater to Woolf, we can define a tradition in which an ambiguous configuration of aesthetic perception itself gave life to art. We can define an Impressionist tradition, in which the strange status of a figure for perception made writers aspire to new territory and balk at new alliances – in which a dynamic figuration became a protean literary theory and, in turn, a mother of modernist invention.

II HUME'S (LITERARY) IMPRESSION

As metaphor for perception, "impression" has always confused the issue, keeping other metaphors from keeping perceptual moments distinct. The metaphor helped to provoke the originary controversy between the Skeptics and the Stoics, because it implied both *striking* and *passing*: to the Stoic, impressions constituted knowledge, because they had a seizing (cataleptic) force that guaranteed validity; to the Skeptic, impressions did not seize so much as print and pass, and therefore could not wait for confirmation.[29] The disagreement in this instance followed upon disagreement between aspects of the "impress" – between the push and remove which together make up the act of impression. Inversely, such disagreement could solve problems, as it did in the Renaissance *impresa*. As a way "to remember a spiritual intention through a similitude," derived as Frances Yates has noted from Aquinas's hope to transmit spiritual intentions through their corporeal counterparts, the *impresa* exploits its parent metaphor's obscure linkage of what brushes by the mind and the physical impress it leaves there.[30] In this and other instances the metaphor elides or confuses, so that in both Plato (*Theaetetus*) and Cicero (*De Oratore*) it makes a unity of the two moments in which the mind receives and reads an imprint, and in the history of perceptual theory likewise blends sensation and thought.[31]

Before that mediation becomes Impressionism, it primarily encourages simple imprecision. Before Hume makes it play a major role, Locke (for example) lets the impression muddy the ground between himself and his philosophical opponents. Locke joins in the tendency to use "impression" nonspecifically as a synonym for perception; he does not, that is, fix the term to any specific place in the epistemological scheme. He does, however, tend to split the term between two particular opposed types of perception: innate ideas and basic sensations. In his *Essay's* initial attack on the innatists, Locke refers to "*innate* impressions," but alternately "impressions denote the most basic *sensations* or "impression on the body."[32] A nonspecific word that nonetheless gravitates into these two specific usages, "impression" rhetorically endorses a oneness of sensing and non-empirical thinking. Empirical sense and ideal thought are yet kept separate by adjectival modification. Locke's impressions are always "sensuous" or "innate." In Hume's system, modification falls away, and Impressionism's proper mediations begin.

Whether or not to attribute Impressionism first to Hume has been a matter of ample debate. Many critics trace Impressionism back to Hume's distinction between impressions and ideas – most prominently, Ian Watt, whose *Conrad in the Nineteenth Century* likens Conrad's foregrounding of sensuous and passional information to Hume's emphasis on the priority of feeling.[33] Watt is also typical, however, for the way he makes little distinction between impressions and sensuous perceptions, and for the way he therefore makes of Hume a precursor only to a skeptical kind of Impressionism. When critics trace Impressionism back to Hume, they do so selectively, interested only in the Hume whose irrationalism, radical Empiricism, and flux-philosophy reduce knowledge to perceptual habit. But that Hume is a caricature, with little to do with the impression invoked by modernist writers, for whom skepticism is rarely more than a pretext. If Hume's impression helped to initiate their Impressionism, it did so not because it represented the skeptic's flux but because it gave centrality to the tendency, already at work in classical philosophy and in Locke's empiricism, to make metaphorical ambiguity a theoretical problem-solver.

In Hume's *Treatise of Human Nature*, "impressions" are the perceptions that "strike upon the mind" with most "force and violence," preceding ideas and determining the degree of certainty about them. But the impression has corollary effects beneath and beyond this usage. Neither sensation nor idea, the impression enables Hume to find continuity where Empiricisms otherwise face partition; both evanescent and permanent, the impression enables Hume to bridge skepticism and pragmatism; both process and object, the impression lets Hume develop a world–mind relation that initiates Empiricism's surrender to forms of idealism and, much later, to Phenomenology.

The *Treatise* begins with a schematic discussion of the "origins of our ideas" in which Hume makes the crucial distinction: "All the perceptions of the human mind resolve themselves into two distinct kinds, which I shall call *Impressions* and *Ideas*."[34] This distinction follows from Hume's signature belief that "we cannot go beyond experience" (xvii), that all ideas are perceptions rather than know-ledge innate to us, that "to hate, to love, to think, to feel, to see; all this is nothing but to perceive" (67). Impressions differ from ideas only in degree of force or vitality, a difference equivalent to "the difference betwixt feeling and thinking" (2). Impressions and ideas, in their "simple" forms, always appear as reflections of each other: "every simple idea has a simple impression, which resembles it; and every simple impression a correspondent idea" (3). Impressions have priority in this relationship: "All our simple ideas in their first appearance are deriv'd from simple impressions . . ." (4). As the prior "feeling" to every "thought," the prior impression verifies the subsequent idea, because "'tis impossible perfectly to understand any idea, without tracing it up to its origin, and examining the primary impression, from which it arises. The examination of the impression bestows a clearness on the idea . . ." (74–75).

Offering this kind of certainty, the impression becomes the focus of the middle portions of the *Treatise*, where Hume focuses on those impressions with most significant influence: the "passions." This focus divides impressions into two categories: "impressions of sensa-tion" and "impressions of reflection" – also called "original" and "secondary" impressions. Hume explicitly disregards the former, leaving study of them to "anatomists and natural philosophers" (8). He then divides impressions of reflection into two kinds: the "calm" and the "violent"; the "violent" – or the passions – may be either "direct" or "indirect" (275–76). Devoting the second book of the *Treatise* to the investigation of the passions, Hume produces his characteristic antirationalist account of human understanding and activity, based on the belief that "reason is, and ought only to be the slave of the passions, and can never pretend to any office than to serve and obey them" (415). He effects what Norman Kemp Smith calls his "resolute reversal" of thinking and feeling, his great contribution to modernity's epistemological trend.[35]

Choosing "impression" to effect this reversal – to stand for "feeling" as opposed to "thinking" – Hume matched the species of perception "that wants a name in our language" to a word that had long wanted some more precise referent.[36] He made deliberate what Locke had implied: that perception reconceived according to the impression-metaphor could include the range from what is experienced to what is innate. But the accomplishment, rhetorical rather than logical, is mixed, because Hume also argues against it. Locke had de-emphasized the mind–body split by calling *all* perceptions "ideas." Hume felt that Locke's " 'idea' idea" misrepresented the nature of understanding, and so his coinage of the impression comes with an attack on Locke's totality: "I here make use of these terms, *impression and idea,* in a sense different from that which is usual . . . Perhaps I rather restore the word, idea, to its original sense, from which *Mr. Locke* had perverted it, making it stand for all our perceptions" (2n.1). Because Locke's "idea" had in fact unified all perception, Hume's return to a distinction among perceptions curiously entails both oneness and division: the impression, combining "sensations, passions, emotions," may, as we will see, bridge sensations and ideas, but it also reinforces a difference between thinking and feeling. What unified also divides – giving the impression the kind of double effect that will make it both a boon and a problem in the future.

Also double is the impression's relation to sensation, its temperamental mood, and (most fundamentally) its grammatical mode. On the one hand, *difference* from sensation gives the impression its real philosophical importance. When Hume calls impressions "feelings," he does not mean sensational ones, for, as R. J. Butler notes, "the all-important contrast is not between feeling a sensation and thinking, but between feeling *that* and thinking *that,* where in feeling *that* we are focussing upon an immediate awareness."[37] The contrast, in other words, stresses the dedication of immediate perceptions. Impressions can therefore be reflective: in fact, when Hume makes the further distinction that divides them into "impressions of sensation" and "impressions of reflection," he focuses exclusively on the latter, which sounds paradoxical only until we understand that impressions remake reflection such that it attains to immediacy. But if the impression therefore differs from "sensation," it is also essentially sensational, because the way it "strikes upon our senses" is what defines its behavior. Hume may choose to leave explanation of the "ultimate cause" of "those *impressions*, which arise from the *senses*" to "anatomists and natural philosophers," believing that "'twill always be impossible to decide with certainty, whether they arise immediately from the object, or are produc'd by the creative power of the mind, or are deriv'd from the author of our being" (1, iii, 5; 84), but he also makes the striking of the sensuous impression the pattern for all others:

An impression first strikes upon our senses . . . Of this impression there is a copy taken by the mind, which remains after the impression ceases; and this we call an idea. This idea of pleasure or pain, when it returns upon the soul, produces the new impressions of desire and aversion, hope and fear, which may properly be called impressions of reflexion, because derived from it. (7–8)

Deriving from sense in manner as well as order, even the "ideal" impression of reflection derives from sensuous obscurity. What Hume concedes to uncertainty – whether impressions originate "immediately from the object" (empirically), from "the creative power of the mind" (ideally), or "from the author of our being" (innately) – he therefore builds into the impression's mediation.

It may not jeopardize Hume's system, but this uncertainty makes it difficult to say for sure what it means to be a "slave of the passions." Such slavery may be, in mood, a matter either of skeptical regret or naturalist contentment, subjecting reason either to random forces, human being, or god's will. For this reason, even though Hume says that "reason is, *and ought only to be*, the slave of the passions" – with the emphasis here of Norman Kemp Smith's watershed proof that Hume is a naturalist rather than a skeptic – his temperament has seemed uncertain.[38] His impression's ambiguous source makes him naturalist and skeptic both. Similarly, it gives his Empiricism an idealist leaning. In the *Enquiry Concerning Human Understanding*, the impression becomes a way to recuperate the notion of "innateness." Innateness, Hume notes, is a fallacious category only when it means to designate the "inborn"; if by contrast it designates "what is original or copied from no precedent perception," then it is valid, for then it becomes the distinction according to which "all our impressions are innate, and our ideas not innate" (22). The impression here verges on idealist behavior, suggesting at least rhetorically a compromise with idealism, and it does so because it comes to occupy two otherwise separate moments in human understanding. As that which "strikes" and that which is "original," the impression mixes moments and combines separate claims to validity.

This mixture and its ambivalences derive from a basic grammatical ambiguity. As a metaphor for perception – in Hume but also before and beyond – the impression refers simultaneously to two perceptual moments. In the passage, for example, in which Hume describes the progress from impressions of sensation to impressions of reflection, he writes both that an impression "first strikes upon the mind" and that "of this impression there is a copy taken by the mind." These two phrases use grammatically different versions of the word "impression": the first describes a process, a striking, where the second refers to an object or marking, something from which a copy may be taken. An impression is therefore both the process of experiential input and the mark it leaves. *The Oxford English Dictionary* can offer its kind of clarification here. Its first definition of "impression" is "the action or process of impressing"; its second is "a mark produced upon any surface by pressure." Hume claims only to deal with the latter: "By the term of impression I would not be understood to express the manner in which our lively perceptions are produced in the soul, but merely the perceptions themselves" (2). But because the impression-metaphor connotes both process and object, it conflates the manner in which perceptions are produced and the perceptions themselves, making the impression's status dynamic in productive and confusing ways.[39]

This conflation gives the impression its appeal and also undermines the modernist aesthetic it encourages. The appeal derives from the way the impression's ambiguity lets Hume elide a persistent gap in empiricist thinking. Where Empiricism notoriously has trouble explaining how primary sense experience ever gels into ideas, or how, as Hazlitt put it, perceptions ever "club together," the impression accomplishes that development by making one metaphor refer both to object and process.[40] The impression's double nature accomplishes in metaphor what Empiricism has difficulty making consciousness achieve in fact. Similarly, the impression's double meaning implicitly solves the problem of solipsism. Hume characteristically denies certainty that mental acts are contingent upon input from the world. The impression, by implying at once input and inner sense, contrives the contingency ultimately necessary for Hume's pragmatic return to the world after skepticism's negations. As Stephen Everson puts it, "Impressions could be then defined as those 'perceptions' which cause us to have beliefs that we are perceiving," or those perceptions that link mind and world in spite of Hume's solipsism.[41]

These metaphorical conflations do more than close empiricist gaps: they strain Hume's philosophy beyond Empiricism. The impression-metaphor even predicts, for example, the change Bergson makes when he describes the falsity of conventional consciousness: claiming that "sensations and tastes seem to me to be *objects* as soon as I isolate and name them, and in the human soul there are only *processes*," Bergson crosses the epistemological threshold the impression straddles.[42] The impression also moves consciousness toward an *intentional* structure – which, after Brentano, becomes the hallmark of Husserlian phenomenology. The theory of intentionality holds that "this universal fundamental property of consciousness" is "to be consciousness *of* something; as a *cogito*, to bear within itself its *cogitatum*."[43] Contriving oneness of perceiving and perceived, Hume's impression simulates *intention*, and makes Impressionism reach toward phenomenology.

But the reach has no grasp. R. J. Butler excuses the inconsistency in Hume's impression by noting that Hume "was grappling ahead of his time with an idea which had no touchstones in contemporary philosophy or that of his predecessors."[44] The grappling – the fumbling for better touchstones – is what the Impressionist inherits. Those writers who followed his lead found in the impression a dynamic metaphor for consciousness, for better and for worse. The impression enables the Impressionists to imagine a juncture of subject and world through feeling, to move from "objects" to "processes," to debunk the rational, and gain in the process a revitalized medium. But the impression's uncertain relation to sense, and the consequent vacillation in the temperament it encourages, makes this medium hard to sustain.

III LITERARY PHENOMENOLOGY?

Impressionism is therefore hard to explain in terms of either Empiricism or Phenomenology. The impression comes out of Hume and leads beyond him, but not so far as Phenomenology, which has a

certainty about its syntheses that Impressionism must lack. It is
essentially this problem – the way Impressionism hesitates between
two landmark philosophical traditions – that makes a new account of
literary Impressionism necessary. When literary criticism imports
phenomenology's terms into the study of Impressionism, as the best
studies of the subject have done, they replace the literary impression
with terms that achieve with systematic clarity what it achieves only
through rhetorical contrivance. Critics including H. Peter Stowell,
Paul Armstrong, and Maria Kronegger have noted the similarity
between what we call Impressionism and the phenomenological
theories of Bergson, Husserl, and Merleau-Ponty, in particular. They
define Impressionism as the belief that "we cannot know reality
independent of consciousness" and that reality itself is "a synthesis of
pure sensations, modulated by consciousness and changed into
impressions," and that the value of impressions lies in the fact that
they are phenomenological "experiences of the qualities of things."[45]
Considering Impressionism a phenomenological link of subject and
world – what Stowell calls a mode of "subjective objectivism" –
critics go so far as to make Impressionism the harbinger or counterpart of "Bergson's *durée* and Husserl's phenomenological time, the
Empiricism and epistemological indeterminacy of William James,
the uncertainty principle of Heisenberg, the relativity of Einstein's
space and time, the phenomenologists' recognition of reciprocal
perceptual reality between subject and object, and the Gestalt
psychologists' model of an inexplicable synthesis based upon
dynamic patterns of perceived fragments."[46] But each of these
reciprocities and syntheses depends upon an enormous amount of
self-conscious philosophical ingenuity: does the literary Impressionist
have it?

Those who would say so note similarities between the descriptive
orientations, psychologies, and world views of Impressionist writers
and those at work in efforts – roughly from Bergson's 1883 *Time and
Free Will* to Merleau-Ponty's 1962 *Phenomenology of Perception* – to root
out the many bad results of epistemological dualism. Simply put,
such similarities might include that between Pater's impressions of
Renaissance art and what Bergson calls "intuition" – "the kind of
intellectual sympathy by which one places oneself within an object in
order to coincide with what is unique in it and consequently
inexpressible";[47] that between Hardy's living landscapes and Husserl's "noematic content" – the object reconceived phenomenologi-

cally as an intentional correlate to human consciousness;[48] that between Henry James's subtlety and his brother's blending of modes of sagacity, their shared sense of the way discrimination comes from "immensely varied instincts, practical wants, and aesthetic feelings;"[49] that between the nausea characters feel in Conrad and in Sartre alike due to the radical freedom of existence and the consequent responsibility of consciousness to make its world; and finally (though the list could continue) the similarity between Woolf's interest in seeing "the world without a self" and Merleau-Ponty's conviction that selfhood only falsifies the true unity of body and world, and that "to be a body is to be tied to a certain world" for "our body is not *in* space: it is of it."[50] In all of these instances writers and philosophers share the mediatory impulse summed up in the impression. But is it possible to equate the writers' impression with the theoretical terms and enterprises through which the philosophers find unity?

To equate them is to attribute too much philosophical systematicity to the outlook of the Impressionist writer, who could never aspire to transcend error in the manner of his or her philosophical counterpart. Husserl, for example, worked hard to refute solipsism, in the fifth of his *Cartesian Meditations*; Conrad, by contrast, wants to show how and why his characters lack the temperamental and theoretical powers to do so. James might have written psychological portraits of his brother's sort of "vagueness," were it not for the competing modes of vagueness he inherited along with the novel from other traditions. Woolf may have wanted to find, as Merleau-Ponty does, a way to theorize embodiment such that it becomes a continuity, but her own body's frightening continuities made her unable to want such a theory without ambivalence. And so it is the ambivalence that characterizes the Impressionist's use for the perceptual theories systematically achieved in phenomenological philosophy. We need not therefore rule out phenomenology, but rather place it at a distance, and think of it as the horizon toward which Impressionism reaches as it looks beyond its empirical ground.

At the same time, however, we should recognize that the Impressionist's ambivalence is no failure to achieve phenomenology's sophistication, complexity, or thorough thinking. For in that ambivalence there is also critique – critique perhaps not unlike that in Derrida's 1967 refutation of Husserlian phenomenology. In *Speech and Phenomena*, Derrida proves there remains in Husserl's phenomenology a certain metaphysical bias, a metaphysical distinction between subjectivity and world, which enables false notions of "presence." The belief that experience makes the world present to the subject is, according to Derrida, wrongheaded, because it fails to see that nothing ever comes unmediated; nothing stands outside of the subject–world relation in such a way as to have the immediacy of presence. This argument is of course a big turning-point in intellectual history, as a basis of the post-structuralist turn. It is important, however, to remember that the argument is less a turning away from Husserl than an extension or correction of his phenomenology: denying the distinctions that make presence possible, Derrida really just completes the phenomenological deconstruction.[51] He knows that the phenomenology, when free of metaphysical baggage, would have to deny the possibility of presence. It would have to disallow, or deconstruct, the last false-logic commonplace distinctions between self and world. It is precisely this outcome that Impressionist writers fear: it is precisely the deconstructionist result that leads the Impressionist writer from enthusiasm about the impression's mediations to strong doubt that they really want to face the loss of conventional selfhood and presence that the impression would ultimately entail. Derrida sees that phenomenology derives its power to interpret the world only through presuppositions that are false to its own premises; the Impressionist writer sees that the impression's mediations, like their phenomenological counterparts, would, when fully followed through, actually undermine literature's power to interpret the world.

If the impression therefore falls "between" Empiricism and Phenomenology, it might make sense to account for it in terms of those empirical psychologies that intervened between these two more conspicuous traditions. Judith Ryan has shown that the theories of perception held in common by Pater, James, Woolf and others resemble and draw inspiration from the "early psychologies" of such figures as Hermann Barr, Ernst Mach, and the early William James. In Ryan's account, these early psychologists argued against nineteenth-century positivism by reviving and modifying Empiricism, making the mechanical human subject "purely evanescent," a bundle of sensations, attention to which required new psychological procedures.[52] Those procedures became literary, as writers – many of them Impressionists – made the evanescence of the self, its sensational make-up, and the life of its streaming consciousness the focus of narration. In the spirit of empirical psychology, writers relocated themselves to the uncertain place "between subjective vision and its dissolution," in the epistemological drama of the perpetually dissolving self.[53] And this uncertainty, that of representation caught between the pleasures and terrors of radical subjectivism, might well explain the uncertainty of the Impressionist. But the impression has meanings beyond and apart from those that empirical psychology assigns it. In empirical psychology, the impression is the basic stuff of sensational evanescence, only different from "sensation" in its connotations of flux. This impression lacks those other connotations – of judgment, abstraction, and longevity – that gives the literary impression its appeal. In other words, empirical psychology's uncertainties cover only half of those in question; the Impressionist's ambivalence casts a wider net. Extending from sensational evanescence to timeless essence, or from the empirical psyche to anti-psychologistic thought and creativity, the impression's literary ambivalences extend beyond psychology's early territories.

IV IMPRESSIONIST MEDIATIONS

Beyond Hume but prior to Husserl, with greater breadth than empirical psychology, the impression's perceptual aspirations and uncertainties match those at work when idealism tries to subsume Empiricism by distinguishing a faculty, synthetic in function and dialectical in process, through which the transcendent and the real interact. The Kantian tradition, in other words, best reflects the problem of the impression, for the impression would play the part Kant assigns to the subjective imagination, mediating between reason and understanding and their many analogously opposed realms.[54] It plays this part, however, not simply according to Kant's plan for the synthetic imagination, but according to the many plans that surround and vary his sense of how such synthesis might work. The impression is corollary to the Kantian imagination, but also corollary more broadly to the Kantian imagination as preceded in British Empiricism and aesthetics and followed in such revisionists as Schiller, the Schlegels, Hegel, and even Marx and Adorno. It works, that is, as Kant might have expected, bridging reason and understanding only in the subject, and not implying that the worlds to which those faculties correspond could themselves unify; but it sometimes works differently – as Schiller might have expected, in the beautiful object of the imagination, or, in the Schlegels' terms, so subjectively that the imagination becomes ironic. It works in Kantian fashion but also in Hume's accidentally rhetorical way, or in an Hegelian dialectic, and this potential variety explains Impressionist uncertainty. For to invoke the impression is sometimes to invoke the rhetorical contrivance that surreptitiously gets Hume from sensations to ideas, sometimes to verge on ironic subjectivism, and sometimes to set a course for the Hegelian Absolute; it is sometimes to advocate "aesthetic education," and sometimes to worry that no such education can overcome alienation (that caused, in Marx, by money), or even begin to address its cultural effects. These different impulses combine, because the impression vaguely promises perceptual unity, and, in the minds of writers only vaguely concerned to theorize that promise systematically, does so with the range of different implications of different philosophical schemes.

For this reason the best characterizations of the impression come through individual attention to the way each Impressionist collocates the powers and limitations of its mediatory effects. What we find, in seeking such characterizations, are strange combinations of (for example) Kantian aesthetics and Marxist critiques, or we find Schiller's educational impulse devolving into irony and then to Empiricist irrationalism; we find the impression leading modernist writers back and forth along the trajectories of philosophy, and only now and then achieving the certainties that make the impression purely and successfully Kantian or Marxist, or comparable to phenomenological and empirical psychologies.

The terms of the impression's basic mediation give the subtitle to Pater's *Marius the Epicurean*. "His Sensations and Ideas" makes a promise to tell us everything about Marius, but also more ambitiously to join disparate realms of knowledge. This goal of course makes the novel sequel to Pater's effort in *The Renaissance* to model full receptivity to impressions. In *The Renaissance*, Pater first invokes the impression, claiming that Matthew Arnold's account of aesthetic response overlooks the fact that good objective judgment of art begins in subjective intuition. He uses the term "impression" to name this subjective intuition, and, it becomes clear, to restore to aesthetic judgment full claims to sense and reason. "Sensations and Ideas" come together: the impression is both a part of the flux of sensuous life and the key to discretion in art – at once pure pleasure and the basis for good judgment. But Pater's public distrusted the combination, which was at least partially an excuse to bring indulgence in sensuous male physicality into the world of serious thought and behavior. In response to Pater's public (and also to himself), Marius's "Sensations and Ideas" revise the impression's way of joining physical feelings and rational thought. *Ascesis* – an ascetic abnegation, a winnowing of the impression – changes the impression's interrelations, and Pater's Impressionism is the diverse theory that results. That theory begins as an ardent belief in the unity of aesthetic response, runs afoul of social obstacles to such unification, and returns as a qualified synthesis, leading in the process to early-modernist writing and, as we shall see, ever further stories about the impression's mixed appeal.

Henry James's impression joins *contingency* and *freedom* to make an "art of fiction." Walter Besant's essay on that subject, the one to which James's invocation of the impression responds, restricts fiction to the record of direct experience. Besant had argued that "everything in Fiction which is invented and is not the result of personal experience and observation is worthless."[55] James corrects Besant by saying that the imagination often richly augments, or even constitutes, experience. The impression helps him to make this point, because it has one foot in experience and the other in the imagination. When James writes that fiction "is in its broadest definition a personal, direct impression of life," he both agrees and disagrees with Besant. He agrees that experience is basic, but broadens the category, extending it into the realm of the imagination on the bridge the impression provides. Connoting both a contingent sense of the outside world and a free inner feeling, the impression makes contingent experience and free imagination indistinguishable. It therefore enables James to outflank Besant on both sides – and also to extend the realm of fiction in both directions. Fiction, theoretically, becomes at once more "artistic" and more true to life than other metaphors for perception could make it. But since the juncture of experience and imagination makes unclear demands on the creative mind – since real-life receptivity might limit the imagination, and since imagination might yet distract from real life – James's theory has problems. These problems become his plots and themes. James's stories often put the arch and the fresh into perilous collaboration. His "international theme," in fact, makes his Impressionist uncertainty a matter of international relations, and his young female characters often suffer for the uncertainty behind his confident refutation of Besant's theory of fiction.

Sensation and *perception* combine in Conrad's impression. In his tribute to the "sensible universe" (in the Preface to *The Nigger of the "Narcissus"*) Conrad complains of fiction's absence of sensation. What should bring sensation back in, Conrad suggests, is writing that makes sensation continuous with emotion. Conrad admires fiction's power to go from the sensible world to the "secret spring of responsive emotions" in each of us to the "solidarity" we enjoy when our emotions respond together. The impression enables these linkages by its metaphorical tendency to "convey" sensation into perception. The "impression conveyed through the senses" makes a conveyance from inchoate sensation to perceptual input; it joins primary data to the capacity to take it in. "To make you *see*" – Conrad's famous hope – gets its double meaning (to make you *sense* and to make you *understand*) from the impression's power to ride consciousness through. In confident moments, this movement breaks down the walls of solipsism, and delivers "solidarity"; in less confident moments – in fictions that thematize the breakdown of conveyance – it runs amok. Perceptive characters find themselves grotesquely dependent on sensuous counterparts; solidarity gives way to cruel misunderstanding, and the universe becomes the implacable thing Conrad so often decries.

For Proust, as we have seen, the impression is something that reality prints but that the writer must labor to decipher. It therefore combines invention and description; and it combines past memory and present experience, becoming that connection through which the writer closes the gap between reality's effect and the way memory records it. For Ford, the terms are *fact* and *value*. Facts are what modernity produces in excessive abundance; value is what the artist makes of them, through impressions, which are facts rendered publicly assimilable.

For Woolf, the impression unites *experience* and *essence*. Forever troubling to Woolf is the difference between full participation in life and the power of insight into its essence – the bad difference between living and being. What promises to solve the problem is the impression's way of coming from within and without. When Woolf contemplates "Mrs. Brown" in her famous essay on modern fiction, she speaks of the "overwhelming impression" that Mrs. Brown gives off – and then finds that impression legible within herself; the impression from without keys a counterpart within, drawing something like the line of "solidarity" that Conrad hopes his fiction will draw. But because she shares her impression with a person of another class, the new unification of experience and essence becomes an old hard relationship, and brings new difficulties to "modern fiction."

In this fashion the Impressionists court mediation but worry about its consequences, unsure what ancillary effects come with the impression's perceptual unity. Even as the impression's strange perceptual and rhetorical status encourages writers to believe in continuity between sensations and ideas, contingency and freedom, experience and essence, its ambiguities encourage them yet to seek the stability of epistemological dualism. Wanting mediation, but also wanting to forestall it, Impressionist writers seek a way to imagine it happening with familiar distinctions intact. They therefore figure the impression's mediation as a matter of a partnership between – rather than union of – human faculties. These "figures for mediation," to revise Geoffrey Hartman's phrase, indicate that mediation has become *collaboration*.[56] Through collaboration, the Impressionist enjoys integration of intellect and sense without giving up intellect's independence, and gains the validity of contingency and experience without losing the "higher" powers of perception, essence, and freedom. But the Impressionist consequently suffers the new alienation entailed in this peculiar recuperation of epistemological dualism.

So basic is this collaboration that it becomes a human relationship. The mixture of togetherness and alienation finds perfect figuration in the relationship between people of different kinds – people whose different social backgrounds put them into agonistic combination. The major Impressionist critical statements feature this figuration. In the Preface to *The Nigger of the "Narcissus"*, Conrad ends his description of Impressionism by invoking a distant laborer, a working-man's body through which Conrad at once claims and projects embodiment. Ford's "On Impressionism" similarly turns to a peasant cabman, whose "virgin intelligence" becomes its author's mindless counterpart. Woolf's "Mr. Bennett and Mrs. Brown" fixes on Mrs. Brown's suffering womanhood and manifest class-decline to generate the impressions that "modern fiction" requires. And Pater's "diaphanous" young-male ideal, James's "woman of genius," and even Proust's grandmother's maid all serve similarly as counterparts in the impression's mediation. Such collaborations personify Impressionist uncertainty. Instead of a clean shift away from dualistic habits of thinking, we get a form of reconsideration, which, by becoming figural, becomes an object as well as a theory of representation.

In the works of each Impressionist writer, a counterpart is chosen; Impressionism's ambivalences personify themselves in the relationship between implied author and this counterpart; Impressionism *sublates* the counterpart, but what the counterpart enables in theory falls apart, thematically, in fiction. Impressionist fictions become splendid imaginative palinodes – "metanovels" that make remarkable efforts to shore up, or take down, the weak structures of theory.[57] So Woolf turns from her use for Mrs. Brown to satire of that use in "An Unwritten Novel" (1920), where prejudicial thinking about a figure much like Mrs. Brown leads to error; and so Woolf turns, finally, from need for embodied counterparts to independence of such a need, as Clarissa Dalloway and Lily Briscoe overcome dependency on the bodies of other women. So Henry James begins with admiration, in "The Art of Fiction," for the "woman of genius," but then moves to meditate on the problem of exploiting women's impressionability: that exploitation becomes the force that traps Isabel Archer, a force finally defied when Lambert Strether stops idealizing the youth of Chad Newsome. In Conrad and Pater as well, collaboration starts as a need, enables a style, and becomes a theme, reflecting Impressionism's aesthetic potential, its correlative uncertainties, and the imaginative effort writers make to manage them.

Of course these collaborators are not equals. Key to the history of Impressionism is what the status of the laborer, the cabman, and Mrs. Brown reveals: that Impressionism's epistemological totality corresponds, for aid and to its detriment, to the social whole. In order to imagine sensations and ideas fully working together, the Impressionists seem also to need to imagine collaboration of the social beings to whom sensations and ideas correspond. Uncertainty about the impression's perceptual status derives in large part from the conviction that certain people naturally correspond to certain faculties – specifically, that women and lower-class people have special access to contingent, sensuous, concrete existence.[58] The association of people with perceptual powers feeds Impressionist uncertainty, creating the worry that perceptual unity will be to art what radical politics are to social life. This conflation in turn makes the Impressionist forestall unity with new dualism, which would join perceptual opposites in more familiar social relations. In circular endorsements these associations compromise Impressionism, disallowing mediation and remaking it in strange new difficult forms.

The question then arises of ideology: what do we make of the politics of Impressionism, if its mediations are inhibited by their associations with threatening social changes, if those mediations therefore become unequal collaborations, and if those unequal collaborations become a basis of Impressionist theory, theme, and plot?

The answer to this question demands a wider context. No failure simply of early-modernist theory, the politics of collaboration partake of a long and unimpeachable effort on the part of literary and aesthetic theory to make up for the significant form lost with religious belief. As such it is a symptom of modernity, and, as such, a formidable opponent for the Impressionist sensibility.

In large part Hume needs the impression to contrive perceptual dynamicism because he does not rely on what had long supplied dynamicism as a matter of course: spiritual allegory. Hume's precursors and successors very often borrow perceptual movement from religious quest. As so many historians of eighteenth- and nineteenth-century thought have shown, epistemology, metaphysics, and the theory of the imagination were often "displaced and reconstituted theology,"[59] in which the processes of mind building itself from small things to great or of imagination creating its world were often patterned toward the infinite "I Am." Imagination and salvation were "virtual synonyms," and the traditional Christian plot survived into the secular system, so that the problem solved by Hume's impression more often got solved from the outset.[60] No local metaphorical dynamicism was initially necessary to propel the "secular" system, because it moved within a metaphor of spiritual aspiration.

Even psychology in its earlier moments was allegory. Subordinate to theological designs – "theopathic," to use David Hartley's term for the way the association of ideas leads to God, or a "theodicy of the individual life" – early accounts of mental life often cast it as religious romance.[61] Sensations combine by association, reflection makes them reasonable, and conscience makes them ethical in turn all within a divine plan; a process toward God subtends what might seem more properly a material affair, because God has planned a course of development from material response to faith. One major strain of psychology depends upon spiritual quest to justify its account of the interactions of mind and matter: picking up from Leibniz (as opposed to Newton), proceeding through Shaftesbury, Hutcheson, Butler, Hartley, and Whytt, this tradition makes a theological endpoint organize the story of the way basic elements make up human reason, ethics, and belief. The story is allegorical in that it tells a more important larger story: in Hartley's theory, for example, "vibrations" associate and form faculties, which combine to constitute moral education, which in turn leads to grace – in a story that plots God's chain of being.

What happens with Hume is that skepticism breaks the chain of being and requires new links – a different "plot" for the process of perception. One way to explain Hume's use for the impression is to point to the dynamicism lost not simply with "causality" but with psychology's religious teleology. And one way to explain the belated emergence of Impressionism from the romantic philosophy so similarly interested in "mediation" is to point to the *persistence* of the religious teleology. Even with the Romantics, theories of perception and imagination yet plot their progress toward God, and it is only when the religious totality fully gives way to "organicist" social totality that Impressionism emerges. It is only then that the impression emerges to initiate Modernism's post-romantic effort to remake the synthetic imagination – and then that the vexed totality of the social whole heightens the modern crisis with which Romanticism had engaged.

Coleridge theorized an imagination that had the impression's power of metaphorical conveyance. As that "reconciling and mediatory power," "incorporating the Reason in Images of the Sense, and organizing (as it were) the flux of the Senses by the permanence and self-circling energies of the Reason,"[62] Coleridge's imagination would seem to subsume the work of Hume's impression and the Impressionism follows suit. But Coleridge's imagination derives from an analogy between the primary imagination and divine creation. To find an active role for the imagination, improving upon mechanistic empiricist materialism without falling into purely subjective idealism, Coleridge turned to the best possible model for creative perception: "The primary IMAGINATION I hold to be the living Power and prime agent of all human perception, and as a repetition in the finite mind of the eternal act of creation in the infinite I

AM."[63] The imagination works as a "tertium aliquid," partaking of counteractive powers, because its repetitional stretch toward the infinite happens in each of its moments; it becomes dynamic in humble imitation of the divine act of creation. This dialectical imagination has as its analog the romantic *symbol* – that "conductor" harmonious with itself and consubstantial with the truth it conveys.[64] Once humble imitation ceases to motivate the imagination, the work of the symbol is taken up, far less successfully, by the impression, which corresponds to an imagination which can only repeat mundane acts of secular organization.

Coleridge might have had to go from symbol to impression – from "esemplastic" romantic unity to one impressionistically contrived – if not for the analogy between the totalities of the imagination and the divine. Similarly, Ruskin might have had to become Pater had he not believed that aspiration toward the beautiful matched aspiration toward God. Ruskin spoke against calling the sense of beauty "aesthetic." He thought it "theoretic," because religious: no "mere operation of sense," perception of beauty is perception of God's benevolence, and therefore appreciation of it is "exulting, reverential, grateful," and something that combines operations of sense and reason toward that higher end.[65] Like Coleridge, Ruskin can believe in the possibility of such a "tertium aliquid" by believing in its aspirational movement. Joy, seeking issue as gratitude, moves sensual pleasure to the "idea of beauty"; what motivates psychology is, again, allegorical, a sequential progress from what is pure and right, averting "mere appetite and lust," toward something analogous to grace. If Ruskin speaks of "impressions of beauty" where Coleridge spoke in terms of the symbols that are the imagination's product, Ruskin nevertheless leaves the term inert. Ruskin yet enjoys the sort of faith that moves theory upward.

Even the more secular aspirations of Hazlitt's organic sensibility, Shelley's "Defense," and the Wordsworth who discovers moral good and evil in "one impulse from a vernal wood" do not doubt unity such that they require the impression. It is important to stress this relative certainty, since it distinguishes Impressionist mediation from an overwhelming host of prior integrations. What distinguishes the work of the impression's conveyance from that of the infinite striving of opposites in Fichte, the mediator Schelling finds in the imagination, the juncture of ideal and sensuous natures in Schiller, and the imagination which in Goethe "hovers above sensation" but then, seeing reason, "attaches itself firmly to this highest guide,"[66] is work done secretly: with no sure model for totality, the impression resembles other fusing and transferring powers only through pretense. The Impressionists will share the hopes of their precursors but not their faith. They, too, will want beauty that moves upward from sense but locates itself somewhere short of the intellect, and they too will hope that the heart will serve as a third term. But no "reverence" will make them "theoretic": religious analogies will give way to other motivational forces, so that where Coleridge and Ruskin could rely on religious devotions to structure psychic work, the Impressionists will look to *social* analogies, and find in them connections that are effective only to the degree that impressions resemble symbols.

On the way to the social analogy certain writers are signposts. Schiller, for example, is already describing the aesthetic education in terms of collaborations between social types, and Wordsworth regarding the solitary reaper and other such figures begins to draw on social differences to theorize aesthetic wholes. Believing, however, that such differences could vanish into whole aesthetic passion, these writers think within "romantic ideology." Real and troubled movement toward the social analogy comes with writers who can not.

Mary Wollstonecraft knew that perceptual parts and wholes had already cleaved to social ones, for she knew that women's subordination was in large part a product of the distinction between reason and passion. Because "understanding has been denied to women," and because reason was thought "inconsistent with . . . their sexual character," women were confined to a low place in the epistemological chain of being. "To their senses," Wollstonecraft writes, "women are made slaves," and that slavery had much to do with their social servitude.[67] Seeing the social corollary to the dynamic distinction between sense and reason, Wollstonecraft sees through to the style of relation that would increasingly inform perceptual theory. Such insight has greater dramatic effect in the work of her daughter. Writing a grotesque parody of the allegory of perception – a story, that is, in which the progress from matter to grace along the chain of being emphasizes only the grotesque unassimilability of the material, and does so in recognition of the problem of *female* imagination – Mary Shelley turns further critical scrutiny upon the social reconstruction of perceptual totality.

Edgar Allan Poe is a transitional figure here: he speaks of

impressions, but finds in them a totality in which romantic and social bases easily overlap. Poe is like his romantic precursors in his interest in "totality of effect," an interest he expresses in his reviews of Hawthorne and in his "Philosophy of Composition." In those essays, Poe argues that the best works of literature are those most likely to convey a strong single effect. The best writers are those that ask themselves, "Of the innumerable effects, or impressions, of which the heart, the intellect, or (more generally) the soul is susceptible, what one shall I, on the present occasion, select?";[68] and their best products are those that can be read in a single sitting, are not so "original" that they "task or startle the intellect," and have intensity strong enough to strike up a bond of sympathy between writer and reader.[69] More pragmatic than his more theological precursors, Poe invokes the impression, for he needs to say how the "total effect" can be at once sharp and continuous without reference to the spiritual allegory that would make what is sharp continue: writing of a "unity of impression" in which "there must be the pressing steadily down of the stamp upon the wax," Poe returns to classical means by which to theorize the lasting imprint, and draws on the impression's double status as stamper and stamped.[70] Poe also turns to social totality to ensure unity. He judges "totality of effect" by its likely appeal to the mass of readers, who, for him, are a homogeneous lot: notoriously, Poe presumes that readers are all alike not only in their reading rates but in the leisure time available to them – uniform, that is, as a social body, within which effects can prove total.[71] Poe could not have his total impressions without this presumption, which falls between the theopathic presumptions of romantic unity and the problems that arise when social life patterns perceptual allegory.

Poe's place between spiritual and social unities marks the emergence of Impressionism: post-romantic in his need for the impression's contrived conveyance, but pre-Impressionist in his certainty about the social whole, Poe stands between Coleridge and Conrad, beyond the former's wish for an aesthetic secularization of the Christian creed, but before the latter's fear that the secular alternative invites social discord into the soul. The solidarity Coleridge presumes to follow from "the One" and the lesser solidarity Poe attributes to the reading mass devolves into the unlikely solidarity Conrad hopes impressions will create; but placing such hopes in impressions, Conrad depends upon a sort of perceptual unity already questionable in Poe, and never necessary to Coleridge.

Is Impressionism therefore the romantic imagination played out –
what is left once modernity has fully defied "integration"? If so, the
advent of Impressionism would be an intermediate phase in the
process through which, in so many accounts, Romanticism becomes
and even encompasses Modernism. Lest this confirmation make
Modernism derivative and Impressionism merely a last gasp, it is
important to stress that to come after Romanticism in this way is also
to change it. Or rather it is possible to reverse the priority, by saying
that Impressionism really creates the romantic imagination (for the
modernists) by confronting modernity without theopathy. Without
theopathy, and with recourse to baser models for integration,
Impressionism takes on the project of romantic synthesis without the
strength of Romantic symbolism.

We might contrast Wordsworth and Conrad, both of whom call up
figures of distant laborers to figure the aesthetic imagination.
Wordsworth's effort to reground poetry in the language and subjects
of common life, in the context of his romantic interest in synthesis,
predicts the tendency in Impressionism to imagine such synthesis in
social terms. His worry about the poet's alienation from poetry's vital
sources – the sense that "his situation is altogether slavish and
mechanical, compared with the freedom and power of real and
substantial action and suffering." His consequent wish to "confound
and identify his own feelings" with those of others – is a precursor to
Impressionist collaboration; and his consequent ideological charac-
teristics – those for which he is by turns admired or criticized, his
broad sympathies or opportunistic condescension – would be those
we might expect to find in Impressionism.[72] But whereas Wordsworth's laborers are effective "displacements," Conrad's return
brutal senses: counterparts in Conrad struggle and switch roles, and
their interdependence tends toward disaster, indicating far less sense
of security in the structure whereby one "identifies" with another. If
Wordsworth thinks love of men can arise from the poetry grounded
in the common feelings he imputes to other kinds of people, Conrad
finds others destroying solidarity because of the way social forms
remake perceptual distinctions.

As a belated and self-critical Romanticism, Impressionism has a
politics different from what we might expect from the structure of
collaboration. Collaboration seems like primitivism, that mixture of
idealization, condescension, and exploitation through which much of
Modernism got in touch with what it newly took to be real. To cast

women and workers in the role of the impression's sensuous or concrete aspect is, perhaps, to gain aesthetic inspiration at the price of stereotype and objectification. If so, Impressionism's ideology might match that which many see in Romanticism – that which puts art first, and gets its innovations through projections that make the disadvantage of others an advantage of its own. But just as Romanticism features, if not directly, its own inevitable part in such affairs, Impressionism makes its need for collaboration a subject of inquiry. When its "figures for mediation" become patterns for plot, Impressionism takes on the problematic connection between basic epistemology and the social order, and does so with greater sustained attention to the crux of that connection than we find even in those philosophical accounts openly focused upon it. For the Impressionist engaged in theoretical collaboration has what Hegel called "unhappy" or "contrite consciousness" (unglückliches Bewusstsein) – is beset by "the unwon unity of the two selves" that would together be complete; but his or her writings are *acts* of contrition. They confess in detail their culture's inequities.[73]

How this is so – how what seems like primitivist projection subjects such projection to critique – will become more clear once we put the problem of Impressionism in the context of the larger political history of fiction. Chapters Three and Four argue that Impressionism's recourse to figurations of women and workers ought to be understood as critiques like those advanced in two of the most influential recent treatments of narrative and ideology: Fredric Jameson's *Political Unconscious* and Nancy Armstrong's *Desire and Domestic Fiction*.

Jameson argues that Impressionism offered, in part, a kind of utopian compensation for capitalist rationalization and reification. Impressionism partially restored the sensuous life that economic rationalization had largely destroyed, but in a manner unthreatening or even helpful to capitalist culture. Jameson, however, defines Impressionism as sensuous presentation. Redefined as a theory of perceptual unity, Impressionism becomes itself something that addresses the problem of restoring sense to rationality – itself the Jamesonian theory that makes Impressionism one of its examples. Collaboration then amounts to a test of utopian impulses, and, when it fails, an exposition of the factors that make such impulses inadequate. Similarly, Impressionism's use for women tests a kind of feminism. Nancy Armstrong argues that female subjectivity and the novel form grew up together. She describes, for example, the codevelopment of novelistic interiority and the authority of female emotion in private life, and so proves that the novel helped to delimit female capacities. Impressionist collaboration brings that delimitation to a crisis: implying that women (at least figurally) make impressions contingent, concrete, and sensuous, the Impressionist reduces to absurdity the logic whereby the novel form had defined its emotional authority, and insofar as the Impressionist's subsequent work suffers the consequences, it is a feminist critique of novelistic subjectivity.

Engaged before the fact in these feminist and neo-marxist forms of critique, Impressionism is just prior to the Modernism T. J. Clark describes in his *Farewell to an Idea*: it takes a last but already ambivalent stand against modernity's triumphant reduction of life to materialist distinctions.[74] Impressionism likewise contests the triumphant rationalization Jonathan Crary describes in his *Techniques of the Observer*, the rationalization whereby the compartmentalization of perceptual life served regimes of sociopolitical control.[75] These are, of course, the grandest arguments on its behalf – grandly put here to dispute with greatest possible vigor the prevailing viewpoint, which relegates Impressionism to precious, detached, pretty self-involvement. But this line of argument will not rule out less partial evaluations. As necessary as it may be to stress Impressionism's critical engagements, it is also necessary to note the extent to which Impressionist theory serves other purposes. When, for example, the Impressionist claims that "fiction *is* an impression," he or she often does so to make vague the procedures through which good writing gets produced – in defense against the rapid professionalization of fiction-writing. As Louis Menand has noted, writing fiction became a profession at this moment, a development certainly reflected in Impressionist essays, which most often respond to the professionalisms of middlebrow writers.[76] James and Woolf, replying to Walter Besant and Arnold Bennett respectively, make the impression's vagueness a way to reject the step-by-step rules through which anybody might enter the profession.[77] Guarding fiction, the impression becomes a force for highbrow exclusivity, lending Impressionism a political character very different from that which engages in critique of social division. In the chapters that follow, that character plays a lesser role, but contributes nevertheless to improve upon Impressionism's prevailing definition – giving "detachment" some more specific motivations and results.

To read Impressionist collaboration primarily as a basis for neo-Marxist and feminist critique, as Chapters Three and Four aspire to do, is to choose from a wide range of theoretical possibilities. The structure of collaboration, in which the authorial mind projects an aspect of itself onto the body of another and apparently lesser being, might emerge more clearly (for example) through the lens of psycho-analytic theory. Psychoanalytic theory has much to say about the use of this kind of "other" – but then again, so does existentialist theory, which makes its claims through schemes alternative to and even basically antagonistic to the schemes of psychoanalysis. The personi-fication at work in Impressionist collaboration might throw us back onto older, even classical rhetorical analysis, or take us right up to the current moment of cultural studies, which has in many ways exposed the *essentialism* at work in culture's beliefs about embodi-ment. Out of this variety of possibilities, I have chosen the Kantian tradition as subject to key theories of "ideology," because it seems best to connect fiction's epistemological theory and its social product. If, as I want to suggest, Impressionism begins as a percep-tual theory that then falls into the realities of social structures and social plots, ideology is its crucial point of complication. For further insight into that complication, I turn, as I have said, to the poststructuralist critique of phenomenology, relevant here as well for the way it explains not only the Impressionist's return to old epistemological distinctions, but for its power to explain what comes next. To describe those fictions in which the problem of Impres-sionism becomes a theme, I will be using the term *allegory*. I use the term loosely, to some degree, to refer to texts really (or also) "about" something else; but I will also be borrowing a use of the term from another deconstructionist touchstone.

Angus Fletcher writes that a certain kind of allegory "always demonstrates a degree of inner conflict," which, for the allegorist who "is constantly ruminating about his own desires," gives narra-tive form to structural conflict.[78] When desire presses toward the resolution of conflict, it often has to turn to forms better able to work through possible outcomes. It often inspires the imagination to make up stories which work through conflict by giving conflicting elements the behavioral tendencies of characters, places, and things. And such allegory happens with particular urgency, as Fletcher also notes, when conflicting elements reduce themselves within a word. There are certain "antithetical primal words" – words with basic double

meanings, whose doubleness literalizes conflict – that most vigor-
ously drive the allegorist from inner conflict to public allegory.[79]
When I discuss Impressionist allegory, I will define it as a form of
allegory that responds in this fashion to the primal conflict within the
antithetical word "impression." I will also, however, get my definition of allegory from a more fundamental definition of the allegorical
impulse. In his "Rhetoric of Temporality," Paul de Man claims that
allegory is really the basis of a very general way of thinking about the
relationship between self and world. When allegory dominates –
when poetry and fiction choose allegory over symbol – representational forms have taken a turn toward recognition of the modern
predicament. They have turned to recognize "an authentically
temporal destiny,"[80] one in which temporality fully asserts *distances* of
various kinds in places where oneness had seemed possible. Since
allegory is that which narrates divisions, following loss of belief in the
possibility of a symbolical oneness, it makes a lot of sense that
allegory is what happens as Impressionists lose faith in the oneness of
the impression. De Man's account, in other words, will help to prove
that there is a very necessary relationship between the problem of
the impression and the allegorical impulse. Along with Fletcher's
account of the way allegory responds to a primal antithesis, de Man
will prove that the allegories of Impressionism have a vital claim to
their form.

To characterize Impressionism in terms of the allegory motivated
by the impression's indeterminacy is to stray far from what has most
often defined it. As we turn, now, to replace old definitions with new
ones, the relative complexity of the new might elicit an embarrassing
question: why define Impressionism as some problematic and com-
plexified theoretical category, when it might be defined so simply in
terms of its relation to *painting*? Impressionist painting might, after
all, give all the definition we need of Impressionism's "subjective"
mode, and has the virtue of historical, terminological, and even
popular priority. And it is hard to deny that literary Impressionism
owes a debt to painting. Any pragmatic approach to the question
must admit that for better or for worse literary Impressionism takes
its name from its counterpart, and will always evoke that counterpart
in the public mind. This introductory account therefore ends with a
word about the right way to think about the relation between the
two Impressionisms. It ends by trying to remove any last doubts in
this regard – by explaining why painting's impression would make us

get the literary impression exactly wrong. It is important to return to the interart analogy because that analogy can help to define, *by contrast*, the nature of the literary impression.

VI SISTER ARTS?

The Impressionisms of painting and literature share an interest in subjective perception. This shift from object to subject, with its emphasis on point of view, seems to have entailed in both arts attention to evanescent effects, radical fidelity to perceptual experience, and a consequent inattention to what had been art's framing concerns. Out were plot, schema, and other forms of rationalizing conceptual knowledge; freedom, informality, and emphasis on the experience of the senses enabled the artist to make art more perfectly reflect lived experience. And freedom from all other goals allowed the artist to get at the moment of perception, from which all other forms of experience follow. Such fundamental insight brought new adeptness with the basic procedures of art: comparable to the Impressionist brushstroke, it seems, is the writer's impression, which makes something slight and sketchy stand for some larger experience, and blends with other impressions to produce a whole more evocative than any more formal set or series of representational details. A similar relativism links both arts at the general level, as well, as each abandons faith in larger systems in favor of faith in what seems personally true.

What do these strong affinities suggest about the relationship between the two arts? Are they *analogous*? Did Impressionist painting *influence* writers, and inspire them to develop a literary counterpart? Or do the two take part in a larger Impressionist *period-style*, with common ancestors in prior traditions? What exactly is the nature and extent of the affinity between literary Impressionism and Impressionism in painting?

Analogies between the arts are always suspect.[81] Beyond the pleasure and usefulness of basic interdisciplinarity, important warnings begin to sound, and these gain special authority when it comes to Impressionism, primarily because such analogies have often supported claims that Impressionism is not literary. Superficial sensation may work well in painting, but it trivializes literature: this has been, as we have seen, the argument behind misunderstandings of the literary impression – the argument that led Max Nordau, for example, to conclude that "Impressionism in literature is an example of that atavism which we have noticed as the most distinctive feature in the mental life of degenerates."[82] But when, by contrast, the interart comparison argues more generally about an Impressionist period-style, it falsifies literary Impressionism in another way. Then, the common ground of "subjective perception" grows so large that it ceases to have any explanatory depth. Looking between analogy and period-style for some account of influence does not do much better, often in fact proving only that Impressionist painting inspires *non*-Impressionist modes of writing. What seems necessary, finally, is some better analogy, one that does not equate impressions with superficial sensations, that could bring out those specific actual affinities that would really help the two Impressionisms to explain each other. That better analogy will be the goal here – not of this introduction, but of this book as a whole, which in defining the literary impression will aim implicitly to contribute the necessary *fourth term* to an Impressionist interart analogy.

Current analogies are compelling but confusing, suggestive at best but at worst misleading. The comparison seems most often to make literary Impressionism a literary *pictorialism*: *ut pictora poesis*, the comparison suggests, made writers try in prose or poetry what they saw in galleries and studios. Local, uncorrected, transient visual perception – what Monet shows of the water at Argenteuil – is then what we look for in Impressionist writing: Conrad's Congo becomes Impressionist for its reticulation of color and light, its intense hazy atmosphere, and a book like Woolf's *The Waves* becomes, like Monet's haystacks, an effort to present the world of objects differently lit by changing angles of sunlight.[83] The definition of literary Impressionism in terms of pictorialist influence typically follows a series of historical connections, stressing connections between Monet and Zola, Manet and Mallarmé, Sargent and James, Whistler and Wilde, and Fry and Woolf. Zola admired the Impressionists, defended them in print, and imported their methods into literary representation (albeit into what we tend to call naturalism); Mallarmé wrote in praise of Manet, indicating the inspiration for his writing's dark disorder; the Goncourts, who painted and wrote, directly made writing painterly with *"écriture artiste."* James, who initially dismissed Impressionist painting as something "incompatible . . . with the existence of first-rate talent"[84] wanted in "The Coxon Fund" to "make an *Impression* – as one of Sargent's pictures is an impression."[85] And Woolf, for whom modern fiction begins in 1910, seems to have borrowed her visuals from those which Roger Fry presented to England in his first (1910) exhibition of the Post-Impressionists. All these connections seem to indicate decades of major *ut pictora poesis* activity. To those who prefer to divide credit more equally, the connections suggest a "far-reaching cultural phenomenon" called "impressionist culture," in which the shared efforts of figures from Monet to Woolf are the style of a whole period's perception of reality.[86]

Two modes of explanation are at work here: those of influence and period-style. The "period" in question extends too far forwards and backwards to have the heuristic value that period styles need. As David Scott has recently noted, the period that would take in all of Impressionism's implications extends too much into coincidence with that of Romanticism.[87] It would wrongly hypostatize "the subjective," which, after all, means many things that only resemble each other in very schematic opposition to what is "objective." The "subjective" justifications for color-theory, for example, differ from the "subjective" justifications for Pater's personal responses to works of art. The former come, via Michel-Eugène Chevreul's *Law of the Simultaneous Contrast of Colors* (1839), from physics; the latter come, as David Bromwich has shown, from Hazlitt and Hume, and reflect a romantic tradition of resistance to scientific explanation. The two, then, are as different as the science of perception and the philosophy of emotion, and relate to each other only within a category as broad as the whole post-Enlightenment unfolding of idealist and empiricist traditions. And the "period" loses even that specificity in light of arguments against Impressionism's historical specificity: since Impressionism in painting was in fact not the dominant art of its moment, and is rather a tendency that some art historians attribute to any number of moments of mimetic crisis, it cannot anchor a period of related Impressionisms in the specific culture of the nineteenth century.

As for influence: should the influence of Monet on Zola, or Fry on Woolf, make us describe literary Impressionism in terms of its counterpart in painting? The Monet–Zola connection, of course, indicates the problem here. Zola saw Impressionist painting and in appreciation wrote – in, for example, *L'Oeuvre* (1886) – naturalist novels. Inversely, a nineteenth-century British writer could produce Impressionist writing in response to Renaissance painting: Walter

Pater of course invoked his impression five years before Monet named his *Impression: Soleil Levant,* and seven years before Louis Leroy coined the name for Monet's style. The Fry–Woolf connection indicates, at the other end, a similar ambiguity: Fry influenced Woolf by exposing her to Post-Impressionism, which differs enormously from Impressionism (in definition) in ways for which Fry was himself largely responsible.[88] These challenges to the story of influence suggest not that painting and writing had nothing essential to do with each other, but that we cannot rigorously define literary Impressionism as a result of the influence of Impressionist painting.

Even where such influence is explicit, it does not help. Take for example the case of T. E. Hulme, who attributes modern poetry's innovations to the influence of Whistler:

... the modern ... no longer deals with heroic action, it has become definitely and finally introspective and deals with expression and communication of momentary phrases in the poet's mind . . . There is an analogous change in painting, where the old endeavored to tell a story, the modern attempts to fix an impression. We still perceive the mystery of things, but we perceive it in entirely a different way – no longer directly in the form of action, but as an impression, for example Whistler's pictures. We can't escape from the spirit of our times. What has found expression in painting as Impressionism will soon find expression in poetry in free verse.[89]

Hulme here calls literary Impressionism a result of a wish to do in writing what Whistler does with paint. If his view is typical, we should explain "the modern" in literature as a result of painting's historical influence. But there are endless complications. Hulme gives us at least three different configurations of this influence. He speaks at once of "a spirit of the times," informing painting and poetry alike; an "analogous change," happening simultaneously in painting and poetry; and of an Impressionism in poetry that will *follow* its expression in painting. For the change to be strictly "analogous," it would have to have happened when Whistler made it – around 1870. To "soon find expression," it would have to happen more than forty years later. And for it to be the product of "the spirit of the times," it could have happened any time from before 1800 to our present day – at any time in which "expression and communication of momentary phases" has been an aesthetic goal. To the degree that Hulme's view is typical, it authorizes an impossibly wide context for influence. Hulme contributes further complication when he moves, with Imagism, from "impression" to "image." Then the impression ceases to inform modern poetry's future and becomes very quickly an element of the past. Impressionism's window of opportunity, that is, shrinks to something like three years – whereas Hulme's description of the example of Whistler's pictures would give it a range of more than a century.

Such argument against interart definition might be pedantic were it not for the special need to disqualify conventional analogy in this case. Despite the fact that the arts are, as Alastair Fowler puts it, "ineluctably familial," and despite the famous fellowship of writers and artists throughout the nineteenth and twentieth centuries, both Impressionisms occurred at a time when the arts thought it important to stress their singularities.[90] Casual analogies would do no harm were it not for the fact that writers who invoke the impression are not imitating their counterparts in painting as much as clarifying the unique requirements of the literary medium. Any similarities really belie the subjunctive mood of *ut pictora poesis*, and it is this drive toward distinction that is overlooked in misconceived assertions of interart analogy: what seems imitation is imitation's opposite; what seems painterly, in the impression, is in fact a movement away from painting's theory of experience and representation.[91]

The analogy itself – based in influence, period, or ahistorical connections – therefore fundamentally distorts the literary impression. This kind of distortion is not uncommon: Wendy Steiner has noted that terms often applied as synonyms in interart comparisons are really *homonyms*. Words such as "rhythm," for example, only sound the same when applied to different arts, but actually mean different and even incompatible things.[92] Despite their common parentage, and despite certain similarities, the impressions of painting and literature are *antonyms*. And we could live happily with the vagueness of period-style and *ut-pictora-poesis* definitions if such definitions did not make synonyms of antonyms – if they did not thereby falsify the literary impression and perpetually make "literary Impressionism" an oxymoron.[93]

Why antonyms? Painters rendering impressions defined them as visual sensations. Seeking impressions meant bracketing everything except immediate visual perception. The impression therefore moved aesthetic perception toward "sensation"; the mediation of the impression-metaphor led painters to pitch key experience further into sensation's territory. For writers, by contrast, the impression moves experience in the opposite direction. Pater, James, and Woolf invoke the impression to argue against precursors – Arnold, Besant, and Bennett, respectively – who focus too exclusively on direct perceptual experience. Arnold would regard the object itself, where Pater wants to see it through the filter of response; Besant insists on direct experience, where James makes imagination intervene; and Bennett would describe everything about Mrs. Brown, where Woolf favors evocation through selection. These writers use the impression, that is, to move aesthetic experience *from* the realm of sensuous perception back toward that combination of (or middle ground between) sense and thought always at work in the "aesthetic." Painterly associations have always obscured this fact. They have led critics to expect rich sensuousness in writing that is notoriously "bloodless"; not finding it, and finding abstraction instead, criticism has been unwilling to admit the possibility of literary Impressionism. But abstraction is that toward which the impression moves literary representation – how it changes the novel, which had always been, as Ian Watt notes, a matter of recording the "directly apprehended sensum."[94] The false likeness of the two impressions leads us to expect greater devotion to visual sensation, when impressions really lead writers to make experience conform to the structure of the aesthetic imagination.

How can impressions mean abstraction, when vivid atmospheres, diminishment of conceptual order, and concrete detail seem proof that Impressionism in literature, like Impressionism in painting, stresses sensory perception? Joseph Conrad certainly seems to contradict the claim in his Preface to *The Nigger of the "Narcissus"*: "All art . . . appeals primarily to the senses," and "may be defined as a single-minded attempt to render the highest kind of justice to the visible universe" (ix, vii). But according to Conrad, art appeals to the senses in order to "reach the secret spring of responsive emotions." It does justice to the visible universe by "bringing to light the truth, manifold and one, underlying its every aspect." The artist does make his appeal through the senses – but, more precisely, with "an impression conveyed through the senses." Conrad in fact uses the word "impression" to distinguish "the senses" from the proper location of good writing. He might have spoken of the senses themselves, but he emphasizes the impression, and thereby links the senses to capacities and needs that are to Conrad too often left out of the literary endeavor. The impression reaches to the senses with one hand, but reaches with the other toward Conrad's greater goal:

"solidarity" (x). Making you *see* is all about making you feel that you belong. Conrad's writing might intensify visual effects, but its Impressionism does so because the impression connects intensity with improved community. Other literary modes might try at one or the other; trying at both, Conrad's Impressionism moves away from the styles proper to either, toward the middle ground that the impression occupies. Conrad therefore falls in with writers who invoke the impression to move the ground of experience from sensuous perception to abstract possibilities not formerly granted to fiction.[95]

The distinction here between painterly and literary impressions ought not to suggest that the impression itself cannot involve intensification of visual effects. It means that the impression is a dynamic metaphor for perception that acts differently depending on what E. H. Gombrich might call its "context of action."[96] The impression's mediation is a metaphorical adjustment whose activity depends largely upon the conditions of what it adjusts; the impression is essentially the same in its painterly and literary guises, but those guises change its ways. What we need, then, in order to define the two Impressionisms in terms of each other, is an analogy that allows for two different versions of the impression – an analogy with *four terms*. Most interart analogies, as Leonard Diepeveen has noted, have only three. They contrive connections on a false pivot, depending on a term allegedly taken from both arts but really only the property of one. The analogy between the Impressionisms is such a "muted, three-term analogy" – forcing the painterly impression into the realm of the literary.[97] A proper four-term analogy would define both the painterly impression and the literary impression in their relation to the two Impressionisms and thereby find the analogy between the arts.

This account of literary Impressionism aims to define the fourth term in the Impressionist analogy. It has, with respect to Impressionism as a "period-style," that limit, reserving for a brief conclusion, and then to other projects, discussion of the interart analogy for which it provides a basis. But it is important finally to emphasize the fact that the problem of the three-term interart analogy is particularly difficult to solve when it comes to Impressionism. The slippage from four terms to three – that slippage that secretly ruins analogies – is strongly encouraged by the impression's rhetorical uncertainty, which would, it turns out, collapse the distinction between the arts. Jean Hagstrum notes that one hope of the *ut pictora poesis* impulse is a unification of faculties: sister-arts discourse (after the Renaissance) aspires toward a "union of body and soul, picture and word, sense and intellect," in the hope that "by assuming the voice and air of her sister" poetry would "attempt to understand with the senses, to feel with the intellect."[98] A common element of this discourse has been the sense that "poetry needs to be supplemented with physical presence to be fully aesthetic" – that sister-arts connections could accomplish the very mediation that the impression itself exists to contrive.[99] Even if literary Impressionism does not necessarily move literature in the direction of greater physical presence, it tries to gain, through the impression, just the kind of unification of faculties that sister-arts connections have tended to want. Moreover, the impression, in its tendency to mediate movement and stasis, even collapses Gotthold Lessing's fundamental distinction between the spatial and temporal forms of painting and writing respectively.[100] So if sister-arts connections secretly collapse analogies in order to advance their cause, they do so, it might be said, in the spirit of the impression; the better impression-analogy therefore fights itself to be born. The analogy to painting, has yet one more role to play: it is essential not only to a definition of literary Impressionism, but to our understanding of the very possibility of interart relations.

CHAPTER 2

Pater's homoerotic impression

The impression marks Pater's place in the advent of modernity. It is his pivot in that progression that revolutionized British aesthetics: Matthew Arnold famously sought to "see the object as in itself it really is"; Pater, revising Arnold's dictum, wrote that "in aesthetic criticism the first step towards seeing one's object as it really is, is to know one's own impression as it really is"; and for Oscar Wilde, notoriously, the critic's job was "to see the object as in itself it really is *not*."[1] Refuting Arnoldian objectivity and enabling Wildean caprice, Pater's impression contributed the conviction that knowledge in and about art must be subjective. His place here between Arnold's Victorianism and Wilde's Postmodernism makes him what Harold Bloom calls the "hinge upon which turns the single gate" in nineteenth-century literary history – and it makes his Impressionism a decisive (if not fully strong) precursor to modernist aesthetic innovation.[2]

This turning point, however, is otherwise and better known for its social life. In Pater's case theorizing the subjective also meant taking the first misstep down the slippery decadence of public homosexuality. The history of *that* decline more memorably goes from Arnold to Pater to Wilde: there is Arnold, sure of the public value of aesthetic discretion, who maintained a respectable eminence as Inspector of Schools and Professor of Poetry; there is Wilde, given to idiosyncracy, ending in the bad eminence of hard labor for gross indecency; and, in between again, Pater – the "demoralizing moralizer," not chosen to succeed Arnold as Professor of Poetry, and author of the book that Wilde first read for consolation in prison.[3] Pater's middle ground between the object as it "is" and "is not" becomes in this version of the progression a place somewhere between Oxford and Reading Gaol.

What links these two histories? Only vague opinions currently answer this question. We tend presumptively to associate the rise of "the subjective" with the relaxation of art's moral imperative and in turn to see this amorality as homosexuality's opportunity, or, to see "the subjective" as the special talent of the impassioned outsider and therefore more likely to prevail in a homosexual subculture. But there is a more necessary connection – and a less tautological one – between sexual and epistemological orientations in this case. That more necessary connection is the structure of Pater's impression, which figures the aesthetic union of intellect and sense as a homosexual relationship.[4]

To Pater the impression meant an aesthetic criticism that could fuse intellect and sense, that could move in and out of consciousness, that could find an object's fixity in the veracity of subjective flux. But when Pater invokes the impression in *The Renaissance*, its characteristic indeterminacy leads to confusion about *impressionability*: wanting to receive impressions, Pater cannot decide where such receptivity lies, since it seems on the one hand a power of the fresh young body but on the other hand a power of the mature discriminating mind. So he imagines that receptivity as a collaborative affair; he ensures the impression's juncture of intellect and sense by making it a function of desire felt by intellect for sense – by a connoisseurial mind for an idealized object of masculine vitality. It is this juncture that makes the impression at once a turn to the subjective and a license for homosexual love – something that might encourage Wilde simultaneously to defend the whim of the critic and the nature of "unspeakable" love. This, then, is the more necessary connection between Pater's sexual and epistemological orientations.

The coincidence of these two histories is basic to literary Impressionism, for a number of reasons. It initiates a characteristic tendency to join social and theoretical urges – the structure of collaboration, which begins in Pater and persists throughout the Impressionist tradition. Moreover, it initiates Impressionism's career of doubt and controversy. What enabled Pater to imagine Impressionist mediation became Impressionism's subtext, legible to hostile critics and, in turn, a force for revision. *The Renaissance*, famously, was a scandal, largely because readers could detect the sexuality of Pater's aesthetic. Responding to the scandal, and to his own doubts about his collaborative desires, Pater revised his Impressionism, producing in *Marius the Epicurean* an allegory of the process through which his Impressionism's synthesis of faculties repented of its scandalous devotions. Homosexual desire therefore gives structure both to the theory and to the history of Impressionism, enabling the impression's mediation of sense and intellect but also forcing their separation.

Pater's Impressionism found stability in desire, and so brought on scandal. Here is the early cause of Impressionism's problems – but also cause to rethink the category of the aesthetic. Influential current theories of "aesthetic ideology" tend to accuse the aesthetic of false consciousness, of quietism, and even collusion with forces of political oppression. Aesthetic judgment has been discredited as a cover for privileged detachment and as an opiate through which capitalist culture makes alienation a pleasure. But as Pater's impression sets it up, aesthetic judgment means turning inward and finding one's capacities for judgment incomplete; it means discovering self-alienation, and trying to correct the problem through engagement with another kind of person. However limited this engagement might seem, its outreach puts sociality where "aesthetic ideology" sees isolated, introverted, and irresponsible selves. Its recourse to collaboration puts social intersubjectivity at the heart of the aesthetic: this, perhaps, is what made the progression from Arnold to Pater to Wilde hard for the public to take, and what gives Impressionism, even when its collaborations seem suspect, its special dissidence.

How does the impression make Pater a hinge figure, if it had already been part of the aesthetic currency? In "On Poetry in General" (1818), for example, Hazlitt had called the impression "that uneasy, exquisite sense of beauty or power that cannot be contained within itself; that is impatient of all limit" and that strives "to enshrine itself, as it were, in the highest form of fancy."[5] Hazlitt had already used the term to describe the conveyance from sense to fancy, so that it is possible to say, as David Bromwich does, that Pater only brings to more triumphant popularity a unit of romantic terminology.[6] Pater's impression, however, is new – made new, that is, by intellectual contexts newly unsympathetic to the romantic imagination. More than ever, deterministic science threatened to reduce the human faculties to mechanistic forces. As Billie Inman and Anthony Ward, among others, have shown, Pater read deeply in theories asserting "the physical basis of life, or the absence of any force but chemical forces in all of life's processes," and theories confident of finding the "mechanical equivalent of consciousness."[7] Spencer's *Principles of*

Biology (1864–67), Huxley's discourses on scientific truth, George Henry Lewes's essays on Darwin – this evidence of physiological determinism confronted Pater's intellectual moment with new challenges to any theory of life or art that tried to distinguish human thought and feeling from animal or chemical impulses.[8] Romanticism met that challenge, in its earlier form, by affirming idealist and transcendentalist distinctions. What Pater does – through the impression – is make science itself fundamental to aesthetic freedom.[9]

Readers rarely note that Pater uses "impression" in two different ways. In the Preface to *The Renaissance*, the impression is a unit of subjective aesthetic response – single, substantial, and a mode of judgment. When he writes that the first step in aesthetic criticism is to realize one's impression, he speaks the language of romantic theory. When, by contrast, the Conclusion to *The Renaissance* describes the fleeting impressions that swirl around us in a world of flux – the "instable, flickering, inconsistent" impressions "in perpetual flight" (187–88), he speaks the language of "perpetual flux" popularized by Spencer, Lewes, and others. It is of course well known that Pater speaks these two languages, and also well known that he plays a large part in the synthesis of their contexts (idealist and empirical). Far less well known is the part that the rhetoric of the impression itself plays in that synthesis – the way that Pater's two uses of the impression become one and thereby enable "perpetual flux" to become a basis for anti-deterministic aesthetic theory.

Wolfgang Iser has noted that Pater's impression is "a mixture of subjective perception with objective perceptibility."[10] It mixes these things, characteristic of different discourses, because the arbitrariness of the objective flux produces strange associations which in turn produce unique moods. When random impressions associate, they produce feelings that are special to certain moments, certain people, and certain discriminations. The unique aesthetic response therefore is intensified, rather than diminished, by mechanized consciousness.[11] Were the impression not able, however, to stand both for fleeting inconsistency and subjective mood, Pater might not have been able to discover this continuity through which biological science becomes aesthetic theory.

The pages that follow here will describe the consequences of this peculiar continuity, this contrivance, not unlike that in Hume, through which Pater blends different perceptual moments, even from different theoretical discourses. What needs emphasis, however, is the nature of Pater's need for such a contrivance, and the way it proves that his impression really is an original "hinge" moment in the history of literary aesthetics. Hazlitt may have made the impression a way to run from perception to the highest form of fancy, but when Pater revives it, he accomplishes a *rapprochement* in which the romantic imagination absorbs its new positivistic nemesis. This accomplishment makes his impression new – remakes it, that is, for Impressionism, and for the early moment of Modernism's renewal of the romantic cultural agenda.

Pater's turn to the "subjective" impression does more than make the aesthetic personal. It takes part in long-standing debates about the history of mind, the nature of perception, and the way art plays upon human faculties. More specifically, it tries for a synthesis of two strains in philosophy which seemed so ruinously incompatible in the nineteenth century: German idealism and British Empiricism. As scholars often note, Pater largely devoted his intellectual life to this synthesis, hoping in particular to find ways to undo the disintegration through which abstract thought had lost its basis in or connection to concrete sense. Anyone who would call his Impressionism facile overlooks this distinguished role in intellectual history. But anyone who would credit it with any great synthesis of empirical and idealist traditions forgets that Pater philosophizes only idiosyncratically. If he finds, through the impression, a way to return thought and sense to a state of happy reciprocity, he does so only through recourse to theorization which is, after all, personal. In Pater, that is, empiricist and idealist thought work together as a result of an analogous union of Empiricist and idealist personhood; they come together insofar as the alienated metaphysician loves an Empirical body, and takes his desire to be a philosophical mediation.

This personalization of the philosophical begins in one of Pater's early unpublished essays, "The History of Philosophy." The essay sees philosophy from the Greeks to the present as a conflict between the claims of abstract thought and concrete sense. It looks regretfully back to the prelapsarian moment of perfect knowledge – when no "thoughts about thinking" spoiled the integrity of human faculties – and it looks forward to the restoration of such perfect integrity through some new philosophical disposition. What gives Pater's essay its modern equivalent to lost integrity is the "subjective idealism" of Berkeley. But as we will see it is less Berkeley's philosophy that leads to this end than something peculiar about Berkeley the man – the way the man was, effectively, two men, who could together join what philosophy kept asunder.

An Hegelian phenomenology of mind gives form to "The History of Philosophy." It begins with a look back at an old ideal – that great " 'unconscious' period of human mind, a period in which, though with full enjoyment of their receptive and active powers," men were "as unsuspicious as children as to any abstract questions of what might be beneath their immediate experience."[12] In what follows – as in Impressionism – this lack of distinction between abstract questioning and immediate experience is Pater's preoccupation. But (also as in Impressionism) this simple integrity can be no simple goal, because "that mind which has once broken the smooth surface of what seemed its self-evident principles can never again be as natural as a child's" (3b). A commonplace regret keeps Pater from any facile primitivism, and demands from him some strategy, beyond escape into a world of children, to regain sense-certainty. In the beginning of the essay, he invokes Goethe to formulate the terms of the strategy, wondering how it might be possible to "[regain] just that state of unsuspecting receptivity of mind by an artificial act of reflection" – how "an all-accomplished philosophy" might "put one back into the state it had originally superseded" (2a). He asks, in other words, how artificial reflection might lead back to natural receptivity and how a finished philosophy might lead back to beginnings.

Philosophy begins, in Pater's account, with skepticism, which limits the bad effects of man's fall from unconsciousness. In the ancient world, skepticism made a virtue of necessity by turning awareness of immediate experience into a kind of "secondary consciousness," in which experience becomes subject to "dispassionate criticism." This form of skepticism, however, led to the development of an excessively sophisticated system of abstract thought – to an idealism that came to require new reference to the corrective experience of the senses. Modern skepticism therefore inverts the tendency of its predecessor, and subjects thought to experience. In all this Pater sees improvement: the skepticisms of Hume, Berkeley, and Fichte, by working counter to the forces of "narrow metaphysical speculation," tend to push consciousness back into patterns of unified knowledge. But nevertheless a dualistic tendency persists – the tendency to distinguish, to whatever lesser degree, the sensation from the idea. Because his interest lies mainly in the resolution of such differences, Pater's essay does not simply give an appreciative account of the development of the empiricist skepticism through which experience grounds reason; rather, it dwells on the way idealist philosophers, at their best and perhaps in spite of themselves, made invigorating concessions to individual, concrete, perceptual experience. What most compels Pater's admiration are those moments in idealist philosophy when the "white light" of the ideal is "refracted" into the colours of "earthly or material phenomena," when "dry abstraction" is "variegated" in the "dynamic element" of concrete reality (14b, 15b). The history of philosophy, which has been a history of the development of divergent philosophical schools, becomes a history of moments in which consciousness has asserted its need for integrity in spite of theoretical divisiveness. The hero of the history is "the irrepressible instinct of our minds for intellectual sympathy everywhere," the efforts of an "illuminated reason," the growth of a "natural ideal" – the tendency of consciousness to deny philosophical division by wanting unions we can only express in oxymoronic phrases (16a).

Because the efforts of the oxymoronic mind are aberrational – because they tend to embellish rather than found the philosophical arguments in which they appear – Pater has a hard time describing them. No single philosopher or philosophy can stand for that activity of mind through which we might regain that receptivity lost with the fall into self-consciousness. Or so it seems, until Berkeley assumes pride of place in the essay, and carries Pater toward hopeful conclusions. In Pater's account, Berkeley's skepticism about the reality of objects leads, later on in the philosophical tradition, to skepticism about the reality of the mind; the mind becomes "but a stream of impressions over the supposed but wholly unknown mental substructure which no act of intuition or reflexion could ever really detect" (23b). Here is a notorious end point in skepticism, which seems an unlikely point of departure for a positive conclusion to "The History of Philosophy." It leads nevertheless to a sense of purpose not unlike that which Pater describes in his major texts: "That we cannot really know the mental substance in ourselves and still less in others might make us so much the closer observers of the *accidents* of the mind[,] the phases and phenomena of its actual and concrete trains of thought in ourselves or in others as still further varied and expanded by the influence of the imagination in art[,] in poetry[,] or fiction" (24a). Let the *flux itself* revive perfect, artistic sensitivity: in this vein, the essay ends having found theoretical restoration of Goethe's "receptivity of mind," the philosophy through which to reintegrate consciousness.

That it does so, however, is strange, since nothing in Berkeley's philosophy authorizes such a theoretical achievement. What inspires Pater's optimistic conclusions is less Berkeley's skeptical philosophy (and less the later influence of that skepticism on theories of the unknowability of other minds) than a certain enabling doubleness in the person of Berkeley himself: "[W]hat is really remarkable about Berkeley's position in philosophy is not as so many have thought the paradoxical character of the theory he maintained but that so simple a line of scepticism so revolutionary because so simple . . . should have found a prelate of the church for its expositor" (21b). As it turns out, it is the combination of the substance of Berkeley's skepticism and the human source of its exposition – the combination of skepticism and religious devotion – that makes Berkeley remarkable; it is this "accidental circumstance" that turns a purely "logical consideration" into an "incisive paradox." Berkeley becomes, through his doubleness, an inspiration both to negative skepticism and to a kind of positive ardor; he becomes the philosopher through whom Pater can make radical unknowability an occasion for the positive enterprise of his aesthetic; he becomes, in spite of his subjective idealism, the thinker through whom Pater can imagine experience both real and ideal.

Berkeley enables Pater to imagine a salutary synthesis because he is not a single philosopher. He is a collaboration of two persons – the empirical skeptic, who brings skepticism to its most notoriously radical conclusion, and the "prelate of the church," whose faith turns skepticism into paradox and lends it a positive and sincere intensity.[13] Just as it takes two different Berkeleys to solve philosophical problems, it will take two different kinds of people to effect the philosophical synthesis of the impression. Just as it takes both Berkeley the skeptic and Berkeley the prelate to inspire conclusions in which mental substance is at once unknowable and the proper subject of our devoted aesthetic attention, it will take the participation of two kinds of persons to inspire an Impressionism in which alienated intellect and sensuous intensity converge. In "The History of Philosophy," no pressing need demands anything more than Berkeley's doubleness, but in Pater's more central aesthetic statements and products, Impressionist mediation borrows from and endorses the more paradoxical union of persons at work in homo-sexual desire.

Like "The History of Philosophy," the Preface to *The Renaissance* would join abstract and concrete forms of knowledge; but where "The History of Philosophy" uses semi-oxymoronic phrases ("intel-lectual sympathy," "natural ideal") to express such mediation, the Preface taps the oxymoronics natural to the impression. The impres-sion does its work for Pater in two stages. In the Preface to *The Renaissance*, it brings Hume into the realm of the aesthetic, to ensure that thoughts about art defer to the feelings art produces. In the Conclusion to *The Renaissance*, it extends this verificatory ground back from the realm of art into the realm of life (leading apparently to hedonism). In both of these stages, the validity of the impression's effects in art and life depends upon the fact that the impression is not, as so many readers thought, simply sensuous – the fact that it is a third term born out of a refusal of a long-standing alienation of intellect and sense. As we will see, however, as Pater moves from the first to the second stages of his theorization of the impression, its status as a third term is threatened by uncertainty about its proper provenance.

The Preface to *The Renaissance* uses the word "impression" pri-marily to replace abstract definitions of beauty with temperamental ones. Responding implicitly to attempts to define beauty by Arnold, Ruskin, and strains of German idealism, Pater notes that beauty "is relative," and so must be defined "in the most concrete terms possible" (xix). These concrete terms are not dictated by the object, but by subjective response – through the realization of impressions. Pater quotes Arnold, writing that " 'to see the object as in itself it really is,' has been justly said to be the aim of all true criticism whatever." He then upends Arnold's injunction by suggesting that the impression comes at a stage crucially prior to Arnold's endeavor: "In aesthetic criticism the first step toward seeing one's object as it really is, is to know one's own impression as it really is, to discriminate it, to realise it distinctly" (xix). The power to discrimi-nate and realize distinct impressions supersedes intellectual and ethical judgment, as the rejection of "a correct abstract definition of beauty for the intellect" makes room for "a certain kind of tempera-ment, the power of being deeply moved by the presence of beautiful objects" (xxi). Describing this power, Pater adumbrates a faculty "aesthetic" in the earlier sense of that term: it mediates sense and reason to produce a form of knowledge that transcends the distinction between mind and body. The impression, as its correlate, mediates sensations and ideas.[14]

At its most flamboyant, this temperament became the famous pose of the aesthete. Pater's special contribution to that pose, however, largely appears in *The Renaissance*'s Conclusion. The Preface modestly takes an aesthetic stand available since Kant wrote, in the *Critique of Judgment*, that in judging the beautiful "we refer the representation to the Subject and its feeling of pleasure or displeasure" in what "is not a cognitive judgment, and so not logical, but is aesthetic – which means that it is one whose determining ground cannot be other than subjective."[15] But this subjective turn becomes newly exciting and potentially dangerous when the Conclusion extends its range. There, the temperament of "he who experiences impressions strongly" is not something deployed in aesthetic judgment but a way of life – the life lived as a "hard, gem-like flame" (189). Aiming his theory beyond the work of art, Pater describes a world "not of objects in the solidity with which language invests them, but of impressions, unstable, flickering, inconsistent" (187). The abstractions that falsify art, it seems, would falsify this life as well, so that it must be everyone's goal always to court "new impressions" (189). The initially subtle and modest modification of Arnold's aesthetic becomes a whole new way of life, lived in the spirit of aesthetic synthesis.

We see the important novelty of the shift – its significance in the history of Impressionism if not quite in the history of thought – when we pick up the impression where we left it (and where Pater found it) in Hume's Empiricism.[16] Pater read Hume in 1861; his grounding of abstract ideas of beauty in some initial impression owes a great debt to Hume's theory of the way impressions initiate and confirm ideas. From Hume, Pater gets his sense that impressions have greater vivacity than the ideas abstracted from them, that feeling is more reliable than thought and a better basis for belief, that sense is a necessary corrective to errant metaphysical speculation. But this debt to Hume only superficially grounds Pater's aesthetic in the rigor of skeptical empiricist methodology. For while Hume takes great pains to stabilize the impression through emphasis upon "custom," Pater endorses perceptual novelty; and whereas skepticism is for Hume a pretext for a more systematic science of knowledge, it is for Pater a pleasure in itself. We have seen that Hume's impression encourages representational dynamicism by conflating diverse moments in consciousness. Dismissing the constraints of custom and system, Pater intensifies both the dynamicism and the indeterminacy of the Humean impression, and makes Impressionism out of Empiricism.

For Pater, the vitality of the impression itself is the source of the impression's significance rather than the proof of it, an end in itself rather than a means to relative certainty. This difference in emphasis creates a crucial overall difference of mood. For Hume, skepticism reduces us to a world of impressions; for Pater, a more Epicurean spirit makes the flow of impressions the most gratifying world of all, so that he does not need the stabilization Hume achieves through the experiential habits of custom. The basis of Pater's Impressionism only seems to resemble Hume's skepticism: yes, Pater describes the "flood of external objects" that "dissipate" into "groups of impressions . . . unstable, flickering, inconsistent" (187); this inconsistency and dissipation seemingly leads to doubt and isolation, as "experience, already reduced to a group of impressions, is ringed round for each one of us by that thick wall of personality" (187); and this problem appears to produce a state something like that into which Hume falls at the end of Book I of the *Treatise* – "the most deplorable condition imaginable, inviron'd with the deepest darkness."[17] For Pater, however, the dissipation of impressions is no source of despair; it is the basis of art and the essence of life. Whereas Hume's "philosophical melancholy" is cured only through distraction from the implications of skepticism in the "game of backgammon," Pater revels in the "continual vanishing away, that strange, perpetual, weaving and unweaving of ourselves" (188). David Bromwich has suggested that "where Hume had described his resolution of the object into impressions as a philosophy that could be believed but never lived, Pater shows us how to live it."[18] That demonstration requires, in fact, a denial of that which makes life livable for Hume. Pater thinks that "to burn always with this hard, gemlike flame" requires that we do not "form habits" or allow customs to stifle our burning, since "the theory or idea or system which requires of us the sacrifice of any part of this experience . . . has no real claim upon us" (189). Stripped of custom and its skeptical source, the Humean impression becomes, in Pater's writing, an Epicurean passion, and a bridge from the skepticism of mechanistic science to the pleasures of love and art.

This intensification happens, essentially, because Pater makes the impression aesthetic: combining Hume's terminology with aesthetic concerns derived primarily from Hegel, Pater elevates Hume's verificatory impression to the strange status of an ideal passion. When he writes, in the famous last lines of the Conclusion, that one must "seek a quickened sense of life" and that art best promises that sense because it "comes to you proposing frankly to give nothing but the highest quality to your moments as they pass" (190), he has snuck empirical fact into the proof of aesthetic "quality." He "aestheti-cizes," and thereby departs from the spirit of, the Empiricist impression/idea distinction, while nevertheless making that distinc-tion justification for aesthetic experience. This is literary Impressio-nism's moment of genesis. Whereas the impression existed before, was current in romantic theory, and current at Pater's moment in the languages of physiology and psychology, here it becomes a keyword. Pater took an empirical impression – made rigorous but flawed in Hume, made more rigorous but unsympathetic in the language of mid-Victorian science – and found its aesthetic essence, effecting a juncture that would repeat in a tradition of writers with similar blendings of Empiricist and aesthetic temperaments.

The new impression has two significant results: it initiates the Impressionist strain of literary Modernism, and it gives that Impres-sionism a homoerotic disposition. How it initiates literary Mod-ernism has been shown by F. C. McGrath, who considers Pater's invocation of the impression "one of the opening salvos of the Modernist movement in literature and the arts."[19] The impression's analogs and effects everywhere in Pater's writing prove McGrath right: in the "Essay on Style" (1888), for example, Impressionism leads Pater away from "facts" to seek the "soul-fact," that hybrid of object and perception that is the representational analog to the intense impression.[20] It is the "soul-fact" he seeks most often in his accounts of Renaissance artists, where truth becomes a matter of inner feeling rather than historical fact. When he wants to describe Leonardo as a "bold speculator," despite the fact that "words of his, trenchant enough to justify this impression, are not recorded" (*Renaissance* 77) Pater nevertheless affirms that "a lover of strange souls may still analyse for himself the impression made on him by those works, and try to reach through it a definition of the chief elements of Leonardo's genius" (78). Seeking the thing itself through his impression of it, Pater discovers truths other than facts. Rather than the facts about Leonardo Pater seeks a sense of the ways he shared in the flux of life: ". . . if we think of him as the mere reasoner who subjects design to anatomy, and composition to mathematical rules, we shall hardly have that impression which those around Leonardo received from him" (84). Having that impression requires methods characteristic of Modernism: narrative procedure that dispenses with chronological ordering, axiomatic logic, and detached description, demanding instead a kind of mimicry of life's unfolding.

Elsewhere, Pater calls the impression's essential, experiential truth the *"vraie vérité,"* and theorizes its expressive style. He seeks this truer truth in describing Giorgione: trying to account for the "Giorgion-esque," Pater writes, "Something like this seems to be the *vraie vérité* about Giorgione, if I may adopt a serviceable expression, by which the French recognise those more liberal and durable impressions which . . . lie beyond, and must supplement, the narrower range of the strictly ascertained facts about it" (*Renaissance* 121). These impressions guarantee both greater general truth and more effective style. They can give an essential sense of things: ". . . beyond all those strictly ascertained facts, we must take note of that indirect influence by which one like Giorgione, for instance, enlarges his permanent efficacy and really makes himself felt in our culture. In a just impression of that, is the essential truth, the *vraie vérité* concerning him" (122). The *vraie vérité* also descends to the level of the particularities of what Pater calls "expression:" in the "Essay on Style," he writes, "In the highest as in the lowliest literature, then, the one indispensable beauty is, after all, truth . . . truth here as expression, that finest and most intimate form of truth, the *vraie vérité*."[21] The impression's intimate form of truth makes it a species of metaphor – a style of figuration that would reproduce the inchoate feelings that Impressionism locates between sensing and thinking. A typical moment of such figuration, taken from *Marius the Epicurean,* suggests that impressions bring to consciousness the same kind of truth that metaphor brings to language. Considering the quality of his service to the emperor, Marius thinks, "Yet it was in truth a somewhat melancholy service, a service in which one must needs move about, solemn, serious, depressed, with the hushed footsteps of those who move about the house where a dead body is lying. Such was the impression which occurred to Marius again and again."[22] Marius's impression here delivers a truth more true than the actually true, and in doing so, participates in Impressionism's epistemological

reversal: overtaking the literal, such metaphorical impressions proliferate in Pater to prove that, just as all language ultimately proves
metaphorical, all knowledge proves not to begin in "facts."

"Soul-fact," "*vraie vérité*," and "expression" make up Pater's
Impressionism – the aesthetic temperament at the foundation of the
strain of Modernism that thusly expresses its interest in "life itself."[23]
Giving credit to Impressionism here is important because this
temperament is typically attributed to Aestheticism, in classifications
that mistake Pater's aesthetic priorities. While Pater will stress "art
for art's sake," his version of *disinterestedness* takes him in another
direction: in his peculiar way of making the aesthetic a way to *live*,
Pater significantly denies the real existence of the aesthetic artifact, of
the work of art itself. His goal in seeking impressions is less to reify
the artifact than to affirm the process of life as an end in itself; art
helps to do this, not because it exists in a realm apart from life, but
because it excites, in an extreme but not different degree, the
passions that affirm vitality. At the same time, however, Pater's
affiliation with that vitalist strain in Modernism has its limits.
Revising Hume's impression, Pater enables Modernism, but he also
creates a complication that ensures that he himself will not achieve it.
The complication is the problem of impressionability – the problem
Pater solves, only tenuously, by making the impression a kind of
reciprocal and homoerotic relationship between intellect and sense.

Having dismissed even the limited stability of Hume's antiration-
alism, Pater loses the power to know exactly how the receptive
temperament exists. A quick reinterpretation of the deployment of
the impression in *The Renaissance* will explain the nature and
consequence of this confusion. The impression serves Pater's qualifi-
cation of Arnoldian discretion by founding aesthetic judgment fully
upon individual subjective interpretation: rather than learning some
authority's account of the beauties of cultural touchstones, one feels
them for oneself. The need for Arnoldian or Ruskinian abstractions
seems to return, however, despite this shift to impressions: who says
what the "finest" impressions are? The Preface to *The Renaissance*
suggests, in answer to this question, the intensity of the impression
itself: the best impressions are those most strongly felt. The near
physicalization of discretion lends Impressionism its authenticity and
its universality. But this mode of aesthetic distinction becomes
problematic in the face of the need to maintain it. Pater's explicit
aim in *The Renaissance* is to encourage "aesthetic education," which

"becomes complete in proportion as our susceptibility to these impressions increases in depth and variety" (xx). Education, then, is necessary to develop impressionability – despite the fact that Pater's doctrine of intensity also suggests that education would deaden it. Is it possible to educate a sensibility without developing the abstract categories of judgment that Pater seeks to refute in the Preface? Or does keenest receptivity end where education begins? Pater writes, in the Conclusion, "A counted number of pulses only is given to us of a variegated, dramatic life"; he then asks, "How may we see in them all that is to be seen in them by the finest senses?" (188). He seems to answer, at times, that education will develop that capacity, but at other times to favor unspoiled openness. Perry Meisel has asked whether the Paterian artist is a "martyr of *ascesis*" or some "unconscious flowering"; the Paterian Impressionist, Meisel might say, is perhaps impossibly both.[24]

In Pater's aesthetic, the martyr covets the flower. Although he does not mean to recommend unreflective hedonism, the state of "unconscious flowering" – what Pater calls in "The History of Philosophy" an "unreflecting and unsuspecting receptivity of mind" – emerges as the superior means to receptivity. It is not, however, a means that Pater's narrative voice can actually claim. Necessarily reflective, that voice aligns with the "educated" mode of receptivity, and demonstrates the split between itself and its ideal even as it speaks it. In the tension between the ideal of unreflective receptivity and the narrative voice of aesthetic education, the erotic dynamic in Pater's Impressionism begins to appear. In other texts Pater explicitly resolves the problem of impressionability by constructing collaboration between an "educated" self and some embodiment of pure receptivity; he develops, that is, that new version of epistemological dualism that seeks its resolution through an erotic grounding of the authorial mind in another's sensuous body.[25]

In "The History of Philosophy" Pater solves the problem of dualism in the spirit of Berkeley's paradoxical personality, finding mediation of Empirical sensations and abstract ideas in the combination of Berkeley's religious and scientific lives. When pressed, however, to find such mediation not only in the history of philosophy and religion but in the lives he recommends for himself and for others, Pater must find a real-life equivalent of Berkeley's doubleness, one that includes himself as a participant. Himself much more likely to have "thoughts

about thinking" than strong feelings of physical living, Pater naturally plays the part of the impression's intellectual component; for his
sensuous counterpart, he looks to that which best gives him a sense
of physical vitality – that which gives, through desire, greatest proof
of physical being.

It is in just such a combination that Pater finds a way to describe
ideal receptivity in "Diaphaneitè." An early, unpublished essay,
"Diaphaneitè" describes the perfect human being. It is well known
that Pater modeled this perfect being on a young man for whom he
felt no small desire: Charles Shadwell, whose famous beauty and
relation to Pater made him the perfect candidate for collaboration.
Read at once as aesthetic theory and amorous tribute, "Diaphaneitè" shows how Impressionism and eroticism interact: Pater seems
to project his own strong feelings, remaking them into the perceptual
capacities of the object that erotically causes them. His physical
attraction to Shadwell becomes, in the aesthetic version of its
processes, a combination of the physical and the intellectual. As the
male body he desires becomes palpitant *his* passion – as his narratorial voice represents desire as the object's heightened receptivity –
that body serves as his link to the passional flux that is, in
Impressionist epistemology, life itself.[26]

To make these connections among erotic, intellectual, and aesthetic endeavors, Pater drew on certain key sources, worth mentioning
here because they throw the homoeroticism of "Diaphaneitè" into
high relief. One of these sources is Winckelmann, whose "temperament . . . nurtured through and invigorated by friendships which
kept him always in direct contact with the spirit of youth" helped
Pater find a model for homoerotic collaboration (*Renaissance* 176).[27]
Another version of the same dynamic has a longer history, going
back to the Greeks and going on at least as far as the moment in
which Oscar Wilde, in court, glorified the model of love in which
"the elder man has the intellect, and the younger man has all the joy,
hope, and glamour of life before him."[28] Linda Dowling has recently
found the Greek model of *paiderastia* everywhere at Victorian
Oxford. Homosexuality at Oxford, Dowling notes, gained substantial self-justification by styling itself after the love "by which an older
man, moved to love by the visible beauty of a younger man, and
desirous of winning immortality through that love, undertakes the
younger man's education in virtue and wisdom."[29] Pater clearly
participates in this mode of justification in his tribute to "Diapha-

neitè"; moreover, he lends the model modern specificity, and grounds Impressionism in it. He lends it modern specificity by implying that the younger man's beauty and vitality can give the alienated modern intellect new access to "life itself," and by implying that an older man's reflectiveness can make love a way to advance along the stages of an Hegelian phenomenology of mind. Impressionism's *paiderastia* makes the love of an older man for a younger man not only a Greek ideal, but a modern way to return to the Greek ideal of "perfect knowledge."

Pater read "Diaphaneitè" to the Old Mortality Society at Oxford in 1864 – three years before he wrote what would become the Conclusion to *The Renaissance*. The essay describes the type of being that, by its "transparency of nature" or unity of perception and expression, offers the creative artist the most inspiring model. The diaphanous ideal has every advantage: in stintless praise Pater celebrates its perfect intelligence, its utter disinterestedness, its beauty, and its potential even to redeem culture from worldly vanity and error. As always with Pater, the ideal is one long ago lost with man's fall into consciousness, with the ruinous separations of modernity, philosophy, and other modes of alienation. And, also characteristically, the way back to this ideal is uncertain. Pater seems confused about the genesis of "diaphaneitè": on the one hand, it seems a natural talent; on the other hand, it seems one given by a special "grace"; and the extent to which one not given it by nature or grace can achieve it seems to vary. This confusion, in turn, requires *paederastia*. Not sure how someone like himself might achieve "diaphaneitè," Pater draws it to himself along an erotic connection, and thereby makes Impressionist receptivity an amorous affair.

Who is diaphanous, and how? "Diaphaneitè" is, at one point in the argument, "the mental attitude, the intellectual manner of perfect culture, assumed by a happy instinct" – "by a happy gift of nature, without any struggle at all."[30] But at the same time, somehow, it comes "as it were in the order of grace, not of nature, by some happy gift, or accident of birth or constitution" (210). The extent, then, to which the power is *natural* seems to vary – as does the extent to which *anyone* can earn it. While aesthetic culture might be, in the Preface to *The Renaissance*, a matter of education and refinement, "that truthfulness of temper, that receptivity, which professors often strive in vain to form, is engendered here less by wisdom than by innocence" (211). Impressionability, then, cannot be learnt. It is the unreachable goal of a range of knowledgeable types: "Not the saint only, the artist also, and the speculative thinker, confused, jarred, disintegrated in the world, as sometimes they inevitably are, aspire for this simplicity to the last" (210). The more the artist and the thinker want and need "diaphaneitè," the less likely they are to attain it, since it depends upon unawareness. Only the simple innocent can be diaphanous; and he becomes diaphanous by the most obscure absence of knowledge.

But "Diaphaneitè" holds out a crucial hope for the "professor." A salutary link approximates him to the diaphanous ideal, one that emerges finally as Pater locates his ideal in the perfection of youthful manhood: "Often the presence of this nature is felt like an aroma in early manhood. Afterwards, as the adulterated atmosphere of the world assimilates us to itself, the savour of it faints away" (213). Here is the eroticism of "Diaphaneitè," the language of which is purposefully ambiguous. The passivity of "felt" makes all the difference: is this nature present to all men in early manhood, or is it felt by all those who come into contact with young men? And the strange synaesthesia of a felt aroma and a fainting savor seems to let Pater confuse the difference between the feelings of early manhood and the feelings it inspires. The result is a passionate attachment, present in the occasion for and tone of the essay's narration: whereas the "professor" may not have a chance if he works for "diaphaneitè," the appreciation of it, if erotically charged, seems to produce the desired effect. It seems in fact to produce "diaphaneitè" itself, insofar as that character is a result of Pater's effort indirectly to express his love for another man.

But this does not mean that we ought to consider Pater's homosexual desire for Shadwell prior to or causative of his aesthetic. Rather, it seems that Impressionism and homosexuality help to create each other: Pater's version of desire between men derives its structure from his sense of where "life" is. His epistemology determines the total projection of passionate desires onto the object of desire, informing the homoerotic structure that would pair innocence and sophistication. The structure of this projection explains in turn – and in indistinct dialectic – the Impressionism of the Conclusion to *The Renaissance*. The experience of liveliness for its own sake as a mode of life and as a first criterion for aesthetic appreciation has its basis in a repression of passion to inarticulacy and a projection of it onto an idealization of the young male body. What results is the connoisseur who seeks to simplify his own nature in imagined contact with an ideally simplified version of embodiment. In numerous essays and portraits, Pater seeks to realize impressions through young men whose simple beauty would enable his own complex eloquence.[31]

This view of the oneness of homoerotic and Impressionistic structures in "Diaphaneitè" builds on – but departs from – recent criticism that has also found the essay suggestive. Like Richard Dellamora, Linda Dowling, and Denis Donoghue, I mean to say that "Diaphaneitè" expresses Pater's sexuality; I proceed, however, with a different sense of the way that the erotic and the aesthetic interact. Dellamora, Dowling, and Donoghue read Pater's aesthetic theory as a "coding" of homosexual desire. Dellamora claims that "Diaphaneitè" intentionally encodes desire, intending to communicate it to those in sympathy with homosexuality while eluding those oblivious to its possibility: " 'Diaphaneitè,' which articulates this ideal [expressive of desire between men] at an early stage in its development, is discreetly coded so as to 'miss' some of Pater's listeners while reaching men sympathetic to expressions of desire between men."[32] Similarly, Donoghue calls parts of the essay "homosexual code," and Dowling writes that Pater, in this and other work, "devis[es] a 'coded' version of liberalism in which its more radical implications became visible to anyone who knew how to read."[33] The "code" theory gives undue prominence to sexuality. It seems more accurate, if less usefully political, to believe that in "Diaphaneitè" Pater sought earnestly to express an aesthetic ideal, and that it was in fact the greater sincerity of the effort that brought the erotic into play – and then to believe that Pater's version of the erotic was equally implicated with his artistic sense of the structure of life itself.[34]

Only this tighter implication can account for the combination of erotic and aesthetic Impressionism as it appears, for example, in "The Age of Athletic Prizemen" (1894). Here Pater praises a certain age of classical art for its fidelity to physical detail, a fidelity that shows greater truth in mute physicality than more ambitiously didactic art finds in religious or political themes. Praising the art of Myron for this far-reaching representation of the athletic body, Pater writes, "Yet if the art of Myron was but little occupied with the reasonable soul (*animus*), with those mental situations the expression of which, though it may have a pathos and a beauty of its own, is for the most part adverse to the proper expression of youth, to the beauty of youth, by causing it to be no longer youthful, he was

certainly a master of the animal or physical soul there (*anima*)."[35]
Myron's genius is his ability to suspend all representation of conceptual knowledge in his sculpture of the male body. Pater likes the
way he creates a point of access for the "speculative thinker" to the
inspiration of primitive being. Admiring Myron's art, Pater expresses
aesthetic prerogatives that neatly coincide sexual desires, since the
body gains its artistic appeal just insofar as its utter embodiedness
offers the artist or spectator imaginary access to impressions. As he
continues to praise Myron's "peculiar value" in the development of
Greek art, Pater betrays this more complicated kind of predilection
for the mindless athletic body: "It is of the essence of the athletic
prizeman, involved in the very ideal of the quoit player, the cricketer,
not to give expression to mind, in any antagonism to, or invasion of,
the body . . . to disavow that insidious enemy of the fairness of the
bodily soul as such" (286). Pater admires the mindlessness in Myron's
representations because it admits his own mind, otherwise alienated
from the bodily life that athletic prizemen enjoy.

Such merging of aesthetics and desire explains the peculiar way
that "The Age of Athletic Prizemen" lingers so lovingly on the
bodies – the expanding bosoms, the parting lips – in Myron's art.
The "code" analysis might claim that Pater chooses his subject
opportunistically; a reading more sensitive to the erotics of Impressionism finds instead that there is no space between sex and art for
Pater to make such a choice. "The Age of Athletic Prizemen"
demonstrates the oneness of lust and the search for impressions, as
Pater makes the claim of masculine youth to "Empirical" authenticity the basis for the truest mimesis:

Now, this predominance of youth, of the youthful form, in art, of bodily
gymnastic promoting natural advantages to the utmost, of the physical
perfection developed thereby, is a sign that essential mastery has been
achieved by the artist – the power, that is to say, of a full and free realisation.
For such youth, in its very essence, is a matter properly within the limits of
the visible, the empirical world; and in the presentment of it there will be
no place for symbolic hint. (282)

Pater links radical-empirical truth to youthful male beauty; the
essence of that youthful form, Pater claims, is phenomenal, making it
the exemplary matter of experience for the artist. And because of its
denial of "symbolic" or conceptual representation, its actual realization requires the mind of the artist. Once granted this pure and
necessary access to the empirical world, Myron can achieve artistic

truth through a dynamic that resolves the problem of impression-ability. For, if unrepresented, the youthful form is meaningless; if lacking access to the empirical world, the artist sees nothing; in the conjunction of Myron and his athletes, however, artistic mind and sensuous body achieve the "essential mastery" in perfect representa-tion of vitality. What results, in Myron's art, is a perfect impression of life: "It was as if a blast of cool wind had congealed the metal, or the living youth, fixed him imperishably in that moment of rest which lies between two opposed motions, the *backward* swing of the right arm, the movement *forwards* on which the left foot is in the very act of starting" (287). If such a description and others like it – of, for example, the "very turn and texture of the crisp locks" and "the very feel of the tense nerve and full-flushed vein" (282–83) – ring with the language of sexual fetishism, it is because sexual fetishism, insofar as it seeks to reify the vital, shares the specific ambivalence of Pater's Impressionism.

The oneness of aesthetic and sexual motives is important here for a number of reasons. It places the aesthetic – or more specifically, Impressionism – within social life, rather than in the rarefied or detached remove to which critics of aesthetic ideology would assign it. It explains not only the disposition of Impressionism, but the unenthusiastic reception it received in certain quarters. And, by extension, it explains what Impressionism becomes. For the combin-ation of aesthetic and sexual motives was clear enough in Pater to worry the Oxford establishment. *The Renaissance* famously raised eyebrows, its call for aesthetic intensity sounding at least obscurely like a call to hedonism and homosexuality. The result is well known: in response to criticism Pater removed the Conclusion to *The Renaissance* from the second edition, and only included it in the third edition with a disclaimer. Why he did so has been the subject of extensive debate.[36] But the fact that we cannot decide whether it was because he feared retribution against homosexuality (as some say) or because he felt strictly intellectual reservations about the Conclu-sion's philosophical arguments (as others argue) is a fact very significant to the history of Impressionist uncertainty. Pater himself seems to have been unsure of the full import of his turn to the impression; moreover, he turned against it, to a certain degree, by editing out the Conclusion, and then turned again in writing *Marius the Epicurean*. In the disclaimer with which he restored the Conclusion in the third edition of the Renaissance, Pater writes, "This brief

'Conclusion' was omitted in the second edition of this book, as I
conceived it might possibly mislead some of those young men into
whose hands it might fall. On the whole, I have thought it best to
reprint it here, with some slight changes which bring it closer to my
original meaning. I have dealt more fully in *Marius the Epicurean* with
the thoughts suggested by it" (186). All this turning – all this omitting,
changing, and further dealing with the thoughts suggested by the
impression – is proof of the impression's productive indeterminacy,
and an excellent record of its result.

As we will see in Chapter Five, *Marius the Epicurean* makes this
indeterminacy itself an argument in the impression's favor. Critics
have read the novel as an autobiographical reflection on Pater's
problems with *The Renaissance*, but that reflection takes as its object
the very essence of Pater's aesthetic – not just the scandal of *The
Renaissance*, or Pater's personal life, but the problem of perception
from which both scandal and success proceeded. *Marius the Epicurean*
charts the progress of its protagonist through the claims of different
philosophical systems, and thus apparently reflects Pater's own
changing theoretical affiliations. The allegory, however, is less a
biography of Pater's self than of his impression: the claims of different
systems differently configure the relation between sensuous feeling
and abstract intellect, so that *Marius* begins in homoeroticism,
proceeds through varieties of the finest education, and ends back in
the kind of religious allegory the homoerotic one had tried to replace.

Chapter Six will show how. To round out this present account of
the homoerotic collaboration at work in Pater's impression, it
remains to discuss one last text – one in which the collaboration at
work in "The History of Philosophy," "Diaphaneitè," and "The Age
of Athletic Prizemen" goes tellingly bad. The text is "Apollo in
Picardy" (1893), a late "portrait" in which *paiderastia* leads to murder.
If *Marius* allegorizes *The Renaissance*, "Apollo in Picardy" allegorizes
"Diaphaneitè," for it tells the story of a teacher whose need for
rejuvenation ends up killing his student. If *Marius the Epicurean* works
out the theoretical uncertainties of Pater's Impressionism by subjecting them to biographical allegory, "Apollo in Picardy" makes
biographical allegory a means to admit that there may be violence in
Impressionism's conflation of aesthetic and erotic motives.

The protagonist of "Apollo in Picardy" has too much intelligence
and too little sensuous vitality. Unhealthy, the Prior is sent to "the

Grange or Obedience of Notre Dame de-Pratis . . . for the benefit of his body's health, a little impaired at last by long intellectual effort."[37] With him is his young pupil and charge, Hyacinthus, whose name prepares us for a characteristically Paterian allegory – mixing, now ominously, Christian and pagan themes. Their destination promises recuperation for the Prior, its reputation saying that "the mere contact of one's feet with its soil might change one" (188). The pair's arrival at the Grange confirms this likelihood, as "from the very first, the atmosphere, the light, the influence of things, seemed different from what they knew" (189). Establishing this enervated protagonist's arrival at a place of mysterious plenitude, the portrait prepares to set up the structure of Impressionist collaboration. To come is the productive and erotic contact of mind and body, which occurs with the appearance of Brother Apollyon, whose natural brilliance, inspiring vigor, and radically sensual masculine beauty earns the loving rhetoric of "Diaphaneitè": "Prior Saint-Jean seemed to be looking for the first time on the human form, on the old Adam fresh from his Maker's hand. A servant of the house, or farm-labourer, perhaps! . . . a serf! But what unserflike ease, how lordly, or godlike rather, in the posture!" (190).

In "Diaphaneitè," such primal and easy fineness of form gives life to the authorial mind. In "Apollo," that consummation is but the early climax of the portrait, as the Prior undergoes a transformation explicitly attributed to Apollyon's inspiration: "Thenceforth that fleshly tabernacle had housed him, had housed his cunning, over-wrought, and excitable soul, ever the better day by day; and he began to feel his bodily health to be a positive quality or force, the presence near him of that singular being having surely something to do with this result" (194). This relationship sounds erotic but remains curiously detached, as if to maintain the structural purity of Impressionist collaboration, in which passion is felt as epistemological enhancement. The Prior, that is, does not feel desire as much as a refutation of abstract ideas; he feels as if some river "had carried away from him all his so carefully accumulated intellectual baggage of fact and theory . . . the hard and abstract laws . . . deserted him" (200). Apollyon helps the Prior dispense with the kind of abstractions that the Preface to *The Renaissance* finds so numbing, and the fact that appreciation of Apollyon enables this escape from dogma shows that aesthetic culture, even after Marius's *ascesis*, may yet parallel erotic stimulation. Revitalized, the Prior begins to do great work; his abstract ideas disappear and return as impressions – "to be revived in him again however, at the contact of this extraordinary pupil or fellow-inquirer, though in a very different guise or attitude towards himself, as matters no longer to be reasoned upon and understood, but to be seen rather, to be looked at and heard" (200). Now the Prior physically hears and hopes to record "the singing of the planets," acquiring knowledge through a "beam of insight," an "astounding white light" (200–01).

What has changed since "Diaphaneitè," however, is Pater's ingenuous confidence in this dynamic of vitalization. In "Apollo," bliss only briefly prevails before it becomes known that Apollyon is "not only a thief, but a homicide in hiding from the law" (195). As much as he might be a "natural inspiration," he also scatters "the seeds of disease" (195) and breaks the backs of animals for pleasure. He comes to seem part of that "irredeemable natural world," as natural sympathy shades into unregenerate savagery (196). His power to inspire comes not, as "Diaphaneitè" might believe, from an innocent harmony with nature but from a "sort of heathen understanding with the dark realm of matter" (197). On the other side of Pater's brush with scandal, "Apollo in Picardy" expresses this different view of masculine sensuality.

The combination of Apollyon's power to inspire and his proneness to violence leads to a double climax. Just at the moment in which the Prior achieves his white-light epiphany, Apollyon and Hyacinthus play naked in the moonlight. Throwing "devil's penny-pieces" – discuses, like those tossed with such aesthetic appeal by Myron's athletes – Apollyon kills Hyacinthus, launching a discus that goes "sawing through the boy's face, uplifted in the dark to trace it, crushing in the tender skull upon the brain" (203). In this double climax, the terms of Paterian impression reach their fully fascinating expression: if, as these works suggest, desire takes the form of the epistemological impetus that enables aesthetic insight, its climax would be this ambivalent one – this simultaneous consummation of genius and sexual violence. Since Pater's Impressionism depends upon an idealization of the primitive, it makes sense that the primitive should escape primitivism at the moment of consummation, to do the work of death inverse to the impression's seizure of life.

It makes sense, too, that Pater would imagine his Impressionism's consummation to mean the death of a pupil, and that the Prior's inspirations should quickly appear to be the delusions of a madman accused of "the charge of having caused the death of his young server, by violence, in a fit of mania" (204). The Prior's conviction on this charge seems an allegorical confession of guilt, an admission of Pater's immorality. The contemporary fear that the Conclusion to *The Renaissance* might "mislead young men" finds its expression in this portrait as a guilty sense that an erotic aesthetic does in fact constitute a crime against society. The Prior's final bewilderment is Pater's despair that his vision of Impressionism should devolve so inevitably into his detractors' version of it, that the threat of scandal should have turned his diaphanous ideal into the murderous and diseased destroyer of youth. In the split between the Prior's bliss of essential insight and the violation of his pupil, there appears a duplication of the inversely parallel Arnold–Pater–Wilde progressions. That the happy coexistence of "the subjective" and homosexuality should split into madness and death indicates the extent to which Pater himself came unwittingly to encourage our misunderstandings of his place in the aesthetic tradition.

"Apollo in Picardy" therefore perhaps best explains why the progression from Arnold to Pater to Wilde corresponds to a progression from respectability to a criminalized homosexuality. The argument here has been that the impression and homosexual desire share a common structure. The impression's mediation of sense and intellect, troubled by the problem of impressionability, demands conceptualization in terms of that human relationship which seems most fittingly to join the sensuous and the intellectual. Pater's relation to the diaphanous ideal significantly combines different attributes of availability and distance: relative mindlessness offers no resistance to a kind of intellectual takeover; but prized receptivity is, as we have seen, largely a projection of Pater's passion; and social sanction keeps the diaphanous ideal even imaginatively at a definite distance.

The impression could become justification for sexuality too far beyond the norm. What Wilde did was make otherness so necessary a part of his sexual ideology that his circle widened out beyond those who could believably play the diaphanous ideal. As Wilde's circle widened from Lord Alfred Douglas to those he would later call "panthers," he let Hyacinthus give way to Apollyon the Destroyer, and finished out that sequence according to which we now conflate aesthetic and sexual decadence.

Impressionism does not really follow that sequence, however, since it does not properly go next to Wilde. Henry James diverts it, inheriting it from Pater but also from other sources that change its character. Where Pater has Hume and Hegel, and Arnold to react against, James has his brother, and the questionable advice of Alphonse Daudet. And where Pater has his diaphanous ideal, James has for his counterpart the tremendous receptivity of the woman writer. For him, it is the "woman of genius," specifically Anne Thackeray Ritchie, who serves as the enabling example of impressionability. His Impressionist plots consequently correspond better to those which his culture might expect to read. The difference is an advantage: where Pater's way of thinking about impressions required of him great expenditure of strength in apology, James could let more conventional plots carry him from vexed mediation to happier junctures of art and life.

CHAPTER 3

The woman of genius

I "CALL DOWN DOLLY"

In volume two of *Tristram Shandy*, Tristram tries to explain why his Uncle Toby, who is "no fool," is nevertheless "at the same time such a confused, pudding-headed, muddle-headed fellow."[1] He turns to Locke's *Essay Concerning Human Understanding*, the authoritative "history-book . . . of what passes in a man's own mind" (vol. I, p. 98). The *Essay* teaches, Tristram says, that "the cause of obscurity and confusion, in the mind of man, is threefold" (99). Obscurity and confusion arise because of "[d]ull organs . . . slight and transient impressions made by objects when the said organs are not dull . . . [and] a memory like unto a sieve, not able to retain what it has received." Tristram faithfully reproduces Locke's description.[2] He goes on, however, to improve upon Locke with an illustrative figure for the way impressions sometimes fail to make their mark.

"Call down *Dolly* your chambermaid," Tristram commands, wanting to make her a figure for perception: "When *Dolly* has indited her epistle to *Robin*, and has thrust her arm into the bottom of her pocket . . . take that opportunity to recollect that the organs and faculties of perception, can, by nothing else in this world, be so aptly typified and explained as by that one thing which *Dolly*'s hand is in search of" (99). The thing is "an inch . . . of red seal-wax," but a dramatic pause has made us think it will be Dolly's clitoris; and the "typification" that follows is a frolicsome parody of Locke, in which Sterne extends to absurdity the metaphor through which Lockean Empiricism figures human perception. In Tristram's description, Dolly tries to melt her wax onto her letter and imprint it with her thimble, but fails: she may have waited too long, and let the wax harden; or the wax may be have been of an inferior kind ("of a temper too soft"); or Dolly she may have quit too soon. Whatever the cause, "the print, left by the thimble" comes out "as unlike the prototype as a brass-jack." Tristram has made his point – he has dramatized three possible types of pudding head – and so doing has brought Locke down along with Dolly.

Using "Dolly your chambermaid" to make fun of Locke, Sterne does something that Impressionist writers will do years later: suspicious about the rhetoric of impressions, he makes a female body absorb its promiscuity, so that he can at once have and disclaim its version of human perception. James will do something like this in "The Art of Fiction"; Woolf will do it too in "Mr. Bennett and Mrs. Brown." Dolly is an early Impressionist "woman of genius" – an early example of the tendency of the impression's mediation to come undone according to distinctions of sex.

Dolly makes a good introduction to this tendency because of the extent to which her sex comes into play. When Tristram describes her thrusting her arm into her pocket, fumbling for her thimble, thrusting against the wax, and leaving off in haste at her mistress's call, he does so as if he were also describing a scene of female masturbation. With its thrusting and fumbling, the scene comically debases Locke's "history of mind." But in so doing the scene also more seriously discredits Locke by bringing out certain implications in his epistemological shift. Locke, as Ernest Tuveson notes, taught Sterne and others "how mind and body are one nature," how bodily impulses determine mental and spiritual being – in short, that "the *body thinks.*"[3] As a figure for that juncture, Dolly justifies and jeopardizes the thinking body, in unequal measure: association with the masturbating girl makes the thinking body vital but self-consuming. Sterne's use of Dolly suggests that what Locke gains for the body he loses for the mind.

It is to express similar reservations about a similar exchange that Impressionist writers call down figures like Dolly. For them, too, impressions entail a theory of perception in which the body thinks, and they too find the prospect as exciting and as limiting as female sexuality. No Impressionist will go so far as to figure that combination in a scene of female masturbation, but many make the excited vitality of such a scene the implicit basis of the Impressionist aesthetic. The essence of Impressionism is often an isolated femininity, one set apart and intense, whose appeal is at once enabled and undermined by perceptual limitations. Reproducing Dolly in the "woman of genius," Impressionist writers follow Sterne in associating impressions with female strengths and weaknesses, and in making that association a way once again to anatomize the perceptual life of the thinking body.

For while Sterne initially uses Dolly to explain the perceptual life of Uncle Toby's pudding head, he finally denies the applicability of the example. "[N]ot one of these," it turns out, "was the true cause of the confusion in my Uncle *Toby*'s discourse" (100). Tristram only tells the parable of the impression "to shew the world what [the confusion] did *not* arise from." Uncle Toby's confusion is not that which Dolly represents, but "the unsteady use of words." Turning to this other explanation, Tristram turns to another aspect of Locke's epistemology, but of course the initial example stands. Tristram, that is, gets to have the proto-Impressionist explanation of perception, but also finally to confirm intellectual priorities. In similar fashion, the Impressionists will make figures like Dolly at once a way to profess an epistemology based in the impression and a pivot upon which to turn back to the self-contained mind. The unlikely pointlessness of the whole Dolly scenario – its peculiar elaboration and retraction – gets repeated later in the way Impressionist writers use the "woman of genius" to affirm and deny the impression. The scenario and its dismissal prefigure the *apophasis* in the Impressionist use for femininity.

Apophasis affirms what it denies. It governs the logic of the impression when the impression leads writers to find advantage in limitation – when, in other words, they look to women's lives for the impression's link to vitality. To explain this dynamic, it is important to remember that *apophasis* also rules as a tendency in larger theories about the role of women in the history of representation. Many feminist histories of the novel, as well as histories of the place of the female sensibility in philosophy and in the other arts, have described the way various cultural forms develop through reference to, exploitation of, or even the creation of the feminine.[4] In doing so, however, these critics at once exalt and debase femininity, insofar as they consistently note that it has been for these various cultural forms an advantageous limitation: culture has depended upon it, but typically in order to *abject* itself in response against authority too great to be right or artistic. Culture has used femininity to justify itself – in the process feminizing itself, debasing femininity, and producing, for real women, a paradox. Women get cultural authority, but from epistemological and social restriction, so that their authority is always *apophatic*. It is always the affirmation of a denial.

The paradox gets most attention in "standpoint feminism." As Helen Longino describes it, "standpoint theory reflects the view that women (or feminists) occupy a social location that affords them/us a privileged access to social phenomena" and includes among a range of corollaries to this basic premise "the romantic idea that women come, by nature or social experience, to be better equipped to know the world than are men."[5] Because such social experience equips women with knowledge at the expense of power, standpoint feminism has a basic paradox at the center of its logic (or its object); exalting limitation, standpoint theory pinpoints that reversal around which much feminist theory combines advocacy with abjection. For this reason, standpoint theory (and the kinds of feminist inquiry that implicitly use its logic) makes a good touchstone for the study of Impressionist *apophasis*. The Impressionist who would collaborate with feminine sensibilities is a standpoint feminist, believing that women have privileged access to phenomena while knowing also that the privilege is a liability.[6]

To say so is, of course, to overstate the case – James as a standpoint feminist? – but the overstatement saves us from a worse inaccuracy. In the case of James, for example, the "woman of genius" might seem a product of misogynist exploitation, and, for that reason, part of what some call the tendency of James's fiction to "embod[y] a covert act of force directed against women" or to make gains at the cost of real women's lives.[7] But the tendency is really only questionable until feminist cultural history reminds us that the debasement of the feminine is often its claim to power. In other words, standpoint feminism, and other feminisms attentive to the strange history of female sensibility, can remind us that in the world of theory such debasement often aims to undo the bad effects of social difference.[8] To overstate the case, then, and align the "woman of genius" with this form of theoretical insight, is to remember that the Impressionist's use for the feminine is most often self-defeating, and soon subjects itself to negative critique.

The real debasement, by contrast, comes from another quarter: from those who make the same kind of association between Impressionism and female sensibility cause for rejection of both. The anonymous writer of a *Spectator* review of 1886 claims that "the Impressionists are effecting very injuriously the literature of the day" because they cause "a loss of distinct standards of thought and judgment."[9] The reviewer blames the injury primarily on "Miss Thackeray" (coincidentally James's "woman of genius"), who has "undoubtedly sacrificed too much to her delicate feeling for moral atmosphere." Irving Babbitt reinforces the analogy in noting that "with the spread of Impressionism literature has lost standards and discipline, and at the same time virility and seriousness."[10] As Michael Levenson has pointed out, Babbitt blames the lack of virility in the Impressionist impulse for bad developments in aesthetic form; and Babbitt goes on, in *The New Laokoon*, to criticize the "impressionistic flutter" for the fact that "art and literature are appealing more and more exclusively to women, and to men in their unmasculine moods."[11] In his introduction to Frank Swinnerton's *Nocturne* (1917), H. G. Wells praises Swinnerton by distinguishing his technique from the Impressionism of Dorothy Richardson: Dorothy Richardson "has probably carried impressionism in fiction to its furthest limit . . . [Her work presents] a series of dabs of intense superficial impression; her heroine is not a mentality but a mirror . . . [h]er percepts never become concepts . . . But Mr. Swinnerton, like Mr. James Joyce, does not repudiate the depths for the sake of the surface. His people are not splashes of appearance, but living minds."[12] In Wells's account, male and female writers divide up on either side of the percept/concept distinction – as they do for W. L. George, who, in complaining about the popularity of "impression without conception" in the "painter's literature" of the day, pardons "intellectuals" like Joyce and Lewis while scolding Woolf and Richardson for being "guided only by the impressions their characters continually receive" and thus (in a telling metaphor) "tearing a foetus from the womb of time."[13] Frierson's *English Novel in Transition, 1885–1942* (1942) finally says what is implicit here – that Impressionism is, unfortunately, a feminine aesthetic. Frierson divides the postwar novelists into two groups, "Impressionists" and "Freudians," and uses the division to distinguish merely feminine impressions from substantially masculine thoughts. Under the "Impressionists," Frierson groups Richardson, Mansfield, and Woolf, and then makes their femininity definitive: ". . . both imagism and impressionism were presided over by women and were featured by qualities that might be looked upon as 'feminine' – mental agility, a passion for the minute and the fragmentary, a love of color and preciosity, and a feeling for the atmosphere of exaltation. Conversely (and Joyce is not an impressionist) the product of both schools lacked a cosmic, philosophical view . . ."[14] Here is a view significantly different from that which would make the "woman of genius" a help in the production of fiction. Here is sexism – and an attitude in no small measure responsible for the resistance that limits Impressionism to atmospheric and aberrational descriptive occasions. In contrast with it, the Impressionist's use for the woman of genius – even something as unfortunate as Sterne's treatment of Dolly – must mean something different. A continuum emerges, with the anti-feminine anti-Impressionism at one end, feminism at the other, and, in the middle, the Impressionist. In between, the Impressionist is like the feminist who would affirm women's limitation in order to exploit the insight it enables.

This position is not that of those women writers who affirmed impressions wholeheartedly. In 1915 May Sinclair published her *Journal of Impressions in Belgium,* a war record gladly limited to the impressions of its writer. Sinclair tells us that because she had no inside information, and no time to sit and write, her book will be a "Journal of Impressions" and "nothing more."[15] But immediately she claims that less is more: "Solid Facts" and "Great Events" may not appear in her account, but the very fact that she could not record them is what makes her account worthwhile. Because she has no access to the fieldwork of the Ambulance Corps, because she had no place to sit among the wounded and the encroaching battle lines, her views were necessarily incomplete, and she can therefore offer the most psychologically accurate representation of war. The perceptual chaos of war is doubled by the impressions of the woman writer rushed along the sidelines. Confident that this is the case, Sinclair is more confident of her impressions than those writers central to the Impressionist tradition. Similarly more confident is Elizabeth Bowen, whose 1950 *Collected Impressions* is so titled, she tells us, not for the sake of "disarming" ambiguity but for the sake of "precision": collected impressions are impressions rescued, by "collection," from ambiguity, because together they form a sort of critical constellation.[16] Arranged years after their reception, they become something more like Hume's "ideas," since what had struck the presses in the earlier part of the century has faded out of immediacy. Confident of their collected rigor, Sinclair presents her impressions without any sense that any feminine freshness was their key feature.

To place Impressionism among these different attitudes toward the relation between gender and cultural authority is to place it also in the history of the novel. If recent feminist histories of the novel are correct, the novel has been primarily a domestic form, which defines private spaces – both in the home and in the mind – as feminine ones. The anti-Impressionist response against such a feminization reveals that Impressionism prompted masculinization – a wish to counter the trend that brought the novel its authority in the first place. Impressionism, then, pushed the feminization of the novel to a point at which it could no longer seem natural. What follows below ought to explain why. Feminization of a domestic and popular form was one thing, but feminization of the aesthetic itself was another. When Henry James finds the "woman of genius" at the heart of an aesthetic theory, he proves that the art of the novel has made the aesthetic itself feminine. To resist that connection while also exploiting it – to give the feminine its due priority without really letting it *have* art – is the double goal in the pursuit of which James defines Impressionism and redefines the novel.[17]

II JAMES AND THE WOMAN OF GENIUS

James knew that Pater's hard and gem-like flame did not burn very bright. To James, Pater shone only "vaguely, and ha[d] a phosphorescence, not a flame." Not himself burning bright, his place was "to show you, in the darkness, where you can strike a light."[18] And Pater may, in fact, have shown James where to strike *Impressionism*'s brighter light. Pater, as we have seen, modified Matthew Arnold's wish to see the "thing itself" with the observation that to do so one must first realize one's impression – and then had his own wish modified by Oscar Wilde's ambition to see the thing as "in itself it really is not." James intervenes in a similar series. His impression corrects Walter Besant's semi-Arnoldian dogma, and brings on a Wildean remonstrance from Robert Louis Stevenson. Besant had claimed in an 1884 speech, "The Art of Fiction," that "everything in fiction which is invented and not the result of personal experience and observation is worthless."[19] James, writing four months later in his own "The Art of Fiction," exposed the fallacy in Besant's too-strict Empiricism: writing that "a novel is in its broadest definition a personal, a direct *impression* of life," James granted the creative imagination an equal part in constituting the reality that, for Besant, we must merely "observe."[20] Stevenson, subsequently, played Wilde's role, albeit without pose or paradox. In his "Humble Remonstrance," he reminded James that "the artist writes with more gusto and effect of those things which he has wished to do, than of those things he has done."[21] Between Stevenson's romance and Besant's realism, James founded the Impressionist theory of fiction. Like Pater between Arnold and Wilde, James made the impression the basis of an aesthetic vision that discovers truest realism in the most fertile imagination. He then made that inspired compromise a way to call fiction an art.

But if the impression brought James to something like Pater's place, it also found him in something like Pater's dilemma. James's central equivalence – "impressions are experience" – stakes everything on shaky ground, and the effort to make it steady raises some of his most pressing questions: Does receptivity to impressions, what he calls "the finer grain," require natural openness or cultured discretion? If it favors the former, where does Impressionism leave the sophisticated mind so much at home in James's art? If it favors the latter, how does Impressionism keep up its link to "life"? The questions are Paterian, but James transposes them, by trying at different sorts of answers. He too seeks a compromise between different styles of receptivity and seeks it through an appropriative admiration for the kind of person who embodies a receptivity he himself cannot claim. And he too makes the compromise the subject of speculation of other kinds. Whenever America goes to Europe, for example, or children face corruption, or an artist must choose between life and art, James worries about his Impressionist compromise. But James finds a different kind of counterpart. His is the "woman of genius," who, in "The Art of Fiction," has that power to "guess the unseen from the seen" and spin out stories on the basis of the smallest possible experience. James invokes her to prove that imagination is itself a form of experience – that a woman with just an impression of "life" might see more in it than a man who has life always before his eyes. That he needs her to do so, however, qualifies the logic of the impression, in "The Art of Fiction," and then also beyond.

The need gets rougher in fiction that finds Gothic (or comic) horror in the marriage of fresh female insight and male sophistication. When Isabel marries Osmond, James repeats his collaboration with the woman of genius, but now with an eye to its costs. If the impression's juncture of faculties is like a marriage, that marriage is a bad one, and through the bad marriage of Isabel and Osmond,

James reflects upon the imprudence in his theory of fiction. That reflection turns out to be productive: with it, or alongside it, James finds better ways to think about the relationship between art and life. In *The Portrait of a Lady*, the impression's mediation fails; in *What Maisie Knew*, it becomes an absurdity; and in the Preface to these and other novels that James wrote for his *New York Edition*, it gives way to the belief with which James had to be more comfortable, once he could give up coveting other sensibilities: the belief that "art *makes* life."

This development makes James's use for the "woman of genius" a kind of strong negative critique. The point here, for the most part, will be to see how this personification brings out problems in the theory of Impressionism, and then participates in all the second-thought meditations that constitute Impressionist literature. But the point will also be to see how this personification places James and his Impressionism in the larger history of the novel. It would be easy to call the woman of genius a throwaway bit of semi-sexist condescension, or to fault James for some kind of exploitation. But in fixing on the woman of genius in trying to characterize the art of fiction, James lays bare the mechanism that had always put stereotypical femininity and novelistic subjectivity into collaboration. Persisting, then, to deconstruct that mechanism, James changes the terms of novelistic subjectivity in a feminist fashion, by working to undo the tendency to make an aesthetic strength of women's weakness. His use for the woman of genius is therefore an important moment in the history of the novel – both a touchstone in the Impressionist theory through which James would influence fiction for years to come and a moment of note in fiction's feminine genealogy.

Pater's impression precedes James's, but James's use of the term is not just an instance of what Richard Ellmann calls "Pater's pied-piping."[22] Two other guides helped lead James to the crux of "The Art of Fiction": his brother William, and Alphonse Daudet. In 1868 – five years before *The Renaissance* became notorious, four years before Monet's *Impression: Soleil Levant*, sixteen years before "The Art of Fiction" – William wrote Henry a letter which, in its assessment of Henry's fiction, shows how nineteenth-century psychology helped put "impression" into the literary vocabulary. And in 1883, Daudet got from James an appreciative review, in which James attributes to Daudet the theory that a writer must make impressions his "most precious source of information." Where William passed the impression on to his brother from empirical psychologies, and Pater handed it on from his reaches into Hume, Daudet apparently got it from the French painters, and in the combination of these sources (and, as always with the impression, untraceable vernacular reference) James found words to describe the literary imagination. But the diversity of these sources makes James look beyond logic for theoretical stability. This he finds in the "small cornerstone" of female sensibility, which, in collaboration with the authorial mind, lends the impression's theoretical diversity the justification of sexual difference.

In his letter, William, having read Henry's "The Extraordinary Case," reflects on the goals of Henry's fiction. He notes that "one of the objects you have had in view has been to give an impression like that we often get of people in life," when people come and go and leave us "with little more than an impression of their reality and a feeling of baffled curiosity as to the mystery of the beginning and end of their being."[23] Writing this in 1868, William has not yet fully developed his way of saying that such impressions *are* reality, for all practical purposes. Still wanting a "reality" of which an impression is only a curious and inadequate part, William seems to give to his brother a *skeptical* impression, and not the impression that would in "The Art of Fiction" take its place at the center of Henry's exaltation of the imagination.

William's letter goes on, however, to find elegance in this skepticism, and in its second thoughts perfectly exemplifies the Impressionist's two minds. "You expressly restrict yourself, accordingly, to showing a few external acts and speeches, and by the magic of your art making the reader *feel* back of these the existence of a body of being of which these are casual features." William already does know, then, that to give "little more than an impression" is more magically to suggest the whole; his skeptical impression is on the way to pragmatism. While still caught up in pre-pragmatic distinctions between appearance and reality, William's view of Henry's fiction shows such distinctions in the process of collapsing into the syntheses through which William would later correct his empiricist predecessors. Impressionism, however, does not properly belong to that later moment, but rather to this earlier moment of indecision. In "The Art of Fiction," Henry associates impressions with "the magic of art," but also preserves an older skepticism about the fulness of the impression's connection to "reality."[24]

From Daudet, James gets a different uncertainty. In the early 1880s, James reacquainted himself with the "young French school," of which Daudet was a member.[25] In 1885, James refers to a conversation he had "some time ago" with Daudet, in which Daudet said that "the personal impression, the effort of direct observation, was the most precious source of information for the novelist."[26] Without question these words are the source of the similar words James would write in "The Art of Fiction." The similarity, however, is not in itself conclusive, because James seems in fact *not* to have agreed with Daudet on this point. In his 1883 essay on Daudet he doubts the range of Daudet's impression.[27] The essay praises Daudet both for "an extraordinary sensibility to all the impressions of life" and for his power of imagination, his "quick, instantaneous vision" but also a "divination" that makes ideas spring up "with a whirr of wings."[28] It turns out, however, that Daudet's impressions fail fully to run this range. James quotes with admiration Daudet's comments about the "personal impression," but then questions that impression's depth and extent. It seems superficial: "Daudet's weakness has been simply a want of acquaintance with his subject. Proposing to himself to describe a particular phase of French Protestantism, he has 'got up' certain of his facts with commendable zeal; but he has not felt nor understood the matter, has looked at it solely from the outside" (237). Whereas in "The Art of Fiction" James's impression will partake equally of experience and imagination, here he faults Daudet for letting the latter falsify the former; whereas "The Art of Fiction" will call imagination itself a mode of experience, here James emphasizes experience of a more conventional kind. He concludes that Daudet "has a quick perception of many things, but that province of the human mind cannot be *fait de chic* – experience, there, is the only explorer" (238). James has yet to make Daudet's impression something that can make imagination itself perceptive – that can make experience a better explorer. He will get his help in this regard not from Daudet but from the "woman of genius": as we will see, when *she* looks at "French Protestantism" from the outside (James will in fact use the same example) she sees the depths in a glimpse.[29]

From Daudet, then, as from William, James gets "impressions" of mixed appeal. William's impression finds things to doubt and things to praise in appearances; Daudet's has a certain quick vitality but not the kind that would know things artistically. The inheritance here is crucial background to "The Art of Fiction," and, by extension, the Impressionist theory that that essay would make so central to the "great tradition." For, somehow, between the moment of that inheritance and that of "The Art of Fiction" James gains the confidence to say that "a novel is an impression." Somehow, that is, he makes the doubtful depthless thing he inherits from Daudet and his brother into an adequate basis for a defense of fiction. Unless of course the questionable impression persists despite and beneath James's confident tribute to it – unless the impression never really becomes the adequate basis it seems to be in "The Art of Fiction." This is what the context of William's skepticism and Daudet's superficiality can help us to see: that James's watershed theory of fiction comes with its own built-in resistances.

"The Art of Fiction" tries to unify two divergent goals of the Victorian novel: to mimic life and to fashion art. The impression emerges as the unifier, helping James to outflank Walter Besant on both sides of the issue. In response to Besant's notoriously banal defense of fiction, James wants to prove that fiction, if more a matter of artful imagination than Besant allows, can be more vitally realistic than Besant guesses.

James begins the essay with the nominal intention merely to "edge in a few words under cover of the attention which Mr. Besant is sure to have excited" – before delivering the many words he has to offer in disagreement with Besant's advice to the aspiring writer of fiction (165). Besant's essay tries to promote fiction, and to elevate it to the status of art, by offering a system of rules for its properly artistic production. But it is just such rules, James argues, that would keep art out of fiction. His "single criticism" of Besant is that "[h]e seems to me to mistake in attempting to say so definitely beforehand what sort of an affair the good novel will be" when "the good health of an art which undertakes so immediately to reproduce life must demand that it be perfectly free" (169–70). Calling for freedom, speaking the dialect of the Kantian aesthetic, James most vehemently rejects the rule that would allow circumstantial necessity to give the rule to "experience." Besant argues that fiction must come from personal experience and not from invention, and he illustrates the point with the claim that "a young lady brought up in a quiet country village should avoid descriptions of garrison life; a writer whose friends and personal experiences belong to what we call the lower middle class

should avoid introducing his characters into Society."[30] James denies
such limitations by widening "personal experience" into a faculty
more like Kantian judgment – a process of estimation that bridges
understanding and freedom as it activates creative capacities. In this
version of "experience," direct participation is not necessary,
because the "seriously artistic attempt" leads to an "immense
increase" of understanding, so that even a provincial artist – and,
most significant for the present argument, the "young lady" – finds
that "the province of art is all life, all feeling, all observation, all
vision" (177). What "observation" is to Besant's version of experience, "impressions" are to James's; they are the indirect perceptions
that lead more directly to life as art sees it.[31] By claiming that "a
novel is in its broadest definition a personal, direct impression of
life" and that "impressions *are* experience," James widens experience
so that it properly connects art and life, reconciling the belief that
"the only reason for the existence of a novel is that it does attempt to
represent life" with the belief that the novel can enter art's autono-
mous sphere.[32]

The impression allows James to say about the novel that it has a
"large, free character of an immense and exquisite correspondence
with life"; it allows him to make mimesis "exquisite." Enjoying this
synthesis, James produces his famous images of the imagination at
work. If an artist has a great "capacity for receiving straight
impressions" (178), his or her art will have "the power to guess the
unseen from the seen, to trace the implications of things, to judge the
whole piece by the pattern, the condition of feeling life in general so
completely that you are well on your way to knowing any particular
corner of it" (172). To illustrate this power in action James offers his
famous metaphor of the "web" – a metaphor significant, in this
context, for the way it imagines a "consciousness" both active and
passive, contingent and removed, empirical and *a priori*: "Experience
is never limited, and it is never complete; it is an immense sensibility,
a kind of huge spider-web, of the finest silken threads suspended in
the chamber of consciousness, and catching every air-borne particle
in its tissue" (172). This famous and influential summation makes
mimesis an art, through the impression's metaphorical power to be
an "air-borne particle," something simultaneously borne from the
world and caught by consciousness.

But here, in these splendid images, a problem emerges: when
"web" meets "particle," art traps life; or, to alter the metaphor,

impressions fade to too exquisite faintness. James writes, for example, that genius "takes to itself the faintest hints of life" and "converts the very pulses of the air into revelations" (172). Impressions, as "hints" and "pulses," are important now for their slightness, which better proves the power of genius to convert them into revelations. The exaltation of the imagination of genius demands that impressions diminish. The diminution of impressions then causes a problem in the logic of "The Art of Fiction" – conflicting with James's claim that a novel's value "is greater or lesser depending on the *intensity* of the impression" (170; emphasis added). Not quite contradictory, "faintness" and "intensity" compete for aesthetic primacy, with confusing results.[33] "Faintness" exalts the active intelligence; "intensity" speaks for the power of feeling. If by emphasizing the faintness of the impression relative to the discernment of the mind James limits the impression's intensity, he undermines what he himself claims is the "value" of a novel. If intensity overwhelms discernment, compelling it in spite of itself, James concedes too much to the world beyond the authorial imagination. Does fiction's life depend on the power to convert faint impressions or the power to receive intense ones? And, since each of these capacities differently favors "art" or "life," does the impression's great synthesis devolve again into division? James's conclusions about the art of fiction beg these questions, returning us to the problem of impressionability. When he finally qualifies Besant's command that one "write from experience and experience only" with the famous exhortation, "Try to be one of the people upon whom nothing is lost" (173), he recommends a divided endeavor.

Impressions, then, connect art and life, but may also merely divide them differently. They may unify what is perceived and what is imagined, but the act they require on the part of the subject varies. "The Art of Fiction" therefore goes on to cast about for some way – apart from theoretical criticism, which seems to lack adequate terms – to encompass this variety and define the temperament or talent to which impressions correspond.

It is worth pausing here, before getting to this definition, to note just how much James's fiction features the variety it would encompass. Doubt about the impression's new art/life distinction appears in the contrasting ways James elsewhere uses the word – sometimes to mean vital experience and sometimes to mean artistic discretion. For every moment in which a Jamesian character has a direct intuitive impression of life, another has an impression that is a refined act of taste: Hyacinth Robinson in *The Princess Casamassima* (1886), for example, may perceive the essence of London in "the reflexion of the lamps on the wet pavements, the feeling and smell of the carboniferous London damp" as he "move[s] in the midst of these impressions," but impressions mean something crucially different in "The Madonna of the Future."[34] In that story, Theobold steps out of the shadows of the Palazzo Vecchio and, as the narrator recalls, "in a tone of the most insinuating deference he proceeded to appeal to me for my 'impressions'" (XIII, 439). In scare quotes here, 'impression' is hardly the name for the primal stuff of experience; rather, it is a hackneyed word for effete discretion. Richard Ellmann notes that in "The Author of Beltraffio" James actually mocks the Paterian impression, having the narrator ask Mrs. Ambient of her husband, "I suppose London's a tremendous place to collect impressions . . . Does he get many of his impressions in London should you say?"[35] Written in the same year as "The Art of Fiction," "Beltraffio" oddly undermines the essay's sincerity: if "impression" is a word James puts in the mouth of a cynic, how can he himself write it earnestly? If cynical, the term may be part of what Jonathan Freedman calls James's "aesthetic will to power," his urge to mystify social domination through artistic distinctions actually empty of meaning and meant really to maintain fine art's exclusivity.[36] The impression has this potential. It gives art a link to life but also justifies detachment, potentially redefining the art/life distinction as a division between vitality and connoisseurship.

"A New England Winter" (1884) makes this new distinction a basis for satire. Florimond Daintry comes home to Boston from an extended stay in France, having gained questionable artistic talent but a glamorous label: "His power of rendering was questioned, his execution had been called pretentious and feeble; but a conviction had somehow been diffused that he saw things with extraordinary intensity . . . It will have been guessed that he was an impressionist."[37] Whether or not he deserves the label seems unimportant, for, as James puts it, "the reader will probably feel that he was welcome to this ambiguous privilege" (115). Ambiguous, the privilege seems not to mean that "extraordinary intensity" has the claim to life or to meaning that it would seem to have. To Lucretia Daintry, his "impressions" render not life, but something much more narrow: "In pursuance of his character as an impressionist, he gave her a great many impressions; but it seemed to her that as he talked, he simply exposed himself – exposed his egotism, his little pretensions" (119). The plot of "A New England Winter" turns on Lucretia's interest in proving how unlike life Florimond's impressions are. She confronts him with a woman whose more credible claim to "extra-ordinary intensity" – that, perhaps, of a "woman of genius" – would give his impressions some real experience: "She should like Rachel to tell him at the end that he was a presumptuous little boy, and that since it was his business to render 'impressions', he might see what he could do with that of having been jilted" (124).

And on the level of theme, as well, this new version of the art/life duality preoccupies James – particularly the fiction that he wrote in the 1880s and 1890s. Nona Vincent, an actress, needs a visit from the real woman upon whom her character is based in order to perform well; the Monarchs, the genteel couple who seem such good models for aristocratic illustrations in "The Real Thing" (1892), prove too real for good art; Neil Paraday, the great writer of "The Death of the Lion" (1894), gets worn out when he becomes popular at house parties, and is just one of many Jamesian artists who find that an excess of life is deadly to art. These and any number of other examples prove that James has revised the old art/life distinction in terms dictated by the impression's ambiguity: behind them is the conviction that the best sensibilities combine artful perceptions and the act of living, but that such combinations could also cause new and strange catastrophes.

Knowing in advance that Impressionism may divide again what it ought to join, "The Art of Fiction" takes additional measures. At first, in describing the web of experience, James refers to the superior receptivity of the "*man* of genius." The conversion of the "pulses of air into revelations" occurs "when the mind is imaginative – much more when it happens to be that of the man of genius" (172). When he turns to specific arguments against Besant's advice, however, he tellingly singles out Besant's "*young lady* brought up in a quiet country village" as the unlikely possessor of the Impressionist imagination. He seems to choose her because, of Besant's examples, she is the least likely candidate for an aesthetic renovation. To make his point most powerfully, he claims that *even she* can have the aesthetic experience good novels require: "The young lady living in a village has only to be a damsel upon whom nothing is lost to make it quite unfair (as it seems to me) to declare to her that she shall have nothing to say about the military. Greater miracles have been than that, imagination assisting, she should speak the truth about some of these gentlemen" (172). Even she, James implies, can envision what she does not actually see. But given the argument that minimal real experience leaves most room for imaginative activity, such a "young lady" becomes the exemplary, rather than the marginal, aesthetic imagination. Having spoken against direct understanding in art, James has implied that the greater relative freedom allowed in its absence enables greater receptivity. If greater receptivity depends on lesser factual encumbrances, the "young lady" becomes "a damsel upon whom nothing is lost" not despite her limiting circumstances but because of them. The argument here becomes *apophatic*, as James values a limitation, or affirms what is denied. As a result, in James's reorientation of experience authority slips from the "man of genius" to the young lady; that slippage appears, in the essay's narrative, in the rhetorical displacement that turns James from the man to the girl.

This displacement turns the man of genius into the "woman of genius." After redeeming Besant's young lady, James extends her into a more substantial example of impressions at work. The "young lady" becomes, more specifically, Anne Thackeray Ritchie, and James's admiration for her becomes his essential figuration of the Impressionist imagination:

> I remember an English novelist, a woman of genius, telling me that she was much commended for the impression she had managed to give in one of her tales of the nature and way of life of the French Protestant youth. She had been asked where she learned so much about this recondite being, she had been congratulated on her peculiar opportunities. These opportunities consisted in her having once, in Paris, as she ascended a staircase, passed an open door where, in the household of a *pasteur*, some of the young Protestants were seated at a table round a finished meal. The glimpse made a picture; it lasted only a moment, but that moment was an experience. She had got her direct personal impression, and she turned out her type. She knew what youth was, and what Protestantism; she also had the advantage of having seen what it was to be French, so that she converted these ideas into a concrete image and produced a reality. (172)

Here is the figure that perfects the Jamesian impression. Where Daudet had left James with a bad combination of experience and imagination, Anne Thackeray Ritchie shows him how to connect those two categories – how a certain kind of experience inspires, rather than excludes, the imagination. Her "opportunity" to experience French Protestant life is actually drastically limited – she only glimpses it – but it is for that very reason aesthetically limitless. Obliged to "produce" what it perceives, her sensibility processes slight concrete experience through a network of abstract relations: she has abstract functions for "youth," "Protestantism," and "French"; she has had a glimpse of something which, when plugged into the equation these abstract functions constitute, creates the "reality" which necessarily intervenes between the concrete and the abstract. Her "impression," in other words, "converts ideas" into "concrete images" and "produces reality": it is the equation through which the vaguest of abstractions meets the merest of glimpses and produces, through the very gap between these two modes, the most convincing mimesis.

For James, then, Anne Thackeray Ritchie's "peculiar" limit of experience illustrates what he elsewhere calls "that odd law which somehow always makes the minimum of valid suggestion serve the man of imagination much better than the maximum" (XII: vii), and that law, as opposed to any Besant can formulate, epitomizes James's sense of what makes fiction an art.[38] Once this is clear – once we see that James's Impressionism depends upon the peculiar experiential life of inexperienced femininity – we find the same dependency in James's fiction more generally. James's interest in the woman of genius is the basis of his interest in what one critic calls "the elemental fineness of girl nature," his interest in the possibilities that fresh girlhood brings to fiction more generally.[39] Maisie, of course, who "couldn't be with verisimilitude a rude little boy" (II: viii), is the best example here.[40] According to the Preface to *What Maisie Knew,* James initially felt that it would be hard to make Maisie "presentable as a register of impressions." He felt, that is, that it would be hard to register a novel's requisite extent of theme and value through the consciousness of someone even younger than Besant's "young lady," since her impressions would be limited and shallow. But then James realized that she would make a perfect "ironic center": her "obscure notations," as the "one presented register of the whole complexity" would beautifully emphasize that complexity, in ways clearer notation could not. Readers have long agreed that Maisie epitomizes "point of view," featuring the greatest possible complexity in her simple sights. What readers tend less often to notice is the way Maisie transforms from "ironic center" to Impressionist genius. In his Preface, James recalls changing his mind – thinking at first that

Maisie would work ironically, but then coming to see, through the same apophatic logic that led him to exalt the woman of genius, that Maisie would work well beyond his original plan.

Maisie's limited experience becomes a wealth of imagination. She does not just "remain fresh, and still fresh," but has "even a freshness to communicate," and "treats her friends to the rich little spectacle of objects embalmed in her wonder" (xi). Objects are not just more present to her friends and to us because she transmits them to us unchanged. They become "embalmed in her wonder" – transformed by a purer receptivity, so that her inexperience becomes artful. Maisie's "undestroyed freshness" is a "vivacity of intelligence," and James's final evaluation of her leaves little doubt that for this reason she embodies his mediatory impression:

> She is not only the extraordinary "ironic centre" I have already noted; she has the wonderful importance of shedding a light far beyond any reach of her comprehension; of lending to poorer persons and things, by the mere fact of their being involved with her and by the special scale she creates for them, a precious element of dignity. I lose myself, truly, in appreciation of my theme on noting what she does by her "freshness" for appearances in themselves vulgar and empty enough. They become, as she deals with them, the stuff of poetry and tragedy and art; she has simply to wonder, as I say, about them, and they begin to have meanings, aspects, solitudes, connexions – connexions with the "universal!" – that they could scarce have hoped for. (XI: xi–xii)

Here is the balance, at the level of person, that "The Art of Fiction" wants for the novel. Maisie takes the poor persons and things of life and, by involving them in the "special scale" of her fresh intelligence, transforms them into art. Empty and vulgar appearances – what life might be if untransformed – take on those meanings, connections, and universality in just the way impressions improve upon "mere" particular perceptions. "Losing" himself in rhapsody over this peculiar advantage, James reveals that he has lost authorship to Maisie's condition. Just as Maisie treats her friends to the rich spectacle of objects embalmed in her wonder, imagining Maisie gives to James himself the power to say how he embalms the objective world in the wonder of art. She lets him endow the prosaic with "meanings, aspects, connexions" that *his* mind alone "could scarce have hoped for," not in fact, perhaps, but in the terms of his aesthetic theory.

Maisie, then, like Anne Thackeray Ritchie, is the female genius through which James loses excessive sophistication without losing "meanings." Through this "girl nature" James finds a way to make sophistication a function of innocence, and thereby to make sophisticated art vital. But why should the experiential limitations of the woman of genius prove so serviceable, if very similar limitations – a similar "want of acquaintance" – makes Daudet's depiction of French Protestant life merely superficial? How does she turn a want of real acquaintance into an advantage, where he ends up with just a scattering of quick perceptions? The difference, it seems, is one of opportunity. As a woman, Anne Thackeray Ritchie could only pass by what Daudet could have entered into more fully. As a result, James implies, she diverts her energies into the imagination, and gives life to the little she has seen by giving her own life to it. Faint perceptions produce intense imaginings, but not for everybody. Daudet, for example, is too experienced to bring real life to his imagination. And James is too experienced, as well, so he must use Anne Thackeray Ritchie to exemplify his own aesthetic, and he must profess it only by making her imaginative vitality a partner to his experienced sophistication. He can claim her as such a partner because the rules of another system – the system of gender relations – encourages it. Where the difference between his faculties and hers might otherwise be a problem, when personified into the difference between the sexes, it becomes amenable to unions like that of the separate spheres.

In other words, James makes a familiar social contract a helpful theoretical reciprocity; he turns to a commonplace social plot to prop up a weak theoretical structure. He wins unity for his impression, but depends on another mode of difference to do so, thereby hiding a lingering duality within a theory of synthesis. This lingering duality may seem only a very slight challenge to James's refutation of Besant, but it signifies more powerfully in three ways: it persists as a precondition to the connection between life and art, so that when James treats that connection as a theme, it crops up as a complicator; inversely, it persists such that James's treatment of relations between the sexes takes on the stakes of aesthetic theory; and the combined effect of these socio-aesthetic meditations makes James's Impressionism a key moment in the larger history of the novel's role in the formation of female subjectivity.

A number of feminist histories of the novel have noted a correlation between the form of the novel and the nature of female subjectivity. In the boldest, Nancy Armstrong calls subjectivity itself a novelistic creation. To promote middle-class interests, she argues, the novel idealized female virtue, a mystified merit meant to compete with that of aristocratic "blood." Armstrong "links the history of British fiction to the empowering of the middle classes in England through the dissemination of a new female ideal."[41] This idealization entailed the separation of spheres – the creation of middle-class domesticity – and an analogous distinction between male and female subjectivities. Female interiority, a key feature of women's dominion over private emotional space, developed as a result of the new emphasis on private female virtue, and in turn became the model for interior life more generally. It became the realm of the novel – or, more precisely, the novel and female interior life grew up together, as fiction itself made foundational contributions to the creation and idealization of female subjectivity. In this history – this combined history of the novel and of subjectivity itself – femininity's fortunes are mixed. On the one hand, female subjectivity emerges as some-thing restricted and powerless; on the other hand, it has authority over affect, and the full power of feeling. The paradox that results is basic to the novel, which tends to tell the story of women's subordination while at the same time representing the triumph of a female epistemological mode. Inheriting this form, James inherits a form in which femininity signifies both restriction and insight – in which restriction *enables* insight, and women get authority from isolation. But in his apophatic stress on female receptivity, James seems to expose the terms of the feminization of the fictional imagination. Narrowing the basis of the novel down to the impres-sion, James also narrows fiction's ideology down to its basic social dynamic, and, by associating that dynamic with the impression's aesthetic instability, moves toward a deconstruction of novelistic subjectivity itself.

It may be hard to see such deconstruction at work in "The Art of Fiction," where James seems happy enough to make female recep-tivity play its part in the exemplification of Impressionist genius. But the kind of collaboration through which Impressionism brings the social history of novelistic subjectivity to a crisis comes under skeptical scrutiny in other texts – in major novels, as we will see, and in one essay that turns "The Art of Fiction" inside out. In 1885, just one year after writing "The Art of Fiction," James wrote a review of Cross's *Life of George Eliot*. Assessing Eliot's body of work, the review also replays much of "The Art of Fiction" – returning to Daudet's impression, considering its place in the art of fiction, and exploring once again the sensibilities of a "woman of genius." In this version, however, things change: whereas the earlier essay has full faith in impressions, the later one does not; and where the earlier essay is happy to attach the sensibilities of the woman of genius to the male literary intelligence, the later essay sees that very attachment as a real violation.

That Eliot is a "woman of genius" is for James a foregone conclusion. Some critics, he writes, would refuse her the title, and say "that she only had a great talent, overloaded with a great store of knowledge," but James insists, despite his own serious reservations about her excess of "mind," that she has every important "characteristic of the mind *possessed*."[42] He will criticize, but always with a basic sense that "one must speak respectfully of any theory of work which would produce such fruit as Romola and Middlemarch" (673). But he finds cause for disrespect in order to distinguish different sources of Eliot's genius. What makes people think that she overloads her books with a great store of knowledge is the excess of "reflection" there – an excess not hers, but imposed by certain fateful circumstances. Is it possible, James seriously wonders, that the problem was her partnership with George Henry Lewes?

For James, Eliot's career is one long struggle between the claims of perception and reflection. Her best success would have come had she been able always to balance them. At first, she could: "The truth is, perception and reflection, at the outset, divided George Eliot's great talent between them" (674). Writing her first stories, Eliot made direct use of her own fresh perceptions. But with *Romola*, the "equilibrium" is lost; the book "does not seem positively to live," and is instead "overladen with learning, it smells of the lamp, it tastes just perceptively of pedantry" (675). With *Romola*, Eliot lost a basic vitality; she "proceeds from the abstract to the concrete," producing life too "deeply studied and elaborately justified," "not *seen* in the irresponsible plastic way" (673). What has changed, it seems, is that Eliot ceased to run the impression's range from concrete perception to studied reflection. She lost its balance of faculties, and the loss seems egregious enough for James to want to find an explanation for it. This he finds vaguely in many circumstances but primarily in one: " 'perception' and 'reflection', at the outset, divided George Eliot's great talent between them; but, as time went on, circumstances led the latter to develop itself at the expense of the former – one of these circumstances being apparently the influence of George Henry Lewes" (674). Really ready to blame Lewes, James makes his lovely appreciation of Eliot also a melodramatic regret that nothing rescued her from Lewes's influence. In this regret is regret for his own will to make male and female faculties collaborate, and, ultimately, regret that ideologies of gender condition the art of fiction.

James's regret comes primarily in reflection upon Eliot's strange domestic arrangement – her strange parody of standard feminine domesticity. James speaks of the unfortunate effects of her "sequestration" – the enforced exile from social life brought on by the perceived immorality of her life with Lewes – and defines those unfortunate effects primarily as a sacrifice of superficiality. "She was unable, in the premises, to be sufficiently superficial" (671). Endowed with a "deep, strenuous, much-considering mind," Eliot was from the outset in danger of becoming more thoughtful than a female writer of fiction should. Her femininity might have saved the balance had it not been for "her action in 1854," the choice to take up residence with Lewes, and the fact that by it "she committed herself to being nothing if not reflective . . . to a plan of life, of study, in which the accidental, the unexpected, were too little allowed for" (671). To some degree, it was worry about the appearance of frivolity that made Eliot too serious; but for the most part, James implies, it was the influence of Lewes's emphatic "reflection," for "the contagion of his studies pushed her further than she would otherwise have gone in the direction of *scientific* observation, which is but another form of what I have called reflection" (674). And so James seems to describe some grotesque exaggeration of the complementarity basic to Victorian domesticity: where the shared life of domestic "sequestration" ought to entail mutually enriching influence, in this case it has the man spoiling a mutuality that already exists within the woman herself. According to the logic of gender distinctions upon which James's Impressionism depends for its model of collaboration, male and female ought to give each other what each perceptually lacks. But the happy complementarity in "The Art of Fiction" – the good way Anne Thackeray Ritchie serves as James's example – rules out Eliot's Impressionist intensity.

"The Life of George Eliot" therefore contradicts the logic of "The

Art of Fiction," and the two essays – with just one year between
them – represent contradictory theoretical alternatives. And the
framework within which James often imagines human possibility has
Anne Thackeray Ritchie and George Eliot as its defining features.
The two women of genius figure both the happy possibility of an
integral relation between art and life and one in which experience
and imagination are at odds – on the one hand, the possibility that
fresh life will grow naturally together with sophisticated creative
projections, and on the other hand the fear that the mind that
creates and the vital sensibility will fight each other for life.

This opposition reflects the uncertainty that makes Impressionist
writing in general so productively indecisive. And in James's case the
uncertainty has more than two poles – more different theoretical
positions, even, than the two occupied by the perfectly Impressionist
Ritchie and the excessively reflective Eliot. We will turn momentarily
to those fictions and additional critical works in which James's
uncertainties manifest themselves, and in which James's critical
priorities change. But first we need to see what happens to Impressionism in the rest of "The Life of George Eliot," which continues to
lament Eliot's loss of balance, but ends affirming that loss, and
preferring it to what works so well in "The Art of Fiction": Daudet's
Impressionism. In this last reversal James's Impressionist uncertainties really multiply.

The Conclusion to "The Life of George Eliot" wholly reconfigures
"The Art of Fiction." There is, first of all, a return to the strange
basic question of Lewes's influence, as James finds it "impossible not
to let our imagination wander in the direction of what turn her mind
or her fortune might have taken if she had never met George Henry
Lewes" (677). Would we, James wonders, have had more of *Adam
Bede* and less of *Romola* – something "less systematic, more irresponsible, more personal?" (677). James seems ready to say we would, and
to wish we had. But then, perhaps remembering his admiration for
Eliot's last novels, he takes a turn, and seems to decide that in giving
herself over to reflection, Eliot really discovered impressions of the
most valuable kind. He comes to this conclusion by contrasting
Eliot's priorities with those of Daudet. He repeats what he had said
in "The Art of Fiction," now explicitly attributing to Daudet the
belief that "the personal impression, the effort of direct observation,
was the most precious source of information for the novelist" (677).
Now, however, James adds context that makes this statement mean

something very different. Daudet, we now learn, emphasized the
personal impression in contrast to that which comes from books – in
a complaint about the way books produce second-hand impressions
that block perception from reality. "Ah, les livres, ils nous débour-
dent, ils nous étouffent – nous périssons par les livres!": "the effect of
books," James says, now paraphrasing Daudet, "was constantly to
check and pervert" the effort of direct observation, so that "a
second-hand, a third-hand, tenth-hand impression was constantly
tending to substitute itself for a fresh perception," with the result that
"we were . . . seeing everything through literature instead of through
our own senses; and that in short literature was rapidly killing
literature" (677). With this new information, Daudet's impression has
a different status and ceases to be something James can affirm.
Before, in "The Art of Fiction," it was an alternative to too-direct
experience, a kind of detachment in which imagination and experience could play equal parts. Now, it has become a resistance to
representation, or to the form of experience that comes mediated
through representation; it has become part of an anti-reflective
aesthetic of radical immediacy. As such, it loses its mediatory power,
and as such it entails an Impressionism that James must reject. As
would his woman of genius: "if impressionism, before she had laid
down her pen, had begun to be talked about, it would have made no
difference with her – she would have had no desire to pass for an
impressionist."

This remark is one of James's two explicit references to the
possibility of a literary Impressionism. Despite his interest in the
impression, this reference is negative, alleging that a fully inspired
writer could not find Impressionism appealing. George Eliot, it
seems, knew that books themselves, as well as other vehicles of
reflection, could be good sources of impressions, and in this interest
in impressions of all kinds – this interest in even the third- and tenth-
hand impression – she manifests a temperament too broad even for
Impressionism's range. Admiring her for it, James seems to discredit
Impressionism, and certainly to contradict anyone who would want
to call him an Impressionist.

Unless of course we notice that impressions still define Eliot's
work. She may not limit herself to Daudet's immediacy, but what she
gets tenth-hand is still an impression. As long as the definition of the
impression allows for such diversity – as long as it can, as it should,
bridge immediate perception with detached reflection, or bring

passion to her reading life – she might yet have been happy enough
to pass for an Impressionist. She earns, after all, exactly the same
kind of praise James gives to Anne Thackeray Ritchie:

There is much talk to-day about things being 'open to women'; but George
Eliot showed that there is nothing that is closed . . . What *is* remarkable,
extraordinary – and the process remains inscrutable and mysterious – is
that this quiet, anxious, sedentary, serious, invalidical English lady, without
animal spirits, without adventures, without extravagance, assumption, or
bravado, should have made us believe that nothing in the world was alien
to her; should have produced such rich, deep, masterly pictures of the
multifold life of man. (678)

As much as excess "reflection" may have spoiled her writing, she
nevertheless remained "open" in the manner of the isolated woman
of genius. The point here is not to insist that Eliot was, after all, an
Impressionist, but to show that James's categories vary a great deal
according to his various definitions of the impression's perceptual
status. In "The Art of Fiction," the impression mediates perception
and reflection, or, to shift the terms a bit, experience and imagination; in this account of things, James would be an impressionist, and
Daudet and Eliot would seem practitioners of impressions too given
(respectively) to perception and reflection. But in the essay on Eliot,
the impression is redefined in terms of Daudet's excessive interest in
pure perception, and the scale of categories shifts accordingly,
pushing Impressionism off the edge of aesthetic credibility. "Impressionism" is defined in terms of the immediate impression; the fuller
impression, that which extends to the tenth degree, gets no "ism" of
its own; James discredits the former, and fails to name the latter, and
his own theoretical placement migrates among the possibilities.[43]

James's place among Impressionism's possibilities migrates as
follows: in "The Art of Fiction," the impression has a mediatory
status, but one apparently not well suited to James himself, so he
reframes that mediation as a collaboration with that female sensibility best able to make an art of receptivity. That collaboration,
however, may itself limit receptivity – a possibility explored through
the example of George Eliot – leaving James still unsure about the
terms of the impression's mediation. Moreover, the limitation of
receptivity might in fact produce the best impression, that which
truly involves the reflective intellect in perceptual experience. This is
what George Eliot's career ultimately suggests to James, and the
suggestion discredits the impression which, in the first place, inspired

"The Art of Fiction." Tracing his way around this epistemological circle, following his women of genius, James involves himself perpetually in disorienting epistemological twists.

The twists emerge clearly if we contrast this account of the Jamesian impression with one that sees it straight. John Carlos Rowe reads James's impression as proof that James has a proto-deconstructionist disbelief in the immediacy of perception. According to Rowe, James's fictions often show how people who commit themselves to what they immediately perceive go wrong, and only redeem themselves once they learn that experience is always mediated – that there really is no such thing as a "direct impression." James knows "how 'perception' is always already governed by a will-to-meaning," and impressions therefore "depend upon prior determinations of our conceptual faculties."[44] Clearly, the James who admires George Eliot knows that this is the case, but the James who hopes for some compromise between the perceptual and the conceptual hopes that the latter is not "prior" to the former, and that fiction could therefore be equal parts life and art. James's impression does entail a deconstructionist refusal of the immediate, but sometimes it does not: it is the vacillation here, as we will now see it in James's fiction, that makes things really interesting, and it is the movement toward the deconstructionist refusal – again, that turn to the conviction that "art makes life" – that gives James's career its most interesting twist.

"She had an immense curiosity about life and was constantly staring and wondering. She carried within herself a great fund of life, and her deepest enjoyment was to feel the continuity between the movements of her own soul and the agitations of the world" (III: 45). Isabel Archer's talent for continuity nicely personifies the contingency that "The Art of Fiction" wants impressions to bring to fiction. Isabel has a fetching "comprehensiveness of observation" that seems to involve her body as much as her mind: "her head was erect, her eye lighted, and her flexible figure turned itself easily this way and that, in sympathy with the alertness with which she evidently caught impressions. Her impressions were numerous, and they were all reflected in a clear, still smile" (21). Her manifest impressionability – it is important that she *evidently* catches impressions – accounts for her tremendous appeal, which, like the smile that reflects it, brings on an array of admirers. "Isabel certainly has devotees," as Countess Gemini notes, and they have different uses for her great fund of vitality. Jamesians have often remarked, as R. P. Blackmur puts it, that "everyone tampers with Isabel," acting, as Millicent Bell notes, like "generous or tyrannical novelists."[45] These admirers only imitate their creator, though, as they use his woman of genius. Ralph Touchett, Madame Merle, and Gilbert Osmond successively do with Isabel Archer what James hopes to accomplish in his invocation of Anne Thackeray Ritchie – what he hopes the impression's synthesis will accomplish – and, as things go from good to bad to worse, as things look more like James's version of the marriage of Eliot and Lewes, the bad behavior of these tamperers perform key theoretical flaws in James's Impressionist aesthetic.

That Ralph acts as an "author's delegate" is clear. "Planning out a high destiny" for Isabel, and then endowing her "fund of life" as far as he can with his father's money, Ralph helps James give Isabel "the high attributes of a Subject," and, complementing her vitality in this fashion, helps *Portrait* constitute a complete imaginative capacity. Ralph wants to help Isabel "meet the requirements of [her] imagination" (III: 261) – in other words, to make her freshness signify. In doing so, he establishes with Isabel something very much like that "odd epistemological interaction" between Maisie and her narrator. He gives her means, or meaning, and she gives him the sense of life he lacks. "What kept Ralph alive was simply the fact that he had not seen enough of the person in the world in whom he was most interested" (IV: 146); she is his link to life, and is moreover equated with his own faculties' simpler use: "With the prospect of losing them the simple use of his faculties became an exquisite pleasure," a pleasure Ralph finds also with "the advent of a young lady who was evidently not insipid" (III: 53–54). Making up a single Impressionist faculty, Ralph and Isabel enact what is for the moment a good synthesis, with the result that Ralph sees art made more artful by life: "'A character like that', he said to himself – 'a real little passionate force to see at play is the finest thing in nature. It's finer than the finest work of art . . .'" (III: 86). Once again the "little passionate force" – the faint intense impression, the ingenious innocent Maisie – makes of nature a finer art.

Of course, the collaboration between Ralph and Isabel produces no great destiny. The money he gives her in fact threatens the vitality he wants to watch and win, and makes her prey to Gilbert Osmond. In the passage from a kind collaboration to a cruel one, James wonders if the impression's juncture of art and life might not kill life.

He wonders again, in other words, if the "intense" impression might not have to give way to the "faint" one as the aesthetic imagination gets going, and makes Isabel live out that change as she gives way to Osmond's authority. The change, however, is forecasted by Ralph, when he jokes about Isabel's need to suffer. Early in the novel, Ralph tells Isabel that she probably will not be able to see Gardencourt's ghost, because her great powers of observation have certain limits: "I might show it to you, but you'd never see it. The privilege isn't given to every one; it's not enviable. It has never been seen by a young, happy, innocent person like you. You must have suffered first, have suffered greatly, have gained some miserable knowledge. In that way your eyes are opened to it . . ." (III: 64). Here is a hard apophatic solution to the problem of how to become the kind of person upon whom nothing is lost. Here, the gap between vitality and artful discretion has widened, so that to cross it requires more sacrifice than James anticipates in the bluff confidence of "The Art of Fiction."

As the villain who turns this international-theme comedy into aestheticist melodrama, Gilbert Osmond has earned all kinds of hatred and has even (in some recent readings) made James himself look bad. As a figure for Jamesian authorship, Osmond seems to figure the nasty rarefication at work in James's aesthetic. But it requires only slight variation on a common theme in James criticism to prove that Isabel needs Osmond to torture her: where the critical tradition sees Osmond's connoisseurship as an unqualified aestheticist evil, the novel has him to thank for Isabel's refinement. In a manner predicted by Ralph, and predicted as well by the structure of the impression's mediation, chapter 42, which famously shows Isabel's mind "finely aware and richly responsible," is significantly initiated by Osmond's command, "think that over" (IV: 185). Then follows Isabel's reverie: "Isabel had hitherto not asked herself the question, because she had not been forced; but now that it was directly presented to her she saw the answer . . ." (186). The forcing is awful, and the marriage is a terrible mistake, but it makes an ironic kind of sense within the context of the logic of the impression. The marriage follows but renders grotesque that logic, by turning productive mediation into strange collaboration: "It was a strange opposition, of the like of which she had never dreamed – an opposition in which the vital principle of the one was a thing of contempt to the other" (IV: 189). Where Ralph had lived for the spectacle of Isabel's vitality, Osmond lives to hate it, but love and hate here mirror each other. The two have a similar structure, observed by Osmond in the early moments when things are good: "you're remarkably fresh, and I'm remarkably well-seasoned" (81). Here is the familiar collaboration, and Osmond plans to make it work as it should, knowing that "he could tap her imagination with his knuckle and make it ring" (79), and that Isabel will both "feel with him and for him" (200). "Her mind was to be attached to his" – but, it turns out, "like a small garden-plot to a deer park" (200). The juncture of sensibilities here will once again be an unequal one. While Osmond does at first want Isabel to be "richly receptive," their collaboration soon ceases to be that between the "fresh" and the "well-seasoned." Isabel's gem-like flame does not remain a source of light once she enters the Palazzo Roccanera, where Osmond can say with offhand perspicacity, "we're as united, you know, as the candlestick and the snuffers" (309).[46]

Another good image for this unity appears in a description of the relation between Osmond's mind and Isabel's body. Aware, finally, that Osmond's mind complements her sensibility only by torturing it into lucidity, Isabel sees that his house is for her "the house of darkness, the house of dumbness, the house of suffocation" (196). In this house – one that builds upon James's "house of fiction" – Osmond's mind is distant and unforthcoming: "Osmond's beautiful mind gave it neither light nor air; Osmond's beautiful mind seemed to peep down from a small high window and mock at her" (196). If distance within a figure indicates anything, the distance here perso-nifies a new dualism. Making Isabel "[throw] away her life" (203), the novel kills the thing it loves, undermining itself by breaking its link to life and prime measure of authenticity. But this gap is also that which creates the better Isabel: ending Isabel's life gives her that "miserable knowledge" she needs to "guess the unseen from the seen" – to see Ralph's ghost, but also to see the ghost that is the novel's great "impression": that of "her husband and Madame Merle unconsciously and familiarly associated" (IV: 205). Despite Osmond's snuffing effect, he helps her finally to see things in a finer light, as the resolution of the problem of impressionability reaches consummation in the novel's epiphanies: "Now that she was in the secret . . . the truth of things, their mutual relations, their meaning, and for the most part their horror, rose before her with a kind of architectural vastness" (IV: 390–91). The fraught joining of Isabel and Osmond –

and, consequently, the faculties they stand for – creates scenes which, more than any "bewilderment" or superficially "impressionistic" knowing, represent what Impressionism means in James: instant, perfect, and deep insight through a glimpse of what is given.

One such scene occurs in Isabel's impression of the association of Osmond and Madame Merle; another occurs in the silent and complete communication that passes between Madame Merle and Isabel at the end of the novel, when Madame Merle guesses "in the space of an instant that everything was at an end between them," and Isabel "[sees] it all distinctly as if it had been reflected in a large clear glass" (IV: 378). That James writes for such moments is clear; but what enables them is less so: does Isabel finally see so clearly because of the way Osmond has invested her "great fund of life," or does that fund carry her through to new opportunities despite Osmond's malignance? Is Isabel another Anne Thackeray Ritchie, able to "guess the unseen from the seen, to trace the implication of things" due to the grace of female limitation itself, or is she another George Eliot, made wise at the cost of her freshness by a bad marriage?[47] Of course we never know. The novel, it has often been noted, is open-ended, a fact most often adduced as evidence of James's modernist resistance to closure. Such resistance is, in fact, fairly unique to this case: while James's plots do not often end conventionally in marriage and death, they rarely fall into the kind of deep obscurity that shrouds Isabel's return to Rome. *The Portrait of a Lady* defers the answer to the novel's key question: what Isabel, affronting her destiny, will do. We know she returns to Rome and Osmond, but we do not know what the terms of that return will be; we do not know what she will make of her marriage. But this we cannot know, because Isabel's return to Osmond is an impossible compromise. Isabel must lose her freshness to vie with Osmond; she must vie with him to remain true to her destiny; but her destiny requires her to maintain her openness. In the missing, impossible playing out of those events, James places the burden of what remains unreconcilable in his solution to the problem of impressionability.

In Maisie, who virtually *is* her strange power to "remain fresh," James finds a better solution. At first a pawn in her parents' divorce, she, too, comes to full receptivity through a kind of collaborational torture – like Isabel Archer and George Eliot, she suffers for her insight – but James finds in her childhood a better theory of the way

that impressions might draw at once on opposite sensibilities. The
product of superior aesthetic engineering, Maisie learns above all
else to understand abstract structures through reference to concrete
everyday phenomena. Despite her age she thinks with all the
conceptual sophistication of James's canniest protagonists; but
because of her age she thinks in terms of the sights and sounds of
things intensely seen and heard. This is not to say what readers have
often noticed about Maisie – that her fresh confused perceptions
make *What Maisie Knew* a triumph for the fiction of "point of view." It
is to say that Maisie's consciousness is unique and productive for its
facility with *abstract* thought, which she owes to the vast ready stock
of concrete images. The delight she provokes in James comes from
the ease with which he can imagine her at once transmitting signs of
life and transforming them into the fine shapes of art. More talented
in each regard than any other woman of genius, Maisie gives James
unmatched Impressionist opportunities, and, *reductio ad absurdum*,
pushes those opportunities so far that they lose any credible claim to
his attention.

Maisie's claim to significance, what makes her worth a short novel,
seems to be her tendency "to see much more than she at first
understood" (xi: 9). Her bewilderment, it seems, heightens fiction's
mimetic power by presenting the world undistorted by judgment.
But while Maisie's "fate" is to see more than she understands, it is
"also even at first to understand much more than any little girl" (9).
Immediately we learn that Maisie is not just a funny foil; she "does
things," as James notes in his Preface, transform what she sees. Not
just an innocent, Maisie has "an innocence . . . saturated with
knowledge," and the fact that knowledge does not dissolve her
innocence is her triumph. The plot of *What Maisie Knew* presents
Maisie's combination of knowledge and innocence as a strange result
of very peculiar circumstances. The novel's pattern of description,
however, suggests that the combination is not really something that
Maisie has "more than any little girl." She combines opposite modes
of experience in ways that girl-children always do.

Readers have always noticed that Maisie's childish "bewilderment" makes her an effective center of consciousness.[48] What really
makes her work for James, however, is the way her bewilderment
short-circuits the false distinction between concrete and abstract
experience. Rudolph Arnheim – another aesthetician interested in
the perceptivity of children – finds many of the best examples of

what he calls "visual thinking," or thought that is at once conceptual and perceptual, in children's drawings. Wanting to argue that we think best when we think in images and wanting to prove that simple drawings often contain more knowledge than complex theoretical explanations, Arnheim sees in children's drawings the power of very thoughtful abstraction. Abstraction, for him, is not any airy form of knowledge, but that which detects the common pattern of concrete experience. Children, who do not yet detach abstraction improperly from its concrete instances, are Arnheim's great concern: they prove his point, and would, were his theories applied in educational policy, never grow out of their talents for concrete abstraction. James shares the concern when it comes to Maisie, from whom he gets what Arnheim gets from children's drawings: an example of the style of thought in which "innocence" clarifies the essence of knowledge, and proof that knowledge is richest when grounded in a theory of perception that will not distinguish the concrete from the abstract.[49]

From Maisie James gets a natural source of the kind of metaphor he loves. James notoriously writes abstractly; "life" in his fiction is an etiolated, detached thing, happening among the fine distinctions of consciousness. His figures, however, are often almost parodically concrete. He will figure the movements of consciousness as fairly simple movements in space, for example, often ironically to convey their complexity, but more often to offer a helpful diagram. When these diagrams cease to be helpful – when James's concrete diagrams of abstract thought processes become as complex as what they mean to simplify – the aesthetic failure is telling. Very often when a consciousness eludes diagrammatic representation it also makes moral mistakes, or proves otherwise unperceptive, so that a failure of "visual thinking" marks a failure of good thinking. But when James's diagrams of consciousness succeed, James makes the breadth of the distance between the terms of his metaphor a sign of genius. When a complex act of consciousness has an analog in a simple geometrical diagram, it proves its power, and James pulls off a certain virtuoso aesthetic performance. The match between this performance and that of the impression's connection between art and life defines James's Impressionism, and indicates as well how a little girl like Maisie might have a lot to do with aesthetic success. Maisie is the best proof that for James, impressions, despite their reputation, are abstractions, but abstractions which require the simplicity we associate with (and figure as) concretion.

For Maisie brings the specific complications she sees into the clarity of simple abstraction. Early on, for example, when facing a difficult situation Maisie "held her breath with the sense of picking her steps among the tremendous things of life" (70). As complex situations become "tremendous things," and Maisie imagines walking about among them, James exploits a species of concretion that sounds childish only until we properly measure the distance between its simplicity and the complexity of the problem it figures. The distance would not be as great were this metaphor to describe an adult's process through the world of life; but a little girl's little steps, and the way holding her breath would enlarge her body yet to a size far smaller than life's "tremendous things," produces a diagrammatic discrepancy as abstract as concrete. The concrete image, in other words, is really more important for the abstract shape it conjures; and the abstract shape is the best possible diagram for the moral problem that would otherwise require far more extensive and elaborate description. It is this effect – the way the metaphors Maisie conjures are abstract concretions – that makes her sensibility such a fine producer of impressions.

James clearly enjoys writing "Maisie received in petrification the full force of her mother's huge painted eyes – they were like Japanese lanterns swung under festal arches" (143). Such a metaphor might not violate the fine mind of an adult, but James knows that it is a shame that they would not, since the metaphor shows fine visual thinking. Because she is unfamiliar with cosmetics, Maisie sees that her mother's eyes are what "painted" implies, and her mind runs more incisively to the broad image than to subtler thoughts about the tawdriness of make-up. So we get the tawdriness of make-up in "full force." Maisie makes a reach that broadly joins the abstract and the concrete again when her mother gets angry, and "her mother's drop had the effect of one of the iron shutters that, in evening walks with Susan Ash, [Maisie] had seen suddenly, at the touch of a spring, rattle down over shining shop-fronts" (166). In this figure for Mrs. Farange's mercenary mood-swings Maisie's visual thinking again makes a concrete experience an abstract interpretation – and again James gets to indulge in a metaphorical style otherwise unavailable to his fictional tone. Only when he writes comedy can James write such metaphors, and to write them seriously, and therefore have their energy without their absurdity, James needs to collaborate with the sensibility for whom such metaphors yet remain signs of good thinking. One last example – again the effect of Mrs. Farange's stare – shows just how far Maisie can go into the realm of complexity without departing from seriousness or from life: "Her mother gave her one of the looks that slammed the door in her face; never in a career of unsuccessful experiments had Maisie had to take such a stare. It reminded her of the way that once, at one of the lectures in Glower Street, something in a big jar that, amid an array of strange glasses and bad smells, had been promised as a beautiful yellow was produced as a beautiful black" (223). The connection between the personal and the scientific "experiments"; the movement from a glower to its counterpart on "Glower Street"; the grace of calling the black solution "beautiful" as well – all of these things tell of an unusually advantageous fit between the concrete image and the abstract interpretation within it.

The best evidence that Maisie extends the reach of metaphor is in words that often *qualify* her metaphors. When Maisie thinks that one thing is "like" another thing, her inexperience often qualifies "like" with "something," or turns "as" into "as if." But these qualifiers do not weaken her connections as much as enable connections broader than those that metaphor might typically sustain: they become pivots upon which Maisie reaches more deeply into the fantastic, for diagrammatic figures even more effectively clear of the kinds of adumbrations that would overshadow them. Inversely, Maisie often takes things literally: when Mrs. Wix announces that Sir Claude "leans on me!," Maisie gets "the impression of a support literally supplied by her person" (96). The comic misunderstanding of course sees to a truer truth, insofar as Mrs. Wix's belief *is* farcical, and insofar as much of Mrs. Wix's excitement comes from imagining Sir Claude's body on her own. Refusing any distance between the literal and the metaphorical can be a way to emphasize the healthy oneness of the concrete and the abstract – especially in this case, in which Maisie's mistake sees realities at once more theoretically fundamental and more physically detailed than the one Mrs. Wix has meant to describe.

Maisie's wonderful responses are *impressions* of the highest order. More than any, they connect "vulgar appearances" with "universals"; more than any, they give the art of fiction vital junctures. When James writes that "she seemed fairly to receive new information from every brush of the breeze" (281), he recognizes an impressionability that, to use the words he uses to describe Anne

Thackeray Ritchie, "converts the very pulses of the air into revelations." He sees in Maisie a power to "convert" without any tendency to stop feeling the brush of the breeze, a tendency in fact to convert by making the brush of the breeze itself a diagram for abstract thought. Writing a novel about this power and its sources, James extends his thinking about the way impressions join experience and art.

He also, however, extends that thinking's dependence on the example of a debased femininity and pushes Impressionist *apophasis* beyond the pale. *What Maisie Knew* extends itself beyond any real hope for aesthetic ingenuity, as James strays into a personification too much like what Sterne gives us in *Tristram Shandy*. Like *Portrait of a Lady*, *What Maisie Knew* makes impressionability the result of circumstances not only peculiar but painful – indicating that the fruits of impressionability come to people like James himself only through an aesthetic process analogous to real-life cruelty. As Impressionist collaboration takes child-abuse as its occasion, however, James also admits to the evil of it – not its real-life evil, of course, but the evil of its fairly inartistic manicheanism. James lays bare the basic mechanism of "domestic fiction," and, finding it yet dominant in fiction that had begun to aspire to more subtle arts, must resolve to try to excise it. And there is at least one sign that he begins to do so in *What Maisie Knew*, in Sir Claude's apparent suspicion that Maisie is no little girl at all. Sir Claude often jokes and calls Maisie "old chap," "old man," or (and the last example proves that the others are not simple endearments) "my dear old woman" (83, 85, 122). He calls her these things mostly to flatter her precocious wisdom, but also with the effect of suggesting that the essence of her intelligence is something imputed rather than natural. Sir Claude would cajole James out of the sentimentalizing projection of his own metaphorical ingenuity onto this woman of genius. His way of teasing Maisie in fact predicts the moment in which James rejects the logic of *apophasis* – the moment in *The Ambassadors* in which Lambert Strether discovers that his old self is also a fresh one, and discovers this possibility in its opposite: young Chad Newsome's grey hair. *The Ambassadors* devotes itself to a chiasmus of the terms of Impressionist collaboration and to a final result that finds receptivity to impressions fully available to a single older man. Lambert Strether's great epiphany in that novel undoes, to the degree that one epiphany could, the logic through which novelistic subjectivity sequestered its essence and divided itself.

The Ambassadors is *Portrait of a Lady* written backwards. Where the latter makes a vital young woman give up her life, the former lets a lifeless older man find his; where the latter novel begins in comedy and moves to melodrama, the former begins in melodrama (the furor over Chad's corruption) and ends in comedy (the spirit of epithalamion in which Strether finally expresses his liberated joy).[50] The years between the latter and the former, then, see a development that proceeds through three stages. In the first, marked by the collaborations in *Portrait of a Lady* and "The Art of Fiction," James imagines Impressionist unity as a collaboration whose theoretical complications match the real complications of a bad marriage; in the second stage, James perfects the collaboration, but only by pushing the analogous social dynamic – the dynamic also essential to "domestic fiction" – to the absurd extremes of *What Maisie Knew*; and in the third stage, that marked by *The Ambassadors*, James happily gives up on the collaborative solution, by making what fiction had reserved for limited femininity something at once universal and free. To some degree these "stages" are crude. But James himself delineates them in his Prefaces to the New York edition. James's Prefaces chart a change in attitude towards the impression, so that despite his own belief that they represented "the continuity of an artist's endeavour" (and despite Blackmur's corroborating claim that the Prefaces have the "consistency of a mathematical equation"), they feature the discontinuity through which James's Impressionism changed.[51]

In response to Stevenson's "Remonstrance" to "The Art of Fiction," James wrote to him, "My pages, in *Longman*, were simply a plea for liberty: they were only half of what I had to say and someday I shall express the remainder."[52] James expressed the remainder twenty years later in the Prefaces to the New York Edition of his collected works. The Prefaces stress (as James puts it in his debate with H. G. Wells) that it is "art that *makes* life,"[53] as James calls for the artist to "dramatise," emphasizing now not receptivity to impressions but the power artistically to work them up. That power is James's "other half," but it is really an extension of the first, since "to dramatise" is to take the impression's "liberty" and thus to make life anew.

Similarly, the Prefaces extend, rather than speak against, "The Art of Fiction," and in fact they do so gradually. They begin reiterating what the essay says about the need to justify fiction through the

intensity of the initial impression and end with the need to dramatize; and they pass, in this progress, through something like what
"The Art of Fiction" implies about the important faintness of the
impression and the way it requires the play of female sensibility. The
result is a kind of retrospective survey of the way the problem of
Impressionism plays itself out in James's work: the Prefaces take us
from mediation that requires collaboration and the renewal of
dualism to mediation that happens at the liberty of the artist
himself.[54]

James very apparently repeats "The Art of Fiction" in his Preface
to *The Portrait of a Lady*, where he again argues that a fiction must be
"some direct impression or perception of life" (III: ix), and again
ascribes the impression to womanhood. But it is with the Preface to
The Princess Casamassima that James sets a form for the Prefaces to
many of his early fictions: this and later Prefaces begin with an effort
to find the first impression – to recollect the moment (sometimes an
impression, sometimes a "germ") in which each fiction had its slight
but promising beginning. Apophasis characterizes these recollections, insofar as slightness and smallness make for the best first
impressions, and insofar as the best first impressions are those related
to a specifically feminine "frailness." "Anything more than the
minimum spoils the operation" (x: v); and something suggested by a
lady at dinner, or the "light lamp" of girlish enthusiasm, really sets a
good fiction going. But somewhere after the Preface to *The Aspern
Papers*, James ceases to stress the way the "novelist's imagination
winces as at the prick of some sharp point" (x: v). He shifts, at this
point, from that emphasis to "expressing the remainder" – to
stressing the need for the good writer to "dramatise." "Owen
Wingrave," for example, is a "seedless fable," where the need to
"Dramatise it!" prevails as the better aesthetic imperative (xv:
xxii–xxiii).

The shift in question runs parallel to that with which James gets
over his fascination with what Maisie represents. It runs parallel to
the shift with which Lambert Strether comes to revel in his mature
sensibilities, and it therefore makes sense that the Preface to *The
Ambassadors* should be that in which James strikes a balance: "Never
can a composition of this sort have sprung straighter from a dropped
grain of suggestion, and never can that grain, developed, overgrown
and smothered, have yet lurked more in the mass as an independent
particle" (xxi: v); "Nothing can exceed the closeness with which the

whole fits again into its germ" (XXI: vi). Having come to believe that "its only into thickened motive and accumulated character . . . that the painter of life bites more than a little" (XXI: viii), and yet having come to think as well that such accumulation does not obscure the particle within, James also comes to theorize impressions that run that fuller range. At this moment he abandons Impressionist mediation. To mix more metaphors with those James mixes: to want to be a painter of life who bites into more than a little is to disbelieve that the small cornerstone founds the best house of fiction; to rejoice in maturity is to find joy where Impressionism tends to worry that no such vivacity can exist, and to want thickening and accumulation is to worry no longer that such developments would deaden impressionability. Had James written his review of Cross's biography of Eliot at *this* moment, he might have been less likely to believe that Lewes spoiled Eliot's art by thickening it with science; had James written "The Art of Fiction" at this moment, he might not have made Ritchie the example of the way that fiction runs life into art. He would not have needed collaborations to make impressions work. But then he would not have needed impressions at all. If the impression is the term that writers use to describe the imagination when the imagination's synthesis is uncertain – if they require its ambiguous connections to have both synthesis and separation – then the impression is not a term writers will use when they are happy enough to conflate aesthetic and experiential perceptivity. Its work done, the impression departs – or, rather, passes into vernacular anonymity.

When James does refer again to impressions, it is to regret that they meant duality as much as synthesis. In his late *Notes of a Son and Brother* (1914), James recalls the thrill of that early moment in which "To feel a unity, a character and a tone in one's impressions, to feel them related and all harmoniously coloured, that *was* positively to face the aesthetic, the creative, even quite wondrously the critical life and almost on the spot to commence author."[55] In his recollections of his earliest aesthetic life James describes the way that impressions scratched audibly at the door of vocation, and the way their intensity and appeal distracted him from thinking them through and figuring out what they "were for." "Impressions . . . were the dearest things in the world" (254), but a guilty indulgence, because of "the troubled view that they were naught without a backing, a stout stiff hard-grained underside that would hold them together and of which the terrible name was simply science, otherwise learning, and learning exclusively by books." James almost seems to remember Daudet's complaint here – the worry that books would kill impressions and thereby kill themselves. Like Daudet, he had held to the paradoxical belief that impressions and books were antagonists. The older James sees the error: "Never did I quite strike it off, I think, that impressions might themselves *be* science – and this probably because I didn't then know them, when it came to the point, as anything but life." What James admits here is that impressions made thrilling connections that were also false distinctions. They seemed to be "aesthetic" in the full sense of that word, but were really limited to "life," and largely depended on a defensive inattention to the very aspects of life that led to aesthetic connections. In fact James's "liveliest" impression was the belief that "life and knowledge were simply mutual opposites, one inconsistent with the other" – that, in other words, the parts of art were divided by the very impression that ought to bring them together.

What follows, in *Notes of a Son and Brother*, is a distant memory of Impressionist collaboration, now with personifications more at odds and problems more present. James writes that he thought that life and knowledge were opposites despite also observing

the anomaly that when knowledge impinged upon life, pushed against her, as it were, and drove her to the wall, it was all right, and such was knowledge's way and title; whereas when life played the like tricks with knowledge nothing but shame for the ruder, even if lighter, party could accrue. There was to come to me of course in time the due perception that neither was of the least use – use to myself – without the other; but meanwhile, and even for much after, the extreme embarrassment continued: to whichever of the opposites one gave one's self it was with a sense of all but basely sacrificing the other. (254–55)

What had always gone on in secret is here revealed: we see "knowledge" forcing "life," as a man might force a woman, according to his right and his title, and all for the good; and we see that a woman trying to do the same would be a shame for her. Not to put much weight on the metaphor – since the point throughout has not been to take the impression's collaborative relations literally, but rather to see that such figurative relations endorse a self-alienated aesthetic, and to see that James outlines the "embarrassment" of all this figurative bad behavior. For his dealings with the impression metaphor lead him to want to stop the base sacrifices it seems to require, and to know that it really ought to prove that when it comes to the parts of the life of the aesthetic, "neither . . . was of the least use without the other."

James finally regrets that one's faculties were prone to harass one another, but then also notes that the conflict itself was a source of interest: "However, the conflict and the drama involved in the question at large was doubtless what was to make consciousness – under whichever of the two names one preferred to entertain it – supremely intense and interesting" (255). Consciousness may have gone by two conflicting names, and so may have made it harder for James to justify art properly or live life well, but then again the conflict itself was impressive. It was itself of the highest value – and of no small use.

As James's last personifications of "life" and "knowledge" suggest, the conflict led to representation of an analogous social conflict, to the point where James could only disclose the social basis of his form. In other words, the best way for James to make sense of the conflict was to see it socially, and doing so inevitably led him to wonder what gender relations had to do with novelistic subjectivity. That this was, in fact, a kind of "deconstruction" is affirmed by James's late suspicion of the need to choose between epistemological opposites. His early hope for the impression's mediation was a hope for some immediate relation between experience and the higher powers of the imagination. But his later wish that he had always known that life was "no use" without knowledge constitutes a deconstructionist sense that life is not present to consciousness. If the hope for the impression's mediation was a hope for a phenomenological synthesis, James's final sense that "impressions might themselves *be* science" is a productive resistance to mediation, productive for the way it allows human alienation itself to figure as a basis for good art.

If James ends calling impressions science, does he not after all discover the true "impression?" Here things get more complicated, perhaps, than they should: I have argued, on the one hand, that the impression is itself a way to deconstruct dualistic arrangements of the human faculties, but then I have argued on the other hand that deconstruction comes in when James demystifies the impression's immediate presence. It seems, on the one hand, that James's hope for unity comes when he believes that impressions combine sense and intellect where experience and imagination meet; but then on the other hand it seems that James finally achieves unity when he can believe that impressions are science – that the opposed faculties really always work together, because "neither . . . was of the least use without the other." The difference between these two "unities" may be the difference between phenomenological holism and deconstructionist deferral: turning to a mode of unity that exists when no sign-system has priority over another, James ends up with a kind of totality that is, if less blessed, more authentic, and perhaps as such a better basis for the "sacrifice" of representation.

III HARDY'S DEFENSIVE IMPRESSION

Had James written an allegory on the basis of his last description of the relation between impressions and ideas – had he sharpened the melodrama of *Portrait of a Lady* such that Osmond really "drove her to the wall" – he might have written Hardy's *Tess of the D'Urbervilles* (1891). Even more than Isabel, Tess has the "fund for life" with which an Impressionist writer must want to endow his work; and even more than Isabel, Tess finds herself despoiled as a result. Moreover, Tess like Isabel is coeval with the "impression" of her book: just as Isabel "is" the impression that was the occasion for *Portrait of a Lady*, Tess has everything to do with the impression Hardy defends when he defends *Tess* from criticism.

Hardy invokes the impression to explain *Tess* after the fact, in his 1892 introduction to the novel. He defends *Tess* from blame through indirect reference to James's theory of fiction (though he might not have James in mind): to those who see an unpleasant "argument" in *Tess*, Hardy says "that a novel is an impression, not an argument."[56] He says, in other words, that there is no gap between life and fiction in which "argument" might make its way. As an impression, a novel may sound like an argument, because it does have the depth of thought; but as an impression a novel has no intentions, because it has the immediacy of sensation. Staking out this position, however, the impression fares less well than it does in "The Art of Fiction." In Hardy's case, the impression stands too close to its source: too much the sensuousness of Tess herself, this impression seems less to mediate than to adulterate.

Hardy always refused to theorize, and so it might seem inappropriate to ascribe to him any Impressionist theory. He always called any substantial amount of intellectual doctrine a danger to art

– even preferring reckless inconsistency to any systematic approach to fiction. This skepticism, however, is itself an Impressionist theory, insofar as it primarily resists the way doctrine would detach fiction from the world of concrete reality. When Hardy speaks against theories, he is never anti-intellectual; he may not have had his peers' formal education, but he certainly read around, and probably devoted more time than did his peers to thoughts of a "philosophical" nature. He resisted theory in a very specific context: the moment in which the artist adjusts his temperament to the task of creation. At that moment, Hardy felt, theory would give fiction an unreal systematicity. Wanting by contrast to find a temperamental location between the detachment of intellectual abstractions and the immediacy of concrete life, Hardy sought an Impressionist compromise. For as much as he wanted to refuse theory, Hardy wanted to refuse fact. "The 'simply natural' is interesting no longer," Hardy wrote in 1887, indicating an interest, inverse to his distaste for theory, in "[translating] the qualities that are already there" by some power of the imagination.[57] As Morton Zabel puts it, Hardy perpetually sought to maintain "a precarious balance, in art as in intelligent life, between the necessities of personal, practical, and localized experience, and the knowledge of universals which transcend all individuality."[58] This effort was the basis of his "incongruity," his tendency apparently to move haphazardly between "philosophy" and what Tony Tanner calls his "graphic crudities of effect," between the different claims of thought and sense.[59] It might make sense to see Hardy's "incongruity" as an Impressionist's uncertainty. Wanting to disclaim both abstract doctrine and simple nature as guides for fiction, and yet to have both in a way that make imagination their mediator, Hardy was an Impressionist.

Otherwise, we have to contend at once with Hardy the Naturalist and Hardy the Symbolist. Otherwise, we have a writer who alternates incongruously between the view that the will of nature determines all and the view that nature's effects exist simply to communicate the idea at the back of them. Without the terms of Impressionist mediation to make sense of Hardy's movement within this duality, we have a writer who seems inconsistently to devote himself to visual effects and to fatal forces – to sensuous urges and to the higher powers that destine those urges differently for good and bad results. This is not to say, however, that attributing to Hardy an interest in Impressionist mediation would fully reconcile his inconsistencies. In a sense, it just makes them stand out more prominently. But it makes them stand out as aspects of a single endeavor – as the farthest poles (and Hardy does place them farther apart than any other Impressionist) of the impression's ambiguity.

Hardy seems to encourage this categorization when he says that a novel is an impression. But he also encourages some more unique classification, given the fact that his references to the impression – in the Preface to *Tess* and also elsewhere – are always very defensive. Hardy repeatedly defines his art as one of impressions at moments when others demand of him some more thorough explanation. The Preface to *Tess* contains the first example of this defensive Impressionism (which, as we will see, responds against Mowbray Morris's famous attack on *Tess*). A second comes with the Preface to *Jude the Obscure* (1896), in which Hardy responds to lingering charges of immorality by calling his book "simply an endeavor to give shape and coherence to a series of seemings, or personal impressions, the question of their consistency or their discordance, of their permanence or their transitoriness, being regarded as not of the first moment."[60] More such defensive impressions follow: in 1917, in response against W. L. Courtney's effort to "treat my works of art as if they were a scientific system of philosophy," Hardy emphasizes again that "the views in them are *seemings*, provisional impressions only, used for artistic purposes because they represent approximately the impressions of the age, and are plausible, till somebody produces better theories of the universe."[61] In 1920, Hardy writes, in response to a friend who has "[objected] to what he calls my philosophy," that "I have no philosophy – merely what I have often explained to be only a confused heap of impressions."[62] But the best example of Hardy's tendency to use the impression as a defense against calls for some more consistent, rigorous, or moral outlook is his response to Joseph McCabe's wish to include Hardy in his *Biographical Dictionary of Modern Rationalists*. Hardy, who was ill at the time, had Florence Hardy write to McCabe as follows: "He says he thinks he is rather an irrationalist than a rationalist, on account of his inconsistencies. He has, in fact, declared as much in prefaces to some of his poems where he explains his views as being mere impressions that frequently change . . . So that he cannot honestly claim to belong to the honourable body you are including in your dictionary, whom he admires for their straightforward sincerity and permanent convictions, though he does not quite think they can claim their title."[63]

These defensive impressions make a difference because they show us how Impressionism got its reputation. When Hardy refuses to explain himself or avers his irrationalism by saying his writing is *only* a matter of impressions, he does two things: on the one hand, he expresses a theory of fiction which is not only valid but would best ensure balanced productions. But on the other hand he seems to admit that he works without any theory at all, and that his writer's mind is all confusion of provisional semblances. His Impressionism might have sounded better, and satisfied critical demands, had he been able to say how impressions have their own rationality, and how their apparent deficiency of theory is really an unusual surplus of life. But Hardy could not offer this explanation, due to no deficiency of his own. What his defensiveness indicates is that the best way to describe Impressionism, for him as for others, was not to describe it at all – that somehow to "rationalize" it would be to spoil its power to combine reason with sense and remake the fictional imagination. Hardy's peculiar and cryptic references to impressions suggest that Impressionism had to remain a kind of anti-philosophy and that as such it could only remain unsatisfying to critical reason.

The anti-social anti-philosophy in Hardy's defensive Impressionism determined the production and reception of *Tess*. It is behind the characterization of Tess and her place in the conflict between nature and society. And, consequently, it caused certain key negative responses to *Tess* and defined the terms in which those responses would become a cultural debate. Once again, then, a "woman of genius" serves as Impressionism's vehicle. In Hardy's case, however, she is a more sensational heroine – more remarkably grounded in the sensuous confusion through which literary doctrine can lose itself, but also therefore more deeply embedded in controversy.

The context of the debate over *Tess* gives us, yet again, a critical trio: where Pater had his Arnold and James his Besant, Hardy had Mowbray Morris, who wrote the attacks on *Tess* that made Hardy mimic James and say "a novel is an impression." Where Pater had his Wilde and James his Stevenson, Hardy had Andrew Lang, coming back at him with claims that extend Impressionism into idiosyncrasy. Once again the impression takes part in a controversy over the "proper sphere" of art (and by no strange coincidence Morris names his attack on *Tess* "Culture and Anarchy"). Again the impression helps a writer defend his imagination but then sets him up for reproach from one who proves that stress on the subjective imagination can cut more deeply – that it can detach fiction and its justification from all reliable contingency on real life.

What Mowbray Morris said about *Tess* is well known. "Mr. Hardy has told an extremely disagreeable story in an extremely disagreeable manner": this attack – made more specific in descriptions of the "pure cant" of Hardy's opposition to conventional morality, the excess of his stress on "poor Tess's sensual qualifications," and the like promiscuity of Hardy's style – provoked Hardy to add a defensive Preface to the novel's 1892 edition.[64] What is less well known is the fact that Morris's attack on *Tess* was just part of a larger attack on the "New Culture." Morris thought that Hardy's novel partook of a bad new trend toward aesthetic anarchy. That Hardy should have responded to the chaos in "anarchy" with the ambiguous unity of the impression, and that he did so in a debate over a woman's "sensual qualifications," makes this particular exchange a culmination of what we have seen of the impression's causes and effects in prior debates.

Morris makes his review of *Tess* part of an attack on "the great aesthetic epidemic we are at present suffering from under the name of culture" (338). The problem, Morris tells us regretfully, is at least partially the fault of Matthew Arnold, who promoted aesthetic culture in an England where "there is no native instinct to guide us, no recognized standard of right and wrong in such matters." Culturally unaesthetic, England could only go wrong in following Arnold's lead – especially because Arnold advocated, along with the spread of culture, a "New Democracy." Aesthetic excitement combined poorly with the spread of personal liberty; the vulgarization of art followed, and "our struggle after culture has developed into anarchy" (340). In ways Arnold did not foresee, "the element of culture was not sufficient to leaven the whole mass," and the masses – especially the masses of women misled by "that foolish misconception of woman's true place in the world which goes by the name of Woman's Rights" (341) – "combined to defeat Mr. Arnold's plan." The defeat has had even worse results for fiction, Morris argues, because the proponents of the New Culture chose fiction for their form. And here the argument takes on a complexity peculiarly relevant to the question of the impression: the proponents of the New Culture have no real aesthetic discretion, and they conceal this lack by "affecting to change the purpose of fiction" (342). They "claim for it now the stern offices of the preacher, the law-giver, and the judge," without, however, full commitment to intellectual rigor. In these times of "mental dissolution," fiction's allegedly "stern offices" get taken over by the "animal instincts," so that those trying to exalt fiction really end up preaching the doctrine of gross sensuality. Thus, as a result, come all at once Hardy's "inartistic blunders and improprieties" and subject matter "such as no clean-minded reader can get through without disgust" (343).

Hardy could only respond to this "manipulator of *Tess*" with the observation that those with "causes to advance, privileges to guard, traditions to keep going" must always be disappointed by the "mere tale-teller" (6). But Hardy's response also knows the great justi-fication that lies at the back of this modesty, and repeats Pater's response to Arnold in order to make that justification indisputable. He denies the motives that Morris would assign to him, saying that *Tess* was designed to be "neither didactic nor aggressive" but "representative simply" and "charged with impressions [rather] than with convictions" (4). And then he says it again: "Let me repeat that a novel is an impression, not an argument; and there the matter must rest" (5). The impression's characteristic indeterminacy works very well for Hardy here, since it helps him disclaim conscious motives, but also because it indirectly answers Morris's charge in the best manner possible. Nothing like a thought, an impression cannot have the "sternness" of argument; and yet it is more than any transcribed sensation – no mere product of the "animal instinct" that is to Morris the other cause of culture's new anarchy. Hardy argues brilliantly here, in other words, by letting the impression's mediatory meaning answer Morris's charges: where Morris fears a brazen didacticism emboldened by primal passions and a horrible betrayal of Arnold's legacy, Hardy finds that combination of thought and feeling that had been, even long before Arnold, the focus of the highest hopes for cultural good health.

In other words, where Morris fears a preaching based in animal instincts, and sees *Tess* as an example of it, Hardy suggests in the impression a different, positive, and even "aesthetic" version of the combination of "preaching" and "instincts." And it makes sense that Hardy should first come up with this defensive impression in the Preface to *Tess*, for Tess herself embodies this same combination. Just as the impression answers Morris's charge of cultural anarchy, Tess answers those cultural norms that would dismiss her as a fallen woman and see her rape as her destruction: a better grounding in sensuous life refutes bad faith in moral argument. Perhaps the boldest example of the way this argument works in and through *Tess* is Hardy's claim, in reference to the rape, that "Tess's passing corporeal blight had been her mental harvest" (129). If a terrible moment of sensuous anarchy can ennoble Tess's mind, then her sensibility has a "native instinct" that surely helps in England's "struggle after culture." This is the boldest example, but there are many others that prove that Tess embodies for Hardy a natural harmony of the corporeal and the mental, which in turn justifies his impression.

That Tess embodies nature, against a wrongheaded culture, is clear enough. What may be less immediately obvious – what thinking in terms of Impressionism might help us to see – is that the "nature" Tess embodies is in not simple sensuousness but a natural combination of sense and wisdom (and that Hardy opposes it to its inverse, a wrongheaded combination of hypocritical morality and empty sensuous indulgence). As many critics have noted, *Tess* seems to make two arguments about Tess's "virtue." The novel wants to absolve her from guilt both because she is innocent of any crime and because the crime is no crime; that is, Hardy seems to say both that Tess is sinned against, and therefore pure, and that she is pure because nothing sinful has happened at all. But there is a third argument, more radical than these other two – an argument implicit in Hardy's claim that "Tess's corporeal blight had been her mental harvest": the argument that in nature's ethical system, there is no consistency, and that a woman who is fallen at one moment can be virtuous again at the next. In one of her more cheerful moments, Tess asks herself, "Was once lost always lost really true of chastity?," and thinks in response that "the recuperative power which pervaded organic nature was surely not denied to maidenhood alone" (103). It is due to this recuperative power, stressed again and again throughout the novel, that Tess can always be chaste. Sometimes Hardy calls it the "invincible instinct toward self-delight" (104); sometimes it is the " 'appetite for joy', which pervades all creation" (191). Wherever he notes it, Hardy pays tribute to an intelligence in vitality itself, an instinct whose judgment is fine, which does not stop at what Morris called Tess's "sensual qualifications" but proceeds to the synthesis Hardy expresses in terms like "mental harvest."

That it proceeds far, but is thwarted, is clear in one of Angel Clare's moments of admiration for her:

He was surprised to find this young woman – who though but a milkmaid had just that touch of rarity about her which might make her the envied of her housemates – shaping such sad imaginings. She was expressing in her own native phrases – assisted a little by her sixth-standard training – feelings which might almost have been called those of the age – the ache of modernism. The perception arrested him less when he reflected that what are called advanced ideas are really in great part but the latest fashion in definition – a more accurate expression, by words in *-logy* and *-ism*, of sensations which men and women have vaguely grasped for centuries. (129)

Tess can "shape" all kinds of "imaginings" – she can give sensuous form to "advanced ideas" accurate enough to "be called those of the age." But Angel, whose tragedy is that he cannot give up on culture sufficiently to appreciate Tess's natural wisdom even to the point of its troubling source, cannot quite appreciate the mode in which Tess's imaginings work. He still thinks in terms of "sensations" and "ideas": for him, there are fashionable advanced ideas (the kind Hardy resisted) and primeval sensations (the "simple nature" Hardy also resisted), but not the combination at work in Tess (the combination also at work in Hardy's defensive impression). He is less impressed, that is, when he is able to divide Tess's impressions back into sensations and ideas – to restrict her to a simple nature to which advanced ideas only distantly correspond. Here, and especially once he turns against Tess, he thinks like Mowbray Morris, and does not see the merit of the native instinct of Tess's Modernism.

Hardy's impression, then, is not only an appropriate response to Morris's vision of cultural anarchy, but one that corresponds to the "argument" against cultural anarchy in *Tess* itself. The impression backfires, however, when it is subsequently used against Hardy by Andrew Lang. The Preface to the 1892 edition of *Tess* responds not only to Morris, but also to Lang's criticism of Hardy's bitterness. Lang liked *Tess*, but pointed out the bad theology in the novel's melodramatic observation that Tess is but sport for the "President of the Immortals." In the Preface Hardy criticizes in turn this "gentleman who turned Christian for half-an-hour," noting that "to exclaim illogically against the gods . . . is not such an original sin of mine as he seems to imagine" (5). Lang then raised the stakes: willing to match illogic with illogic, he borrows the terms of Hardy's self-defense, and, acknowledging that *Tess*'s popularity proves him wrong about the novel, writes "So I confess myself in the wrong; and yet a reviewer can only give his own impression, and state his reasons, as far as he knows them, for that impression."[65] The impression had allowed Hardy to restructure Morris's description of the "New Culture" according to a more respectable plan, but the impression also allows Lang irresponsibility. Because impressions are indeterminate, one is unlikely to know one's "reasons" for having them. A fiction-writer needs no reasons – they might only make him or her "didactic" – but a critic can use unreasonability as a cover for malicious intent or poor insight. Lang seems to know this, and to make his right to resort to impressions a criticism of the way Hardy's Preface pleads ignorance. Lang seems almost to raise the specter of Wilde: hide behind the impression, he seems to say, and I will read you wholly as I please, without respect for the requirements of serious public engagement.

What we have, then, is the following sequence: Morris misunderstands Tess's virtue, and calls it an argument for cultural anarchy; Hardy responds with an analogy, in which *argument* is to *impression* as the fallen woman is to Tess, and redefines fiction, in response against Morris's claim that it has been taken over by the "animal instincts," as a force for the anti-social renewal of natural vitality; but then Andrew Lang plays the part of Alec D'Urberville: finding in *Tess*'s popularity proof that natural "reasons" are prey to any and all justification, he takes advantage of Hardy's analogy, and makes the impression a good excuse for recklessness. It is through this sequence that female virtue plays a central role in the definition and reception of the impression: natural female virtue inspires Hardy to see argument for social change as something best accomplished in terms of Tess's relation to convention – in terms of the anti-social "structure of sensations"; arguments therefore become impressions, but as such their new isolation makes them subject to an opportunistic removal from rational context. Impressions become irrational, not because of their distance from "ideas," but because of their refusal of social argument.

And this is what the "woman of genius" becomes to Impressionist thought more generally. When Impressionist writers let the melodrama of gender difference serve as a form of argument – when they use women's presumptive distance from reason as a term in the aesthetic argument against reason – they make their cases too strongly and too well. The melodrama of gender difference may dramatize the stakes of Impressionism very well, but that melodrama makes Impressionist theory as clumsy as it is clear. In other words, recasting the binarism that impressions would resolve as another binarism resolved only through conventional cultural plots subjects Impressionism to a certain conventionality. Unconventional writers find their aesthetic innovations subject to standard fictions. But they subsequently make those fictions, somehow, equal to the task, and this is the remarkable thing about the "woman of genius" in James and Hardy. She outgrows "argument"; she lives, not only because her vitality is an aesthetic necessity, but with the result that she undoes rather than fulfils the need.

CHAPTER 4

The distant laborer

I PROUST IN EULALIE'S LITTLE ROOM

At the climax of *A la recherche*, when Proust makes the epistemological shift that will enable him to write – when he looks finally into that "inner book of unknown symbols," which is "the only one of which the 'impression' has been printed in us by reality itself" – he pauses.[1] His mode has been theoretical, pursuant to a long train of thought that leads him from the "gloomy thoughts" in the courtyard of the Guermantes mansion (where he steps on the paving stones, and the long reverie begins) to the moment in which he enters the party there. He has realized that what will restore the past, and call up realities beyond the vicissitudes of time and error, is the essence common to two sensations, present and past, found in the impression. And at the moment in which his thoughts turn from the impression's perfect truth to what he will need to do to discover it, he pauses for a parenthetical recollection. From the Guermantes mansion of the present, he swerves into an episode in his early childhood (of which he has not since then given any thought) in which he had been "made to sleep in Eulalie's little room" (276). The episode has no clear relevance to what precedes and what follows – seeming perhaps intended to illustrate the way present feelings call up past ones to produce, together, an impression. But Proust's parenthetical swerve into Eulalie's bedroom in fact has all the relevance of a necessity, for it adds to Proust's impressions a necessary quality they might not otherwise have had.

For Proust, impressions reveal timeless essences, and construct their "deathless analogies," because of a peculiar doubleness in sensational life. When we have a sensation, adventitious circumstances keep its essential meaning from us; that meaning only comes to us later, when another sensation with the same essence brings to mind what adventitious circumstances had hidden. Sensations are double, then, in that they have an essential truth, a basic accurate perceptivity, beneath the cover of qualities that only seem to characterize them. What must worry Proust, it seems, is that this inner perceptivity, this true feeling, might entirely disappear within its outer circumstances. Especially given his ill health and the thick mesh of social forms that dictate his movements and wishes, Proust must worry that inner sensations may after all be nothing other than their outer conventionality. He needs the guarantee of true proximity to sensational life. Like Pater and James before him, he needs to find some additional way to imagine for himself a contingent sensorium.

He gets this contingency in Eulalie's bedroom. He ends up there, he tells us, because his aunt Léonie has a fever, possibly typhoid. To avoid his catching it, he is sent to another part of the house, and to a room that has none of the abundance of furnishing to which he has become accustomed. Eulalie's room has "nothing but rush mats on the floor and over the window a muslin curtain that was always buzzing with a sunshine to which I was not accustomed" (276). Because it is just a "little old-fashioned servant's bedroom," it is not well protected from the sun, and, because of its location, it is open to sound: at night, "one heard the hooting of the trains." These unusual sights and sounds make a crucial difference to Marcel's impressions. They supply the difference necessary to give sensations a life apart from convention, and necessary in turn to give impressions their claim to truth: ". . . seeing how the recollection of this little old-fashioned servant's bedroom suddenly added to my past life a long stretch of time so different from the rest and so delicious, I thought by contrast of the nullity of the impressions which had been contributed to it by the most sumptuous entertainments in the most princely mansions." Sumptuous privilege, it seems, nullifies impressions, because it is an adventitious circumstance; the essence of sensation, by contrast, seems to require the openness to the world Marcel gets when sent to the servants' quarters, where cheap curtains and a bad location let real sensations in.

The parenthetical digression therefore serves a central purpose, finding in Eulalie, or at least her bedroom, necessary contingency. Proust seems able to find this vital basis in Eulalie's bedroom because it is the bedroom of a servant – a place lacking in the trappings that, in Proust's reckoning, encumber sensibility. To what extent, then, is

Proust's Impressionism dependent on class difference? To what extent does his house of fiction need a servant's room within it?

Class difference matters beyond the parenthetical digression, as Proust distinguishes Impressionism from other forms of art. The fact that "true life" is hidden within sensation proves for Proust the "falseness of so-called realist art" (277). Since we have "the habit of giving to what we feel a form of expression which differs so much from . . . reality itself," there is little point in looking for truth in the outer movements of social life. Such things as "great working-class movements" – so popular in literature, or at least literary theories, since the Dreyfus case dragged the artist out of his "ivory tower" – do not make for "authentic art"; reality is more likely to reside in "that clink of a spoon against a plate, that starched stiffness of a napkin, which had been of more value to me for my spiritual renewal than innumerable conversations of a humanitarian or patriotic or internationalist or metaphysical kind" (279). Moreover, "popular art" is a mistake, because it mistakes the nature of the working classes. They do not need the condescension of a form that sacrifices refinements for their sake: "the working classes are as bored by novels of popular life as children are by the books which are written specially for them" (280). They want, like all readers, to "be transported to a new world, and working men have as much curiosity about princes as princes about working men." If anyone needs the simplicity of realist art, it is "fashionable society," which is where one finds illiteracy – as one does not, "let us say, among electricians."

Electricians, like household servants, *preoccupy* Proust's Impressionism. At one end of the process of literary creation, the working classes are a model for authentic sensation; at the other end, they are a model for literate reception. And the place where one expects to find such models – the novel of popular life, or of working-class movements – somehow does not serve them nearly so well as the novel of clinking spoons and stiff napkins, since the latter depends upon their rich sensational life to get written, and depends upon their imaginative needs to get read. Proust takes an interest in the working classes that seems tangential but is really fundamental. In them he finds twin bulwarks of aesthetic authenticity. It is here that Proust makes the claim that a writer "goes astray" only "when he has not the strength to force himself to make an impression pass through all the successive states which will culminate in its fixation, its expression" (279). Does he get this strength, in a sense, from the working classes?

What would it mean to say that he does? Would it make Proust guilty of the failure that often goes by the name of "primitivism"? Would it, in other words, mean that Proust is exploitative, exercising a class privilege that makes lesser figures serve his purposes, thereby trivializing or stereotyping their actual counterparts? We have had questions like these before: James's treatment of women – his similar use of female figures to round out the Impressionist complex – also seems to partake of the kind of conceptual exploitation that, through its connections to real-life exploitation, would endorse social inequities. In the case of James, however, we saw that this exploitation corresponds to a form of feminism. In its exaltation of feminine limitation, its annexation of that limitation to link masculine intellect to life, and its discovery, as a result, of the bad reciprocity at the heart of novelistic subjectivity, James's use for female sensibilities is also a feminist discovery of the role of the feminine in culture's epistemological fantasies. Proust's use for the working class – however less significant to him than the use for the feminine is to James – may have this same critical force, not in a feminist spirit, but in a Marxist one.

Marxist theory everywhere associates the aesthetic unification of sense and reason with a utopian reintegration of the social world. Parallel to the good outcome of the class struggle is an undoing of the division, created by capitalism, of instrumental reason and vital sense. From Marx to Lukács to the present position most prominently occupied by Frederic Jameson and Terry Eagleton, the evil of capitalism virtually is its disintegration of the faculties, its dissociation of sensibility, to which class distinctions inevitably correspond. And for these theorists, a key feature of Marxist subversion is the assertion, against the rule of alienated rationality, of a vital and vigorous sensorium, toward the reintegration that would by analogy forever discredit social hierarchy. If Proust's impression, like that of all Impressionists, drives at some similar reintegration of faculties – if it seeks the common essence of sensations, and to produce that sense of things that has the value of an idea without an idea's arbitrariness – then perhaps its aesthetic objective is also a Marxist one. Perhaps its mediation would undo, at some level, the divisions upon which capitalist hierarchies depend. Its use for the working class, in that case, would mean something very different from "exploitation": it would be the sign of an effort to recognize the value, to thought, of sense, and to make the aesthetic conjunction of these faculties a return to lost social unity.

In *The Ideology of the Aesthetic*, Terry Eagleton entertains both this possibility and its opposite. Eagleton reminds us that "aesthetics is born as a discourse of the body" (13) – that it got its start as a theory of the way art grounds reason in sense, and that it therefore promoted embodiment as an ideal.[2] This origin, however, means that the political thrust of the aesthetic can go in two different directions: it can challenge the authority of reason with the un-reasonable energies of the body, or it can put those energies to reason's use. As Eagleton puts it, the aesthetic "signifies a creative turn to the sensuous body, as well as an inscribing of that body with a subtly oppressive law; it represents on the one hand a liberatory concern with concrete particularity, and on the other hand a specious form of universalism" (9). Aesthetic ideology renders reason sensuous, and champions concrete particularity, or it rationalizes sense, and universalizes the particular in such a way as to control it. What Eagleton proves, as he goes on to find both possibilities in the history of aesthetics, is that the aesthetic has always been a question of the unification of faculties, and a question with two sides. The two sides are those that make up the question of Proust's use for the working classes: does his bid for working-class sensibilities signify a return to the sensuous body, with a liberatory concern for concrete particularity, or does it inscribe the working-class body with an oppressive law, and speciously universalize Proust's own interests?

These questions are basic to the study of Impressionism insofar as the impression may be the very focus of "aesthetic ideology." The impression is that subset of the aesthetic that specifically concerns the aesthetic's subjective function with regard to human faculties. Whereas the larger term takes in much other than that subjective function – the status of the artifact, for example, and the relation of art appreciation to other areas of human endeavor – the impression focuses attention specifically on what Eagleton calls the "dream of reconciliation" (25) that would make aesthetic theory also utopian ideology. To ask, then, what the impression means in Proust when it makes ambiguous reference to working-class sensibilities gets at the crux of the aesthetic dream of reconciliation, for it is to inquire into the possibility of such reconciliation precisely at a moment in which its possibility and failure coexist. If Proust's bid for a new middle way between the arbitrary idea and the contingent sensation simply reproduces the division that is, according to Eagleton, at the basis of aesthetic ideology, then its apparent reconciliation may have the effect of reinforcing division at a more basic level; but if Proust's reconciliation makes reference to the difference between working-class sensibilities and those of Proust himself in order to reveal the distinction between arbitrary idea and contingent sensation, then that reconciliation may rank high among those ideologies which, in Eagleton's account, best realize the potential of art.

The way to decide is to see what happens with Proust's new division. He wants to make the impression's discovery of the common essence of two sensations a form of transcendence that has an idea's generality without an idea's arbitrariness; he pauses, on the way to such a discovery, to enlist the aid of some contingent subjectivity. What happens next? As we have seen, Proust does make the working class a resource, but takes pains, immediately following the swerve into Eulalie's bedroom, to emphasize working-class literacy. Making the "electrician" his reader as well as his resource, Proust attributes full capacities to working-class subjectivity. And that extension has a crucial analog in the further development of his Impressionism. Proust turns to working-class subjectivity, it seems, out of some worry that he may not "have the strength" to register and develop impressions fully on his own. But he then turns his weakness in this regard into a different kind of strength. What causes his worry is the shocking appearance, just at the moment in which he understands how the impression can work as a deathless analogy, of death: suddenly, his friends at the Guermantes party seem old, and the quick passage of time is a "serious reason" for "distress": "I had made the discovery of this destructive action of Time at the very moment when I had conceived the ambition to make visible, to intellectualise in a work of art, realities that were outside Time" (351). But he makes a crucial recovery, when he sees that he can consider this "destructive action" an "effect of Lost Time" (447); human debility itself becomes a feature of the gap across which Proust can construct impressions. Once weakness itself serves Impressionism, Proust no longer needs the strength of another kind of person – with the result that he can begin to see his own writing as a form of "work." He imagines himself writing "under the eyes of Françoise, who like all unpretentious people who live at close quarters with us would have a certain insight into the nature of my

labours" (509). Whereas before the turn to the working class was a
movement to another person's space, here the labors are Proust's
own, and he fabricates his own book with his own full material
engagement: "I should work beside her and in a way almost as she
worked herself . . . and, pinning here and there an extra page, I
should construct my book, I dare not say ambitiously like a
cathedral, but quite simply like a dress." It may seem that Françoise
is still just a servant who supplements Proust's work, but there is
evidence that some more thorough "sharing" is at work here, when,
for example, Proust asks: "had she not acquired a sort of instinctive
comprehension of literary work, more accurate than that possessed
by many intelligent people, not to mention fools?" Here is the analog
to the earlier moment in which Proust extends to the "electrician"
the power also of readership. He makes Françoise a determinant of
his "work" – work he does himself according to her pattern, and
work, which she both accurately and instinctively comprehends.[3]

Here, then, is some proof that Proust works toward aesthetic
reconciliation in the full sense, and that his use for working-class
subjectivity brings what Eagleton calls the aesthetic's "incipient
materialism" to fuller realization (196). He realizes it much in the
way that James realizes a kind of feminism – not with the full
advocacy of any credible political position, but with the attention to
epistemological fundamentals that may perhaps be the most credit-
able literary contribution to credible politics.

Things happen differently in Conrad. Whereas Proust's parenthetical excursus into Eulalie's bedroom is a short departure from a
substantial theory, Conrad's use for working-class subjectivity comes
at the climax of a theory of far less substance. The difference means
that Conrad's laborer will cause him much more trouble. Conrad's
laborer is, like Eulalie, a supplement that fleshes out the body where
the body may be weak. But Conrad's version of Impressionist
mediation depends with more weight – and less certain willingness –
on the faculty of sense. The laborer's body represents a somatic urge
that elsewhere turns somatophobic, keeping Conrad from getting to
the point where he feels sure of the physical strength to drive
impressions through.

Conrad's effort relates aesthetics and ideology more centrally than
that of Proust, because that relation has already been the subject of
the best and most influential treatment of Conrad's aesthetic practice. Fredric Jameson has argued, like Eagleton, that the relation

between sense and reason is crucial to the fortunes of capitalist culture: like Eagleton, he argues that capitalism has largely succeeded by sundering overdeveloped instrumental rationality from more purely perceptual energies, and cultivating those perceptual energies to compensate for the loss of the better wholeness. Aesthetic experience, he argues, is a compensation for capitalist rationalization and reification, one that works, as it does in Eagleton's account, in two ways: it may work as a "utopian compensation," undoing in certain ways the effects of capitalism, or an "ideological" one, that furthers those effects. Conrad's Impressionism figures prominently in this account. It perfectly emphasizes Jameson's paradox of "utopian ideology": "Seen as ideology and Utopia all at once, Conrad's stylistic practice can be grasped as a symbolic act which, seizing on the Real in all its of reified resistance, at once and the same time projects a unique sensorium of its own."[4] Jameson asks that we respect the "ambiguity value" of Conrad's Impressionism – its tendency at once to make sensuous experience merely a gratifying aspect of capitalist rationalization and to make it a fully utopian antidote to capitalist dehumanization.

The following account of Conrad's Impressionism will build on (and argue against) Jameson's account in two ways. The "ambiguity" Jameson sees in Conrad's Impressionism is different from the ambiguity I see in the impression itself. In Jameson's account, the impression is sensuous: it is a matter of "sense data," and not the juncture of sense data and intellectual function it becomes when Impressionist writers refer to it. The following account therefore asks what difference it makes, to Jameson's theory, if the impression is not simply the flip side of capitalist rationalization, but more ambitiously itself a Jamesonian theorization of the juncture between rationality and sensuous experience.

Again, this last question will have a different answer than it does when asked about Proust. To begin to say why it will, we might turn to a moment in Proust's work in which there is the threat of a different outcome. As we have seen, Proust worries that death will, after all, disallow the deathless analogy of the impression; he asks, "was there still time and was I still in a fit condition to undertake the task?" (511). He wants to make a "profound study of impressions," but his memory is "old and tired," and, moreover, the wish to transpose sensations seems to confine him to a body not up to the task. "For the fundamental fact was that I had a body, and this meant that I was perpetually threatened by a double danger'': having a body, it seems, brings on the necessary sensations in the first place, but may then defeat the purpose in the last crucial moment. "Indeed it is the possession of a body that is the great danger to the mind" – even if that very possession is fundamental to what Proust elsewhere calls the mind's perfection. Proust finds a way to consider the decay of the body a positive part of his larger enterprise. Conrad does not, and his Impressionism therefore brings on more extensive and ambivalent meditations upon the place of the body in the representation of life.

II CONRAD'S DISTANT LABORER

Soon after writing the Preface to *The Nigger of the "Narcissus"* Conrad found that trying to "make you *see*" could backfire. In March 1898, a bad case of writer's block made him unable to express "impressions conveyed through the senses," and brought him instead a nauseating awareness of his own body:

. . . that story I can't write weaves itself into all I see, into all I speak, into all I think, into the lines of every book I try to read . . . You know how bad it is when one *feels* one's liver or lungs. Well I feel my brain. I am distinctly conscious of the contents of my head. My story's there in a fluid – an evading shape. I can't get hold of it. It's all there – to bursting, yet I can't get hold of it no more than you can grasp a handful of water . . .[5]

This bad feeling inverts the perceptual philosophy that Conrad has just described in his Preface. There, impressions would convey sensations into stories, but here, feeling blocks the imagination. Conrad feels his organs rather than feeling with them; his mind is just a brain, and his own body, his source of sensation, has become an antagonist who betrays the mind into sensing only its own brute matter.

This *somatophobia*, however, is nonetheless a moment in Conrad's Impressionist theory. His Impressionist project seeks strict fidelity to the visible universe in order to encourage human solidarity. The project seems possible when impressions create their continuity between the literary mind and the sensuous body – or, more specifically, between the moments of physical sensing and interpretive perceiving that intervene between body and mind. But distrust of what such conveyance will bring of mere corporeality, and the fear that such corporeality will in fact persist as untransformed and intractable materiality, gives Conrad's project a contrary urge. It makes Impressionism also a matter of protecting thought from sense, and recreating some new version of the old mind/body split. In his Preface, Conrad advocates an empathic Modernism, one based in certainty about the oneness of consciousness and its material context; but beneath this advocacy is a contrary urge to abstraction, an anti-empathic will to free consciousness from materiality. This conflict of urges compels much of Conrad's writing to ask hard questions: how to get from what is sensed to what is perceived, without letting matter dictate mode? And how to go from sensations to solidarity, in a literary project fearful of its own need to unite them?

The first sign that *somatophobia* will complicate Impressionism comes at the end of the Preface itself, when Conrad invokes a "laborer in a distant field." The laborer is what other such figures have been for Pater, James, and Proust: a way to claim Impressionist receptivity and range without making full commitment to its collapse of epistemological distinctions. As an embodied counterpart to his authorial mind, the "distant laborer" brings a division of labor to the impression's mediation, and strikes a compromise between competing attitudes toward the perceptual presence of corporeal materiality. If we turn now to the Preface, we will see how what begins as faith in the impression's conveyance reveals its doubt, and subsequently how a range of Conradian touchstones – the longing for solidarity, the dedication to work, ambivalence about affect, and indulgence in *similic* excess – array themselves around the compensatory structure that doubt builds.

According to the Preface, an artist's effort begins with and consists in the attempt to "render the highest kind of justice to the visible universe by bringing to light the truth, manifold and one, underlying its every aspect."[6] Truth, then, begins in what the senses perceive. But doing justice requires an attempt to find *in* forms, colours, light, and shadows "what of each is fundamental, what is enduring and essential" (vii). The senses perceive enduring essences; essences, therefore, do not exist apart from appearances but in the crucial way an object impinges upon consciousness – in that "one illuminating or convincing quality" about it that strikes the viewing eye. By "descending within himself," and exploring his own subjective responses, the artist discovers what Conrad calls his "appeal" – the essential truth that he formulates in an intersubjective call to the community of human temperament.

The impression plays a crucial role in this appeal. Conrad writes that "such an appeal to be effective must be an impression conveyed through the senses" (ix). By this he means that the artist's response to the visible universe must be a feeling initiated by, but not equal to, sensuous experience. What can convey the truth, then, is not sensation but impression, that unit of perception that conveys sensing into thinking and can therefore put seeing into writing. Rendering impressions enables the writer to reach what Conrad calls our "secret spring of responsive emotions"; and Impressionism, defined as a theory of responsive emotion, leads Conrad to his sense of a writer's calling. According to Conrad the writer "speaks to our capacity for delight and wonder, to the sense of mystery surrounding our lives . . . to the latent feeling of fellowship with all creation – and to the subtle but invincible conviction of solidarity that knits together the loneliness of innumerable hearts . . . which binds men to each other, which binds together all humanity" (viii). Impressions suggest to writers that they can knit together human hearts by doing justice to the visible universe. With this affective range, the impression has as its correlate neither the faculty of sense nor that of intellect; rather, it has to do with a faculty of "subtle but invincible conviction" or "latent feeling," a site of empathy at which fiction might reach greater representational immediacy.

In its great faith that there is meaning in creation, available to literature, this mode of authorship seems unlike Conrad, and it also seems unlike Modernism, which we most often define as disbelief in these things. But Conrad seems less interested, here, in exploring the limitations and solipsism of subjective experience – less interested in noting, as he has Marlow famously put it in *Heart of Darkness* (1902), that "we live as we dream – alone" (82). Impressionism is therefore not at this moment what Albert Guerard, for example, calls a "technique of evasion"; it is not, as Ian Watt thinks, an expression of Conrad's skepticism.[7] Skepticism and a wish to evade of life's ravaging forces may enter into Conrad's theory, but they do so, as they do with Pater, as a pretext for (and then a persistent testing of) the development of a very different philosophical temper. Conrad, that is, only half admits "the flux": "To snatch in a moment of courage, from the remorseless rush of time, a passing phase of life, is *only the beginning* of the task" (x; emphasis mine). The "task" itself entails great faith in insight and permanence: it is "to hold up unquestioningly, without choice and without fear, the rescued fragment before all eyes in the light of a sincere mood" (x). As a "sincere mood," Conrad's Impressionism has the advantage that Lionel Trilling attributes to "sincerity": the "single-mindedness" of integrated consciousness.[8] It therefore ought to render moot those various critical dissatisfactions that fault Conrad's Preface for failing to say how the "notoriously fallible evidence of the senses" or the "evanescent concrete particular" attain to accurate and stable meaning.[9] If there is such a failure in Conrad's logic, it comes later; and it comes not because he fails to say how sensuous particulars play a part in larger literary meaning, but because he himself subjects the process to skeptical undoing. The difference is crucial: as a "sincere mood," Impressionism emerges, in line with Michael Levenson's sense that Modernism develops through very different stages, as an early, salvific, empathic Modernism; and it is the failure of it – foreshadowed, in the Preface, by the appearance of the distant laborer – that leads in Conrad and in Modernism more generally to the isolation, suspicion, and dread for which both are better known.

Prior to or apart from that skeptical undoing, however, Conrad's impression makes a lot of sense, and determines his characteristic stylistic practice. Teasing apart the positive and the negative in this regard clarifies Conrad's priorities: it can, first of all, help us to redeem his "temperament" – to forget the schizoid Conrad, who "overwhelm[s] us with sensations, in saturating us in colors, in sounds, in human voices," but on the other hand gives us vast symbolic reflections.[10] In place of the schizoid Conrad, we get a writer who grounds vast symbolic reflections in colors, sounds, and voices, by exaggerating (often to excess) what is perhaps the most basic tendency of rhetorical figure. When Conrad wants to "make you *see*," he wants less to devote writing to surfaces and sensations than to renew a classic mode of figuration: he is less concerned with something new than with the very familiar effects of *simile*.

Aristotle's *Art of Rhetoric* called the form of expression that "[sets] things before the eyes" *energeia*. In *energeia*, "things are set before the eyes by words that signify actuality," and as an effect, give a crowd a common cause.[11] Conrad uses the technique toward different ends, but in seeking to reach that "secret spring of responsive emotions" he shares Aristotle's wish to be "convincing." Moreover, he takes part in the substantial tradition that makes such a wish basic to the theory of metaphor – a tradition that would combine ethics and aesthetics in the belief that art creates sympathy and promotes right action primarily to the extent that its local techniques create a sense of shared perceptual feeling. It is important to emphasize this tradition for two reasons: first, to assert that Conrad's Impressionism is no sensationism; and second, to begin to show how fear that it *might be* leads Conrad to rethink literary "labour" and thereby make his peculiar contribution to metaphorical practice.

Throughout Conrad's writing are examples of words that signify actuality to create common cause. Conrad describes the endeavor itself in a description of one "impressionist phrase" in *The Mirror of the Sea* (1906). About an archetypal sailor, Conrad writes,

> He is the man who watches the growth of the cable – a sailor's phrase which has all the force, precision, and imagery of technical language that, created by simple men with keen eyes for the real aspect of things they see in their trade, achieves the just expression seizing upon the essential, which is the ambition of the artist in words. Therefore the sailor will never say, "cast anchor," and the shipmaster aft will hail his chief mate on the forecastle in impressionistic phrase: "How does the cable grow?" (20–21)

The mode of expression idealized here begins with a keen eye for the real aspect of things, but does not then describe it simply to reproduce that reality in superficial sensuous fashion. The keen eye for the real seizes on the essential, not the superficial thing, and therefore will not settle for sensuous description; nor, however, will it settle for an abstraction ("cast anchor"), but instead tries for the "imagery" through which the sensuous object and the rational concept combine. This imagery – produced in the precision of technical language, but with a "force" that is "simple" – will at once focus the attention of its recipient on the sensuous object (the cable) and the necessary evaluation of it. The overall effect matches Conrad's in his Preface: the figure, which is the rhetorical correlate to the impression, conveys through precise sensuous detail a solidarity-producing concept, a common enterprise beyond the sensuous which has the sensuous as its shared currency.

Impressions produce this and similar patterns of figuration, what has always really been the effect of *simile*. Impression is simile, for example, in one moment in *Under Western Eyes* (1911). Conrad describes the impression that Razumov makes on the teacher of languages: "The next moment he gave me a very special impression beyond the range of commonplace definitions. It was as though he had stabbed himself outside and had come in there to show it; and more than that – as though he were turning the knife in the wound and watching the effect. That was the impression, rendered in physical terms . . ." (350–51). The "impression" here is the feeling conveyed to the teacher of languages, who is especially sensitive to Razumov's mood. Its epistemological peculiarity is matched by its status "beyond the range of commonplace definitions," its unavailability to literal expression. It requires as its mode of expression "physical terms," a clause followed by the similic "as if" which offers a conditional comparison grounded in language of sensation. The type of simile at work here translates abstract experience (Razumov's anguish) into a concrete image (the self-mutilation) while *foregrounding that translation*. This foregrounding is what distinguishes simile from metaphor (and what has often marked it as the inferior literary trope). Conrad exploits its power to communicate by making foregrounded similic translation a means of putting another in his fiction's place.

To convey sensation into perception, Conrad's impression works as a "comparative apperception" – Hans Vaihinger's category, in *The Philosophy of "As If"*, for the process from which all fictions derive.[12] Insofar as Conrad's Impressionism presents fictions within fictions by means of a foregrounded "as if", it defines itself in terms of fictionality's pivotal perceptual moment. Vaihinger defines "illustrative fiction" in particular as a type of fiction that "serves the purpose of converting abstract ideas which are, for that very reason, difficult to retain within our mind, into concrete ones which are easier to realize" (217). In this mode of fiction-making the simile's comparative apperception offers greatest concretion. Prompting us "to see," the simile asserts the greater truth of its apperception, and convinces by evoking the "mysterious" process by which our common physical experience "converts." Conrad says that he renders impressions so that "the light of magic suggestiveness may be brought to play for an evanescent instant over the commonplace surface of words" (ix); he attains this magic suggestiveness through tropes that best portray the transition from the common to the suggestive, and would thereby best enact apperceptive activity. Elaine Scarry describes something like this process when she describes the way vivid literary images come to mind: by "producing the deep structure of perception," rather than simply through vivid description, writing brings vivacity to mental life.[13] Conrad's Impressionism is an effort to mimic the structure of perception, by coercing the translational act of apperception. The nature of the effort, however, makes a difference: Conrad's similes may, as Scarry puts it, "have an instructional character that duplicates the 'givenness' of perception" (22), but the duplication has an anxious force which, as we will see, withholds the "given" as well.

To say that Impressionism in Conrad is primarily an emphasis on similic seeming may be to make too modest a claim: as a literary commonplace, simile could be the basis of nothing new, and could not distinguish Impressionism from any number of other literary tendencies. The claim is a bolder one, however, insofar as it subsumes interests broadly epistemological within the structure of a literary commonplace. If Impressionism comes down to simile, Conrad places great weight – the weight of all his combined aesthetic and social aspirations – on a routine maneuver, which must, in turn, depart from its routine. Just as Conrad's "distant laborer" will figure a crisis in the unity of Conrad's Impressionist aspirations, so will his similes broaden to accommodate it. What will distinguish the Impressionist simile from any number of other literary tendencies is the way anxiety widens its range, making it reach broadly from the concrete detail to the existential rumination.

Moreover, this emphasis on broadened similic seeming is important for the way it has misled critics to define Impressionism solely in terms of its excessive reach into the concrete. Not only have critics mistaken Impressionism for sensationism; but even the best interpretation of Conrad's Impressionism – Ian Watt's description of Conrad's "delayed decoding" – pays too much attention to sense. As a mode of apperceptive conveyance, Impressionism would never depend on merely sensuous information; it always greets the sensuous with interpretive intention, and immediately involves it in analogy, so that there would be no gap between sense and interpretation. In Watt's account, however, the central feature of Conrad's Impressionism is the tendency "to present a sense impression and to withhold naming it or explaining its meaning until later."[14] Watt's theory, however helpful in explaining those moments in Conrad's fiction where one kind of interpretation cedes to another, misunderstands Conrad's analogical effects. It forces a "gap" between what it takes to be impression and intellection to emphasize the tenuousness of interpretation, rather than respecting the degree to which explanation and affect coexist in the initial "impression." Watt presumes a skeptical orientation, distorting the process in question by placing teleological stress on the final judgment: the "coding" actually occurs in the fuller nonfigural explanation which follows the impression, not in the impression itself, so what Watt calls "delayed decoding" might more appropriately be called "delayed *en*coding."[15]

Watt is right, however, to see something skeptical about Impressionism, but he mistakes it for something comprehensive. The distinction here is fine but critical: temperamental oscillation, or a kind of epistemological dialectic, is the impression's main theoretical contribution to Conrad's writing, and Conrad's writing gets much of its perceptual drama by following the dialectic through its stages.

To understand the terms of this dialectic, we might turn to that aesthetician contemporary to Conrad who best perceived the Impressionist dilemma: Wilhelm Worringer.[16] In his *Abstraction and Empathy* (1908), Worringer distinguishes two opposing aesthetic directives: "empathy," which "finds its gratification in the beauty of the organic" and "a happy pantheistic relationship between man and the phenomena of the external world." "Abstraction," by contrast, bespeaks the inevitable modern alienation from such external phenomena, reflecting "man's great inner unrest" and his consequent need to "wrest the object of the external world out of the unending flux of being, to purify it of all dependence on life . . . to approximate it to its absolute value."[17] Worringer's dualism can help to characterize Conrad's effort at Impressionist mediation: first, Conrad seeks an empathic unity between human consciousness and the phenomena of the external world, but when the somatic point of connection that seems necessary to enable that unity proves repulsive, Conrad prefers an external object purified of dependence on life. He turns, in other words, from an empathic theory of the impression's mediation to an abstractional one – to one in which impressions come just insofar as physical vitality ceases to ground the mind in the phenomena of the external world. For while Conrad's interest in impressions at first indicates a belief that mind and body can work together, a particular kind of "inner unrest" often makes him doubt that they can. Vacillation between faith and doubt in this regard structures much of his writing – even the Preface to *The Nigger of the "Narcissus,"* where it begins to drive a wedge between the thinking mind and the laboring body.

This split begins to emerge as soon as Conrad considers why it is that our "secret spring of responsive emotions" is so secret. The artist's appeal, he implies, must pierce through something in order to reach it: "His appeal is made to our less obvious capacities: to that part of our nature which, because of the warlike conditions of existence, is necessarily kept out of sight within the resisting and hard qualities – like the vulnerable body within a steel armor" (viii). Putting the body in armor, Conrad begins a return to a division of somatic receptivity and "hard" or abstract judgment. Here and elsewhere, such armor serves as a literal version of what Mark Wollaeger calls Conrad's "sheltering conceptions" – those fictions and beliefs that protect him from the corrosive truths of skepticism.[18] Skepticism, then, and its will toward abstraction, produces imagery that subtly clashes with Conrad's aesthetic aims.

The body/armor image corresponds to a number of tropes in Conrad's writing that link shelter to some hard and masculine corporeal shell. One such image appears in *A Personal Record* (1912), where Conrad explains what rescued him from a stupor of indecision about a career at sea. He tells of seeing an "unforgettable Englishman," whose hard calves inspire confidence and resolution: "his calves exposed to the public gaze and to the tonic air of high altitudes, dazzled the beholder by the splendour of their marble-like condition and their rich tone of young ivory . . . the inextinguishable and comic ardour of his striving-forward appearance helped me to pull myself together" (40–41). The Englishman's marble calves relieve Conrad's dread by implying non-vulnerable embodiment. In his attraction to them, Conrad qualifies the power of the vulnerable body, now within the armor of resisting and hard qualities. Bernard Meyer writes that this incident exemplifies Conrad's "endless pursuit of the quality of solidity in things and people," his obsession with "images epitomizing strength and masculinity," and his tendency, most relevant to this discussion of the Preface, "to array himself in the borrowed armor of powerful men."[19] This tendency, which begins to emerge in the Preface, inhibits receptivity to impressions; as it comes to dominate, Conrad's aesthetic priorities will conflict.

Associating responsive emotions with the body, Conrad begins to back down from his "beginning phenomenologist's" enthusiasm about impressions, toward a retrograde conflation of impressions and sensations.[20] This return to dualism makes Conrad want to hold the body at a distance: in the Preface, Conrad's opposing urges toward Impressionist immediacy and the armor of abstraction combine to create the "distant laborer," a figure that, like Pater's diaphanous ideal and James's woman of genius, puts the body at a comfortable dualistic distance.

The distant laborer appears at the end of the Preface, as Conrad disclaims the theory he has been proposing. Having made bold claims for his artistry, he backs off, to suggest only that we have sympathy for his efforts now that we have some sense of the intentions behind them. As this disclaimer's figural conceit, the distant laborer works, of course, to help Conrad to continue to endorse the theory apparently disclaimed; it also, however, indicates that Conrad disclaims his theory on a deeper level:

Sometimes, stretched at ease in the shade of a roadside tree, we watch the motions of a laborer in a distant field, and after a time, begin to wonder languidly as to what the fellow may be at. We watch the movements of his body, the waving of his arms, we see him bend down, stand up, hesitate, begin again. It may add to the charm of an idle hour to be told the purpose of his exertions. If we know he is trying to lift a stone, to dig a ditch, to uproot a stump, we look with a more real interest at his efforts; we are disposed to condone the jar of his agitation upon the restfulness of the landscape; and even, if in a brotherly frame of mind, we may bring ourselves to forgive his failure. We understood his object, and, after all, the fellow has tried, and perhaps he had not the strength – and perhaps he had not the knowledge. We forgive, and go on our way – and forget. (xi)

Conrad pretends to divert us here, but hardly wants us simply to forgive and forget. The figure proves his point: now that he has likened Impressionism to the work of a laborer, dedicated to honorable toil, his efforts gain dignity; more significantly, now that he has likened his writing to "movements of the body," it seems more likely to begin where writing should. He rewrites what he has written as an impression – beginning with the physical (the movements), adding his "purpose," and producing "understanding." We are brought by our feel for work to a "brotherly frame of mind," if the figure works, and so Impressionism has worked. No merely modest disclaimer, the passage enacts what "the fellow has tried," and has made us see in solidarity.

But the bodies are different: that of the laborer is not that of Conrad. Estrangement (Watt calls it a "serene metaphorical distance") qualifies the association.[21] Conrad gives us only a distant view of what laboring entails, a view with features that neo-Marxist criticism has taught us to recognize and distrust: there is aestheticization of labor in it, a primitivistic nostalgia for physical work and its value, alienation within identification, and, some might say, a will toward exploitation. There is what John Barrell sees in the landscape tradition in which Conrad's depiction seems an ekphrastic participant: an effort to contrive "mythical unity" where division really prevails; and there is what critics of Romanticism see in the reapers and workers whose real-world disadvantages only suspiciously enable the romantic imagination.[22] For Conrad takes a sophisticated view of the simple worker, one that belies any association of his own work with that going on in the field, so that the figure seems ultimately to emphasize dependence on some other's bodily work. Whereas Impressionism should convey itself from the body to the mind (and, more broadly, from the "movements" of the body to a brotherly frame of mind), the figure through which Conrad finally illustrates the process illustrates something else: it figures forth Conrad's somatophobic need to distinguish again the moments of the impression's conveyance, and to do so according to those social distinctions drawn from best at combining interrelation with distance.

Marianna Torgovnick has described the way " 'the primitive' becomes a means of access to 'the essential' " in much modernist writing and thought. Is Conrad's Impressionism a version of primitivism?[23] Even as the image of the laborer seems to create the kind of solidarity sought by Impressionism (creating a "brotherly frame of mind"), the solidarity achieved seems to have the limits set by primitivism's distortions and condescensions. The viewer remains at a distance, and quickly "forgets"; the distance that prevails makes solidarity a sham sympathy, an epistemological exploitation of otherness, and an estrangement within sympathy that must discredit Conrad's Impressionism.

That, at any rate, might be the vulgar Marxist interpretation of the figure. But a fundamental confusion of allegiances makes it hard to criticize Conrad in this way. Aristocratic distance always mixes with egalitarian identification (not to mention a seaman's experience) in Conrad's outlook, as it did when he only regretfully declined knighthood "as a man whose early years were associated in hard toil and unforgotten friendship with British working men," and as it did when Conrad expressed mitigated sympathy for the Labour Party, "glad that they have not got the majority" despite his belief that "the only class really worthy of consideration is the class of honest and able men to whatever sphere of human activity they may belong – that is, the class of workers throughout the nation."[24] In both of these cases, imagined solidarity is a distant admiration, but not therefore a false product of "mythic unity." Likewise, no doctrinaire Marxism can aptly contextualize the distant laborer, and we should turn instead to one capable of assessing the politics of ambivalence.

In *The Political Unconscious*, Fredric Jameson describes Conrad's Impressionism as a mode that includes both the exploitative possibility and its opposite. He takes a mixed view of Impressionism: on the one hand, he writes, it is a result of the nineteenth-century "abstraction and reification" and "deperceptualization of the sciences" – a reduction of the life of the feelings to literary commodities available for contained consumption.[25] On the other hand, he writes, that very consumption and its reactivation of the senses can disrupt capitalist rationalization and reification; it is a "semi-autonomy" that "open[s] up a life space in which the opposite and the negation of such rationalization can be, at least imaginatively, experienced" (236). Conrad's Impressionism, then, confirms rationalization and its effects but is also a "utopian compensation" for our alienation, one through which we can imagine and even achieve postcapitalist integrity. Jameson therefore asks us to "respect the ambiguity value of Conrad's impressionism," to see it as "ideology and Utopia at once"; he seems finally to admire Conrad's Impressionism for its simultaneously nostalgic and revolutionary impulses, for its power to resist rationalism by reaching before it to some prelapsarian sense-certainty. Had Jameson discussed the figure of the distant laborer, he might have seen it as the very embodiment of Impressionism's ambiguity value. Ideological and utopian all at once – a product of a certain alienation of the sensuous body, and yet also a utopian vision of its reintegration – the distant laborer evades "primitivism's" simpler critique.

Even more, if we shift Jameson's theory to recognize the ambiguity value of the impression itself. If the impression is not, as Jameson presumes, wholly a category of sense, then Impressionism becomes less "ideology" and more "Utopia" – less something capitalist and more something that militates against those capitalism's diminishments of sense. For then the impression works not as a compensatory by-product of deperceptualization, but itself a force for reintegration, and Impressionism works more fully toward the utopian ends Jameson sees as one half of its endeavor. Impressionism also, however, becomes more fully a *theory* of utopian consciousness. In Jameson's account, Impressionism is a matter of style: Conrad produces lush sensuous effects, with the twin results of enlivening gratification and narcotic depoliticization. But if Impressionism is rather a theory through which writers address the possibility of reintegration – if, in other words, they theorize in some preliminary fashion as Jameson himself does – then Conrad's distant laborer becomes a sign of the effort to bring the bad effects of rationalization and reification to mind. The laborer then indicates a hope to return to the better labor relations analogous to a happier state of consciousness; and the laborer's distance and failure may be the sign that Conrad knows, like Jameson, that that outcome is at best utopian.

The distant laborer, then, is precursor to Jameson's critique of Modernism, a figural recognition that Modernism's aesthetic aspirations prove undetachable from their political bases. And that critique does not simply emerge in this instance of figural recognition. If we see the distant laborer as the sign of a Jamesonian critique *within* Conrad's writing, then we can see that the sign has analogs at every level in Conrad's writing: the laborer's "ambiguity," its position in relation to Conrad himself, and the dialectical epistemology that produces it also manifest themselves in Conrad's habits of theme, plot, and simile. My reading of *Heart of Darkness* in Chapter Six will prove that the dialectic that leads to the laborer also structures Conradian allegory. What follows here is an account of two other products of the impulse that produces the distant laborer: the *homo duplex* situation that so frequently occupies Conrad's thematic attention, and the "ambiguity value" of the similic semblance that impressions would convey.

Conrad once wrote, "Homo duplex has in my case more than one meaning."[26] But these many meanings group themselves around the one conveyed by Conrad's relation to the distant laborer: in every case – every case in which there is a fraught interdependency between men who think and men who feel, between the vitally young and the old and wise – there is the same collaboration, and the same mixed belief that subjectivity able to run a total range requires partnership, projection, and conflict. Marlow and Jim are perhaps the most famous example of the relationship this mixed belief engineers; and the narrator and Leggatt in "The Secret Sharer" present the relationship in its crudest purity. The critical debate about "The Secret Sharer" remains unsure whether the selves in that story are identical or different. But the *homo duplex* situation in Conrad's writing stresses the different and idealized power of what Bruce Johnson has called the "natural man."[27] Or it stresses the need to project idealized weakness onto some simpler being: Albert Guerard notes that Conrad expresses an "obvious personality conflict" in frequent dyads of "youthful seaman" and "landlocked meditator" – the former "intellectual, probing, moralistic," and the latter "romantic and vulnerable."[28] If Guerard is right to say that Conrad uses "the double" typically to "objectify in a physical outsider a side of the self we sympathize with yet condemn," he recognizes the same ambivalence that produces the distant laborer: that which exiles a somatic self, both weak and strong for its power to feel, in order to have at a distance its simultaneously perceptual and social contingency. The ambivalence resembles that which made Pater idealize young men, and indeed Conrad has his own kind of *paiderastic* affinity for the young man with, to quote Walter de la Mare, "senses unblunted."[29] In "Youth" (1902), there persists the refrain, "Oh, the glamour of youth! Oh, the fire of it, more dazzling than the flames of the burning ship, throwing a magic light on the wide earth" (30); and this refrain is corollary to Conrad's sense that passing from youth over the "shadow line" to maturity means dulling the flame of perception. That sense makes Conrad want to preserve what he calls, in a letter to Cunninghame Graham, the "simple and great" "elemental force" of the "unconscious man" – and to make that preservation also a way conceptually to make that elemental force serve as his prosthetic sensorium.

Conrad gives his characters the same urge – in *The Rescue* (1920), for example, in which Mrs. Travers, a British aristocrat, absorbs the vitality of a native princess. Conrad initially figures the moment as one in which sophistication beats simplicity while the two meet in the "heart":

Mrs. Travers fixed her eyes on Immada. Fairhaired and white she asserted herself before the girl of olive face and raven locks with the maturity of perfection, with the superiority of the flower over the leaf, of the phrase that contains a thought over the cry that can only express an emotion. Immense space and countless centuries stretched between them: and she looked at her as when one looks into one's own heart with absorbed curiosity, with still wonder, with an immense compassion. (140)

On the one hand there is a comfortable duality, of thought over emotion, and the sophisticated over the primitive; but on the other hand there is envy and absorption, and interconnection through the symbolic "heart" that would make "compassion" (like solidarity) the resolution of the thought/emotion duality. And as the scene proceeds, Mrs. Travers moves further towards envy and absorption: "She envied, for a moment, the lot of that humble and obscure sister.

Nothing stood between that girl and the truth of her sensations . . ."
(153). Like Conrad himself, she conflates epistemological and cultural
dispositions, and, as a result, tries to achieve epistemological unity
through an imaginary cultural one. She too undoes alienation
through collaboration: "Thinking of what such life could be Mrs.
Travers felt invaded by the inexplicable exaltation which the
consciousness of their physical capacities often gives to intellectual
beings." In this moment Mrs. Travers becomes an Impressionist; she
enjoys a positive version of Conrad's horrifying sense of "feeling his
brain"; mitigated perceptual unity – that achieved in concert with a
close but distant cultural other – produces mitigated inspiration:
"She glowed with a sudden persuasion that she could also be equal
to such an existence; and her heart was dilated with a momentary
longing to know the truth of things." This Impressionist longing
comes with the Impressionist result, which makes Mrs. Travers feel
"intensely alive . . . with an impression of novelty as though life had
been the gift of this very moment" (165).

But since this gift of life is taken with condescension – since Mrs.
Travers is the imperialist and the *femme fatale* – her "impression" also
conveys Conrad's doubts about the politics that enable this Impressionism. Conrad could write, as he did to W. L. Courtney, that he
"wrote straight from the heart – which is alive" because he "wanted
to give a true impression," but such heartfelt impressions come with
dread of the bad cultural relationships to which the heart's symbolic
crux corresponds.[30]

The Nigger of the "Narcissus" is the best example of the way politics
take back Impressionism's gift of life. For James Wait, the lazy
worker whose dying body focuses the crew's obsessions, is a bad
version of Conrad's distant laborer, and "knits together" a fellowship
of sentimental falsehood. The sequence ought to run from manifest
sense to active perception to shared feeling to solidarity, all through
the working body of another; in this case, however, it runs from
exaggerated sense to sentimentalized perception, and from there to
fraught fellowship and mindless collectivity. At the beginning of this
sequence is a bestial version of Conrad's "natural man," "animal
like," "a thing of instinct," "a scared brute" (118); at the end of it is
decadence and abstraction: "Through him, we were becoming
highly humanised, tender, complex, excessively decadent: we understood the subtlety of his fear, sympathised with his repulsions,
shrinkings, evasions, delusions – as though we had been over-

civilised, and rotten, and without any knowledge of the meaning of life" (139). Brutal instinct and overcivilization spoil the combination of sense and knowledge. That better combination stands aloof in the figure of Singleton, the patriarch both "learned and savage," the "incarnation of barbarian wisdom," with his "head of a weather-beaten sage on the body of an old athlete" (6, 14). His thoughts are "as much a part of his existence as his beating heart" (26), but the crew knows not to emulate his "completed wisdom," his "clearer knowledge" (99, 129). He may hold to the wheel, "profound and unconscious" (130), but more sensational shows draw the sympathies of the crew, as if to suggest that foregrounded sense in fact *distracts* from the good work of the impression, turning Impressionism into "sentimentalism" and making a "sentimental lie" of its truths (138, 155).

Impressionism becomes sentimentalism because the body must sicken and die. Its sensations are headed toward perception, but also toward decay, and this new gap – between perception and decay, rather than mind and body – drags knowledge into pathos. But Impressionism also becomes sentimentalism due to the fact that the body that enables it provokes guilt as well as sympathy. James Wait's racial difference, necessary to the structure of collaboration, gives the impression's mediation the structure of a master–slave dialectic (in Conrad's terms, a "weird servitude" [43]), and founds solidarity upon guilty social estrangement.

How racial difference spoils Impressionist mediation is the subject of my treatment of *Heart of Darkness* in Chapter Six. Here, we will further trace the impression's sequence in *The Nigger of the "Narcissus"*, from bad solidarity back into the foregrounded simile that is the impression's hallmark. Sharing sensations means finding some means of translation, contriving a juncture of perceptual moments according to the pattern of social relations. But because those social relations are hardly consistent with solidarity, solidarity only becomes its opposite, and at worst cycles back into sensational similes that likewise emphasize alienation. Just as James Wait makes solidarity a sentimental lie, the figural mode in which Conrad tells his story conveys estrangement. It ought to foreground the translations through which perception makes meaning; but it extends itself too broadly, needing to reach from brutal instinct to overcivilization, and therefore foregrounds dissonance.

Things take on grotesque life, and people become simple things.

The ship crawls like a black beetle, under a sun restless like a thing in pain, on a sea that moves like a madman with an axe (27, 49, 57); James Wait is like a doll knocked clean of its stuffing, or a black buoy, and the crew moves first and last like "figures cut out of a sheet of tin" (3). Alternatively, abstractions hover, lacking material ground, and matter disintegrates. The crew is often but a collection of disembodied hands, legs, and lips; higher hopes ("ideal beauty," "fellowship") set out toward similic concretion but end back in the abstract. Figural mediation becomes "aesthetic distancing," as if Wait's relation to the crew has infected Conrad's effort to get at our "responsive emotions." Spanning perceptual moments becomes a matter of great leaping, and Conrad's feel for figure becomes (characteristically) as broad as sentimentality.[31]

Enacting the aesthetic process of its Preface, *The Nigger of the "Narcissus"* trips the traps that the Preface so blithely passes over. The distant laborer becomes a present body, enabling Impressionism's empathy but bringing up the problems that face a somatic epistemology when that body loafs, sickens, and dies. It is fear of this eventuality that leads Conrad more generally to his "urge to abstraction." Paul Armstrong explains the problem: Conrad has the "temperament of a monist" but the "sensibility of a pluralist"; that is, his aesthetic convictions are Impressionist while his feelings (ironically) demand absolutes. What results, for Armstrong, is a "ceaseless (and potentially unstoppable) oscillation between an intense desire to overcome contingency and an equally compelling recognition that this can never be accomplished."[32] Something like this oscillation creates the structure of *Heart of Darkness*. A return to Worringer can help explain how: describing the problem with the empathic impulse in art, Worringer writes, "the self-activation demanded of me by a sensuous object may be so constituted that, precisely by virtue of its constitution, it cannot be performed by me without friction, without inner opposition."[33] Conrad resists the self that enjoys sensuous knowledge; "inner opposition" limits empathy, producing what Worringer calls "negative empathy." Conrad then feels what negative empathy produces: the urge to abstraction. *Heart of Darkness* features this urge. Its oscillations take Marlow from naturalist empathy to negative empathy to the urge to abstraction – not from Impressionism to its opposite, but from one to the other of Impressionism's drastically different possibilities. There, however, Conrad will discover an impulse that Worringer's formalism doesn't predict: a kind of *negative abstraction,* in which the "life-denying inorganic" presents consummate horrors.

III FORD'S PEASANT CABMAN

Conrad's laborer and Eulalie's bedroom suggest that Impressionism thrives on class difference but also exposes its hidden roots in perceptual distinctions. Such collaborations augment Impressionism's political "ambiguity value" and, in so doing, shed new light on the politics of Modernism. Analyses of Modernism's politics have shown how often Modernism's aesthetic achievements seem to depend upon defense against the democratization of art; how its interest in form, for example, often gets its vital impulse from a distaste for popular content, and its exalted states of mind seem to depend as well on lofty social bearings. With their comfortable views of the working class, Conrad and Proust would seem to participate in this exclusion. Impressionism, consequently, would intensify the essential dynamic of Modernism's high/low agon, or even endorse at the level of basic perception the social theory that some say led writers to support fascism. In Conrad and Proust, however, we have seen Impressionism's figurative class distinctions lead in another direction: the two writers take lofty views of the working class, but expose the way personification of human faculties strengthens dehumanizing political distinctions. They feature forth the link between power and perception. As we will see in Chapter Six's reading of *Heart of Darkness,* they participate in a perpetual dissatisfaction with possible locations of perceptual authority, a skepticism finally too driving for any political complacency.

If Impressionism sheds light on the politics of Modernism, then, it perhaps helps us to see how Modernism's radical ambiguities can coexist with its faith in aesthetic distinction. The combination is strange: how can Modernism rarify art if it believes that life is aleatory – and give us formalism with formlessness? The Impressionist's position with regard to the working-class other might explain the combination, by showing us how a certain elitism can interact with a skepticism basic to the liberal sense of what is fair. If the Impressionist wants aesthetic distinction to hold the masses at a distance, he does so with an uncertainty about perceptual authority, which in turn elicits endless speculation about the degree to which any single form of experience can stand legitimately for the whole.

This relation to perceptual authority is pivotal to the work of Ford Madox Ford. He aims at a synthesis of fact and value – oneness of modern life's aleatory facts and the forms that would give them meaning. In this aim he makes the impression basis for what Raymond Williams calls "structures of feeling." Williams notes that art often provides the conditions of affect that arbitrate lived social experience; Ford, similarly, describes the impression as the element of response through which the artist channels society's factual experience into human value.[34] But Ford also doubts that an artist's valuation of fact can stand for that of the whole, and so he proposes that the impression's "structure of feeling" corresponds to a social structure of inclusion. It includes the "peasant cabman," since he best embodies openness to the artist's point of view. Thusly built, however, the impression's structure matches not that which, according to Williams, drives practical social life forward into new emergent formations, but one of reactionary nostalgia. It takes Ford back to feudalism, and becomes cause for the "anti-impressionist reaction" still active today.[35]

In "On the Function of the Arts in the Republic," Ford argues that in modernity "life is a thing so complicated that only in the mirror of the arts can we have a crystallized view or any vicarious experience at all."[36] In a classic modernist account of the new overwhelming speed and diversity of modern times, Ford argues that experience itself has become impossible, unless it happen vicariously: ". . . it is only in the pages of naturalistic novels that we can hope nowadays to get any experience of modern life, save that individual and personal experience of our own which comes always too late" (28). If we have experiences at all, they happen only belatedly; the old immediacy, so necessary to good thinking and right action, only comes to us in such novels as can "register the truth" and make it "assimilable by the human perception"; such novels being naturalistic ones, to a certain degree, but more properly those that give a "crystallized view," not simply transmitting facts but changing them such that they feel like old-fashioned experience. When such novels successfully give us the "picture of the life we live," we regain our sense of "proportion," and the State thrives as a result. Ford draws a connection between good art and the health of the state by arguing that in modern times events only become historical expressions through art – that only art, now, can make events politically available and productive to the future of the state. His theory of the function of art describes what Levenson has called a "civic realism," a mode in which modern society might rediscover a shared reality.[37]

Art's reunification of fact and value therefore has from the outset a political goal. Its politics are vaguely utopian, perhaps the aesthetic idealism Ford inherited from the Pre-Raphaelites and shared with figures from William Morris to members of the Bloomsbury group. For the most part, the utopian politics are egalitarian, and elsewhere they endorse the hope to "re-erect in English a literature that shall be really of the masses," and to wrest literary authority away from the "Class of the More Select."[38] Other political associations, however, begin to enter in, as Ford tries to say more specifically how an artist translates modern fact into human experience. There are three stages in the process. The artist registers facts, renders them in impressions, and, through the reader's response, enjoys his role as civic leader. Ideally, Impressionist rendering balances what the artist registers and how the reader responds, but that equation may not work if Ford is right about modernity: if the welter of modern fact has deadened public experiential capacities, what guarantees that those capacities will be any more open to impressions, however well the artist has assimilated fact within them? Inversely, if the public is yet open to experience, and therefore ready to respond to the artist's impressions, why do they really need the artist after all? To answer the first question, Ford alters the "business" of the literary artist, to say that "the first business of the author is to interest." To guarantee that his renderings will compel intense response, the writer must interest – and interest rather than render accurately. "If he be an artist of sufficient attraction, it will convince us of the reality of the story that he tells" (38), and bring us closer to reality than modernity would otherwise allow. But once "attraction" becomes the priority, rendering gives way to "exaggeration," and "civic realism" becomes something else entirely.

The function of art in the republic is civic leadership, but the need for exaggeration defers that leadership to other quarters. The artist himself can no longer be the proper source of vicarious experience. Rather, "it is to the music halls that we must go nowadays, for any form of pulse-stirring – for any form of consummate expression of art" (36). This move sounds populist, and seems to have the same interest in mass art that Ford elsewhere expresses, but when combined with Ford's theory about the civic role of art, it takes on a different political valence. From Shelley to Arnold to Morris and beyond, aesthetic thought has stressed the power of art to make better laws, to close social gaps, and to bring order to thought. Participating in this trend, Ford participates in a belief that a kind of supplemental aesthetic can work against modern alienation. But when art's power to work as this kind of compensatory supplement devolves into "pulse-stirring," its ideology changes. For Ford turns to the music halls not out of any interest in their content, but out of interest in their sensational form. He turns to them because they guarantee the vitality his version of art needs but lacks, so that their "compensation" is not utopian but "ideological": they solve the problem of modern alienation not by mediating between modern fact and human experience, not by making modern fact truly assimilable to experiential faculties, but by contriving vitalization of those faculties by means "sensational" in both senses of that word.

In "English Literature of Today" (1909–10), the terms of this contrivance begin to verge on those of a reactionary politics. Ford returns to the artist's responsibility to bring experience to modern men "too weary to think and too much caught up in the machine to feel."[39] Now, however, he comes up with a new way to deal with the possibility that modern man's incapacities extend to total unreceptivity. Just as music-hall exaggerations are necessary, at one end, to make sure that aesthetic presentation can elicit a fully intense response, some adjustment must, at the other end, intensify reception. So Ford alters his theory about modern alienation such that it becomes "the business of the artist to awake thought in the unthinking" – such that the alienated mind becomes an empty one:

> Tolstoi has said that the writer should aim at interesting the agricultural laborer alone, and the dictum, if it be exaggerated after the manner of this considerable rhapsodist, is nevertheless an exaggeration of great value. What it means technically is that the artist should strive to be explicit. What it amounts to in practice is that the artist should consider himself as writing for the uninstructed man *bonae voluntatis* – for the absolutely uninstructed man who is of his own type. (64)

Ford's point here seems valid and relatively cautious: the artist will write with greatest effect if he imagines himself writing for someone without intellectual preconceptions; that someone was, for Tolstoy, the "agricultural laborer," but not necessarily for Ford, who recognizes the "exaggeration" in that rhapsodic stereotype. But the slip from an audience unable to think because alienated to an audience unthinking because uninstructed is a crucial moment in Ford's turn toward a reactionary Impressionism: moving from an outlook critical of a cultural deficiency, and eager to find some aesthetic supplement for it, to an outlook that affirms the deficiency of a particular type, Ford changes Impressionism's ideology. What is here a "man . . . of his own type" will revert back to Tolstoy's laborer; and what had been a version of the effort, described by Jameson and Eagleton, to make the aesthetic a means to undo the bad effects of capitalist rationalization and reification, becomes itself reificatory. The "uninstructed man" enables Ford to imagine that his impressions will repeat themselves in the reader, but such an idealization would, if it could, also limit the mental lives of real people.

This must sound, itself, like an exaggeration, but there is a good deal of evidence that the ideology in Ford's Impressionism translated at times into a real political position exactly opposite to its "civic realism."[40] Ford was, by his own account, a "Tory Revolutionary," committed to an old-style conservatism which, in the early years of the twentieth century, was losing ground to Labour and conservatisms swayed by capitalist influences. Against the collectivist politics of labor reform, Ford asserted a traditional individualism; against the leveling tendencies of reform, Ford asserted hierarchy; and where reformers stressed the rights of all, Ford stressed the duties of individuals hierarchically arranged in conventional class structures.[41] At its most extreme, and when Ford felt his conservatism most embattled, this commitment to old-style Tory politics made Ford want to "return to yesterday" – to return to the historical moment in which hierarchies best preserved the individual differences and reciprocal duties of the people of Western Europe. Ford's "politics of nostalgia" made him call "the feudal system" the "most satisfactory form of government or of commonwealth," an "enlightened age" which had been unfortunately followed by a bad history of social reform.[42] The politics of nostalgia closes a logical circle which excludes certain classes of people from the ranks of the "instructed." If the problem of modernity was such that it divided fact and experience; if that problem seemed to call upon the artist to heal the rift; if doing so meant conceiving the relation between writer and reader such that the modern artist had to idealize the "uninstructed man"; if that idealization conformed to the hierarchies of the feudal system, and if reform was its enemy, then Impressionism made Ford speak against the kinds of civic improvements he himself elsewhere favored.[43] We might understand the costs of this self-division by returning to the similarity between what Ford finds in the impression and what Raymond Williams finds in "structures of feeling": whereas for Williams the structure of feeling makes art herald to new cultural formations, for Ford the compromised impression makes art look backwards, and try for a return to the past.

In one instance Ford specifically deplores the way reform brought education to the middle classes. In his "Historical Vignettes" written for *Outlook* in the early teens – the essays given largely to the depicted of the "blessings of [the] enlightened age" prior to reform – Ford speaks with regret about those developments which led to widespread "instruction." He calls a piece of bad middle-class writing "the formidable product of Caxton, of Henry V, of Thomas Cromwell, of Edward VI, of the Gordon Riots, of the social disturbances of the last century, and of the Education Act of 1870."[44] Wanting, as a "Tory Revolutionary," to undo these revolutionary moments, Ford shows how his belief that "Literature exists for the Reader and by the Reader" is also a wish for illiteracy – and therefore how his combination of political and aesthetic ideals becomes ultimately self-undermining.[45] It never, of course, becomes undermining to anything other than itself: for the most part, Ford's attacks on reform were ironic and playful, and neither his temperament nor his income suited him for really effective dominations. The important point here, however, is not that Ford's Impressionism led to any diminishments in public education, but rather that it undermined its own sociopolitical goals, and that, by being at cross purposes with itself, it became an untenable theory of fiction.

Had Ford been a politician, his ambiguous attitude toward social hierarchy might have limited the range of public opportunity (though he would then have subjected it to more serious and sincere critique). But since he was a fiction writer, a marginalized polemicist, and the editor of literary reviews, his ambiguous attitudes made themselves felt in another way: they made him a "character," muddled his Impressionism, and subsequently prompted reflection on the conflict between art's social origins and social objectives. Feudal idealism and civic realism go badly together. Based in the former but aiming at the latter, with contradictory beliefs about the nature of the reader and contradictory theories about representation's pragmatic moment, Ford's Impressionism could only make him erratic, ironic, and finally contrite. And it could only become what it was in Ford's personal life, in his best novel, and thereafter: as we will see, in this case ideological ambiguity associated Impressionism with the Ford who was "the peddlar of suspect anecdotes" and with the ruinous irony and contrite skepticism of *The Good Soldier.*[46]

To the extent that Ford defines Impressionism, he says it captures the meaning of its age as it impinges upon imperfect individual consciousness. Claiming that it "is the duty of the poet to reflect his own day as it appears to him, as it has impressed itself upon him," Ford explains how such reflection occurs: a writer "must render, never report," never propagandize, or add "moral-drawing comment," or "correct" haphazard incident. The writer "must not comment; he must not narrate; he must present his impression of his imaginary affairs as if he had been present at them" – always choosing these "impressions" over the "corrected chronicle."[47] The overall goal is to "produce upon you an effect of life." Life, however, comes into Ford's art in different ways.

Ford vacillates, in "On Impressionism," between skepticism and enthusiasm, between a sense that Impressionism means only "showing you the broken tools and bits of oily rag which form my brains" and a very different sense that in doing so he is laying claim to "the sort of odd vibration that scenes in real life really have."[48] Ford vacillates, that is, between regret for Impressionism's limitations and pleasure at its verisimilitude. Similarly, Ford alternates between defining Impressionism as "exaggeration" and precise "presentation"; and he alternates between defining impressions as permanent marks on consciousness and calling them "the record of a moment" (169, 323, 173). Such vacillation appears most prominently in a deliberate paradox: "the Impressionist author is sedulous to avoid letting his personality appear in the course of his book. On the other hand, his whole book, his whole poem is merely an expression of his personality" (323). This paradox reflects no irreconcilable difference – Kant and Flaubert had reconciled it long ago – and nor do Ford's other tendencies to alternate between conflicting moods and explanations. Ford could reconcile personality and impersonality, evanescence and permanence, but he does not, and his inconsistencies culminate as his account of Impressionism concludes.

William Gass notes that such inconsistencies create Ford's *Impres-*

sionisms. As Gass notes, confusion makes Impressionism "the blur a double-vision sometimes makes," and in particular places Ford between different fundamental objectives. Gass makes a list to show that Ford's impression ranges everywhere from "an atom of sense" to "a vague general attitude" to "something that the well-bred say in order not to appear too opinionated."[49] This variety makes Ford's Impressionism "fall into quarreling pieces." Most uneasily, for the present argument, it puts him "between the forward thrust of the art of fiction toward its own internal coherence, independence, value, and validity, and the pull of the bourgeois past," between different ways of conceiving art's relation to reality.[50] Ford vacillates, that is, between believing art can produce its own coherent reality and believing that that power requires deference to some real-life source. This latter belief makes Impressionism fall back into retrograde distinctions.[51]

This regression exacerbates the problems at work in "The Functions of the Arts in the Republic" and "English Literature of Today." Particularly divisive is the conflict between "presentation" and "exaggeration," which reflects the lack of fit between Ford's mimetic and pragmatic priorities. In earlier essays, these priorities were made to coincide by reference to the music halls and the uninstructed mind; here, coincidence comes through the rhetorical contrivance of the impression. For in Ford's usage "impression" means both something that impinges from the outside world and something imagined within; it means something both empirically given and something aesthetically enhanced, that can therefore serve both mimetic and pragmatic purposes. It serves mimetic purposes through its apparent relation to basic factuality, which makes it simply an element of "presentation"; but it serves pragmatic purposes – the purposes that Ford aims to carry out when he speaks of exaggeration and its good effects on the sensibility of the reader – through its distinction from perception empirically conceived. If we look back to Hume, who initially set the pattern for this kind of rhetorical doubling, we find a precursor in the way that Hume makes the impression refer both to the moment of experiential input and the mark left upon the mind. Ford similarly conflates two different moments – the moment at which the artist assimilates modern fact and the moment at which he remakes it such that it has exaggerative impact on the public. Impressionism becomes a good way to address the problem of experience within modernity, despite the fact that it bridges the gap between accurate presentation and interesting exaggeration through doubleness rather than mediation.

This duplicitous mediation keeps the problem alive, so that Ford must still turn to supplementary help to give his Impressionism its necessary justification. As we have seen, Ford's need to imagine an impressionable audience leads him to feel that the "instructed" endanger art: "Intellectuals," he writes, "are persons of very conventional mind" who have "the knowledge of so many conventions that it is almost impossible to make any impression upon their minds" (329). At least initially his anti-intellectualism is mild and leads him only to say that "those are the best individuals for an artist's audience who have least listened to accepted ideas" (331). At first, that is, Ford's need for an impressionable audience sounds like a need for open minds. But something makes him push things further, and make the unconventional or free-thinking audience into one more radically blank. "What the artist needs is the man with the quite virgin mind" (333): Ford ultimately guarantees the artist his function in the republic by guaranteeing that the reader's mind will do, at the level of reception, what the impression does when it conflates representational moments. The "virgin mind" sees to it that "presentation" will get a fully intense reception. And what guarantees that the "virgin mind" is not *un*impressionable – not, that is, virgin because impassable or deficient – is that mind's class status. Now, to be sure that the "uninstructed" is instructable, and even hierarchically available to instruction, Ford resorts after all to Tolstoy's "exaggeration" (even over the protests of a "futurist friend") and claims that the virgin mind is to be found in the "peasant intelligence" – in the "cabman round the corner."

What motivates this turn to cliché? What motivates this pivot upon which "On Impressionism" turns from good practical advice to a cheap primitivism that even Ford recognizes as such? Ford makes his alliance with the peasant cabman, it seems, in response against the politics of reform. Earlier in "On Impressionism," Ford explains the greater effectiveness of the Impressionist version of facts by mocking the plain speaking of the Fabians: to those who favor direct representation of fact, he writes, "You might as well contend that our Lord ought to have delivered a lecture on the state of primary education in Palestine in the year 32 or thereabouts, together with the statistics of rickets and other infantile diseases caused by neglect and improper feeding – a disquisition in the manner of Mrs. Sidney Webb" (170). The Lord delivered no such lecture because he transformed his facts into impressions: "Our Lord was, you see, an Impressionist." His "word" lacked factual documentation but was the better for it; "It is probable that He did not have access to as many Blue Books or white papers as the leaders of the Fabian Society, but, from His published utterances, one gathers that He had given a good deal of thought to the subject of children." Ford tries to prove that while the Impressionist version of fact may seem wholly impractical, it actually makes a more profound statement than any "disquisition." As an aspect of his conservative advocacy, however, this claim aligns Impressionist indirection with an opposition to reform: let the lordly artist improve the world indirectly, Ford seems to suggest, and the world's children will do better than they would if Mrs. Webb had her way. This correlation between Impressionist indirection and anti-reformist politics can explain Ford's turn to the "peasant" cliché because it shows how his conservatism leads him to value archaic relationships. To top the Fabians, Ford alleges that God's Impressionism did more for children than did the Fabians; to continue to prove that Impressionist art could do more for modern society than reformist action, he alleges that his Impressionism is the cabman's better friend.[52]

The cabman, then, is a product at once of aesthetic and political motives: art's role in the republic demands an open-minded audience; the republic ought not to go the way of Fabian reform; so that the open-minded audience would best be the unreformed worker, in whom the writer has the privilege of "awakening thought." Paternalism turns Ford's interest in the aesthetic mediation of fact into a lordly administration of education; and Impressionism becomes a matter of collaboration between the conservative gentleman and his driver. Like other Impressionists, Ford looks to a social relationship to accomplish what Impressionism seems after all unable to accomplish on its own. The best example of what follows is *Ladies Whose Bright Eyes* (1911; 1935), a novel which enacts a conservative gentleman's return to the world of peasant consciousness, and finds in a restored feudal culture a new basis for Impressionist immediacy.

Ladies Whose Bright Eyes imitates Twain's *Connecticut Yankee*, sending a modern Englishman back to medieval times for lessons in authenticity. Mr. Sorrell is a successful publisher, fully proud of his accomplishments and powers, who finds, when a bump on the head transports him to medieval Salisbury, a world of primitive squalor unmistakably inferior to the modern world of clean convenience. But his attitude changes, as he discovers in primitive feudal culture an immediacy and purity of experience unlike anything he knows in modern times. Enacting the change through which Sorrell finds his faculties integrated and his modernity undone, Ford writes a fictional version of his theory of Impressionist mediation. And making that change a function of a "return to yesterday," Ford also shows how much the theory depends upon a feudal structure.[53]

In the first pages of the novel Sorrell briefly considers Ford's thesis about the nature of modern life. For the most part he thrives on the efficiency of modern commerce, but he pauses to note that "the modern man had to know so much that he could not carry it all round in his head."[54] Ford would call Sorrell a modern man in need of art; Sorrell himself overleaps that solution, to think in terms of Ford's medievalism: "Yet there was some mediœval fellow who was said to know all knowledge." Sorrell does not, at this point, take this medieval fullness seriously, for he thinks that a return to the medieval would emphasize modern advantages. Transported into the past, he imagines, he would dominate: "What a bully time he might have had if with all his present faculties and knowledge he could be thrown right back into the Middle Ages . . . What would not he be able to do with those ignorant and superstitious people!" (14). Of course ignorance and superstition will turn out to enjoy a superior structure of faculties, and Sorrell will find a better way to "know all knowledge" when his modern conservatism combines with them.

Life in the Middle Ages at first appalls Sorrell, who finds its "grimness" and "ugliness" astonishing (89). "He observed only noise, dirt, nauseous smells, and great crowds of importunate and ugly people," and so he sets out immediately to make improvements (228). He applies good modern business sense to various problems, and works wonders, ridding the countryside of a "weighty pack of robbers" and otherwise inspiring improvements (279). Improvements, however, primarily work in the other direction, as Sorrell discovers a strength of apprehension that far outstrips that available to the modern businessman. The cathedral at Salisbury, for example, may be surrounded by squalor, but inside it is so full of "violent, crude and sparkling colours" that Sorrell is "overcome": "here was such newness – here was such a brilliant profusion of colours, that even the vastness of the building seemed to be lost" (230). Sounds and smells swirl around him to such a degree that Sorrell reconsiders his modern superiority. He soon gives up the notion that "a modern man with all my knowledge" ought to "occupy very soon a commanding position in these barbarous, ignorant, and superstitious times," and he soon admits the medieval mind's superior construction. He "used to be what we called a good business man," but now he cares only to walk in the fields with his beloved, and when he worries that such pursuits ought not to take up the whole of a man's life, she proves to him the emptiness of his modern version of experience. "Are there not such things as duties, ambitions, and responsibilities?" he asks, and she answers in the voice of a wholly different experiential mode:

I do not know what these things are . . . In the spring the moles come out of the woods and the little birds sing, and we walk in the gardens and take what pleasure we can. And then comes the winter, and shuts us up in our castles so that it is not so pleasant; but with jongleurs and ballad-singers we pass the time as well as we may. (252)

She knows truly practical experience, where he thinks in terms of factual relations; her mode is descriptive, accounting for life in terms of immediate experiential detail, where his replaces such detail with rationalizing abstraction. She does not know "things" not part or product of perception – and he will come to enjoy an Impressionist unity once he can learn to pass the time in the same way.

As he gets drawn into this primitive *episteme*, he finds that his knowledge is nothing: "I am entirely useless, and there is nothing I can do well . . . I am so ignorant" (252–53). He had planned to make his knowledge of history a source of prophetic authority, but he finds that he is even ignorant of his own history. In this failure, Ford dramatizes what he sees as the main crisis of the modern republic: facts no longer impinge upon modern consciousness, so that history happens unperceived. The role of the artist is to make history possible by making fact assimilable, but here Ford circumvents the need for the artist by having his protagonist return to basics. Sorrell will return to foundations, and remake his sensibility such that it is grounded in the full experience of fact, so that history can properly begin again. First, his beloved, Lady Dionissia, tries to rouse him out of his abjection by reminding him that he has known wonders – "the flying of men through the air, or their rushing faster than the flight of swallows beneath the ground" – but he knows that such knowledge lacks all practical immediacy. "All that is nothing," he knows; "I know nothing of my own arts." Sorrell has to admit that the wonders of his culture have only distracted him from the basic arts of life:

. . . it is a condemnation of a whole civilisation. There was not, of the men I knew, one who knew any of these things. There was not one of them who knew that a beefsteak comes from an ox. Or if he had known that it did, and if he had possessed an ox, he would not have been able to kill that ox. Or if he had been able to kill the ox, he would not have known how to cut the steak or to cook it or to make a fire or to light it when it was made. (253)

Not knowing how to kill an ox, Sorrell's "brain is more useless than an empty pot with the wind whistling in it" (254). He needs practical knowledge, and, more specifically, the kind that runs a sequence of facts into a fully productive experience. The kind of continuity at work in Ford's Impressionism here gets expressed as a experiential sequence within an adequately known fact – the process of going from ox to steak, within knowledge of the fact of their relation.

Such nostalgia for plenitude is unremarkable. It characterizes not only much of modernist theory but much of the philosophy of history and the philosophy of mind. But Ford's nostalgia becomes an unusual kind of polemic when it makes special arrangements for Sorrell: Sorrell does not simply return to the Middle Ages to live a happy peasant life, but becomes, due to the very modernity he and Ford both deplore, a knight. His modern know-how has, after all, earned him respect and admiration, so that, with great ceremony, Mr. Sorrell becomes Sir Guilhelm de Winterburne de St. Martin, receiving along with his title "a little castle" and a small but promising fiefdom. It becomes clear that Sorrell's fate presents another version of Impressionist collaboration: the reintegration that it is the job of art to bring to modern life happens here, as elsewhere, only insofar as some incongruous social combination can combine factual and experiential modes. What is unusual about the politics of nostalgia in *Ladies Whose Bright Eyes* is the peculiar way nostalgia draws primitive receptivity into the realm of modern possibility. And what these peculiar tactics reveal about Ford's aesthetic theory is that it must take extreme measures to work: if the fictional corollary to Ford's theory of the function of art in the modern republic entails a "little castle" in medieval Salisbury, what hope is there that that theory will work for the modern artist?

Ladies Whose Bright Eyes ends with a vision of the future that asks this very question. Sorrell, now back in the present, can hardly abide the duties and relationships of his business life. Civilization, it is clear, has atrophied; his associates cannot "throw an axe" or "spear a salmon" (345), and unable to tolerate them Sorrell makes a pilgrimage to the land of his past triumphs. There he meets the modern version of his medieval beloved, and discovers from her the lesson in his trip to the past. It is not, after all, about the past, but the future: going back "to those beginnings" is less about escapist nostalgia than about restoring the epistemological foundations upon which to build a better future. He has learned how to proceed with restored courage and faith toward a future of "hard, unatrophied things and minds" (350). Sorrell therefore anticipates the kind of future Ford wants for the republic; he has discovered in the past what the artist would bring to culture, and, on the basis of this new connectedness, can make the historical distinctions necessary to imagine progress. But can he count on this future only because his trip into the past has enabled him to circumvent crucial elements of cultural incoherence, relocating pragmatic knowledge in a cultural elite by displacing in time what his culture displaces by class? Is *Ladies Whose Bright Eyes* an ideological fantasy that brings the politics of Impressionism into safe territory, making the peculiar collaboration with the peasant cabman a juncture in which a "peasant intelligence" becomes the property of a gentle knight?

One clue that it is not is Sorrel's sense of where he is likely to find his future "little castle." When the modern Dionissia asks if he could possibly "find another little castle" "somewhere where they're beginning [again]," Sorrel answers that he's seen one, "on the side of a valley in the Russian Caucasus." Dionissia notes that, given changes since then, "it would be a ruin now," but Sorrell nevertheless confirms the new "beginning" such a proto-revolutionary ruin would represent. Looking forward to a ruined castle in revolutionary Russia, Sorrell gives us a new revised figure for Impressionist collaboration (349). Whereas his Impressionism otherwise gets its synthesis from primitivism or the nostalgic "return to yesterday," here it remakes collaboration such that it combines tradition and reform, and thereby redeems nostalgia and primitivism alike. Nostalgia now becomes embrace of tradition in acknowledged ruin; primitivism becomes progressive, an interest in new social beginnings. So if *Ladies Whose Bright Eyes* is an ideological fantasy, it also reverses its ideology, finally, and subjects it to the critique figured in a return to a revolutionary present.

But when Ford chooses a subject that allows no such experimental adjustment, and when the capacity to assimilate fact to value remains within modernity, no new beginning commences. In *The Good Soldier*, the problem of Impressionism wreaks its full havoc, driving divisions much deeper than those art would solve for the republic.

Critics have always called *The Good Soldier* proof of Impressionism's failure. Dowell relies on appearances; appearances betray him, and prove that an Impressionist vision of the world gives up on deeper meanings with disastrous results. Or, Dowell's reading of people and events is wholly "subjective"; he is a solipsist, and suffers for his failures to see beyond himself.[55] But this tendency to interpret the novel in terms of the difference between Dowell's "impressions" and "what really happened" does not get to the heart of the problem. Impressionism does not fail Dowell because it necessarily distinguishes between appearance and reality, or between subjective and objective judgment. It fails him because Ford turns Impressionist theory into one of incompatible perceptual moments. The common interpretation of the novel has always been unable to account both for the impossibility of "objective" knowledge and the special insensibility of Dowell himself. Are impressions "all we can know," or is Dowell specifically undone by the fallibility of *his* impressions? If we approach the problem with Ford's conflicted ideology in mind, we will see that it is not impressions that cause the problem, but the way in which Dowell tries and fails to find through them the value of fact: what fails, in *The Good Soldier*, is Dowell's effort to generate experience through collaborative relationships with "virgin minds."

Dowell's is a divided nature: "It is as if one had a dual personality," he thinks, "the one I being entirely unconscious of the other."[56] He has an outer self and an "inner soul" (114), and the inner personality seems to do all the feeling and perceiving without the knowledge of the outer. So it is not really the case that Dowell does not get, for example, the news of his wife's infidelity: as he recalls, he got the news "full in the face," but as he also recalls, "I didn't say anything and I don't suppose I felt anything, unless maybe it was with that mysterious and unconscious self that underlies most people" (100). Perceptual responsibility is simply delegated to another self, in the spirit of the collaboration Ford designs in "On Impressionism." And Dowell's dual personality sets the pattern for a series of collaborations to follow. It creates Dowell's version of Edward Ashburnham, of Nancy, and finally the "silent listener" through whom he desperately seeks a last remedy.

Dowell acknowledges that his obsession with Edward has been a kind of dual selfhood: "For I can't conceal from myself the fact that I loved Edward Ashburnham – and that I love him because he was just myself" (227). Edward, however, has been Dowell's "inner soul" – the one that gets to do the experiencing. As the "large elder brother" Dowell watches "from a distance," Edward is a kind of distant laborer, enjoying by right of simple vitality the experience Dowell cannot himself have.[57] When Dowell admits, "If I had the courage and virility and possibly also the physique of Edward Ashburnham I should, I fancy, have done much what he did," Dowell attributes to Edward the same ground for experience in Sorrell's return to the Middle Ages. He attributes to Edward what he calls his own "right to existence," and thereby alienates his own epistemological foundation. Taking up this ground, Edward plays the role of Ford's cabman. He has, in fact, that "virgin intelligence" (128) – the phrase appears again here – manifest in a face that "expressed nothing whatever" (29) and eyes that are "perfectly straightforward, perfectly stupid" (128). According to the logic of "On Impressionism," this virgin intelligence would make Edward a perfect counterpart for Dowell: together they could constitute a vital, meaningful, and anti-modern perceptual complex. But *The Good Soldier* discovers the flaw in the logic, which it thematizes in Edward's social-class status. Edward, of course, is no sentimentalized peasant; he owns a lot of land. Edward's money makes him not at all subject to Dowell's projections, proving that it is hard to find good mental virginity. Dowell tries to simplify him; his repeated assertions that the Ashburnhams are "good people" reflect his effort to virginize Edward; but that goodness proves ultimately not to come from some exploitable simplicity, but from the very allegiance to conventions that "On Impressionism" ascribes to the worst kind of reader. Edward's virgin intelligence turns out to be purely conventional – leaving Dowell without the vital foundation Ford's Impressionism requires, and consequently more and more subject to skepticism.

In the skepticism that follows the loss of Edward's "goodness" and his death, Dowell turns to another kind of collaboration, now with Nancy Rufford. In that juncture, Dowell finally achieves Impressionism's juncture with a virgin intelligence, only in horrific form. Once Edward and Leonora are through with her, and give her up to Dowell for marriage, she sits silent, but not like Ford's "silent listener." She cannot speak, other than to utter occasional mad interjections. Dowell waits for her recovery, and in the meantime can only dwell on her parodically perfect suitability for the collaborational role. She is, he sees, mindless and vital, but then also utterly unmeaningful: "It is very extraordinary to see the perfect flush of health on her cheeks, to see the lustre of her coiled black hair, the poise of her head upon the neck, the grace of the white hands – and to think that it all means nothing – that it is a picture without meaning" (228). Dowell here discovers the truth about the "quite virgin mind": it is not impressionable, necessarily, but quite possibly incapacitated. Not able to find in it any source of inspiration, Dowell is finally just "an ageing American with very little knowledge of life." Nancy is not the receptive audience that guarantees at once the mimetic accuracy and pragmatic effect of her partner's impressions; she is a senseless body, joined to a desperate mind, for whom "life peters out" (227).

With a more receptive audience Dowell might have been able to make his life make sense. But after failed collaborations with Edward and Nancy, he plunges into a despair exactly opposite to the good result Ford wants from collaboration with the "uninstructed mind." In "English Literature of Today," Ford writes, "Of [our fellow men's] lives and passions we know nothing. So that unless the imaginative writer help us in this matter we are in great danger of losing alike human knowledge and human sympathy" (67). As we have seen, the imaginative writer delivers knowledge and sympathy only with false assurances – through the connections impressions promise but only contrive, and through distinctions among "our fellow men." So when Dowell tries to be the storyteller Ford describes in "On Impressionism," he discovers that distinction in fact makes Impressionist connections impossible, and must ask, "Who knows?" and see that "there is nothing to guide us," that "it is all a darkness" (16, 18). Then – and not simply because appearances deceive – he concludes that he is "alone – horribly alone" and that he knows "nothing – nothing in the world – of the hearts of men" (140). His skepticism, therefore, does not indicate that he is just a part of a larger "valueless and anarchic present busily shoring up its ruins."[58] His is an individual horror, one that occurs as the failure of the structure meant to justify impressions makes "life" recede further from his purview.

When Dowell makes one last ditch effort to contrive that structure, it becomes fully clear that *The Good Soldier* refutes "On Impressionism." Telling his story now after the discovery and loss of Edward and Florence has left him "horribly alone," Dowell seems to feel more than ever the need for some "virgin mind" to help make his story meaningful. Having failed to find it, he doesn't even know how to tell his tale: "I don't know how it is best to put this thing down," he says, wondering "whether it would be better to try to tell the story from the beginning" or to tell it as it became known to him. To answer the question of form, he takes the advice Ford gives in "On Impressionism": he figures to himself a "silent listener." He decides to "just imagine myself for a fortnight or so at one side of the fireplace of a country cottage, with a sympathetic soul opposite me. And I shall go on talking . . ." (19). Later, he calls this sympathetic soul his "silent listener" (114), but by that time this explicit reference to "On Impressionism" – this use of the same phrase – does not so much reflect improvement as prove the danger in the essay's incidental figuration: by now, the choice of the silent listener seems only the repeat offense of a man who ought to have learned not to put significatory power in the silence of another. And then when the type of tale-telling inspired by the silent listener does nothing to put things in order, Dowell can only apologize for Ford's Impressionist theory:

> I have, I am aware, told this story in a very rambling way so that it may be difficult for anyone to find their path through what may be a sort of maze. I cannot help it. I have stuck to my idea of being in a country cottage with a silent listener . . . I console myself with thinking that this is a real story and that, after all, real stories are probably told best in the way a person telling a story would really tell them. They will then seem most real. (167)

When Ford initially advocated the silent listener as a writer's ideal reader, he seemed to imply that that reader's indulgence would allow the teller to tell the tale in the most realistically unprofessional fashion. "Instructed" readers might expect a neater story, but the uninstructed would have the patience for ones told "the way a person telling a story would really tell them." But now the storyteller is one who needs professional help – who would in fact be better off meeting the expectations of an instructed reader. Having idealized a kind of epistemological "silence," Ford has given up too much, and Dowell suffers the consequences. Too much silence – the significatory analog to the peasant cabman's lack of cultural distinction – means too much difference between factual truth and experiential value.

What makes Impressionism fail, then, is the breadth across which impressions must mediate, once Ford decides that they need so full a silence to "seem most real." But to the critical tradition, Impressionism has seemed a failure simply because Dowell does what the Impressionist ought to do and ends up miserable as a result. Dowell might have been a happy Impressionist had the theory which produced him not become, through the politics of nostalgia, one drawn to idealize the experiential purity of an unreformed working class. Then, Ford might not have arrayed experiential truth so far from intellectual engagement; then, Fabianism and Impressionism might not have seemed so much at odds, and Ford might have imagined that a larger populace would be receptive to an artist's impressions. In that case Dowell might have found that telling his story brought the facts in line with experience. Were Dowell so lucky, however, *The Good Soldier* would not be a novel which features in such harrowing fashion the problem of Impressionism's most extreme "ambiguity value." *The Good Soldier* in that case would not dramatize the problem of clashing ideologies, as it does by showing at the level of telling how social distinctions become epistemological divisions and in turn make representation unable to assimilate modern facts into universal experience.

In this, Ford's work is not unlike that of Proust. In the observations that began this account of Impressionism's distant laborer, I argued that Proust's impression ultimately relocates labor in the material work of the author himself. When Marcel makes his book the way Françoise would make a dress, he does his own work, after having come to understand that to alienate labor is to forfeit the strength to see his impressions through. Ford may not quite reach the point at which such understanding dispels skepticism, but he lingers longer over the moment when Proust, at the Guermantes' party, fears that his weakness will leave his impressions unexpressed. Ford makes that moment – the moment in which an alienated strength leaves behind extreme representational weakness – long enough to be both the ruin of Impressionism and one very influential basis of Modernism.

CHAPTER 5

Woolf's phenomenological impression

So winning was Virginia Woolf's argument against Arnold Bennett that it is surprising to find that there is hardly any argument there at all. In her essays against Bennett and his fellow Edwardian writers, Woolf makes a convincing case against the lifelessness of "Materialist" fiction, and she winningly advises modern writers to trade material detail for "life itself," but she does not say what "life itself" is, or how modern fiction will treat it. In fact she ends her essays on modern fiction admitting failure – failure to come up with any alternative, and failure to replace Edwardian Materialism with credible new conventions. Failure, if anything, is her answer to Arnold Bennett, since failure is a sure sign of the effort to make it new. But of new terms for modern fiction Woolf offers none.

She offers no positive alternative to "Materialism" in part because she wants to keep the field open. Her real adversary is less Bennett's writing than his rules: Bennett and others had said she could not create character, and Woolf wanted to defend herself not only by reversing the claim and proving Edwardian character lifeless, but by proving that to specify any single method for characterization (or any other aspect of fiction) is to destroy the freedom fiction needs to thrive. Had she simply switched modernist rules for Edwardian ones, Woolf would have traded one trap for another. *Pace* Wyndham Lewis, Woolf was not "the orthodox 'idealist', tremulously squar[ing] up to the big beefy brute, Bennett, plainly the very embodiment of commonplace *matter*."[1] She does not argue for "idealism": the excess of material detail given in Edwardian novels may have been deadening, but simply to turn from "inessentials" to "essentials" would not have worked. What Woolf wanted was some right combination of the two – some way to have the kind of life that resides in material detail, but yet to make it a part of some more essential vision; some way to have essential insight, but yet stay grounded in material life.

Unable to describe the terms of this combination, Woolf lets "failure" stand at least for the freedom of provisional effort. And the best she can do, to give a name to this freedom, is to invoke the impression. When Woolf famously writes that the proper stuff of fiction is the "myriad impressions" that compose the "incessantly varying spirit" of "life itself," she chooses a focus both material and essential – both empirical and ideal. Such impressions convey the spirit of life itself by transmitting aspects of life as lived. Myriad *ideas* might compose life's pure essence, and myriad *perceptions* or *sensations* might constitute its material experience, but impressions put fiction between essence and experience such that it can have the broadest significance. When Woolf writes, later in these essays, of the need to describe the impression she gets from Mrs. Brown, that impression is "like a smell of burning," but also something that conveys the essence of character. It is an experience of essence, an inessential essential, and therefore a category through which to refute Materialism without giving up its claim to "life."

It is tempting to compensate for the ambiguity here with the specificity of some comparable philosophy. With her tendency to use philosophical language – to refer to "things themselves," to speculate on the reality of objects – Woolf in fact seems to invite this kind of interdisciplinary comparison. So we might call her an Empiricist, and her attack on Materialism a belief that "life" adheres in psychological process. Or we might call her a Neo-Realist, tracing the Bloomsbury connection to G. E. Moore, and see her anti-Materialism as an effort to do better justice to the real existence of objects and others. Or we might define her ambiguous synthesis of materials and essentials as phenomenological and give her argument against Bennett the specificity of Husserl's definition of "intentional" consciousness, of Heidegger's effort to correlate being and existence, of Merleau-Ponty's solution to epistemological dualism, or at least of phenomenology's basic synthesis of empirical and idealist modes.[2] Woolf, however, once wrote, "I don't want a 'philosophy' in the least," and the refusal reflects an elected inconsistency that must disallow philosophical classification.[3] Woolf also wrote, "No critic ever gives full weight to the desire of the mind for change" – meaning that the human mind, as opposed to the critical one, varies.[4] People are collections of different selves: this is one of Woolf's basic beliefs (basic, for example, to *Orlando*, and to *The Waves*), and it is less a philosophy of flux than a belief that some selves are flux-philosophers and some are not – that some see empirically, some are phenomenological, and that they alternate according to moods, which are in turn basic to life. Woolf's philosophical affiliations change with the moods of her characters, which is why no philosophical affiliation can define her vague theory of fiction. It is also why the impression suits her so well: in its indeterminacy, the impression responds well to differences in mood, seeming sometimes to place an empiricist emphasis on the primacy of perception, but able also to stand for phenomenological combinations and less theoretical feelings.

We might nevertheless more decisively characterize Woolf's indecision by relating it to that of another epistemological tradition. When Woolf invokes Mrs. Brown to explain her interests in impressions, she makes her Impressionism a matter of feminist epistemology. Henry James, we have seen, is oddly a kind of standpoint feminist, interested in the way limitation converts to advantage for the women at the basis of his apophatic Impressionism. Woolf, who focuses such consistent interest upon the question of the female standpoint, extends James's implicit critique of the relations among the novel, female subjectivity, and perceptual theory. Indeed such interest is her specialty, the source of her most major contribution to the history of ideas. With regard to Impressionism, it makes her the theorist most likely persistently to question the impression's social collaborations, and to try to work past them to more genuine mediations.

It therefore makes sense that her indecision – the indecision about the theoretical affiliations and implications of the impression – should match that of standpoint feminism. Currently, standpoint feminism vacillates on one central question: is the female standpoint *itself* an epistemic privilege, or is it effective as a way to reveal the perspectival nature of knowledge, *on the way* to the greatest possible objectivity? Woolf wonders the same thing, and this uncertainty, combined with that about the mixed blessings of *apophasis*, is the link between the impression's indeterminacy and Woolf's political aesthetic.

But there is another link – one which connects Woolf to politics of another kind. For Mrs. Brown may mark Woolf's Impressionism as a feminist epistemology, but Mrs. Brown is not only a "woman of genius." Also a "distant laborer," she provokes many of the same questions provoked by Conrad, Ford, and Proust – more strenuously, perhaps, because Woolf is notoriously a self-designated "snob." Does

Woolf invoke Mrs. Brown to have materiality without sacrificing the privileges of ideality – to draw matter into her art of essence without leaving her high ground? Is *this* the source of her indecision – ambivalence about the social location of material life? Is the impression important for its inimitable precious ineffability, and is her attack on Arnold Bennett motivated less by feminist episte-mology than by snobby aesthetics – by a wish to guard the art of fiction against comers from below?

In "Modern Novels" (1919), the essay in which Woolf first speaks of impressions, she moves dialectically through a range of possible perceptual slants, finally to say two things about the Impressionist temperament: it is that which thrives on the thrill of dialectic move-ment itself, and ends happily shaken into negative capability.

The first step is to mock the "ill-fitting vestments" of Materialist rendering – to note that "the essential thing" always eludes it, and to ask the basic question, "[I]s life like this after all?" Sure that it is not, trying to say what life *is* like, Woolf then describes a "vague general confusion" in which clear-cut distinctions get "dissolved beyond the possibility of separate recognition."[5] This confusion is the "incessantly varying spirit" in which the mind "receives upon its surface a myriad impressions"; and Woolf's job, it seems, is to say how the modern novelist renders these impressions.

To define "the task of the novelist" in these terms Woolf turns to Joyce. "In contrast to those whom we have called materialists" Joyce is "spiritual," and therefore gives us what "seems to be life itself" (34). Joyce's spiritualism, however, is just the inverse of materialism. He goes too far in the other direction and "never reaches out or embraces or comprehends what is outside and beyond." If Bennett writes lifeless realism, Joyce writes blind idealism, and Woolf must look elsewhere for a synthetic model. This she finds, temporarily, in "The Russians." They lead her to something between spirit and matter: the "heart." She admires, in other words, their feeling, which she sums up in the following lesson: "Learn to make yourself akin to people. . . but let this sympathy be not with the mind – for it is easy with the mind – but with the heart, with love towards them" (35).[6] Heartfelt sympathetic kinship might be the model; it might combine psychological insight with materialist reality; but having lit on this synthesis, Woolf undercuts it. For the Russians tend toward gloom. They may convey that "general confusion" with real feeling, but they do so in such a way as to turn its "incessantly varying spirit" into incessant anxiety, leaving us "in hopeless interrogation that fills us with a deep, and finally it may be with a resentful, despair" (36).

Not the answer, Russian despair nevertheless does lead somewhere: to the fourth term in the dialectic, and to Woolf's solution, however incomplete. The Russian style of interrogation prompts a "voice of protest," which bespeaks a joyfully synthetic imagination: it is "the voice of another and ancient civilization which seems to have bred in us the instinct to enjoy and fight rather than to suffer and understand . . . our natural delight in humour and comedy, in the beauty of earth, in the activities of the intellect, and in the splendour of the body" (36). This English version of Russian "heart" has perceptual diversity without gloom, and can convey vital impressions. But if Woolf thereby defines the Impressionist temperament, she does so only negatively, for the important thing about this "voice" is that it never ceases to ask "question after question." Answers are forbidden, and "any deductions we may draw from the comparison of one fiction to another are futile, save as they flood us with a view of infinite possibilities." We are left with the belief that the proper attitude of modern fiction is in the *form* of Woolf's essay rather than in its content – in the form that takes natural delight in asking a dialectical series of questions but giving no answers, in the form whose openness excites vitality, ends in negative capability, and *generates* "life itself."

Indirectly performing the Impressionist mode, then, "Modern Novels" ends in a kind of paradox. Happy to fail to reach conclusions, letting the flood of the infinite set the standard, Woolf stakes fiction's success on critical failure. Critical indecision is therefore not only corollary to the theory of the impression, as in other writers, but essential. When critics notice this kind of indecision in Woolf they tend to call it postmodern, or performative in the contemporary sense of that term. Woolf chooses not to choose; in the process, she performs rhetorically the variety fiction ought to have, and commits herself to a postmodern antifoundationalism.[7] But to call Woolf postmodern or performative is to miss her earnest Modernism and the hope in her quest for salvific insight. Woolf commits herself to the free play of the impression not because she revels in *différance*, but out of an effort to adumbrate a new faculty, one that has the freedom perceptually to range. But the impression's tendency to range is not always corollary to good failure. When ranging freely means finding good middle ground between essence and existence – between the life of the spirit and the life of the body – Woolf's voice sounds on in delight, but when ranging freely means that consciousness can slide into brute materiality or utterly lose its ground, Woolf trades freedom for stability, even if it means borrowing it from sources out of sympathy with modern fiction.

When Woolf's Impressionism finds its middle ground, combining what she calls "ordinary waking Arnold Bennett life" with "life itself," it flashes into phenomenological fulness.[8] The impression's free play triumphs when Woolf can believe that it hits on objecthood and essence – when it partakes at once of the phenomenal and the psychic activity of "intentional" consciousness. Then, due to her particular motivations, Woolf rides Impressionism furthest toward its phenomenological horizon. Impressions fail to help, however, and defeat phenomenological insight, when their ambiguous mediations present only impenetrable objects or structureless consciousness. Then, Woolf becomes desperate for the "commonplace matter" of "Arnold Bennett life" and the ground of its conventional material stability.

This oscillation appears in the options for characterization in *The Waves*, for example, where Bernard enjoys the impression's phenomenological mediation and Rhoda suffers for its redivision. Bernard ultimately transcends individualized consciousness, with good results; he is "not one person," but "many people," and corollary to his transcendence of self is full insight into phenomena, as he becomes "immeasurably receptive, holding everything, trembling with fullness, yet clear, contained."[9] Rhoda, by contrast, feels such selfless receptivity as a terror. For her, it does not entail both transcendence and receptivity, but an inverse combination: formlessness and alienation. Too detached, she feels that she is out of life, that "nothing persists," that "I have no face," and finds herself perpetually in need of some material ground (the "rail of the bed" or some such other basis in "lodgment") to have experience.[10] Bernard embodies the voice that speaks in delight at the end of "Modern Novels"; Rhoda embodies one that asks if Bennett's Materialism might not after all be the safer alternative.

Peter Walsh, in *Mrs. Dalloway*, embodies both voices at once, when he becomes the "solitary traveller." Asleep on a bench in Regent's Park, Peter drifts into a visionary mode, in which the possibility that "nothing exists outside us except a state of mind" conditions "visions which proffer great cornucopias full of fruit" and "[take] away from him the sense of the earth."[11] These visions enrich both being and perception – or seem to, until the solitary traveler finds himself "indoors among ordinary things," and there finds himself lost. A landlady asks a question, prompting another question – one Rhoda might have asked: "But to whom does the solitary traveller make reply?"[12] To whom, to what, is the visionary responsive, and is the experience of essence really no form of experience at all? Such questions sound throughout Woolf's creative and critical work, so that hope for phenomenological synthesis is dashed. Wondering perpetually "how to keep the flight of the mind, yet be exact," "is life very solid or very shifting . . .?," "how to give ordinary waking Arnold Bennett life the form of art," and organizing her thoughts according to distinctions between "fact and vision," or "granite and rainbow," Woolf perpetually finds that the impression's mode of representation emphasizes the disparity it would unify.[13]

And she perpetually takes measures to compel disparity into unity – measures that define her career in a number of ways. Such measures define the pattern recognized by many who have looked for the literary analog of Woolf's bipolar disorder.[14] Such measures would define her writing life in the 1930s, when changing times demanded new attention to the material, and Woolf tried to refigure the impression's mediation in the "essay-novel," a hybrid that would have "facts, as well as the vision. And . . . combine them both."[15] Such measures define her relation to Modernism itself, insofar as Modernism at once imitates and defends against modernity, making a new culture of the salvage of old distinctions.[16] And, most importantly for the present argument, such measures are what create Mrs. Brown. For she is what Woolf creates in order to shore up, immediately and to greatest historical effect, the impression's power to emcompass essence and experience. Mrs. Brown is what "lodgment" is to Rhoda, and what would guarantee to the "solitary traveller" someone to whom to make his reply. She is that material supplement that ensures the impression's claim to vital experience.[17] At first, in "Modern Novels," she does not appear, but when Woolf feels the need to lend greater substance to her argument, she draws on the very "Materialism" she seems to attack. When, in "Mr. Bennett and Mrs. Brown," and then in "Character in Fiction," she tries more positively to describe "life itself" – to say what, beyond vaguely conceived free play, a modern writer wants, and to say how the modern soul's impressions have an object – she embodies "life itself" in Mrs. Brown, allegedly because Mrs. Brown is the kind of person Arnold Bennett would describe poorly, but really also because Mrs. Brown is the kind of person "ordinary waking Arnold Bennett life" can guarantee. Mrs. Brown comes to Woolf from her adversary but gets enlisted as a partner. Allegedly a character, Mrs. Brown is also a counterpart, together with whom Woolf is able to imagine impressions to have both their different perceptual bases and their integrity.

So Woolf does what others had done before her, but with a difference. Mrs. Brown is a woman of genius, for her power to guarantee contingency; but she is also a distant laborer, bringing materiality to a highbrow's insight at least to some degree along the lines that separate the social classes. The double partnership makes a difference because it means different incitements and different results: as we will see, Woolf is egged on to create and then to dismantle Mrs. Brown by her feminist affiliations; but what is promoted by a feminist will to inclusion, demystification, and unity is shadowed by social-class conflict. As these social meanings pull in opposite directions, Mrs. Brown's theoretical plots perpetually double up and redouble doubt.

What follows here is an account of the construction and decon-struction of Mrs. Brown, through a series of essays and fictions, focusing primarily on those lesser-known texts in which Mrs. Brown begins. Woolf's confrontation with Mrs. Brown is only the middle moment in a long series of such confrontations. The series begins in texts that feature narrators contemplating some material trace (a "mark on the wall," or a moth) and wondering how to do justice at once to its material life and its larger meaning. Mrs. Brown herself only appears as the need for such justice becomes most pressing – as social arguments demand a female form. Once formed, Mrs. Brown becomes the object of deconstructive energies, as throughout the 1920s Woolf replays with deepening critical scrutiny the scene in which one woman broadens her own epistemological connections in contemplation of the "life" of another. Wanting then to dispel the myth that women embody "life itself" (as, for example, Mrs. Ramsay seems so oppressively to do), Woolf dramatizes the process through which people find the full range of human faculties within themselves. As she does so, she offers a solution to the problems that tend to confuse feminist epistemology; but she also finds that other rifts in the social totality deny this plenitude, and confront even her most ecstatic fictions with the threat of losing ground.

"The Mark on the Wall" (1917) is practice of what "Modern Novels" preaches – a fictional version of what the essay says about fictionality. As the story's narrator-character sits and regards an unidentifiable mark, she engages in wild speculations, all of which prove wrong: the mark is just a snail. The failure here has led many readers to read the story as a solipsist's fall into scepticism, or a self-conscious parody of an aesthete's self-indulgence, or an allegory of the idealist mind's problem with objects. But it is really no more a failure than that of "Modern Novels." For here as well Woolf moves dialectically through a series of different perceptual alternatives, and discovers in the process itself the best one. Unlike "Modern Novels," however, "The Mark on the Wall" does not end happily in the free play of perceptual possibility. It extends that free play to the moment in which materiality reasserts itself like a full-stop, as if to wonder if the state of perception corollary to the impression can run life's range without help.

"The Mark on the Wall" takes Woolf's typical point of departure – departing from the outset from material and ideal extremes in an effort to walk the line between them. As the story's narrator moves through her various *material* conceptions of the mark's status – "a nail, a rose-leaf, a crack in the wood?" – she sinks into a reverie that trades material classification for essential insight.[18] She does so because were she just to "look at" the mark, she "shouldn't be able to say for certain" what it is. "The mystery of life" and the "inaccuracy of thought" prevent such easy investigations, and true insight will require some other mode – just as it does for Woolf herself in "Modern Novels." But "The Mark on the Wall" goes on to satirize *that* mode as well. Exclamatory reverence for "the mystery of life" is as silly as faith in "looking." Saying so, the story sets out to find Impressionism's middle way.

What is wanted is some way to have the definite clarity of the material classification (a nail) with the freedom of association that would trade classification for intimation (what picture hung on the nail, owned by whom, the owners' habits and histories). The combination seems possible as the narrator resolves to leave behind both her ordinary ideas and the ordinary world of facts, proposing a state of mind in which things run together and ideas are solid: "I want to think quietly, calmly, spaciously, never to be interrupted, never to have to rise from my chair, to slip easily from one thing to another, without any sense of hostility, or obstacle. I want to sink deeper and deeper, away from the surface, with its hard separate facts. To steady myself, let me catch hold of the first idea that passes . . ." (85). Steady and slipping, holding and letting go, the narrator aspires to Impressionist mediation but, as in "Modern Novels," finds no positive way to dictate its terms. Trying to "catch hold of the first idea that passes," the narrator discovers Shakespeare. Shakespeare, who figures so prominently as the epitome of "incandescence" in *A Room of One's Own*, here seems at first the answer, but turns out to model only the ideal solipsistic "spiritualism" that "Modern Novels" finds in Joyce. He is "a man who sat himself solidly in an arm-chair, and looked into the fire" as "a shower of ideas fell perpetually from some very high Heaven down through his mind" (85). This is no "shower of innumerable impressions" – nothing that gives ideas a grasp – but a shower of ideas; and it passes not through an open consciousness, but one that sits too solidly in a self. It therefore leads the narrator astray into an attitude once again too ideal, and puts her "upon a pleasant track of thought, a track indirectly reflecting credit upon myself . . . dressing up the figure of myself in my own mind, lovingly, stealthily" (85).

That excess of self-centered solipsism helps, though, insofar as it drives the dialectic to its fourth term. In materialist realism, we see only appearances; in subjective reverie, there is only "mystery"; in Shakespeare, there are ideas so solid they admit no admixture; but together these modes can inspire the novelist of the future: "As we face each other in omnibuses and underground railways we are looking into the mirror . . . And the novelist in the future will realise the importance of these reflections, for of course there is not one reflection but almost an infinite number; those are the depths they will explore, those are the phantoms they will pursue, leaving the description of reality more and more out of their stories" (85–86). This provisional conclusion is important for four reasons: first, for the way it would have the novelist depart both from the description of reality and simple self-seeing, toward pursuit of infinite human depths in their infinite interreflections; second, for the way that pursuit would match the free play "Modern Novels" also endorses; third, for the way that pursuit prepares the pursuit of Mrs. Brown,

also a "phantom," and also in "omnibuses and underground railways"; and finally for the way it is, as a conclusion, only provisional.

What is for "Modern Novels" a fine conclusion is for "The Mark
on the Wall" only a worthless "generalisation" (86). The story does
not believe that vague freedom, however ecstatic, hits the "mark,"
and it pushes on toward some more positive complaint about
conventions. The dialectic redoubles: "generalisation" – even if it
has seemed an answer – now partakes of "habit," and is associated
with "a whole class of things indeed which as a child one thought the
thing itself, the standard thing, the real thing." And what drives
Woolf finally toward something better – beyond her account of a
simply negative capability, toward some substantive Impressionist
method – is the motivation of her feminism.

Feminism is what drives Woolf to turn from "generalisation" to a
renewed effort to theorize fiction, because feminism opposes perceptual divisions. Woolf initially defines "generalisation" in terms of
"the class of things which as a child one thought the thing itself."
She then wonders "what now takes the place of those things" –
what, for adults, gets in the way of essential understanding – and
decides that it is "the masculine point of view which governs our
lives, which sets the standard, which establishes Whitaker's Table of
Precedency" (86). Distinctions by gender and by class replace
perception of things themselves with perceptions merely of distinction: with this discovery, Woolf adds a crucial step to the dialectic
that has moved between empirical and ideal ways of seeing. Both, it
turns out, are fallacies enforced by social distinction, as is the
opposition between them. And once Woolf discovers this iso-
morphism of social and perceptual division she can move beyond her
merely negative interest in free play. Free play becomes important
not simply because of its open indecision, but because it presents
perception with a wholly different object.

"Learned men," now, are nothing "save the descendants of
witches and hermits who crouched in caves and in woods brewing
herbs" (87). Their "generalisations" dispatched, Woolf develops
positive images for Impressionist perception. She imagines, for
example, "a very pleasant world" in which "one could slice with
one's thought as a fish slices the water with his fin" (87). Attributing
material force to thought, and figuring its object as a liquid solidity,
Woolf starts to figure a style of perception unfettered by habits of
distinction. Once perception ceases to observe it own habits, it can

get at the object "in itself," and it is that *phenomenological* goal that Woolf now pursues. Imagining a "tree itself," she engages in a mode of description that is at once abstract and concrete – general without "generalisation," material without "Materialism," and therefore fully unifying:

I like to think of the tree itself: first the close dry sensation of being wood; then the grinding of the storm; then the slow, delicious ooze of sap. I like to think of it, too, on winter's nights standing in the empty field with all leaves close-furled, nothing tender exposed to the iron bullets of the moon, a naked mast upon an earth that goes tumbling, tumbling all night long. The song of birds must sound very loud and strange in June; and how cold the feet of insects must feel upon it, as they make laborious progresses up the creases of the bark . . . (88–89)

Woolf's tree is an important moment in her development as a writer and in the history of literary Impressionism. The "thing itself" has been found through the synthesis the impression has long endorsed but rarely made. Impressionism reaches its phenomenological horizon: very much like the "tree" Sartre uses to explain Husserl's phenomenology, this one is an essence correlative to the *intentional* activity of consciousness.[19] Consciousness here makes its object – but without therefore reducing that object to unreality. The making is reciprocal, and experience of the object is one with its essence; material description has the utter vitality of tumbling laborious processes, and the "ideal" mind finds itself happily well rooted.[20]

For the phenomenologist, this unified mode of perception does best justice at once to the real world and to the life of consciousness. For Woolf's narrator, it is therefore also the best basis for fiction, for it stimulates the imagination to multiply objective possibilities while also expanding itself. The tree, in Woolf's vision, falls, and is made into timber, but "even so life isn't done with; there are a million, patient, watchful lives still for a tree, all over the world, in bedrooms, in ships, on the pavement, lining rooms . . ." (89). Once seen phenomenologically, the tree ramifies into its infinite intentional productions and becomes the basis for countless stories. "I should like to take each one separately," Woolf writes, indicating that she has found her connection between basic materiality through vitalized imagination to infinite literary productivity.

But two things prevent the tree from ramifying into any fully phenomenological orientation. First, Woolf's narrator cannot sustain it. Just when she wants to embark on her many separate visions of the tree's essential experiences, something "get[s] in the way" (89). "Generalisation" returns to thwart her – as does the old empirical attitude. Someone appears and interrupts the reverie with a reminder of the Almanack and the Table of Precedency: "I'm going to buy a newspaper." This someone also supplies a materialist explanation of the mark: "All the same, I don't see why we should have a snail on our wall." Reminded of epistemological standards, and able now to say, "It was a snail," Woolf's narrator has lapsed. So the "story" must end, rather than ramify, because the mark has been materially identified and placed in its proper relation to the news of the world. Ending in this fashion – at a dead end, so unlike the happy failure that ends "Modern Novels" – "The Mark on the Wall" registers doubt about the phenomenological attitude corollary to the impression's synthesis: former styles of perception must inevitably return, it seems to suggest, and return too quickly for the "general" and "material" to change permanently into essence and experience.

Woolf's narrator cannot sustain the phenomenological orientation because what initiates it is weak. In order to depart from what phenomenology calls the "natural attitude," Woolf's narrator depends upon a kind of trick of otherness: it is only because the "mark" is so alien – so minimal, and so meaningless – that investigation of it can enable her to bracket off conventional experiences and conventional ideas. The strange alienation of the "tree" similarly indicates a need for a bracketing so extreme as to be impractical.

These two problems – the difficulty of sustaining the unified vision, and its source in extreme otherness – are familiar, as the basic problems of Impressionism. Woolf's impression would, like the vision of the mark, join opposed modes of perception to stimulate the fictional imagination. But like the vision of the mark, it runs afoul of interruption; something always intervenes to reassert the material or the general, and to force the fictional imagination back into patterns of observed detail and disengaged generalization. And that something always intervenes because the synthetic mechanism deviates too fully from selfhood: impressions come, like the exalted vision of the tree, only insofar as the self puts itself in the place of another, in a projection that enriches consciousness at consciousness's expense.

Before Woolf solves these problems, she exacerbates them, and that is why we get Mrs. Brown. For Mrs. Brown develops out of the enabling alterity of the mark on the wall, and, female, helps sustain synthesis. "The Mark on the Wall" ends in flat disappointment; flat disappointment turns to hope when the mark takes on a female body; but once in a female body, the impetus of Impressionism becomes subject to the revisionary energy of feminism, which makes all the difference. It was a touch of feminism that got the narrator of "The Mark on the Wall" beyond masculine "generalisation" to her temporary phenomenological vision. In later texts, stronger feminist commitment will get Woolf to see the relation between social and perceptual division and to push past the temporary measure of Mrs. Brown.

A next stage in the making of Mrs. Brown comes when Woolf turns her "mark" to a "moth" and brings her Impressionist counterpart to life. "The Death of the Moth" (1917) is the first in the train of fictional scenes in which a narratorial figure faces some manifestation of "life itself," and tries, with very different degrees of success, to find the best way to render life on the basis of it. The moth is a "tiny bead of pure life"; watching it, Woolf's narrator finds a way in to the purer vitality that gets concealed in everyday life.[21] The implication is paradoxical, but familiar from James, and crucial to Woolf's aesthetic: life shows its essence in a being hardly alive, to a being too steeped in life to see it.

The narrator of the piece is torn in a typically Woolfian way. She sits reading by an open window, which looks out into a scene of distracting natural beauty. On the one hand, there is the intellectual work indoors; on the other, there is outdoor vitality. The latter must upstage the former: "such vigour came rolling in from the fields and the down beyond that it was difficult to keep the eyes strictly turned upon the book" (3). How, then, to get work done, and still participate in this rolling vigor? To answer this question she needs to find some point of connection between the life outdoors and her book, and this she finds in a moth that flutters in the liminal space of the window. Whereas the larger life outside has an overwhelming and distracting materiality, the moth focuses life such that its meaning can be life for the mind. Two things give it this status: it is, first of all, no ordinary moth, but one that flies by day, and it is therefore both common and unfamiliar; and, more importantly, it is only hardly alive. "Watching him, it seemed as if a fibre, very thin but pure, of the enormous energy of the world had been thrust into his frail and diminutive

body" (4). The moth is such a little bit of life that it is "little or
nothing but life," and "because he was so small, and so simple a
form of the energy that was rolling in at the open window," it
condenses that energy to its essence. Watching it, Woolf's narrator
gains an insight into "life itself" that could come neither from her
book nor from the world outside: the moth seems to exist to "show
us the true nature of life," which one is "apt to forget" because of the
way it is typically "humped and bossed and garnished and cumbered" (4–5). It is humped and cumbered, it seems, in equal but
different ways by books and by life's full vigor. Both obscure "life
itself" – just as Materialist and idealist approaches to fiction would
do – which only comes clear when "energy" and "form" collaborate.

But there is, in this "queer spectacle," cause for pity: "the thought
of all that life might have been had he been born in any other shape
caused one to view his simple activities with a kind of pity" (5). Pity
for the moth reflects no small worry on Woolf's part about the terms
of this collaboration of energy and form. If you need to pare life
down to the size of a moth in order to see its "true nature," then you
jeopardize that very life in the process. The moth in this sense is not
unlike the femininity James admires for its "frailness": both get their
powers to transmit life into art from a weakness that is in real terms a
liability. James dramatizes the liability of frailness in his plots of
domestic torture. Woolf dramatizes the "pity" of slight life more
immediately. The moth soon fails to fly and becomes awkward with
the "approach of death." Slight life, it seems, passes very easily into
death, ending as well the life outside. "Stillness and quiet had
replaced the previous animation" of the life outside, now, despite the
fact that "the power was there all the same" (5–6). The power of
vitality may persist but without the moth to communicate its nature
it seems "indifferent, impersonal," and now a force of death.
Whereas before a vital essence enriched the narratorial consciousness, now "nothing, I knew, had any chance against death" (6). A
new duality supersedes the one between the book and the life
outside, and while this one also clarifies the meaning of life – while
"this minute wayside triumph of so great a force over so mean an
antagonist filled me with wonder" – the cost is great. Woolf even
figures this cost as a kind of failure of writing itself: as the moth dies,
Woolf's narrator tries and fails to intervene, in a significant way:
". . . as I stretched out a pencil, meaning to help him to right

himself, it came over me that the failure and awkwardness were the approach of death. I laid the pencil down again" (5). To lay down the pencil in the face of death is to discover – not unlike Conrad feeling his brain – the inverse of the Impressionist hope. The Impressionist writer hopes to find both life itself and a spur to the pencil; this writer finds in the moth a death that is an end to writing.

The impression would funnel life into a form slight enough to describe, but it might also reduce life to a nothing before which a writer can only lay her pencil down. Here is Woolf's version of Impressionist uncertainty, and it is an uncertainty which, again, pervades her writing well beyond the year in which she wrote "The Death of the Moth" and "The Mark on the Wall." It is at work when, for example, artist figures like Lily Briscoe stake everything on life that seems too negligible, or when the habit of epiphany endangers Peter Walsh's power to "reply" to life. It is also an uncertainty characteristic of the early reception to Woolf's writing. Readers other than Arnold Bennett, even friends like E. M. Forster, also felt that Woolf's characters had ideality at the cost of real-life presence.[22] But since she too knows that rendering essences might kill the life of her fiction, Woolf worked hard to make her "moth" more substantial. She worked hard to make it an essence better able to bear the weight of existence – and to make her impression, analogously, some more positive link between these two modes.

To make it bear the weight of existence without fully losing the slightness that reveals essence, Woolf next gives the impression a frail body. In "An Unwritten Novel" (1920), the moth becomes "Minnie Marsh," and generates impressions across a railway car. These impressions bring to story form the highs and lows of prior texts – the "mark's" mix of phenomenological excitation and material disappointment; the moth's mix of vitality and death; and "Modern Novels's" sense of lucky failure, negative freedom, and dialectical vertigo. But giving the impression a female body brings it into the critical realm of social plot, and therefore marks a turning point. The stakes are raised, both for perceptual theory (now that error has real consequence) and for social life (now that perception explicitly partakes of the distinctions that determine fate as well as feeling). The result is a conclusion that matches that of "Modern Novels" but brings it, and the problem of Impressionism, to climactic crisis.

Minnie Marsh "looks at life."[23] She suffers – and that quality will make her the vehicle for the narrator's own glimpse of life, much the way the moth mediates vitality. But at first the narrator fears that possibility, and hides behind that which, in "The Mark on the Wall," represented old perceptual conventions: she holds up a newspaper, thinking, "the best thing to do against life was to fold the paper so that it made a perfect square, crisp, thick, impervious even to life. This done, I glanced up quickly, armed with a shield of my own" (112–13). Giving her narrator this newspaper shield, Woolf drama- tizes the fear that revives old epistemological distinctions, and suggests that such distinctions have all the firm prevalence of a tough daily paper.

For the rest of the story Woolf's narrator alternates between looking at Minnie looking at life and hiding behind some shield of details. The newspaper, it turns out, is analogous to the "Materialist" details that keep Edwardian writers from seeing "life itself." When it is up, the narrator notices details; when it comes down, she shares in Minnie's experience, and understands its meaning. When the news- paper is up, for example, the narrator notices that Minnie "twitched her arm queerly to the middle of her back" (112). "Queerly" indicates lack of sympathy. When the newspaper comes down, however, Woolf's narrator shares the twitch: "And then the spasm went through me; I crooked my arm and plucked at the middle of my back . . . one spot between the shoulders itched and irritated, felt clammy, felt raw" (114). Intersubjective experience becomes possible with the fallen shield of detail. Moreover, that experience immedi- ately betrays the very essence of Minnie's life, for once the shield has fallen she "had communicated, shared her secret, passed her poison." The "twitch" between Minnie's shoulders, the physical experience she and the narrator now share, is somehow also her "secret," somehow also the essence of her character. Other things do not matter: "Ah, but the details matter nothing! It's what she carries with her; the spot, the crime, the thing to expiate, always there between her shoulders" (115). Clearly, the "twitch" is an impression – an external perception that becomes an internal feeling, and one which mediates between physical experience and essential meaning. It is both outer and inner, guaranteeing perception of both forms of justification; and it is both a physical detail and the general truth, both the clammy raw itch and a "spot" which is "the thing" itself. Woolf's narrator even describes the spot in such a way as to combine its physical and essential status: she writes, of Minnie's many meanings, "the spot receives them. It's raised, it's red, it's burning" (116). As a spot that burns with insight, Minnie's twitch is an impression.

But the narrator nevertheless worries that the "spot" may not be that focal point of experiential and essential meaning. "Have I read you right?," she asks, wondering if there might not after all be some inescapable difference between the physical detail and the higher meaning. Whereas she hopes that her eye can see in two ways at once, she worries about the possibility that "in the human eye . . . there's a break – a division – so that when you've grasped the stem the butterfly's off" (117). Maybe grasping the "spot" means losing the "thing" – and maybe the unity between the two will slip any grasp. Significantly, the "butterfly" in this image becomes a "moth." Woolf returns to her prior image for "life itself," and has her narrator think of her goal as "this moth that hangs in the evening air over the yellow flower." The image has changed slightly – now the unity of "life itself" is the juncture of moth and flower – but the same fragility obtains. It is now heightened, as Woolf's narrator thinks that to maintain this vision she must not "raise my hand." She must not make a move, since the unity in the "spot" between physical presence and essential meaning is as flighty as a moth on a flower. She cannot "grasp" it; all she can do is beg, "Hang still, then, quiver, life soul, spirit, whatever you are of Minnie Marsh"; for the moment, she can think that she, too, has gained access to life itself – "I, too, on my flower"; but the task of representation will require the "grasp," and what, in that event, will happen?

Unsure, the narrator decides on a different course of action. She decides to enumerate facts after all, "head down, eyes shut, with the courage of a battalion, and the blindness of a bull" (117). She gets materialistic, and coercive, needing now to "lodge myself somewhere on the firm flesh, on the robust spine, wherever I can find a foothold," and making now for Minnie something like the prison of Edwardian detail. She pins Minnie down, and even stops the "twitch" that had been so illuminating before: "Minnie you must promise not to twitch till I've got this straight" (118). What had enabled intersubjective feeling is now squelched in favor of Materialist accuracy. The impression Minnie makes, therefore, has changed. Before, it was the "spot" that was at once the "twitch" and the "thing"; now, because the narrator needs something she can grasp, it has become more materially substantial.

Irony takes over, here, and "An Unwritten Novel" frays into a very telling epistemological diversity. Diverse outcomes reflect the heady range the impression can run. Woolf's narrator seems to get it all "straight," and spins out Minnie's story. But then Minnie gets off the train, to meet a son and return to a life that, in the narrator's account, she ought not to have. The story's structure collapses, leaving the narrator in lifeless despair: "Well, my world's done for! What do I stand on! What do I know? . . . Who am I? Life's bare as bone" (121). With the "robust spine" but a "bare bone," rendering impressions has failed, and Woolf seems to lament the problem of going by Impressionist "appearances." But is it *Impressionism* that has failed? Has the narrator been reading impressions, or has she been reading the *materialist* details that make Bennett's fiction unreal? Grasping the stem and losing the moth – lodging herself in the "firm flesh" of detail – this narrator may be a materialist rather than an Impressionist failure, and it is the strange ambiguity of the impression's location between the material detail and the essential insight that makes it hard to decide.

Moreover, even if we can decide, we have a second ending to deal with. The narrator despairs, and then rallies: "And yet the last look of them . . . floods me anew. Mysterious figures! . . . Oh, how it whirls and surges – floats me afresh! I start after them . . . If I fall on my knees, if I go through the ritual, the ancient antics, it's you, unknown figures, you I adore; if I open my arms, it's you I embrace, you I draw to me – adorable world!" (121). This fresh flood is familiar from "Modern Novels" and its last ocean of possibility. Once again we find that "life itself" comes not from any specific mode of insight but from the way failure to find one forces flexibility – the way the "unknown" becomes the "adorable." But again we have ambiguity, and one inverse to that of the story's "first" ending. There, it was not clear whether the failure was materialist or Impressionist; here, it is not clear whether the success is a success. The second ending may celebrate the "ritual" of pursuing the unknown, or it may satirize "antic" aestheticism, the foolish prostration of those for whom the world is "adorable" rather than real. When crossed, these first and second ambiguities fray the end of "An Unwritten Novel" into so many theoretical possibilities that Impressionism covers the range of perceptual orientations. The story is playful, and the range is therefore playful as well, but it portends serious questions: if the impression's synthesis entails supposition so rangy that it gets its life at the expense of every other good – at the expense of accuracy, certainty, sympathy; of details and meanings alike – what is it worth? And if the inspiration to that synthesis can come only insofar as one makes a collaborative object of an *abject* other – in this case, a woman diminished, not unlike the dying moth, into the suffering that proves that she "looks at life" – does it not get its purchase on character by exaggerating social difference?

That Impressionism takes advantage of female abjection is suggested by two other moments in Woolf's writing. "Modern Novels" ends with a telling figural equation of good fiction and mistreatment: "All that fiction asks is that we should break and bully her, honour and love her, till she yields to our bidding, for so her youth is perpetually renewed and her sovereignty assured" (36). And further reinforcing this *apophatic* logic is a telling moment in *Jacob's Room*. Once again, we get two people in a railway car, only in this case one of them is male. *Jacob's Room*'s version of the railway-car scenario puts a upper-middle-class man in the position of "life itself," and gives to a lower-middle-class woman the job of investigating impressions of him. Young Jacob produces no impressions; Mrs. Norman can make nothing of him; and the scene inverts what goes on with Minnie. In the world of a male protagonist, it seems, impressions have no path to synthesis. They have, rather, a model in which life is on the one hand the material commerce of banks and on the other the unseiz-able force of the economic invisible hand, and any vision of character in itself becomes impossible. *Jacob's Room*, then, is in at least one sense anti-Impressionistic. Often called the most impressionistic of Woolf's novels – for the way it tries to portray a character not in his interior life but on the basis of the impressions of others – *Jacob's Room* documents the inaccessibility of "life itself," and does so because its subject is no impression-inspiring woman of genius.[24]

Before Woolf tries to pin the impression down and to undo its social difference, she makes it even more rangy and even more a matter of female abjection. We have seen her trying to put failure in positive terms; and we have seen how Woolf's feminism has clarified, in brief moments, the need for that failure and the kind of vision it might enable. The major turning point – in the process toward a phenomenological Impressionism, motivated by the feminism that would make Woolf critical of differences at once social and percep-tual – comes when Woolf finally makes explicit the connection between impressions and women's lives. Then, I will argue, Mrs.

Brown appears and disappears: she enables Woolf to see what has *prevented* positive confidence in the impression's mediation, and what would – beyond "failure," and beyond collaborations with the enabling materiality of others – make that mediation a matter of course.

It is worth tracing, now, the way in which feminism provoked Woolf to embody the impression in her relation to Mrs. Brown. That history shows that Woolf's impression and her feminism actually grew up together – both getting much inspiration from resentment toward Arnold Bennett.

The construction of Mrs. Brown began in 1910 – because such things as the Post-Impressionist Exhibition then began the "change" in "human character" that Woolf would use Mrs. Brown to represent, but also because the Exhibition prompted a provocative response from Arnold Bennett. Woolf's quarrel with Bennett began when he visited the Post-Impressionist Exhibition and wrote "Neo-Impressionism in Literature," a review-article which wonders what will do to literature what Cézanne and company had done to painting. These musings virtually invite the attack Woolf launches a few years later: "Supposing a young writer turned up and forced me, and some of my contemporaries – us who fancy ourselves a bit – to admit that we had been concerning ourselves unduly with inessentials, that we had been worrying ourselves to achieve infantile realisms? Well, that day would be a great and a disturbing day – for us."[25] Not only did Woolf soon bring the disturbing day; she even gave him a warning, in his own words, that she would. In 1917, she reviewed his *Books and Persons*, a collection of essays including his 1910 review-article, and lingered over his prediction: "These new pictures, he says, have wearied him of other pictures; is it not possible that some writer will come along and do in words what these men have done in paint? And suppose that happens, and Mr. Bennett has to admit that he has been concerning himself unduly with inessentials, that he has been worrying himself to achieve infantile realisms? He will admit it, we are sure . . ."[26] Bennett failed to "admit it," giving her fiction lukewarm reviews, and Woolf launched her attack. Her terms were his: in "Modern Novels" and "Mr. Bennett and Mrs. Brown" she faults Bennett and his contemporaries for their inessentials and realisms, and even lets Bennett choose the date (1910) on which he became obsolete. Moreover, she makes "Neo-Impressionism" the cause of his obsolescence, using the "impression" to describe modern fiction's turn from inessentials to a more mature realism.[27]

So Woolf may never have used the word "impression," or thought it capable of making details essential, had Bennett not suggested that such a change would compare to that in the world of painting. The connection is important for two reasons: it suggests the odd indirection of interart influence between the Impressionisms, and it is half of what motivates Woolf to attack Bennett's inessentials. The other half of this motivation came when Bennett later shifted his attention from difference between new writers and old to the difference between writers male and female.

Mrs. Brown may never have developed out of the moth and the mark if not for a little flurry of sexist publication that caught Woolf's indignant attention in the years from 1920 to 1922. Bennett published *Our Women* (1920), which celebrated female talent only within the bounds of the assertion that "intellectually and creatively man is the superior of woman." Desmond McCarthy, writing as "The Affable Hawk," gave Bennett's book a favorable review, agreeing that "no amount of education and liberty of action will sensibly alter" woman's inferiority, and that her "indisputable desire to be dominated" proves it.[28] Reading Bennett's book and its reviews led Woolf to consider "making up a paper upon Women, as a counterblast to Mr. Bennett's adverse views reported in the papers."[29] That paper would have to wait, but Woolf did immediately write a series of letters to the *New Statesman* published under the heading "The Intellectual Status of Women," offering Sappho as one example of female genius and blaming lack of education for the rarity of others. Bennett subsequently published a review of *Jacob's Room* (1922), entitled "Is the Novel Decaying?," which explicitly faults Woolf for the lifelessness of her characters and implicitly calls it proof of female literary inferiority.[30] Woolf responded in turn with the new and extended version of her "Modern Novels" argument, which, given the nature of its provocation, is really a feminist document. Not only did Woolf try to redefine the nature of literary "life"; she defined "life" in terms of a new feminine spirit. She developed, in other words, the argument not only that femininity did not prevent her from rendering life, but that it was somehow itself the location of the life that modernity now compelled artists to render.[31]

"Mr. Bennett and Mrs. Brown" argues that fiction has lost its "character-making power" because Bennett, whose novels are "soulless bodies," has no insight into what makes a woman like Mrs. Brown live. He mocks her up in houses but does not say what animates her so that when one "tries to search out her real meaning" she "crumbles" and her house "topples to the ground." And what emerges from the wreckage, when one tries to salvage her soul, is something very much like Woolf's "moth": "She becomes a will-o'-the-wisp, a dancing light, an illumination gliding up the wall and out of the window."[32] The "soulless body" becomes again that point of connection between the two (what were inside and out of the window in "The Death of the Moth"), and therefore a way to connect material substance to "real meaning." As before, the connection does not quite come off, because Woolf satisfies herself with the excitement of the "dancing" freedom that comes when conventions crumble: not now, but *"one of these days* Mrs. Brown will be caught," and "the capture of Mrs. Brown is the title of the *next* chapter in the history of literature" (388; emphasis added). But having given the moth a female body, in response to Bennett's sexism, Woolf comes much closer to saying how to catch "life itself." Having embodied the enabling juncture of materiality and essence in a female persona – aligning that mothlike mediation with the terms of women's lives – Woolf hits on a way of understanding just what such a juncture would require. She realizes what she has implied in prior texts and discovers the problem of Impressionism in reference to the feminization of character.

Before "Character in Fiction," Woolf attributed the inspiration for modern fiction mostly to the example of Russian fiction and to what Samuel Butler revealed about Victorian hypocrisy. Now, she condenses these and other explanations into the strong and famous claim that "on or about December 1910 human character changed."[33] Read repeatedly as a modernist slogan, this statement actually refers more specifically to a change in the way people think about women. Woolf's examples of the change define the emergence of a new human character as a new attitude about female literary characters: she points out that since 1910 when one reads the *Agamemnon* "your sympathies are . . . almost entirely with Clytemnestra," and that in considering "the married life of the Carlyles" one's sympathies make one regret "the horrible domestic tradition which made it seemly for a woman of genius to spend her time chasing beetles, scouring saucepans, instead of writing books" (422). What happened around 1910, then, was that "human" character began to take a *woman's* part. It became newly possible to see beyond archetypal roles to "character itself," and to find that "character itself" is of a nature formerly derogated to femininity.

For the same reason that one sympathizes with Clytemnestra and Mrs. Carlyle, Woolf sympathizes with Mrs. Brown: she suffers as a result of the domination of male interests, and when you take her part she endorses a revolutionary structure of perception. In the case of Mrs. Carlyle, the "domestic tradition" limited a "woman of genius" to horrible material pursuits; in the case of Mrs. Brown, restrictedness similarly features forth genius, albeit genius of another kind – the genius of strong feelings that reflect material conditions but dramatize their essential implications. Discovering in Mrs. Brown this means to be certain to marry details and insight, Woolf discovers what many feminists have currently been telling us about Modernism more generally: that the nature of women's experience gave them a superior claim to modernist insight. As a host of critics have noted, what were formerly liabilities became strengths when Modernism revamped the terms of literary genius; liabilities such as emotionality, irrationality, and proximity to private experience made women seem more likely to produce or at least to inspire the immediate, inchoate, and interior modes of writing that modernists came to value.[34] Just as this critical view has revised the genealogy of Modernism, Woolf sought to revise the Materialist theory of character, to suggest that subordination and suffering could make women the model for characterization most likely to get at "character in itself." Unencumbered by the trappings of a public role (more simply existent, like her predecessor the moth) and intensely emotional (featuring her interiority much like the moth as well), Mrs. Brown helps Woolf defy obstacles and take a phenomenological view. When Woolf does, and when she implies that the impression that happens as a result can be at once contingent on the details of Mrs. Brown's experience and yet revelatory of the state of her soul, she marks 1910 as the date of a momentous convergence, in Impressionism, of feminism, phenomenology, and fiction.[35]

To claim this convergence, Woolf tries to describe the process whereby a writer renders impressions. We get, finally, in the climactic moment of "Character in Fiction," the Impressionist moment. Now with her exemplary character in front of her, Woolf can say what Bennett does wrong. So she gives the material details Bennett would give, and, proving that they only keep her from having to "account" for Mrs. Brown, makes the phenomenological change in orientation: "but details could wait. The important thing was to steep oneself in her atmosphere" (425). Then comes the impression: "The impression she made was overwhelming. It came pouring out like a draught, like a smell of burning. What was it composed of – that overwhelming and peculiar impression?" To some degree the answer to the question – and not just the question about *this* impression – is implied in its terms. Like a draught of air, the impression is an atmosphere the two women share – Mrs. Brown's pain felt as Mrs. Woolf's "pity." Like a "smell," it is an effect produced in the perception of it, but yet with a source – the word "smell" imitating the grammatical ambiguity whereby the impression is at once process and object. And since the smell "overwhelms" it disrupts the habits of perception which might emphasize the process at the expense of the object. Even as it overwhelms consciousness and produces that excess there, it is "peculiar" to its source, with the result that it runs the full range from experiential specificity to fully occupied consciousness. The result, in other words, is perfect and full representational continuity – or, in Woolf's words, an example of "character imposing itself on another person . . . making someone begin almost automatically to write a novel about her" (425). As a source and effect of automatic writing, the impression closes the gap between life and art.

This at any rate is implied in the language that describes the impression's "composition" – composition being, again, a word that emphasizes the immediate relation between the impression's make-up and writing. But saying that the impression makes one automatic-ally *begin* to write, Woolf injects some doubt about that relation, and indeed then goes on to revert back to her negative emphasis on the successes of failure: "The incident had made a great impression on me. But how was I to transmit it to you? All I could do was to report as accurately as I could what was said, to describe in detail what was worn, to say, despairingly, that all sorts of scenes rushed into my mind, to proceed to tumble them out pell-mell, and to describe this vivid, overmastering impression by likening it to a draught or a smell of burning" (431). Here again is the free play that has characterized the last moment of the Impressionist process; and here again is "despair," ironized by implicit confidence that the tumbling of the mind is itself the ecstacy of meaning. Here, however, the combination of failure and success enters a different theoretical realm, for it has been attributed to female abjection. That attribution makes a crucial difference: on the one hand, Woolf now admits that free play will not suffice: "I should have had to go back and back and back . . . referring each word to my vision, matching it as exactly as possible" (432). Binding literary work is necessary after all; and, moreover, there is the need to subvert convention not simply by leaving it behind but by "going back" to some moment when word and vision matched.

The wish to return to some primordial moment prior to the unmatching of word and vision, and to do so through reference to womanhood, is basic to modernist aesthetic theory and practice. Putting this wish in feminist terms, however, Woolf runs up against a problem in feminism which Diana Fuss and Peggy Kamuf describe as the "risk of essence": she risks attributing the phenomenological turn to something essential to womanhood, and thereby restricting womanhood even as she makes it a focus for Impressionist innovation.[36] Suggesting that female "character in itself" might return consciousness to the possibility of a visionary language, Woolf flirts with essentialism, and indeed such essentialism seems to pervade her writing. Makiko Minow-Pinkney has claimed that Woolf's feminist aesthetic tries for contact with what Julia Kristeva calls the *semiotic*, to "disperse the transcendental unified subject that underpins male rationality and narrative" and "to adumbrate the area anterior to the logical, judging, naming subjectivity, to bring in the semiotic."[37] Minow-Pinkney thinks that Woolf brings in the semiotic through reference to a female standpoint, since, according to Woolf and Kristeva alike, women have likelier access to "the world beneath consciousness; the anonymous world to which we can still return . . . which still exists in us, deep sunk, savage, primitive, remembered."[38] Like Kristeva, Woolf endorses "going back," via female semiosis, against phallocentric symbolic restrictions, to a "pre-thetic" stage in which phenomenological syntheses never came undone.[39]

Once drawn, the connection between Woolfian and Kristevan phenomenologies and their essentialisms seems to reveal Mrs. Brown's presence throughout Woolf's work: she then appears again in the "vatic charwomen" who, according to Jane Marcus, have a mute visionary status; and she appears in Sally Seton, in Jinny, in Mrs. Ramsay, and other women through whom Woolf's female characters seem to "[search] for the female *logos* . . . tunneling back to the obscure origins of the female aesthetic."[40] But as soon as we find Mrs. Brown's "essence" in these other women, we see that her essentialism is one Woolf could not long like: for these characters promise essential insight only by humbling the more real women who regard them, and those more real women only thrive insofar as they cease to take the "risk of essence."

Rather than feminist essentialism, Mrs. Brown presents the dilemma of feminist epistemology – specifically, feminist epistemology's question about the perceptual uses of marginality. Whereas essentialist feminism believes that the female perspective confers epistemic privilege, feminist epistemology vacillates between that belief and the belief that such privilege ought only to be a stage on the way to the development of "strong objectivity." Marginality, in other words, may itself be a perceptual advantage, insofar as it lacks the false habitual presumptions of "objectivity"; or, it may better be a procedural position through which the epistemologist "shears away" false objectivity on the way to true – not itself a position to celebrate or perpetuate, but one from which to learn and to depart. We have seen how the theories of "standpoint feminism" complicate interpretation of Henry James's use for the "woman of genius." Here again they come into play, to suggest that Woolf's use for Mrs. Brown vacillates between a kind of primitivist essentialism and an orientation that would make reflection upon essentialism a means to improvements at once aesthetic and social.

"Strong objectivity" is Sandra Harding's term for the outermost goal of feminist philosophy. Harding argues that standpoint philosophy must locate itself between positivist objectivity and the relativisms of subjective strains of philosophical and social thought: neither the local, relative, personal knowledge of the marginal subject nor the general, universal, positive knowledge of science will do; rather, they must combine into a procedure, in which inquiry *begins* with marginalized perspective and reaches toward an objectivity that will therefore pass beyond limited objective standards. Harding advocates "starting off thought" in the marginal mode, using it to shear away the false presumptions of objectivity, and innovating an objectivity that has the advantage of variable perspective: "marginal lives ground epistemology for standpoint epistemologies," but they do not encompass it, for such lives survive into the strong-objective position as that which makes objectivity truly impartial.[41]

But not everyone shares Harding's view – and indeed the point of her argument is to reveal the ambivalence, in feminist epistemology, between the quest for strong objectivity and the interest in marginal perspectives as such. It is this ambivalence that we find in the construction of Mrs. Brown, for Mrs. Brown may be either the marginal life that embodies life itself, or the marginality through which the narratorial consciousness develops its strong objectivity. These options correspond to those of Impressionism: Impressionism similarly presents itself to its practitioners either as a subjective mode that guarantees perspectival, experiential truth, or as a mode of better objectivity. The former is the more limited mode, the latter the more compelling, and to get from the former to the latter Woolf has to make decisions about womanhood. She remains in obscure free play among possibilities as long as she does not; but when she does – when she values the marginal life not for itself but for the way it grounds strong objectivity – her Impressionism reaches a rare positive affirmation.

That affirmation comes whenever a female narrator like that of "Character in Fiction" deconstructs figures like Mrs. Brown. As we will see, it comes when Clarissa Dalloway thinks about the inspiring feminine example of Sally Seton, but then transforms Sally into a ground for a strong perceptual unity of her own. *Mrs. Dalloway* picks up where "Character in Fiction" leaves off in that it extends the parallel developments of Mrs. Brown and Woolf's Impressionism: a theoretical process that began in the celebration of critical failure in "Modern Novels," found points for critical inquiry in the "mark" and the "moth," gained impetus through feminism and then embodied itself in Mrs. Brown, reaches an apotheosis when it is embodied and then revised in Clarissa's relation to Sally Seton. In the outcome of that relation, Woolf thematizes that to which Impressionism and feminism at once aspire: a total perceptivity.

Once achieved, that total perceptivity becomes a recurrent theme, common to three very different structures in Woolf's most important work. The epiphany that allows Lily Briscoe to finish her painting, the turn to androgyny at the end of *A Room of One's Own*, and the perspectival structure of *The Waves* are all results of the deconstruction of Mrs. Brown – the first dramatizing the great aesthetic benefit of moving past essentialist collaboration with womanhood, the second likewise undoing the link between woman's abjection and aesthetic advantage, and the last arriving at the "strong objectivity" that comes when marginal perspectives are a means rather than an end in themselves. Insofar as these three results bring Woolf's impression to unprecedented theoretical viability, they show how persistent inquiry into the social terms of perceptual totality transform those terms from unconscious liability to aesthetic advantage.

Why, then, would such mediation continue to devolve for Woolf into distressing differences between ways of perceiving? Why would she continue to doubt junctures of "fact" and "vision" – and indeed why would the 1930s find her dividing them again? The answers to these questions bring us finally to the problem of class. As a woman, Mrs. Brown leads Woolf from impressions to new dualities to better mediations; as a member of a lower class, however, she stalls this very process, making Woolf recognize and even reaffirm, for better or for worse, the necessary linkage of perception and difference.

For if, as a woman, Mrs. Brown reflects the process through which Woolf's feminism prompted her towards a phenomenological synthesis, as a member of the lower class she reflects a very different sequence of events. In this other sequence Woolf acts not from the subaltern position of womanhood, but from the superior position of the upper-middle class; and she acts not to make gains for a marginalized group, but to protect art from "middlebrow" incursion. The critical tradition has noted that the "whole contention between Mr. Bennett and Mrs. Woolf" can be read in these two ways – Samuel Hynes emphasizing class conflict (Woolf's disdain for the lower-middle-class subject-matter of the Bennett novel) and Beth Rigel Daugherty emphasizing conflict between the sexes (Woolf's outrage over Bennett's condescension toward women writers).[42] If we look at things now from Hynes's point of view, we can see that the impression is not only an aspect of feminist phenomenology, but an aspect of the "highbrow" distinction.

One peculiar result of the impression is the way it mystifies the act of writing. To say that "a novel is an impression" is to leave writers with no clear sense of how to write, since impressions are by definition indefinite. It seems likely that this mystifying tendency attracted writers who, like Woolf and James before her, wanted to oppose the codification of "rules" for fiction-writing. Just as James had resisted Walter Besant's effort to define the novel as a result of direct experience by rendering experience impressionistically free, Woolf tried to resist Bennett's effort to say exactly how to conceive, write, market, and appreciate fiction. Bennett's effort in this regard was extensive: in such books as *How to Become an Author: A Practical Guide* (1903) and *Literary Taste: How to Form It* (1909), Bennett laid out the steps, from learning to spell to earning upwards of five hundred a year even as a "sagacious mediocrity" to how to get hold of literature "as a dog gets hold of a bone."[43] To no small extent, invoking impressions was a way to muddy just such steps. And that obfuscation could take different forms: it could be part of an effort, in the spirit of the sort of distinction-making Pierre Bourdieu has described, to defeat the aspirations of the "professional" writer; or it could be part of an authentic effort to distinguish art from craft. Of course in Woolf's case it was both, and the mix of authentic and reactionary tendencies makes it hard to characterize the politics of Impressionism.

Woolf would have been the first to admit that "being a snob" determined her tastes and judgments. In one essay devoted to the subject, we see how these tendencies could conform to the structure of collaboration. "Middlebrow" is Woolf's response to a reviewer who has called her a "highbrow." It embraces the distinction, and defines a "highbrow" as "a man or woman of thoroughbred intelligence who rides his mind at a gallop across country in pursuit of an idea."[44] But Woolf then denies what one might expect – that highbrows find lowbrows repulsive. On the contrary, she writes, "they honour so wholeheartedly and depend so completely upon those who are called lowbrows" (178). As the "man or woman of thoroughbred vitality who rides his body in pursuit of a living at a gallop across life," the lowbrow is the highbrow's natural and necessary complement. A highbrow like Woolf needs the lowbrow because "I cannot do things myself." She herself cannot "live," and needs the lowbrow to gain vitality; lowbrows, inversely, cannot "see themselves," and need highbrows to "show" them what their lives mean. There is, in other words, collaboration here between the high and the low, and if anyone is repulsive it is the "middlebrow," the "bloodless and pernicious pest who comes between" (184). The middlebrow, of course, sounds just like Bennett, all concerned with material distinctions and the art of show. To the extent that "Materialism" is "middlebrow," it is opposed by Woolf both by the impression's collaborative mediation and by the impression's resistance to those tastes and judgments through which "middlebrow" makes a profession of the art of writing.

In this sense, then, Woolf's collaboration with Mrs. Brown is a highbrow–lowbrow interdependence, which aims to scoop the middlebrow by excluding it and its mediations from social and aesthetic authenticity. To leave it at that, however, is to miss the irony of "Middlebrow" and those other essays ("Am I a Snob?," "Royalty") in which Woolf admits to her respect for social distinctions. In these essays, Woolf uses the fact of her respect for social distinctions as an occasion for playful thought experiments not unlike that of "Modern Novels": distinctions become hurdles over which the active mind (high or low) leaps into liveliness. "Middlebrow," for example, initially distinguishes clearly between upper, middle, and lower classes, but quickly concerns itself more with the subtler things that distinguish people by temperament and mettle. Caught up in subtleties, the essay renders distinctions absurd, and concludes in Woolf's typical affirmation of the free mind. If we treat "Character in Fiction" as another such experiment, we see that the construction of Mrs. Brown is as much an effort to play distinctions out of existence as an effort to construct a highbrow–lowbrow collaboration.

Impressions may be part of what Mary Childers calls Woolf's "advocacy of certain forms of consciousness that are largely dependent on ample access to leisure time," and other high distinctions, but they also undo distinctions; as much as they mystify, they blend, and the result is a strange effect upon the distinctions apparently necessary to their very theorization.[45] For it is not quite true that Mrs. Brown is of a lower class: sometimes she is, but sometimes her class is not given, depending on the version of the essay.[46] Sometimes Mrs. Brown appears in poverty, sometimes as the descendant of gentlefolk, and sometimes and most tellingly both. What we first learn about Mrs. Brown is that "She was one of those clean, threadbare old ladies whose extreme tidiness – everything buttoned, fastened, tied together, mended and brushed up – suggests more extreme poverty than rags and dirt."[47] But then again she "came of gentlefolks who kept servants" ("my grandmother had a maid," she timidly boasts), and she even seems to have some property (which dire straits now force her to give up) (423–25). The property seems to be that of a middle-class "seaside house," but one which "queer ornaments" mark as low to middle. In such diverse class characterization Woolf takes pains to stress ambiguity; moreover, these diverse characterizations are only those of one version of the essay: other versions leave out one fact or another, so that the overall impression is one that blurs class distinctions. And this seems to be the point:

whereas a materialist realism could only represent class in terms of the details that would fix it for certain, Woolf's alternative would let in the ambiguities that would prove class indeterminate and therefore subject to change. The indeterminacy is important here for the way it conflicts with the structure that makes Mrs. Brown appear in the first place: on the one hand there is the need for difference, which enables Woolf to imagine collaboration of the experiential and the essential; on the other hand, there is the preference for indeterminacy, which would replace rigid materialist detail with the fluidity of the essential variety of any real person's class affiliation.

Woolf sums up this conflict nicely in a diary entry for July 31, 1926. She writes of seeing "Two resolute, sunburnt, dusty girls, in jerseys and short skirts, with packs on their backs, city clerks, or secretaries, tramping along the road in the hot sunshine at Ripe."[48] In her response to them, Woolf recognizes the value both of dissolution and division:

My instinct at once throws up a screen, which condemns them . . . But all this is a great mistake. These screens shut me out. Have no screens, for screens are made out of our own integument; and get at the thing itself, which has nothing whatever in common with a screen. The screen making habit, though, is so universal, that probably it preserves our sanity. If we had not this device for shutting people off from our sympathies, we might, perhaps, dissolve utterly. Separateness would be impossible. But the screens are in the excess; not the sympathy.

The "screens" of class instinct are figured here as a bad physical barrier – a husk of materiality that makes the subjective merely solipsistic. They block essence, or the "thing in itself," from the outset, and in saying so Woolf recognizes that class distinction disallows perceptual unity. But then again, screens prevent our utter dissolution: here is Impressionist anxiety about the undoing of distinction, and the wish to preserve it at the social level so as to stay alive. To the degree that Woolf prefers the "thing in itself" to the "screen," her Impressionism would undo class distinction along with the perceptual distinctions that make essence inconceivable; but to the degree that she recognizes the value of screens, she admits that to do away with *all* distinctions is insane, and that to commit fully to Impressionism is to risk doing without the "separateness" that may in fact be perception's basic precondition.

The ambivalence here therefore gives us, in Mrs. Brown, both the derealization of social class "integument" and a distinct separation between classes of perception. Because "the screens are in excess; not the sympathy," the essays in which Mrs. Brown appears tend toward greater and greater derealization, but they never do without the social difference that enables Woolf to imagine her highbrow idealism grounded in and yet distinct from a lower materiality. And whereas texts that follow those in which Mrs. Brown appears deconstruct her in one sense – deconstruct, that is, her *feminine* difference – they do not deconstruct what distinguishes her by class. Woolf's Impressionism yet maintains that consolatory difference, retaining "separateness," as we shall see, in Clarissa Dalloway's relation to Septimus Smith. *Mrs. Dalloway* may mark the turning point that leads to an apotheosis of Impressionist theory in *The Waves*; but it also dramatizes the persistence of the perceptual habits that would yet call upon difference and keep even Woolf from pursuing "life itself" into its full range of reaches.

CHAPTER 6

Three Impressionist allegories

Allegory deconstructs the "symbol." So said Walter Benjamin, and others since, in order to redeem allegory. Coleridge had thought allegory excessively deliberate, inartistic, and rational, far beneath the symbolic mode, which could suggest truth and model transcendent experience. Symbols gave meaning immediately, at all levels; allegory trotted out its emblems over a length of time, and in narrow improvisations, that made art just an "exercise of subliterary fancies."[1] For Benjamin, however, the symbol's unity was false. In *The Origins of German Tragic Drama*, he argues that the symbol's "momentary totality" has nothing true to reveal about human thought or human experience. Symbolic representation pretends to unify the immanent and the transcendent because it cannot face the tension between the two. Allegory makes that tension the route to truth. Allegory extinguishes the symbol's "false appearance of totality"; and it takes the ruined symbol, the fragmented emblem uprooted from the concrete, and makes its "deadness" a ground for truly "pure curiosity."[2] As Bernard Cowan puts it, "In becoming a world of allegorical emblems, the profane world is robbed of its sensuous fulness, robbed of any inherent meaning it might possess."[3] What bothered Coleridge about allegory – its dry and formulaic lifelessness – becomes for Benjamin its advantage, for it is by featuring the falseness of any higher truth that allegory becomes not just some "playful illustrative technique" but the characteristically modern experiential mode.[4]

Allegory's ruins, incisive in the Baroque, virtually constitute modernity, so that Benjamin can appreciate Baudelaire's fragmentary symbols for their oneness with modern discontinuity, and so that Paul de Man can write that "the prevalence of allegory always corresponds to the unveiling of an authentically temporal destiny."[5] For de Man, allegory designates a distance from origins and,

renouncing hope for proximity, bases itself in the very movement
that is temporality. It thematizes the difference that time establishes
as life's painful precondition; it reflects the *dedoublement* through
which consciousness disjoins itself into activity; and it makes narrative the language aware of inauthenticity. Allegory thus leads with de
Man to the broken unity that narrates even the truth about language
– the ironic truth that perpetually debunks the "tenacious self-
mystification" of integral meaning.[6]

My reason for tracing this tradition ought to be half clear. If
allegory follows demystification of perceptual unity, it makes sense to
use allegory to refer to those fictions that indirectly narrate the
redivision of Impressionist synthesis. The use of the term, that is,
may be justified by the connection Benjamin and de Man see
between epistemological dissociation and allegorical narrative. But
then again, is there such justification if allegory proceeds in these
accounts from the broken *symbol*? Does the impression resemble the
symbol sufficiently to give "allegory" this special meaning here?

The standard definition of the impression would suggest that it
does not. If impressions are simply sensational perceptions, as they
seem to be in most accounts, then impressions would be nothing
other than an aspect of the "tenacious self-mystification" through
which we dream of coincidence with substance, rather than something that might break and pitch us into the better knowledge of our
inauthenticity. But if impressions in fact share the symbol's fantasy of
mediation, then they, too, might relate necessarily to the allegorical
mode. In at least one influential account, Symbolism and Impressionism do have matching tendencies: Ian Watt has argued that
Symbolism and Impressionism do the same thing in different directions – that Symbolism aims to manifest the ideal in the real, where
Impressionism aims to derive ideal meaning from real objects and
sensations.[7] If we extend Watt's claim to define the nature of the
impression, and to say that it is the impression itself that reverses the
symbol's unifying tendency, then we might develop a sense of
allegory parallel to that which derives from the broken symbol. We
might, that is, say that allegory debunks the impression much the
way it debunks the symbol, replacing a dream of "momentary
totality" with a reality of ever-unfolding alienation. The only
difference, perhaps, between the allegories that follow upon symbol
and impression might be the difference directionality makes. If it is
true that impressions try for totality in the "opposite direction," then

Impressionist allegory does not have to use its deadening energies to refute a false notion of immediacy. As I have been trying to define it, the impression, which seems to sensualize literary representation, in fact moves it further in the direction of abstractional imagination. It moves, in other words, in the direction that allegory would move the symbol – toward "pure curiosity," to use Benjamin's phrase, and away from curiosity's allegedly concrete stimulation. Impressionist allegory then would not quite share the deadness of post-symbolic allegory. Since the impression does not share the symbol's pretension to incarnate the ideal, the allegory that follows upon its particular pretense introduces a more dialectically diverse mode of curtailment.

When Pater, Conrad, and Woolf propose the impression to unify perception, the unlikeliness of such unification pushes them almost immediately into an allegorical mode. Where the impression's unification ought to enable them simply to describe or enact the production of felt ideas (for Pater), of sense-based solidarity or vital essentials (for Conrad and Woolf respectively), the fact that unification conflicts too strongly with social and epistemological standards produces an impression that is, even almost from the outset, "broken." Allegory asserts itself and turns the impression's unity into a story about difference. So Pater presents his felt ideas as things enabled by *paederastia*; so Conrad has his distant laborer manifest the physicality he ought to own himself, and Woolf grounds essences that ought to be no different from their ground in another woman's vitality. Allegory begins here, and then more fully unfolds in texts in which stories about difference can go into far greater detail.

But whereas post-symbolic allegory would make these details refute the theory, the kind of allegory that begins in Impressionist collaboration has a form to match the greater indeterminacy of the impression's unity. So ambiguously located between sensation and idea, or existence and essence, the impression breaks into pieces that always propose different challenges to unity. So the form of the Impressionist allegory is erratic, and dialectically motivated, hitting at different moments on different reconfigurations. What ultimately blocks unity is a difference that presents itself as social. Post-symbolic allegory denies unity in the deadness of its emblems; the allegory that denies the unity of the impression does so by asserting, in spite of various bids for integration, social specificities that show difference to be anterior to any oneness the Impressionist can propose.

What this means will become clearer as we see it in three

Impressionist allegories. In *Marius the Epicurean*, *Heart of Darkness*, and *Mrs. Dalloway*, impressions become a matter of extensive speculation. This speculation happens on the pattern set by Impressionist collaboration: it leads Pater through various enactments of the way same-sex desire might inspire credible mind–body unities; it leads Conrad to make the exposure of Imperialist horror a sorting through ever more horrible relations between distant labor and shared ideas; and it leads Woolf to see how correlating one's existence to some essential meaning is never permanently possible, but always a trick of social difference. In each case, the theory of impressions becomes less certain but more thorough – less able to believe in unity, and more able to see how and at what cost it becomes temporarily, provisionally, or artificially possible. Each Impressionist finally makes a discovery analogous to that of the post-symbolic allegorist: where the post-symbolic allegorist discovers (if we combine what de Man and Benjamin say) authentic difference and purely human thought, the Impressionist allegorist discovers that some irreducible social distinction perpetually foils the impression, and that human thought thereby advances in ironic or alienated wisdom.

To say, then, that Impressionist writers allegorize the problem of the impression is to say more than that they continue their essays into their fiction. It is to say that there is something necessarily allegorical about Impressionist uncertainty, and that the impression's ambiguity is the engine of a certain narrative drive. To say that Impressionist fiction is necessarily allegorical is also to answer those who might complain that these particular fictions have already had their allegories too much gone over – that the hidden meanings in *Marius the Epicurean*, *Heart of Darkness*, and *Mrs. Dalloway* have been brought to light in pages upon pages of criticism. The Impressionist allegory may be the fundamental one: enacting different fundamental structures of perception, the thread spun out from the impression might be that upon which all other stories hang, in these novels and in the mode of Modernism that equates renewal with new perceptual possibility.

I MARIUS THE EPICUREAN

Pater begins with a combination of erotic longing and aesthetic discontent. They meet in the impression, where the problem of *aesthesis* is solved by desire. Sensuous intensity comes to the intellectual thinker, and subjective feelings gain credibility, as the desire that enlivens the subject is attributed to its object. Pater begins here, but then finds the closed circle of aesthetics and desire broken open in two ways: on his end, desire also alienates what it brings to the intellectual thinker, for its object differs in kind; and in his culture, specifically homosexual desire troubles institutions of intellectual thought, so that his new aesthetic ground is upheaved in scandal. His own doubts demand some way to be sure that the impression is more than amorous passion, and the doubts of others demand passion's retraction. So Pater revises and retracts – and desire gives way to other forces of union.

Everyone interested in Pater has tried to explain why he suppressed and rewrote the Conclusion to *The Renaissance*.[8] Some say the Oxford establishment demanded it; some say Pater felt that his ardent followers had misunderstood him, and that he needed to distinguish his theory from the erotic hedonism for which so many mistook it. Some say that *Marius the Epicurean* is a retraction, motivated by fear, or internalized disapproval; some say that it is a reappraisal, motivated by legitimate intellectual second thoughts. But legitimate intellectual second thoughts and fearful desexualizing coincide here: like the erotic aesthetic to which it responds, *Marius the Epicurean* unifies opposite motivations.

The novel reasserts *The Renaissance* with the peculiar retractive force of allegory. It dwells again on the problem of mediating human faculties, but recasts that problem now as one of an *education* that happens over time. Whereas *The Renaissance* had recommended Impressionism more or less right away, *Marius* suggests that its synthesis is the product only of a career of trying. This does not mean that it takes a lifetime to achieve the proper intellectual development of sensuous nature, but that it takes a lifetime dialectically to test different possible ways of combining sensations and ideas. Marius tests the *paiderastic* model; Marius tests Stoicism, Skepticism, Euphuism, and New Cyrenaicism; the novel becomes a rhetoric of Impressionist syntheses, at key switching points dropping such paradoxes as "material essence," "anti-metaphysical metaphysic," and "unconfused sensation" (as well as "materialist devotee," "medical dreams," and "vigorous ennui"); and when Marius finally comes to the best sort of mediation, Pater has achieved an ingenious retractive reassertion. For he has shown that the impression's synthesis corresponds to many of the best "theories of practice" Western thought has to offer; he has shown that Impressionism is no superficial hedonism, but a course of rigorous education; and he equates it, finally, with Christian sympathy. That is the state in which Marius ends up, in Impressionism's final *ascêsis*, as if to prove to Pater's critics and to himself that what begins as homoeroticism can very well end in grace.

From the outset, Marius's impressions make him more than an Epicurean but less than an idealist. Remarkable for his sensuous "susceptibility," his "exquisite personal alacrity," he is also remarkable for his "almost morbid religious idealism," and tendency to "[construct] the world for himself in great measure from within."[9] In what follows, these conflicting tendencies will have to resolve. And early on Marius gets intimations of such resolution, in the provocative mystery of perceptions that mix modes: ". . . some very lively surmises, though scarcely distinct enough to be thoughts, were moving backwards and forwards in his mind, as the stirring wind had done all day among the trees, and were like the passing of some mysterious influence over all the elements of his nature and experience" (I, 9). Surmises, like impressions, are less than thoughts, and important for their stirring movement. This movement draws Marius onward, always through dialectical reverses and collapses. Every mode he takes on implicates its opposite, as when his initial "subjective philosophy" proves not indulgent but a kind "abstinence, strenuous self-control and *ascêsis*," and as when his Epicureanism entails a system in which "the body [became] . . . but a quiet handmaid of the soul" (25, 28). Oppositions collapse, just as "susceptibility" and "idealism" combine in "surmises," and the mystery of the consequent combination stirs Marius's allegorical development.

The sheer variety of potential combinations answers Pater's critics: the collapse of thought and sense (and their analogs) is multiform and inevitable, and youth will go astray if unprepared for it. Whereas Pater's critics thought his programme likely to "mislead young men," Pater now proves that young men begin unbalanced, and have the best chance precisely when, like Marius, they are prone to "surmises." Impressions, in other words, do not entail decadent sensuality, but the "mysterious influence" of dialectical perception. Their influence is at work when the death of Marius's mother "turned seriousness of feeling into a matter of the intelligence" and "made him a questioner" (43). It is at work when "mere bodily health" operates "as an influence morally salutary" by "counteracting the less desirable or hazardous tendencies of some phases of thought" (41). In both of these cases, albeit in opposite ways, provisional perceptual combinations work correctively, and in turn become subject to new combination. Such crossing and recrossing of faculties is confusing; it makes Marius as uncertain as ardent; but in it Pater argues persuasively that the impression's indeterminacy motivates the best *Bildung.*

And he persuasively argues, in the first important stage of Marius's development, that Impressionism is not simply "aestheticism." When at first Marius is one "who must be made perfect by the love of physical beauty" (32), the vitality he craves seems to come, as it does for Pater in "Diaphaneitè," from attention to the beauty of young men. He is often a "spectator" who reaches temporary perfections by watching the "limited boyish race" before him (46). One particular boy embodies aesthetic perfection: Flavian, who "seemed to have a natural alliance with, and claim upon, everything else which was physically select and bright" (51). Another version of Pater's diaphanous ideal, Flavian has that power "to be forcibly impressed" and therefore justifies a theory that sounds very much like that of the Conclusion to *The Renaissance.* His "theory of Euphuism" devotes Flavian to a "hard-set determination, defiant of pain, to arrest this or that little drop at least from the river of sensuous imagery rushing so quickly past him" (117). Revisiting Impressionism in this fashion, Pater does two things – performing what becomes the novel's characteristic double gesture. On the one hand, he makes Impressionism sound better than it did before, for now it has "this uncompromising demand for a matter, in all art, derived immediately from personal intuition" which "saved [it], even at its weakest, from lapsing into mere artifice" (103). It is, in other words, an Impressionism which does not compromise or lapse from rigor. But on the other hand this new justification does not make this version of Impressionism something permanent. It is better than it was, but Marius is better than it: Flavian dies, taking Euphuism with him, and grief toughens Marius, pushing his Impressionism into new dialectical developments. Grief activates a "genuine virility," which entails an "instinctive recognition" of the importance of "vigorous intelligence" (124). The death of Flavian purges Impressionism of excess sensuality, but not with the effect of purging Marius of any commitment to Impressionist synthesis. Rather, it simply extends the range of that synthesis, further into "intelligence." In similar fashion, Impressionism becomes both less and more homoerotic. With Flavian dies Impressionism's effeminacy, and its interest in the diaphanous ideal, but as we will see its new virilization in fact simply relocates the stimulus of homosexual desire.

With each new system Marius encounters, Pater continues to prove that Impressionism is at once more respectable and more inventive than it has seemed. Anyone critical of his skepticism, for example, would find it not only as well established as Heraclitus, but Heraclitus rigorously reconsidered. Marius, it turns out, shares with Heraclitus a skepticism that is but "the preliminary step towards a large positive system of almost religious philosophy" (130). No more threatening than an age-old physics, Pater's skepticism now also appears as an initial stage of careful piety, something misunderstood because taken out of context. "But it happened, that, of all this, the first, merely sceptical or negative step, that easiest step on the threshold, had alone remained in general memory": as the "sophist" Protagoras had misrepresented Heraclitus, so had critics misrepresented Pater, making him, too, "but an authority for a philosophy of the despair of knowledge" (132). And yet if those who attacked Pater's skepticism found reassurance in this likeness to Heraclitus, they missed the new paganism in another. For Pater not only denies that his Heraclitan flux of things and souls is ground for "the despair of knowledge"; he asserts its better unity of reason and sense. It means that the "ordinances of divine reason" are "maintained throughout the changes of the phenomenal world," so that even as Pater sanitizes his skepticism he makes new gains for the impression's mediation, which now extends from phenomenal flux to supreme intellect.

In this and other similar retoolings of the Impressionist synthesis, Pater develops a wonderfully perfect dialectic. Marius moves perpetually between the claims of the senses and the claims of reason. With each potential configuration of the two, Pater proves both the conventionality and the daring of the combination. Moreover, the two grow ever closer together – each "materialism" more ideal than the last, each "idealism" more grounded, until Pater has perfected the impression's mediation. But then again at the same time each becomes more fully itself – more firmly grounded in sense or more intellectual – so that the mediatory impression also makes the broadest claim to totality. Marius gains focus as his impressions broaden, perfecting knowledge in his story's wake.

The next step in this dialectic, after Marius matures beyond "Euphuism," is "New Cyrenaicism." Like the former, New Cyrenaicism at first sounds like the misunderstood Impressionism of *The Renaissance*: "given, that we are never to get beyond the walls of the closely shut cell of one's own personality . . . then, he, at least, in whom those fleeting impressions – faces, voices, material sunshine – were very real and imperious, might well set himself to the consideration, how such moments as they passed might be made to yield their utmost, by the most dextrous training of capacity" (146). This last phrase, however, indicates an important change. Unable to decide, before, if making impressions yield their utmost was a natural or educated capacity, here Pater comes down on the side of training. And whereas before indecision meant "effeminate" collaboration, "dextrous training" is decidedly manly: "All this would involve a life of industry, of industrious study, only possible through healthy rule . . . for the male element, the logical conscience asserted itself now, with opening of manhood" (156). Virile, industrious, healthy – neither *paiderastic* nor lax nor decadent – this new version of Impressionism corrects *The Renaissance* to the extent that Pater can write "not pleasure, but a general completeness of life" is its goal, and that while "this 'aesthetic' philosophy" may seem to go "against . . . the received morality," it could not be charged with " 'hedonism' and its supposed consequences" (149–50). As before, Impressionism absorbs its antithesis.[10]

And as before it becomes secretly more scandalous in the process. Marius may be more ascetic, but, as Harold Bloom points out, there is an etymological affinity between *ascêsis* and athleticism. "A hedonistic *askesis* is only superficially a paradox" – and a virile Impressionism is only superficially "pure."[11] Homoeroticism returns to Marius's theoretical life even *because* the male element has reasserted itself there. Just as Flavian had represented Euphuism, and just as Shadwell modeled receptivity for Pater himself, New Cyrenaicism has its beautiful male inspiration: Cornelius represents Marius's "own Cyrenaic philosophy, presented thus, for the first time, in the image or person, with much attractiveness . . . a concrete image . . . Meantime, the discretion of Cornelius, his energetic cleverness and purity, were a charm, rather physical than moral: his exquisite correctness of spirit, at all events, accorded so perfectly with the regular beauty of his person, so as to seem to depend upon it" (234). The erotic synecdoche intervenes once again even as Pater apparently retracts "effeminacy" and asserts the male element in its place. What has changed, in effect, is only the meaning of muscularity – from expansive vitality to dextrous rigor.

Impressionism therefore does not give up on the homoerotic. Nor does it rest with its more industrious form: having absorbed its antithesis, it renews its dialectic. New Cyrenaicism may mean that "the beauty of the physical world strikes potently upon . . . wide-open, unwearied senses" with the result of "raising . . . life to the level of a daring theory," but the sense/theory combination proves unbalanced (II, 16). It yet remains to be perfected, now by the stoicism of Marcus Aurelius. Even despite the strenuousness of his Cyrenaic passions Marius begins to feel the need "beyond all others, an inward need of something permanent in its character, to hold by" (18). He finds in stoicism a "duly prescribed corrective" to prior excess, having learned, as he does at each stage of his development, to detect "some cramping, narrowing, costly preference of one part of his own nature, and of the nature of things, to another" (19). Ever more sensitive to such imbalance, Marius shows that tuning mediation is the best education, that impressions not only do not mislead young men, but make for advancement analogous to Marius's rise through the social ranks of antiquity.

New Cyrenaicism excessively emphasizes the physical; it is "a narrow perfection . . . the perfection of but one part of his nature – his capacities of feeling, of exquisite physical impressions" (24). Rejecting it, Marius yearns for the very habits and customs *The Renaissance* speaks against. Customary judgments – those of Matthew Arnold, or even of one's own – had been what ruled out the best possible experience. But here, once Marius feels the need for something to "hold by," he comes to see that such customs actually improve impressionability. He sees the great value of the "world's experience," and realizes that "in attaching oneself to it, one lets in a great tide of experience, and makes, as it were, with a single step, a great experience of one's own" (26). This "world's experience" is a far cry from "one's own impression," and it sounds just like what Arnold meant by "touchstones." But this does not mean that Pater has regressed along that progression that would otherwise lead to relativism and to Wilde, because he has in fact just remade the progression such that both Wilde and Arnold follow from him. Having firmly planted a foot in a strenuous Epicureanism, he can now plant the other in a sensualized objectivity. His phrase proves that this is the case: "world's experience," after all, is another of Pater's Impressionist paradoxes, since it attributes the power of receptivity to abstraction itself.

And "world's experience" is yet subject to further tuning, as Marius turns away now from what is too abstract in it. Reacting against Marcus Aurelius's too extreme stoicism, Marius stops short of the Emperor's belief that the mind should exclude the body: "The philosophic emperor was a despiser of the body. Since it is 'the peculiar privilege of reason to move within herself, and to be proof against corporeal impressions, suffering neither sensation nor passion to break in upon her', it follows that the true interest of the spirit must ever be to treat the body – Well! as a corpse attached thereto" (53). Stoical to the point of somatophobia, this view of reason portends the death of the body, and proves that asceticism can easily be as dangerous as hedonism. Ironically, it is this asceticism, rather than hedonism, that brings Marius to the edge of the "flux": "The purely material world, that close, impassable prison wall, seemed just then the unreal thing, to be actually dissolving away all around him" (70). Not hedonism but stoicism destroys the objective world; excess rigor, in a sense, is dissolute. Marius needs therefore to find a "world's experience" that can include the body, a passionate faith, "the equivalent of that Ideal, among so called actual things" (72). And all this he finds in the novel's final dialectical twist – that which ends in Christianity what had begun so modestly in Marius's surmises.

Seeking now a synthesis that could avoid both the "costly" emphasis on sense and the anti-material severity of stoicism, Marius discovers Christianity in that early form where "there was no forced opposition between the soul and the body" (121). Christianity becomes the "theory of practice" under whose aegis Impressionism finally covers the fullest ground. It effects the juncture of faculties, without letting any of those faculties' bad associations change juncture into new duality; it makes Impressionism irreproachably ethical, accomplishing more successfully than any other late nine-teenth-century theory a combination of aestheticism and religiosity; and it even justifies an aspect of Impressionism's "effeminacy," since Marius finds his Christianity embodied specifically in Saint Cecilia. Everything about Cecilia's mode of devotion models a mediation of faculties powerful at every level. It perfectly matches inner life with outer expression, since "in the entire expressiveness of what is outward, there is for her, to speak properly, between outward and inward, no longer any distinction at all" (93). No distinction between the inner and the outer, and no effective categorical difference between sensations and ideas, since it means "a touching of that absolute ground amid all the changes of phenomena" (184). And, finally, no questionable motive remains – no worrisome sense that Pater wants to make phenomena absolute in order to promote licentious sensuality. Proof of that crucial subtraction comes in one last return to Arnold's dictum about "things themselves." What Impressionism finally becomes, in its Christian version, is a mode of "sympathy." Sympathy is what Cecilia embodies in her connection of soul and body, and in her unification of inner and outer expression. And sympathy is an epistemological help, Pater suggests, because "there is a certain grief in things as they are" (181). Posing the problem of knowledge now as an emotional one, Pater makes Impressionist judgment primarily something that "removes the appearance of unkindness in the soul of things themselves" – something that makes "things" kin to men. That it does so through a feminized Christianity – transforming all evils, honing and heightening every good – shows how ingeniously Pater "reappraises" his Impressionism.

Pater ends *Marius* noting that "throughout that elaborate and lifelong education of his receptive powers, he had ever kept in view the purpose of preparing himself towards possible further revelation some day – towards some ampler vision which . . . might be taken up into the text of a lost epic, recovered at last" (219–20). This look backwards reminds us that the education of receptive powers has worked so well because it has made the experimental arrangement of receptive powers the very basis of education itself; and it reminds us that persistent inquiry into the variety of such arrangement, rather than any single limited one, has been the goal both of Marius's life and Pater's Impressionist theory. But these late observations are also a look forward, toward something that does not and cannot really happen. Marius hopes that perfecting his receptive powers, as he does according to the model of early Christianity, will return him to the totality of "lost epic." He hopes, in other words, that the mediation of faculties at work in early Christianity will be so total that it will extend to that mediation that, as Lukács and others have noted, made epic wholeness possible long ago. But since *Marius the Epicurean* is an allegory of the impression, the best it can do is move dialectically toward some perfect unity that its own existence proves impossible. Pater, after all, is not unlike Ford Madox Ford, in the nature of the effort he makes to circumvent the problems that make Impressionist mediation impossible. Just as Ford must "return to yesterday," Pater must do what historical research is necessary to locate a moment in which "there was no forced opposition between the soul and the body," a time before such oppositions grew stronger and took on the full force of related social and epistemological differences. His hero, in fact, must grow toward that moment, and then die in it. Marius finds only very contrived perfection in his "martyrdom," dying for Pater at the only moment that could accommodate a fully justified Impressionism. History makes possible what history denies – allowing Pater to find a moment for his impression really to work, but, by forcing him to have his hero die there to stay there, proves that it will supersede and convert immediacy into an "authentically temporal destiny."

II *HEART OF DARKNESS*

To find allegory in *Heart of Darkness* is to fall in with a century of criticism;[12] to find aesthetic allegory, moreover, may be to dodge the century's most pressing questions about Conrad – questions about his treatment of racial and imperial issues.[13] But to read *Heart of Darkness* as an allegory of the impression is to refresh the allegorical approach, by tightening the juncture of the aesthetic and the political. For if the journey upriver expresses Conrad's "hunger for the absolute" in response against corporeal contingency, much of what happens along the way can be explained in terms of the problem of Impressionism. Political problems, that is, are more necessarily a problem of Conrad's art when found intrinsic to his effort to do ethical justice to the visible universe. Critics have had much to say about Conrad's treatment of the "black bodies" Marlow encounters in the Belgian Congo, with persistent urgency since Chinua Achebe's claim that "Conrad was a bloody racist."[14] Racism, as a version of the view Conrad takes of his distant laborer, might become something defined more aesthetically, but no less politically, as an attitude through which human attributes are at once shared and disclaimed. In that case, Conrad's wish for sensuous proximity emerges as engagement with the kinds of epistemological distinctions that make racism possible, and to the extent that it fails, there emerges as well an indictment of Imperialism in theory and in form as well as content.

Worringer's "abstraction" and "empathy," which, as I have argued, mark the polar extremes of Conrad's Impressionism, also guide Marlow up the river. He moves repeatedly between empathy and abstraction, always initially finding comfort in the appeal of bodies, but then recoiling when bodies prove brutal, to turn to the different certainty available in abstract voices. This dialectic begins when he sets out. He begins his journey seeming to believe, as Conrad puts it in his letters, that he does not know life and it does not know him; "idleness" and "isolation" seem to keep him "away from the truth of things."[15] What relieves this sense of meaningless is the example of natural embodiment in black bodies at home in the natural world:

Now and then a boat from the shore gave one a momentary contact with reality. It was paddled by black fellows. You could see from afar the white of their eyeballs glistening. They shouted, sang; their bodies streamed with perspiration; they had faces like grotesque masks – these chaps; but they had bone, muscle, a wild vitality, an intense energy of movement, that was as natural and true as the surf along their coast. They wanted no excuse for being there. They were a great comfort to look at. For a time I would feel I belonged still to a world of straightforward facts. . . (61)

Like the laborer's body, these bodies are distant projections of corporeal vitality, and Marlow finds the same kind of comfort in looking at them that Conrad derives from his laborer. "Contact with reality" comes through them, through imagined empathy with bodies engaged in physical activity, due to the way their "wild vitality" physically communicates natural meaning. And if their faces are "grotesque masks," that degree of estrangement exists only to heighten the thrill that difference allows Marlow to feel – the thrill of certainty through another self.

But a scene soon follows that turns the comfort of black bodies into the horror of black corpses. When Marlow reaches the first station he finds not vital bodies but dying ones, in "every pose of contorted collapse, as in some picture of a massacre or a pestilence": "Black shapes crouched, lay. . . in all the attitudes of pain, abandonment, and despair . . . They were dying slowly . . . nothing but black shadows of disease and starvation, lying confusedly in the greenish gloom . . ." (66–67). Marlow discovers empathy's terrible correlative, the other side of the "natural truth" found in "wild vitality";

having staked his sense of reality on the vitality formerly manifest in black bodies, Marlow now feels dread as horrifying as that contact was reassuring. Like Conrad feeling his brain, Marlow finds his way blocked by materiality, so that what once gave him life now gives him death. The "solidarity" achieved through his empathetic response does not mean sharing some "mysterious origin"; it means facing life's common painful end. The cost for representation of this bout of negative empathy is reflected in the striking insignificance of a sign worn by one of these dying bodies. A man who looks at Marlow with "dying eyes" has "a bit of white worsted around his neck," which prompts Marlow to ask, "Why? Where did he get it? Was it a badge – an ornament – a charm – a propitiatory act? Was there any idea at all connected with it?" (67). The world of "straightforward facts" has vanished, replaced by one of obscure questions. In that world now, Marlow stands "horror-struck," desperate to find "ideas," feeling the urge to abstraction.

Marlow deals with his horror in part by finding an abstract image for the heap of dying bodies, seeing them as "bundles of acute angles" (67). But he primarily finds the abstract comfort of "ideas" in something that directly contrasts with the meaningless "bit of white worsted": the highly symbolical clothing of the Chief Accountant. The Accountant's apparent lack of a body calms Marlow's somatophobic horror. His initial appearance suggests the appeal of the shelter he offers:

. . . I met a white man, in such an unexpected elegance of get-up that in the first moment I took him for a sort of vision. I saw a high starched collar, white cuffs, a light alpaca jacket, snowy trousers, a clear necktie, and varnished boots . . . his appearance was certainly that of a hairdresser's dummy; but in the great demoralization of the land he kept up his appearance. That's backbone. His starched collars and got-up shirt-fronts were achievements of character. . . (67–68)

Marlow turns from black bodies to the white armor that is, as Worringer might put it, purified of dependence on life. This white armor recalls the armor that protects the "vulnerable body" in the Preface, and the shift in emphasis that finds more meaning in it reflects the simultaneous retreat from Impressionist insight and interracial sympathy. The whiteness of the Accountant's clothing erases the blackness of the horrifying dying bodies, establishing a dialectical competition between the satisfactions to be found in the vitality of black bodies and the vigor of white armor: the former is the power of sensation while the latter is the strength of abstraction; the former inspires by making contact with natural reality, while the latter reassures by denying that contact in favor of civilized achievements. The problem, of course, with the shift from the former to the latter is that abstraction is not merely a defense against the discomfort that empathy brings: it entails horrors of its own.

The Chief Accountant makes a comment that expresses that horror and breaks the calm of his civilized presence. Referring to the problem of disease (the direct menace to the Central Station and an indirect evocation of the problem with embodied knowledge), Marlow reports, "Once when various tropical diseases had laid low almost every 'agent' in the station, he was heard to say, 'Men who come out here should have no entrails'" (74). Bluntly expressing Marlow's own hope, this statement reminds Marlow of the abstraction's potential to disembowel. Sought as a refuge from dying bodies, the Accountant's apparent lack of entrails now becomes a sign of Impressionism's last failure: it is the point to which Worringer's sense of the passage from empathy to abstraction must be extended, the outcome of *negative* abstraction, made most terrible by the fact that it is the allegorical endpoint of Impressionist empathy.

Heart of Darkness twice repeats this allegorical defeat. The pattern repeats in Marlow's flight from another scene of "wild and passionate uproar," to the shelter of the battered copy of *An Inquiry into Some Points of Seamanship*. Moving upriver, Marlow thinks at first that the movement into primitive territory heightens perception, due to the fact that preconceptions disappear: "Going up that river was like traveling back to the earliest beginnings of the world . . . you lost your way . . . till you thought yourself bewitched and cut off for ever from everything you had known once . . ." (92–93). In this case, the thrill taken in this immediate perceptivity quickly mingles with fear of atavism. In a vision of bodies that follows, Marlow is both attracted and repelled by the suggestion of his affinity with the primitive other:

The earth seemed unearthly . . . and the men were – No, they were not inhuman, Well, you know, that was the worst of it – the suspicion of their not being inhuman. It would come slowly to one. They howled and leaped, and spun, and made horrid faces; but what thrilled you was just the thought of their humanity – like yours – the thought of your remote kinship with this wild and passionate uproar . . . that there was in you just the faintest trace of a response to the terrible frankness of that noise, a dim suspicion of there being a meaning in it which you – you so remote from the night of the first ages – could comprehend. And why not? The mind of man is capable of anything – because everything is in it, all the past as well as all the future, What was there after all? Joy, fear, sorrow, devotion, valour, rage – who can tell? – but truth – truth stripped of its cloak of time. (97)

Once again, a "remote kinship" produces "truth" apparently in spite of the "horrid face" that marks the distant kin. A wild vitality helps Marlow to see a way to strip what cloaks meaning, as a carefully poised difference-within-sameness contrives a juncture of civilized mind and savage body. But this thought of remote kinship immediately lacks the positive sense of "solidarity in mysterious origin" that the Preface glorifies. While Marlow enjoys inspiration here, he also finds "truth stripped of its cloak of time" a horrible revelation. The "terrible frankness" of this scene mixes the earlier visions of black bodies and black corpses, and it therefore leads Marlow once again to long for the cloak of abstraction to fall.

Marlow escapes the sense of savage kinship much the way he finds shelter in the starchy white uniform of the Chief Accountant. On a rude table in a ruined hut Marlow makes an "extraordinary find" – an old book, which has been, not surprisingly, "lovingly stitched afresh with white cotton thread, which looked clean yet" (99). The copy of *An Inquiry into Some Points of Seamanship* is "not a very enthralling book," but its defects are redeemed by "a singleness of intention, an honest concern for the right way of going to work"; handling it, Marlow enjoys "the delicious sensation of having come upon something unmistakably real." Superior to the scene of wild uproar in its clear expression of a simple intention, the book offers a preferable heritage. It is also an "amazing antiquity," but its version of the past reveals no unsettling truths. Rather, it offers a comforting version of the purposefulness of the distant laborer, without the problematic relation to the primeval body that such purpose had seemed to require. Finding such comfort in this not very enthralling book, however, Marlow has scaled back his expectations. Reflecting his own retreat from Impressionism, Conrad has Marlow find in the Seaman's manual the sincerity of a work of art without that which sincerity aims to make us see: the sensible universe, not in its "points," but in its essence. For Marlow, the seaman's manual is reassuring for its abstract signification: most appealing to him are the cipher-notes in the book's margins. As pure signs, they are utterly abstract, like bodies without entrails, protecting Marlow from any repulsive view of the truth.

The cipher-notes, however, soon prove to be no "extravagant

mystery" but merely a fool's scribbling – again, negative abstractions. Just as Marlow's pleasure turns to disgust when the Chief Accountant denies entrails, his satisfaction with the seaman's manual evaporates when it turns out to be the property of the absurd Harlequin. Charmed at first by him, Marlow considers "the essential desolation of his futile wanderings" evidence of stolid virtue: ". . . there he was gallantly, thoughtlessly alive, to all appearance indestructible solely by the virtue of his few years and of his unreflecting audacity" (126). Once the Harlequin declares his devotion to Kurtz, however, "essential desolation" becomes as negative as it sounds: "I looked around, and I don't know why, but I assure you that never, never before, did this land, this river, this jungle, the very arch of this blazing sky, appear to me so hopeless and so dark, so impenetrable to human thought, so pitiless to human weakness" (127). This sense of estrangement, so much the inverse of Marlow's response to the prior "passionate uproar," prepares for the result of Marlow's own encounter with Kurtz. That final encounter comes at the climax of an extended version of the prior dialectics that end in the negative abstractions of the Harlequin and the Accountant. This final dialectic begins with the death of Marlow's helmsman, runs through Kurtz's call to "exterminate all the brutes!," to Marlow's lie to the Intended, and finally to the nihilism that pervades the telling of *Heart of Darkness* (118).

The death of the helmsman is Marlow's worst encounter with the body's brute materiality. Impaled by a spear during the attack on Marlow's steamboat, the helmsman's body produces a flood of blood that soaks through Marlow's shoes. Flinging his blood-soaked shoes overboard, disgusted more than ever with the death of the black body, Marlow longs more than ever for the comfort of abstraction. But now, that desire makes him long to speak with Kurtz: "I flung one shoe overboard, and became aware that that was exactly what I had been looking forward to – a talk with Mr. Kurtz" (113). At first, the helmsman's death gives him a sense of "extreme disappointment," a feeling that he has been "striving after something altogether without substance." He realizes, however, that it is precisely lack of substance that he seeks. Kurtz's appeal, at this moment, lies in evidence of his comparative disembodiment, the fact that he "presented himself as a voice": what "carried with it a sense of real presence, was his ability to talk, his words."[16] Marlow wants not another body now, but a man who can be "just a word for him," forcing a paradox that makes words carry the "presence" that bodies carried before. Seductive through abstraction rather than sensuous concretion, persuasive while denying solidarity, "voice" leads to an alternative model of authorship. Where Conrad's Preface wants words to make us see things, Marlow revels in the fact that "I did not see the man in the name any more than you do" (82); there will be no seeing through Kurtz, and consequently no unsettling reliance on sense. Rather, Kurtz will enable Marlow to find the formalist shelter that Worringer describes as abstraction's "urge to seek deliverance from the fortuitousness of humanity as a whole, from the seeming arbitrariness of organic existence in general, in the contemplation of something necessary and irrefragable" (25).

By contrast, the helmsman seems to figure an Impressionist mode of authorship. In retrospect, Marlow realizes that he cared for the helmsman far more than he thought he did. He expresses this realization in terms that recall the value, to Conrad, of the distant laborer, making it clear that in his urge to abstraction Marlow is leaving Impressionism behind. Marlow thinks that while he cannot forget Kurtz, interest in him requires some correlative betrayal of his helmsman: "No, I can't forget him," Marlow says of Kurtz,

> though I am not prepared to affirm the fellow was exactly worth the life we lost in getting to him. I missed my late helmsman awfully, – I missed him even while his body was still lying in the pilot house. [. . .] Well, don't you see, he had done something, he had steered; for months I had him at my back – a help – an instrument. It was a kind of partnership. He steered for me – I had to look after him, I worried about his deficiencies, and thus a subtle bond had been created, of which I only became aware when it was suddenly broken. And the intimate profundity of that look he gave me when he received his hurt remains to this day in my memory – like a claim of distant kinship affirmed in a supreme moment. (119)

The "life" lost in the search for Kurtz, that body lying in the pilot house, is, like other bodies Marlow has used as an epistemological "instrument," a more vital "help" because it is "savage." The helmsman's work, like that of the distant laborer, creates a bond of fellowship; his "look" carries essential meaning, further establishing that "intimate profundity" to which, for Conrad, impressions enable access; and the total result of the labor and the look is that "distant kinship" affirmed in a "moment" – that "partnership" so vital to Impressionist authorship and meaning.

But Marlow ceases to miss the helmsman as the "look" gives way to the "voice." Marlow seeks meaning in judgment rather than in feeling, and finds it in a form of abstraction explicitly devoted to the eradication of the primitive. It is Kurtz's paper for the International Society for the Suppression of Savage Customs that becomes Marlow's abstractionist manifesto: he calls it "a beautiful piece of writing," and praises it because "It gave me the notion of an exotic Immensity ruled by an august Benevolence" (118). It "vibrat[es] with eloquence," with "no practical hints to interrupt the magic current of phrases" (117–18) – no practical hints, that is, save one, which makes Kurtz the ultimate spokesman for abstraction: "at the end of that moving appeal to every altruistic statement it blazed at you, luminous and terrifying, like a flash of lightning in a serene sky: 'Exterminate all the brutes!' " (118). Like the Accountant's wish to eliminate entrails combined with the "points" of the seaman's manual, Kurtz's pronouncement has enormous appeal. It leads Marlow to reject the helmsman in favor of Kurtz's example, and to hint at a mode of literary communication that is crucially opposed to that of Impressionism: "This is the reason why I affirm that Kurtz was a remarkable man. He had something to say. He said it . . . piercing enough to penetrate all the hearts that beat in the darkness. He had summed up – he had judged" (151). Kurtz reaches the "secret spring of responsive emotion" by "summing up" and "judging" – through abstract means of interpretation and expression. And Marlow's estimation of his power to do so suggests that in "piercing" hearts rather than "binding" them together, Kurtz only coercively "*makes* you see."

That Kurtz turns out to be *just* a voice – the fact that his body has wasted away – emphasizes his status as a figure for abstraction. The fact, however, that his voice is never really heard and that we never really hear what "the horror" is emphasizes abstraction's ultimate impossibility. Kurtz finally proves to stand for abstraction's negativity – a problem whose great symbol is the abstract design that Marlow sees, from a distance, by Kurtz's hut. Through binoculars, Marlow sees "half-a-dozen slim posts . . . in a row, roughly trimmed, and with their upper ends ornamented with round carved balls" (121). Upon closer inspection, these balls reveal themselves to be decayed human heads on stakes. "These round knobs were not ornamental but symbolic," Marlow thinks, indirectly considering such symbolism's violent result (130). These dead disembodied heads arranged in a row parody an abstract design, recalling the "bundles of acute angles" through which Marlow earlier deflects the sight of human corpses, and thereby mark the horror of the kind of shelter sought in Marlow's own flight from embodiment. They are the dead end to Impressionism's allegory.

This is the place to which Conrad's allegory of the problem of Impressionism leads: to the negative abstraction that turns projection of the body into the need to exterminate it. Having arrived here, Marlow is now – in the moment of the story's telling – the bitter man who most characteristically represents Conrad's Modernism. Self-betrayed into negative abstraction, Marlow can only tell the story of *Heart of Darkness* with doubts about his powers to do the work of communication that the Preface to *The Nigger of the "Narcissus"* demands. He considers his creator's wish to "make you *see*" impossible. Asking his audience, "Do you see him? Do you see the story? Do you see anything?" Marlow explains a sense of failure that proves that Conrad's characteristic mood bespeaks the disappointment of his literary-ethical hopes:

It seems to me that I am trying to tell you a dream – making a vain attempt, because no relation of the dream can convey the dream-sensation . . . No, it is impossible; it is impossible to convey the life-sensations of any given epoch of one's existence – that which makes its truth, its meaning – its subtle and pervading essence. It is impossible. We live as we dream – alone . . . (82)

Where Conrad had spoken of using impressions to convey life-sensations, and of producing togetherness in the process, he now has Marlow endorse the skepticism and solipsism for which Conrad is famous. *Heart of Darkness* explains how Conrad moves through Impressionism to reach that mode – how it is in fact his impression's ambiguity become allegorical that moves him with such momentum into its opposite. Because empathy really meant a "distant kinship" for Conrad, and because his impressions could only artificially mediate the mind and its body, Impressionism's inner partnership had to become "inner unrest." And just as such unrest leads Marlow to choose Kurtz as an ally against embodiment, it leads Conrad to end in "mere impressions" of a world of mere abstraction.

III MRS. DALLOWAY

"Distant kinship" is a problem to which Woolf devoted a good deal of thought. When she notes in *A Room of One's Own* that "women have served all these centuries as looking-glasses possessing the magic and delicious power of reflecting the figure of man at twice its natural size" (35), she recognizes that women in particular have been this kind of instrumental projection. This recognition, I have argued, leads her to deconstruct the terms of Impressionist collaboration – to expose the danger, especially to women themselves, of the "woman of genius" – and to write in *Mrs. Dalloway* an allegory of this deconstruction.

When *Mrs. Dalloway* begins, Clarissa Dalloway feels lifeless, and unable to take full part in "existence." Isolated in her attic room, she solves her problem in Impressionist fashion, by calling to mind the exemplary "existence" of Sally Seton, who, unlike Clarissa herself, had a genius for life. Years ago, Sally and Clarissa kissed; remembering that kiss now, Clarissa comes to life herself. But Woolf pushes things a crucial step further: she enacts that process through which Clarissa makes that "life" her own – enabled by Sally's example to imagine vitality, but able herself to see that vitality as a power of her own. The power of the impression, which is in Woolf the power to unify existence and essence, becomes something that stays.

Or rather, it stays at least until Woolf has to reckon with the persistence of otherness in a different form. While it has been my argument that feminism makes Woolf an incisive critic of Impressionist collaboration, it has also been my argument that difference always persists to debunk Impressionist immediacy. It is not the case that insight into the problem of the "woman of genius" leads Woolf to some truer knowledge about the nature of perception; in fact, if anything, it leads her to a realm of fantasy not entirely unlike Ford's medieval Salisbury and Pater's second-century Rome. Perceptual unity, it turns out, is a contrivance of the ambiguity of the "lesbian continuum": an historically specific continuum of female sexuality allows Clarissa to transfer the feeling of a woman's kiss into perception of "life itself." No such continuum exists, however, in the world of class. When Clarissa repeats Impressionist collaboration with Septimus Smith, and does with him what she has done with Sally Seton, class difference sets itself against Impressionist unity, and allegory finally asserts for *Mrs. Dalloway* its divisive but authentic destiny.

Clarissa Dalloway walks the streets of London with a double nature. Like Conrad's *homo duplex*, her faculties are divided, such that her powers in one regard only emphasize failure in the other: "She felt very young; at the same time unspeakably aged. She sliced like a knife through everything; at the same time was outside, looking on. She had a perpetual sense, as she watched the taxicabs, of being out, out, far out to sea and alone" (8). So incisive that she slices right out of life, Clarissa finds that the joy she feels at "loving [life] as she did with an absurd and faithful passion" gives way too quickly, and perpetually, to a sense that "this body she wore . . . with all its capacities, seemed nothing – nothing at all" (5, 10). A vicious dialectic puts Clarissa perpetually in crisis, as her large view of "life itself" only makes her own particular part in it seem "nothing." During her first walk about London, life in general exhilarates her; the nothingness of her body annihilates her; and when she returns home to find an invitation that does not include her, she reads into it her own growing failure to exist. Envisioning Lady Bruton, who has sent the invitation to Mr. Dalloway but not to her, Clarissa "read[s] on Lady Bruton's face, as if it had been a dial cut in impassive stone, the dwindling of life; how year by year her share was sliced; how little the margin that remained was capable any longer of stretching, of absorbing, as in the youthful years, the colours, salts, tones of existence . . ." (30). As we later learn, this "dwindling of life" began for Clarissa even in youth. It is a basic epistemological problem – not one in which age spoils receptivity, but one in which the very power to "read" life, or "slice" through it like a knife, excludes one from participation.

Clarissa dramatizes her own alienation by going up to her attic room, walking upstairs "as if she had left a party," a "single figure" "against the stare of this matter-of-fact June morning" (30). Her voyage upward is a domestic version of Marlow's voyage into the heart of darkness. It becomes, like his journey, a dialectical search for resolution to the dualism that alternates life with lack. In her journey, as in his, the initial goal is a void: "there was an emptiness about the heart of life; an attic room" (31). Clarissa, however, develops her own way to figure to herself the cause and character of this emptiness. The gap between insight and vitality becomes for her a sense of herself as "suddenly shriveled, aged, breastless," like "a nun withdrawing," and unable to "dispel a virginity . . . which clung to her like a sheet" (31) – a sense of herself as lacking in the vitality specifically of female sexuality. Clarissa's problem is a certain lack of perceptual reciprocity. She cannot, it seems, be both "outside, looking on" and inside existence, and the problem seems to give her

the same relation to life as a "nun withdrawing," as a person who
has traded vital involvement for spiritual insight. What she needs, in
contrast to the metaphor of the nun, is a metaphor that recasts
mystic withdrawal as a movement outward as well. This she gets as
she tries to decide what exactly constitutes her persistent "virginity."
She sees that she lacks not "beauty" nor "mind" but "something
central which permeated; something warm which broke up surfaces
and rippled the cold contact of man and woman, or of women
together. For *that* she could dimly perceive" (31). Something that is
central and yet permeates would model a solution to Clarissa's
problem. The closer she gets to figuring to herself a "permeating
center," the closer she gets to being outside and inside at once – and
to patterning herself according to the perceptual status of the
impression.[17] As her initial efforts to produce that figure suggest,
"women together" helps: it helps her concretize vitality, but, as we
will see, only as long as it is something "dimly perceived."

Clarissa's thoughts of the permeating center active in "women
together" lead to a figure for the combination of essence and
experience – one that takes Woolf far beyond what such a combination ever brought in her own encounters with Mrs. Brown. What
had been at once an "overwhelming smell" and a hint at "life itself"
now becomes an "astonishing significance" which is also orgasmic:

> It was a sudden revelation, a tinge like a blush which one tried to check and
> then, as it spread, one yielded to its expansion, and rushed to the farthest
> verge and there quivered and felt the world come closer, swollen with some
> astonishing significance, some pressure of rapture, which split its thin skin
> and gushed and poured with an extraordinary alleviation over the cracks
> and sores . . . (32)

Just as the impression of Mrs. Brown had overwhelmed, this reflection on the feeling of "women together" is something that expands
beyond one's effort to check it – something to which one "yields."
And just as the impression of Mrs. Brown is something that Woolf
had wanted to parlay into all kinds of stories, this feeling leads one to
want to "rush it" as far as possible. From yielding to rushing, the
feeling goes, as the impression does, from external experience to
inner swelling of significance, to produce a complex that confuses the
world and the self. Grammatical ambiguity elides self and world, in
this passage, by making it uncertain whether it is "one" or "the
world" that swells with astonishing significance when one woman
permeates something warm through another.

But this initial revelation passes, and Clarissa returns to lifeless-ness. Another image reflects the change, by recasting the double movement of the permeating center in lesser combinations. She had "seen an illumination," here refigured as "a match burning in a crocus," but now "the close withdrew, the hard softened," and there contrasts with "such moments" "the bed" (with its tight white covers) and "the candle half burnt" (32). No all-consuming allevia-tion or yielded rushing persists past a momentary "blush"; it fades, rather, into figures that make serial what the prior revelation had combined. For the revelation to stay, some more emphatic female presence will be necessary, and this Clarissa will get when she remembers her own specific experience of "women together." It is important, however, that this initial revelation is what typically passes for an impression in common parlance: the "sudden" revela-tion, which flares up and dies out like a quick flame, is what most accounts of Woolf and other writers mean when they describe Impressionism's effects, despite the fact that Woolf quite explicitly presents such sudden revelations as ones that can and should yield to more elaborate ones.

To elaborate her sudden revelation Clarissa returns to "this question of love . . . this falling in love with women" (32). She remembers now that she loved Sally Seton, and describes more specifically the particular value of that passion. It was "not like one's feelings for a man," but "completely disinterested," and derived from a sense "of being in league together" (34). Here we have in miniature the argument through which Woolf earlier exploits the logic of the "woman of genius." When women are in league together, something revelatory happens, because of the way one woman enjoys by example another's special gift for vitality. At first, as Clarissa tries to remember Sally, nothing comes to her: "No, the words meant absolutely nothing to her now. She could not even get an echo of her old emotion" (34). But then she reverses the direction of the effort, to begin by seeking a ground for the emotion, and it begins to come: "But she could remember going cold with excitement, and doing her hair in a kind of ecstacy (now the old feeling began to come back to her, as she took out her hairpins, laid them on the dressing-table, began to do her hair . . ." (34). The nature of this shift suggests that Sally has begun to do for Clarissa what the moth and the mark have tended to do for Woolf: she sets the pattern for a kind of ecstatic physicality, which clarifies by contrast that some "echo" detaches words from their sources. Once Clarissa has followed the pattern into something like the "phenomenological" orientation through which Woolf had gone from moths and marks to "life itself," she makes a second and closer pass at the "permeating center":

> Then came the most exquisite moment of her whole life passing a stone urn with flowers in it. Sally stopped: picked a flower; kissed her on the lips. The whole world might have turned upside down! The others disappeared; there she was alone with Sally. And she felt that she had been given a present, wrapped up, and told just to keep it, not to look at it – a diamond, something infinitely precious, wrapped up, which, as they walked (up and down, up and down), she uncovered, or the radiance burnt through, the revelation, the religious feeling! (35–36)

The diamond is "something central which permeated" – it, also, focuses itself as once inward and outward – but in more portable form. The form matters, since in diamond form the impression gets an objective correlative to allegorize its source, power, and effects. The wrapped diamond, which Clarissa keeps but does not "look at," and whose radiance burns through nevertheless – this image is an apt impression of the impression itself. It is an impression of the impression because it finds a correlate that is at once material and essential, at once something "given" and a revelation, with a radiance able to shine through the encumbrance of the everyday. As a gift from Sally, and specifically the gift of her kiss, the diamond concretizes the process through which Impressionist receptivity comes to one woman from another.

Two things follow from the gift of the diamond that extend its significance even further – beyond the lasting "central radiance" and into an even more permanent model for Impressionist perception. On the one hand, the "religious feeling" of the diamond kiss ends abruptly; on the other hand, its effect extends from the distant past into Clarissa's present. In the past, darkness returns with the reassertion of men and their "words," which, like Whitaker's Almanack in "The Mark on the Wall," interrupt Impressionist reverie with the bald assertion of fact: when after the kiss Peter Walsh and Old Joseph reappear and start giving names to all the stars, "it was like running one's face against a granite wall in the darkness! It was shocking; it was horrible!" (36). And this is the last we hear of Sally's diamond; it sinks into an apparently permanent darkness, because, it seems, of the inevitable reappearance of the "words" of men. Where "women together" might have extended the "woman of genius" into Impressionist success, Woolf chooses again to throw up the "granite wall" of convention. Woolf's "woman of genius," in other words, might have developed from the moth to Mrs. Brown to Sally Seton and then into some permanent essentialist hope for a feminine revelatory mode. As we have seen, however, Woolf in fact prefers the "granite wall" to essentialism: in *To the Lighthouse* and *A Room of One's Own*, something very much like a Kristevan "semiotic" is passed up in favor of attitudes that do not isolate a special vatic femininity. Demystifying Mrs. Ramsay, and turning to androgyny, Woolf chooses to dissociate the "diamond" from the woman's kiss, and to return to the kind of materialism that here strikes Clarissa like a wall in the face. That demystifying turn begins here, as Woolf shows how the "revelation" and "religious" feeling of women together cannot really last.

But this is only one half of what follows the recollection of Sally's kiss. On the one hand, there is this abrupt demystification; but on the other hand there is a transference of the diamond. For Clarissa does keep the diamond – not hidden within a female fantasy, but made public. Looking into the mirror now, in the present, she assembles her "self" in a manner that suggests that she has made the permeating center a real-life possibility: "Clarissa (crossing to the dressing-table) plunged into the very heart of the moment, transfixed it, there . . . collecting the whole of her at one point (as she looked into the glass), seeing the delicate pink face of the woman who was that very night to give a party; of Clarissa Dalloway; of herself" (37). Here is a crucial third stage in the process that begins with Sally's kiss: first there is the gift of the diamond and the enabling example of a sensuous revelation; then there is the interruption, and assertion of brute male fact; and then there is Clarissa "herself," collecting herself to a point, not in imitation of Sally (Clarissa herself is delicate and pink, where Sally was much more robust), and despite the "words" of men. Then there is Clarissa replaying the kiss by kissing herself in the mirror, and becoming, as the subsequent passage tells us, her own kind of "diamond":

She pursed her lips when she looked in the glass. It was to give her face point. That was her self – pointed; dartlike; definite. That was her self when some effort, some call on her to be her self, drew the parts together, she alone knew how different, how incompatible and composed so for the world only into one centre, one diamond, one woman who sat in her drawing-room and made a meeting-point, a radiancy. . . (37)

The permeating center has developed from a barely-glimpsed property of women's love, to a felt gift of a kiss, to become finally the essential thing about Clarissa herself. She herself becomes, in her drawing room, that central radiance, not in some ecstatic removal in which "others disappeared," but in some actual social role. In the long train of texts that begins with "The Death of the Moth" and "The Mark on the Wall," and as a turning point in Woolf's work overall, this moment reflects a great achievement. It figures a self composed such that it can at once participate in things going on and also shape them in essential consciousness – such that it can be both a "meeting-point" and a "radiancy." Moreover, it shows her able to make the social bias in perception productive rather than restrictive: where the social pattern had tended to make the Impressionist writer return to dualism, here Woolf finds a social pattern for unity.

The pattern, of course, is relatively dull. One woman in her drawing room must be less exciting than "women together," but the let-down is significant. For lesbian desire, as a pattern for Impressionist mediation, could only work if "dimly perceived." It was only when "told . . . not to look at it" that Clarissa felt Sally's kiss as a revelation. The silence surrounding lesbianism, and the continuum in women's relationships that obscures the difference between homosexuality and intense friendship, is in large measure what enables love for Sally to bring experience to the level of essence: repression has much to do with Clarissa's tendency to think of that love as a "revelation" and a "religious feeling" – to describe it as a semi-mystical experience rather than a fact of life. That semi-mystical language is another way Woolf demystifies essentialism. Clarissa's memory of Sally is wonderful, but it is also euphemistic, and in her rendering of it Woolf suggests that "women together" brings on essential insights at least partially by closing off the possibility of acknowledged experience.

By contrast, Clarissa in her drawing room is a diamond that she and others can see. What she does there is less exciting, to her and to us, but as a model for perception her place there is really more suggestive. It acknowledges the role of social convention in perceptual theory, and puts that social convention to work in formulating structures that might, despite convention, remake the way perception works. Clarissa in love might subvert convention more obviously, but Clarissa composing herself for the public world does so in a manner that brings Impressionist mediation into the world of real life.

To make a middle-aged middle-class hostess a model for revolutionary perception is a notable achievement in the long history that begins with Sterne's Dolly. To suggest initially that she will work as such a model through lesbian engagement is to fall in with the trend – to do what others had done, by making Impressionist mediation a function of social fantasy. To have that fantasy lead quickly to a mundane reality, however, is to buck the trend, by finding attainable social models for immediacy. Clarissa's party, ultimately, will be that model, insofar as it finds her playing the role of one who composes and enlivens, and one whose sense of "ontological insecurity" gives way to a confidence that she exists and understands. What we find, however, is that Clarissa lapses again. Even at her party she feels once again isolated; confidence that she works like a diamond in the drawing room gives way to that "overwhelming incapacity" (185) and that "awful fear" of lifelessness on one side and meaninglessness on the other. What enables Clarissa to return to the party, and reassume her special role there, is again the "life" of an other – now, Septimus Smith, who seems to die so that Clarissa's party can live.

As many have noted, Septimus is Clarissa's "double." Woolf herself noted that he was "invented to complete the character of Mrs. Dalloway," that the two collaborate to produce a single consciousness, and it is clear that he plays the harder part.[18] He is "the scapegoat, the eternal sufferer" (25), whose terribly heightened vitality seems to make up for Clarissa's deficiency in that regard.[19] Clarissa enjoys the vitality of Septimus's sensitivity without the disaster of his insanity, as other Impressionists make use of distant laborers. Septimus, too, is of a lower class, and it seems that social difference enables Clarissa to strike a crucial balance: social difference separates them enough to allow her to identify with him only up to a point – to have knowledge of his experience, to understand it, just enough to make it useful to her own perceptual life. Remarkably, her collaboration with Septimus repeats the dynamic of her collaboration with Sally Seton. The results, however, are different, because Septimus and Sally derive from divergent aspects of Mrs. Brown.

Clarissa had called Sally to mind after walking upstairs as if leaving a party. Now, after hearing news that Septimus has committed suicide, she walks upstairs from her party – again to try to make the knowledge she has of life something that will not keep life from going on. With Sally, she had begun to join life and insight by going through certain bodily motions. Now, she wonders how Septimus has killed himself, and again "her body [goes] through it" (184). And as with Sally, the gift of the effort is some treasure that makes a center:

> A thing there was that mattered; a thing, wreathed about with chatter, defaced, obscured in her own life, let drop every day in corruption, lies, chatter. This he had preserved. Death was defiance. Death was an attempt to communicate; people feeling the impossibility of reaching the centre which, mystically, evaded them; closeness drew apart; rapture faded, one was alone. There was an embrace in death . . . But this young man who had killed himself – had he plunged holding his treasure? (184)

Like Sally, Septimus makes a gift of a treasure yet radiant, one that makes of experience something meaningful. The language Woolf uses to describe the unavailability of the "centre" is the same as that which described the fading of the "revelation" that suddenly came and went with thought of "women together." Here, the revelation stays, as it did after Sally gave Clarissa the diamond. Clarissa had found an image through which her social reality could enable her to imagine a life at once composed and lived, and it had seemed that the image, the image of herself at the center of a party, had moved Woolf beyond collaboration. With Septimus, however, the need for collaboration is renewed. Moreover, Woolf presents collaboration as something really deadly – something that only brings life to one counterpart while ending the life of the other.[20] When Clarissa asks herself if the "young man" had died "holding his treasure," she sees that his death has "preserved" the treasure. She sees that the diamond, which has the power to make closeness and rapture stay, is preserved and unwreathed insofar as death distinguishes, by difference, life itself. And so whereas Septimus's suicide had at first seemed "her disaster – her disgrace," it becomes her life; it becomes that which enables her, once again, to have both vitality and insight:

> The young man had killed himself; but she did not pity him; with the clock striking the hour, one, two, three, she did not pity him, with all this going on . . . She must go back to them. But what an extraordinary night! She felt somehow very like him – the young man who had killed himself. She felt glad that he had done it; thrown it away. . . . He made her feel the beauty; made her feel the fun. But she must go back. She must assemble . . . (186)

Clarissa regains the sense of "all this going on," the feel of existence, which is also a feeling for beauty, a power to assemble. Here is the goal laid out from the outset – a goal reached intermittently, and particularly with the discovery of her "diamond" self, but now reached through the death of a man "somehow very like." When Clarissa, returning to her party, stands finally at the top of the stairs, and the voice of the narrator thinks, "For there she was," the novel delivers an affirmation only possible, and in a register only possible, because of the way Septimus serves as Clarissa's double (194). The lofty tone of "for" and the emphatic "was" confirm that Clarissa exists transcendently, but she does so finally only because of the way the social system can bring a dead man like Septimus into her home: "somehow," but not really, so she can be glad, and feel the fun.

If this reading makes the end of *Mrs. Dalloway* sound too dark – if it seems out of sync with what otherwise reads as a powerful affirmation – it is important to remember that the novel's ending is double. It is double, first of all, in its compositional history: as Woolf tells us in her introduction to an early Modern Library edition, she had initially intended to have Clarissa kill herself. The reversal of intention, it is clear, is not total. If Clarissa does not die but in fact comes to enjoy "life itself," death nevertheless stalks the scene. As in "The Death of the Moth," the cost of joining essence and existence is death – death to the other whose life must be minimal enough to enable the conjunction. On the one hand there is the achievement of Impressionist unity; on the other, there is the reduction of another life to its merely supplemental feature, in imaginary imitation of the social dynamic that makes some people merely supplemental to others. And in fact this doubleness is so extreme at the end of *Mrs. Dalloway* that the novel is tantamount to a confession. If the two endings, the affirmative and the dark, seem out of sync, it is because Woolf has brought the differential force of allegory to its most "authentic" kind of revelation.

Mrs. Dalloway is double in another sense as well. There is the doubleness of collaboration, but also a doubling of collaboration, since what goes on with Septimus goes on with Sally in a very different way. Septimus dies a martyr, but Sally lives well past the moment when her kiss inspired religious feeling. Her presence at Clarissa's party is very different from her presence long ago at Bourton. "For she hadn't looked like *that*, Sally Seton, when Clarissa grasped the hot water can, to think of her under this roof, under this roof! Not like that!" – and it is important that Sally has lost her power to thrill (171). The change in Sally is the demystification of the "woman of genius." That half of Mrs. Brown ceases to obtain, once

Clarissa has transferred the power of the female other into the realm of her own social life. But by no longer "looking like *that*" Sally only lets Mrs. Brown become Septimus, and makes *Mrs. Dalloway* a combination of two different stories. One is a story of aesthetic success, in which the aesthetic mediation of human faculties rises above the ideology which reasserts division along social lines; the other, again, is an allegory – a story about the inevitability of such division, and the permanent impossibility of any unified perceptual life.

If this our last Impressionist allegory is, despite early promise, so finally allegorical, it seems necessary to conclude that Impressionist fiction always unravels Impressionist theory. Pater's model, depending on a death at a specific lost historical moment, suggests that Impressionist theory must always escape practical occasions; Conrad's model shows just how emphatically sociopolitical difference defines, and therefore mitigates against unity of, qualities of mind and body; and even Woolf, who seems driven by feminism to free human faculties from bad social associations, finds social difference definitive as well. In all three cases, fiction undoes theory and thematizes the way that Modernism itself turns from dreams of perceptual immediacy through allegory to ironical realities.

Allegory's authenticity, however, makes success of these failures. With Pater's failure to reflect a practical solution to the problem of Impressionism comes success in showing how that problem puts special emphasis on basic educational choices. With Conrad's failure to prove that sensuous life works as a ground for human solidarity comes exposure of the limits to the very composition of humanity. And if Woolf's notorious failure to see far beyond the fringe of her own social class reflects an analogous failure to bring all perceptual life within her range, the latter failure very effectively dramatizes the costs of the former. If, as some allege, Woolf's writing suffers for its narrow social bias, her writing itself admits that bias limits its own power to be "modern fiction," not only because it restricts the range of "life," but because it even prevents "life itself" from becoming an epistemological possibility.

Conclusion   Mrs. Brown and Mrs. Bell

In 1925, the painter Vanessa Bell, Virginia Woolf's sister, gave a lecture at Leighton Park School. The lecture says that artists, unlike other people, see the world as form and color. To illustrate – to distinguish this way of seeing from others – she cites "something I read the other day which throws some light on the way in which writers at any rate look at their surroundings."[1] The thing Bell cites is "Mr. Bennett and Mrs. Brown." She uses her sister's essay to make something like her sister's point: some people only see what's very apparently before them, according to some conventional arrangement of details and relations, with the intention of making it serve some instrumental purpose. For Woolf the point had been that Bennett lost the true essence of the person or thing before them in piles of material detail and chatter about social implications. For Bell the point is that writers in general don't "really *see*" – "not in a way that I should call seeing" (155). What they see is things and people refracted through "particular human associations," just in terms of their functions and connections, but never the forms and colors of their individual presence. The difference between the way writers and artists see brings out what is above all necessary to the visual artist: the power not to "go beyond his eyes" (157), insight into pure form, next to which "skill is of no importance," for skills are "habits of hand" that "tend to destroy what is most important to an artist – sensibility" (161).

Bell's lecture is simplistic. She admits that she has not "more than the vaguest ideas of the history of art," and, since she spoke to a group of boys aged fourteen to eighteen, she had no need to make her ideas anything more than vague (149–50). What is remarkable, then, is that her version of "Mr. Bennett and Mrs. Brown" is so much more conclusive than the original. Woolf had to end her essay admitting failure; Bell can say "colour and form," and with those words easily do what Woolf's impression had tried but failed to accomplish. For "colour and form" deliver concrete material with abstract insight: Whistler's portrait of Carlyle, to use one of Bell's examples, shows "form definite, distinct, Carlyle's form, no other old man's" (156). It shows "the shape of Carlyle's head," that concrete particularity, but also, in presenting "its proportion to the rest of him," an abstract interpretation of his mentality and authority. Where Woolf had had to take special measures (and at least temporarily admit failure) to have both "essentials" and material life, Bell can easily claim both. Form is matter and form is essential – bridged in its two modes naturally by the real but ideal presence of shape. In the context of the visual arts, then, the argument about Mrs. Brown goes much more easily, and in fact never even has to come to the point where Mrs. Bell faces Mrs. Brown perplexed about how to render her impression of her.[2]

I address this point of comparison here to begin to draw conclusions about Impressionism more generally. In Chapter One, I argued that the analogy between painting and literature has tended to distort the kind of "impression" Impressionist writers had in mind. Once we presume that the two Impressionisms interrelate, whether by influence, analogy, or some period style, the more historically prominent Impressionism in painting tends to dominate. We know, of course, that writers cannot render perception in the same way that painters can, and yet we presume that Impressionism in writing will be visual, pictorial, or at least sensuous. Even those studies that think differently about the literary impression tend to fall back upon this standard presumption. I have also argued, however, that the impression encourages this kind of mistake, since even if it is not necessarily visual, pictorial, or sensuous, just how it is *not* is never quite clear. When writers invoke the impression, they rarely mean something sensuous, but neither do they seem to know exactly what they do mean. That ambiguity makes it harder to distinguish the literary impression from the painterly impression. That distinction becomes a matter of extensive close reading rather than quick definition, with attention to ambiguity and indeterminacy, rather than confidence that any clear definition will reward the effort. I hope that this book, in its study of the meaning and implications of the impression to those writers who prominently invoke it, has defined the literary impression sufficiently to enable us, now, to distinguish the literary and painterly impressions and to discuss with new accuracy the relation between the sister Impressionisms.

Hume found the term "impression" useful to conflate perceptual moments. He discovered its habit of conveyance, which lent Empiricism a power to run a fuller perceptual range – a range more characteristic of the phenomenological philosophies that would draw on his work in later centuries. But his impression ran a range not otherwise available to his Empiricism, so that it was only a matter of contrivance: it contrived rhetorically what Hume did not propose systematically, and for that reason did not give to intellectual history any stable or reliable mediation of perceptual moments. In later years that ambiguous mediation would become an inspiration and a problem. When Pater, having read Hume, made the impression the basis for his alternative to objective and psychologistic aesthetics, he also found its ambiguous meditation a boon and a liability. It helped him theorize a connection between sensuous response and good judgment, but drew on other ways of relating the sensuous and the intellectual, with the result that the impression's mediation translated into sexual license. To clarify matters – and to prove to his critics that his impression was not only not corrupting, but a relation fundamental to *bildung* – Pater turned the impression's ambiguity into the engine of plot, and produced what would become a standard form: the Impressionist allegory, in which Impressionist unity devolves, for the good of modernist insight, into a dialectic of sense and reason.

Pater found that social relations would tend to make up for the ambiguity in the mediation at work in Hume's impression. The particular social relation in question for him was one that went by the name of "effeminacy." To ground reason in sense, it seemed, was to give up on masculine priorities – in years to come, by abdicating representational authority to women's ways of knowing. James, for a time, thought that the impression could most broadly extend fiction both into reality and into the imagination, but had to call on outside help to guarantee that full extent. Women's ways of knowing – specifically, the apophatic perceptivity of the "woman of genius" – seemed to him a necessary supplement to his authorial imagination. But since that arrangement conceded too much to a kind of sentimentalized limitation, it became, when allegorized in James's fiction, a form for bad marriage. Preferring to emphasize the power "to dramatize" over the power to receive the "seed" of the initial impression, James turned from a sentimental idealization of feminine limitation to a more liberal allocation of "genius." Impressions had balanced art and life, but with strange social effects, so that James finally came to believe that "it is art that makes life" – with or without the impression to provide reciprocity or balance in the process. Thomas Hardy, by contrast, made different use of the impression's interconnections among gender, epistemology, and writing: for him, female sensibilities were the basis of good anti-social iconoclasm, which in turn found polemical representation in the ambiguity of the impression. To say that a novel is an impression for Hardy was to say that it need not make a coherent argument; but not to make a coherent argument was to make an argument of the better kind, according to the pattern of natural female vitality.

Such use for female vitality gives Impressionism a peculiar relation to ideology. Despite claims, for example, that James "exploited" women both real and imaginary, his use for the "woman of genius" suggests that uncertainty about the impression's epistemological relations in fact exposes the way social prejudice limits the imagination. For James's apophatic interest in female sensibilities only brings to a head a reigning tendency in the history of the novel – and, arguably, ultimately speaks against it, by thematizing its bad effects. And that style of critique may be present as well in *Heart of Darkness*, as well, insofar as that novel shows Conrad's need for a distant laborer backfiring. Where the impression would run representation from sense to solidarity, the distant laborer suggests that something primitive is necessary to give it a sensuous ground; in *Heart of Darkness*, that something becomes at once savage and subject to massive cruelty, so that Impressionist uncertainty becomes a force for anti-Imperialist polemic. Such polemic is also made, to less potent effect, in Ford Madox Ford. For Ford, the impression would run representation from inassimilable fact to human experience, but requires, as for Conrad, some supplemental impressionability. This it gets in Ford's "peasant consciousness." To defer to such a consciousness, however, is to cede too much authority to indiscriminate readerly response. As a result, in *The Good Soldier*, Dowell suffers blighting epistemological skepticism, unable to experience fact even with the help of his successive "silent listeners." In a certain sense, Dowell's suffering constitutes a polemic against a reactionary political ideology: Ford's "feudalism," which had been part of an effort to force the mediation wanted in Ford's aesthetic theory. As the mediation of fact and experience gives way to a nostalgia for feudal hierarchies, and as feudalism in turn gives way to severe skepticism, Ford delivers an implicit critique of reactionary ideology.

From Pater to Ford, the impression focuses hope for the kind of unity that has long been the aspiration of the "aesthetic." As a consequence, it stirs up the social and political problems that had also attended that aspiration and its failures. The Impressionists shared with any number of predecessors the hope to integrate human faculties, but found, like them, that the faculties always already had human associations. Difference had the authority of social life and would not be undone, so that even a very capable theorist of difference could not theorize her way out of the impression's new dualism. Even Virginia Woolf, whose perspective on the problem of the "woman of genius" made her eager to deconstruct that mode of collaboration, found herself affirming the "screen-making habit" through which social distinction guarantees consciousness its existence. For Woolf, the impression promised a good combination of material life and essential insight; even she finds, however, that the demands of material life are inevitably social in nature, and therefore determined by difference, so that essential insight must make concessions to that difference in order to live.

The difference that persists despite and as a product of the impression's mediation becomes the theme that characterizes Impressionist fiction. Impressionism may have many other tendencies – time-shifts, delayed decodings, pictorialisms, habits of metaphor – but these may vary, and may not be distinct from tendencies in other literary modes or the tendencies of fiction in general. What characterizes Impressionist fiction is the nature of its allegory. Allegory makes diachronic what the impression hopes to unify, and puts fiction through a dialectical theorization of the impression. In *Marius the Epicurean*, allegory produces a great number of different versions of the impression, only stopping with that which seems most viable when its protagonist dies; in *Heart of Darkness*, the impression's component parts never enjoy any non-allegorical simultaneity, coming rather at impossibly diverse points in Marlow's journey; and in *Mrs. Dalloway* the successful impression gives way to the one whose unity hides the disparity of a collaboration across different parts of London. Finally allegorical, Impressionism is the hope for mediation that gives way to the power to mediate only over the course of narrative time, and only with results that undermine the belief that mediation will ever come naturally.

Mediation does come naturally to some writers. Joyce and Lawrence, for example, seem fairly happy to believe that the body thinks.

But for that very reason they are not Impressionists: Joyce and Lawrence will never invoke the impression in order to take advantage of its power of conveyance, because they do not find such conveyance necessary to imagine the relations of mind and body. Different rhetoric and greater confidence motivate Joycean epiphany and Joycean scatology (those opposite focusings of a "spiritual eye") and Lawrence's question, in response to the problem of duality, "why make a moshy oneness of it?"[3] One great irony in the history of literary Impressionism is the fact that Impressionist mediation happens best in the minds and bodies of those writers who never feel the need to invoke the impression, and the corollary fact that those who do invoke it are those who doubt it will work.

Here, then, is an overview of what we have seen of the activity of the literary impression. If we were now to try to define it, for the purpose of a new sister-arts analogy, we might do so as follows. The impression is a unit of perception that reorients perception such that its different moments convey from one to the next, and, as a result, cease to be; it is a unit of perception that spreads to encompass perception as a whole, and which would therefore bring new immediacy to the literary imagination. It is, nevertheless, a unit, and therefore something that yet participates in the conventional tendency to chart perception as a progress among divisions of human capacity. Those who invoke the impression, that is, still want to know "where" it falls, so that its mediation of faculties still deals in uncertainty about faculties. Such uncertainty draws on lingering unwillingness to do without distinctions, which is in turn reinforced by the social and political associations from which perceptual distinctions take their pattern. What would ideally be synthesis becomes dissociation after all, along social lines, played out in the realm of narrative plot. In sum, the literary impression is that mediatory unit of perception in which perceptual faculties come together to the degree that they can, and with results that defer mediation into allegorical self-consciousness.

What does this literary impression have to do with the painterly impression? What, in other words, can we say about Impressionism more generally as an aesthetic movement or theory? First of all, it is not the case that the impression is essentially different in the different arts. In both literature and painting it is a perceptual conveyance, rather than a static unit of perception, but it does its work differently in its different "contexts of action." As I suggested in Chapter One, the different contexts of action provoke the impression in very different ways: it serves Impressionist painting by enabling perception to slide more deeply into concrete sense; but it serves Impressionist writers by sliding perception further toward abstraction. It moves in these different directions, but is crucially in both cases a term that reorients perceptual theory such that its terms become dynamically continuous. This is crucial because the difference between the two Impressionisms lies in the extent to which each could allow for such dynamic continuity.

To return to the example of Vanessa Bell and Mrs. Brown: able simply to say "colour and form" and with that phrase solve so simply problems that bedeviled her sister, Vanessa Bell indicates the ease with which her art could allow for the impression's dynamic continuity. In the visual arts, the path from sensuous concretion to ideal abstraction was – after merely public resistances fell – relatively clear. The painters turned to impressions wanting sense, but found that they entailed a style of perception that only seemed to devote itself to immediate physical appearances. Impressions set them on the path to abstraction, as the history of art shows: once Monet and his contemporaries found that they could more realistically render "fleeting appearances" in relatively discontinuous brushstrokes, they began the developments that would lead to Seurat's points, Cézanne's shapes, and then to the abstract forms of cubism and full-blown abstractionism. Even as a painter like Seurat tried to turn painting's theory of perception back toward the science of sensation, he produced works of form, and one way to account for that range is to acknowledge painting's power to allow the impression to convey perception most broadly in its opposite directions. And if it seems inappropriate to attribute any interest in impressions to Seurat or Cézanne – inappropriate to see impressions at work in Post-Impressionism – it is also perhaps possible to see the impression as the crucial point of conveyance between Impressionism and its successor: the former leads to the latter in ways that are hard to explain unless we see that the impression does not pertain to the former simply as a unit of perception, but conveys painting from the former to the latter by making mimetic form itself the impetus to formalism and abstraction.

Writing creates a very different context for the impression's dynamic continuity. We might begin to see how by comparing the latter-day attitudes of theorists working in the different aesthetic traditions. Rudolph Arnheim and W. J. T. Mitchell have with confidence promoted "visual thinking" and "picture theory," which are, in key ways, latter-day versions of the impression. Historians and theorists of literature, by contrast, have no foundation upon which to build any such faith in representational unity. The "authentic destiny" of the impression in the reckonings of Benjamin and de Man, as I have suggested, is brokenness, difference, and deferral. This different outcome reflects the different responses provoked by the fantasy of representational unity. It is not simply that writers cannot achieve sensuous immediacy – that is a truism, and a commonplace. It is rather that the literary persona, at least of the historical moment of the impression, cannot allow its writerly detachment to be compromised by continuity with concrete sense. And this is largely because the literary personae in question are such that writing's natural inhospitability to the impression's dynamic continuity is worsened by social refusal.

"Collaboration," as we have seen, is the sign of this refusal. But if collaboration reflects resistance to the impression's continuity, and if that resistance is in fact special to literature, what about the far greater prevalence of Primitivism in the visual arts? Doesn't Gauguin's *D'où venons-nous? Que sommes-nous? Où allons-nous?* (1897–98) betray a far greater dependence upon the primitive, and far greater anxiety about it, than Conrad's Preface to *The Nigger of the "Narcissus"* or *Heart of Darkness*?[4] And wouldn't the comparison prove that the painterly impression, like its literary counterpart, works only through and against social resistances? Much more work – much more extensive comparison of the different primitivisms at work in the two arts – would be necessary to answer this question, but we might make a basic distinction between the degrees of *secrecy* involved in each case. It may be true that in Impressionist writing and painting both the primitive "served as a kind of stimulating focus, a catalytic which, though not itself used or borrowed from, still helped the artists to formulate their own aims because they could attribute to it the qualities they themselves sought to attain."[5] It seems also true, however, that primitivist painters tended openly to include the primitive in their productions, and to emphasize the extent of the catalyzation. This difference and its implications appear perhaps most clearly for our purposes in the different ways primitivism is at work in the essays by Virginia Woolf and Vanessa Bell. Woolf's primitivism, insofar as Mrs. Brown exemplifies it, is covert; Mrs.

Brown might enable her to imagine "the qualities she sought to attain," but Mrs. Brown also does so only under the cover of a different enterprise. Bell, by contrast, openly admits the primitive nature of her primary endeavor – not in her relation to Mrs. Brown, but in what she has to say about the formal genius of children: "If we could see our end clearly at the beginning as children do – and state it, and leave it – our pictures would no doubt be as lovely in technique as are those of the old painters in fresco who had to do so on account of their medium" (165). Bell in fact encourages the adolescents in her audience to be more like the children they have recently been, without any fear that such encouragement will infantilize their work. Fear of that kind leads to Woolf's collaboration with Mrs. Brown; lack of it makes primitivism more present in Bell's theory, and makes it also unlikely to impede Impressionist mediation.

Is this then to say what literary Impressionism's detractors have always said – that, in Pound's words, "Impressionism belongs in paint" and nowhere else? How is saying that writing resists the impression's dynamic continuity really any different from saying that writing must exclude the merely sensuous impression? The difference lies not only between the mediatory and the sensuous impression, but between "resistance" and "exclusion." To say that writing necessarily excludes the immediate report of the senses is to make a simple point (and, in certain ways, an inaccurate one), and to leave little else to say about the writing that would try to include it. But to say that certain writers try to make the impression a way to create the connections that would change writing's relation to sense is to leave much to say, even if – especially if – the effort fails. In that case, the analogy between the sister arts is not simply one that proves that one art succeeds where the other fails, but one that encourages us to look for "success" in other places. Impressionist writing may not as success-fully create the connections that change art's relation to sense, but its formal difference gives it a different and productive critical purchase on the problem of *aesthesis*. Where the impression led painters to ever broader perceptual extensions, it led writers to regret the ways in which the "political unconscious" of their own form made such extensions of aesthetic perception a reflection of differences destruc-tive to aesthetic mediation. Such regretful reflection, however, became a kind of success, if not for aesthetic perception itself, then for the aesthetic record: it became a highly productive record of the linkage, in representation, between perception and politics.

Perhaps the major difference, then, between the sister arts of the impression is the difference between each art's secondary form. If the painterly impression leads onward to abstraction, the literary impression leads onward to allegory; if the former runs strangely as a matter of course into its apparent opposite, the latter runs into something really opposite to it – its own allegorical complication and undoing. These secondary results, however, really only intensify the essential difference between the arts. If it is true, as Clement Greenberg has claimed, that modern aesthetics made it seem that "each art had to determine, through its own operations and works, the effects exclusive to itself," then the impression might be one key force for this new exclusivity, due to the way it overdetermines the "operations" special to each of the arts.[6] Encouraging diachronic allegory in writing and abstraction in painting, the impression emphasizes pre-existing differences between the arts, so that it undoes the affinity that its common appearance in the two arts would seem to create.

This effect is ironic, not only because the Impressionist arts seem so "familial," but because the impression begins as a force for mediation of perceptual "operations" that inform the special operations of the arts. As I suggested in Chapter One, the impression would collapse those distinctions which, at least since Lessing's *Laocoön*, have served to distinguish writing from painting. Its way of partaking both of flux and of instantaneity, and its potential to blur the line between the abstract and the concrete, would seem to disallow the kind of distinctions Lessing (and the subsequent record of sister-art differences) tends to make. Moreover, the impression is in this sense a version of the aspirations of sister-arts comparisons more generally, implying in its ambiguity what sister-arts borrowings try to achieve by bringing the talents of one art into the other. If we combine these contradictory tendencies – the tendency, on the one hand, to blur the difference between the arts, and on the other hand ultimately to emphasize it – we hit on what makes it most difficult to construct a sister-arts analogy in this case.

Difficult, but enlightening: for if the analogy is one that seems to expand and contract so elusively, it is one that sheds light on the theoretical problem of aesthetic periodicity itself. If we ask, finally, whether or not there exists an Impressionist period style, our new analogy gives us the following answer: because the impression at once presumes and limits the sharing at work in periodicity itself, it constitutes a period style in which the difference between the arts becomes the sign of their interrelation.

This last paradox is perhaps analogous to the paradoxical inter-relation of the arts of Virginia Woolf and Vanessa Bell. With so much in common, the Stephen sisters found nevertheless that a common aesthetic interest could produce very different temperaments de-pending on its context of action. Their differences – Bell's relative serenity, not unrelated to the easy plausibility of her account of aesthetic unity; Woolf's relative duality, at once aesthetic and temperamental – reflect (if not derive from) the different effects of the impression in the different arts, which create divisions despite their familiality. And since the impression has such a tendency toward personification, and since its personifications are the key to its problems, it might not be inappropriate to end here by making these sisters stand for the strange sisterhood engendered by the problem of the impression.

Notes

INTRODUCTION

1 Marcel Proust, *In Search of Lost Time*, trans. Andreas Mayor and Terence Kilmartin, 6 vols. (New York: Modern Library, 1993), vol. II, pp. 539–40. All future page references will be given parenthetically and refer to the same edition.

2 For Proust's reference to literary Impressionism, see "Les Eblouisse-ments par la Comtesse de Noailles," *Contre Sainte-Beuve, precede de Pastiches et mélanges et suivi de Essais et articles*, ed. Pierre Clarac and Yves Sandre (Paris: Gallimard, 1954), pp. 542–43.

3 The reading of Proust which follows here generally conforms to the common view of the way Proust regains lost time, and the interpretation specifically of Proust's impression aligns with Julia Kristeva, *Time and Sense: Proust and the Experience of Literature*, trans. Ross Guberman (New York: Columbia University Press, 1996), pp. 255–57; and Martha Nussbaum, *Love's Knowledge* (Oxford University Press, 1990), pp. 267–73; against Gilles Deleuze, *Proust and Signs*, trans. Richard Howard (New York: G. Braziller, 1972).

4 Walter Pater, *The Renaissance: Studies in Art and Poetry* (1893), ed. Donald Hill (Berkeley: University of California Press, 1980), p. xix.

5 Henry James, "The Art of Fiction" (1884), *The Art of Criticism: Henry James on the Theory and Practice of Fiction*, ed. William Veeder and Susan Griffin (University of Chicago Press, 1986), p. 170.

1 IMPRESSIONS OF MODERNITY

1 See Louis Leroy, "Exhibition of the Impressionists (L'Exposition des impressionistes)," *Impressionism and Post-Impressionism, 1874–1904*, ed. Linda Nochlin (Englewood Cliffs, NJ: Prentice Hall, Inc.), pp. 10–14. As Meyer Schapiro notes, Leroy also "may have had a pun in mind, for the phrase *'peinture d'impression'* once meant house painting," (*Impressionism: Reflections and Perceptions* (New York: George Braziller, 1997), p. 21. See also the alternative coinage by John Rogers, who invented "Impres-sionism" with similar intent to ridicule Hume's Empiricism: he wrote in

Antipopopriestian (1839), "All hail to Berkeley who would have no matter, and Hume who would have no mind; to the Idealism of the former, and to the Impressionism of the latter!" (*OED*). For the history of the terms "impression" and "Impressionism" in French painting see John Rewald, *The History of Impressionism* (New York: The Museum of Modern Art, 1973), pp. 212, 318, 330, 421, and 521.

2 Walter Pater, *The Renaissance: Studies in Art and Poetry* (1893), ed. Donald Hill (Berkeley: University of California Press, 1980), p. xix.

3 Henry James, "The Art of Fiction" (1884), *The Art of Criticism: Henry James on the Theory and Practice of Fiction*, ed. William Veeder and Susan M. Griffin (University of Chicago Press, 1986), p. 170.

4 Thomas Hardy, Preface, *Tess of the D'Urbervilles* (1892; London: Penguin, 1978), p. 5; Joseph Conrad, Preface, *The Nigger of the "Narcissus"* (1897; London: J. M. Dent, 1950), p. x; Virginia Woolf, "Modern Novels" (1919), *The Collected Essays of Virginia Woolf*, 4 vols. to date, ed. Andrew McNeillie (New York: Harcourt Brace Jovanovich, 1986–), vol. III, p. 33.

5 Vernon Lee, "On Novels," *Baldwin: Dialogues on Views and Aspirations* (London: T. Fisher Unwin, 1886), p. 202; Oscar Wilde, "The Critic as Artist," *The Artist as Critic*, ed. Richard Ellmann (Chicago: University of Chicago Press, 1969), p. 370; Hamlin Garland, "The Productive Conditions of American Literature," *Forum* 17 (1894): p. 690. For T. E. Hulme's reference to the impression, see "The Sister Arts," below. For those of May Sinclair and Elizabeth Bowen, see Chapter Three.

6 See Richard Ellmann for an account of the way "the word 'impression' agitated against pat assumptions and preconceptions," Introduction, *The Artist as Critic: Critical Writings of Oscar Wilde* (University of Chicago Press, 1968), p. xiii.

7 Peter Stowell, *Literary Impressionism: James and Chekhov* (Athens: University of Georgia Press, 1980), p. 9.

8 Three of these critical accounts – Frederic Jameson's *The Political Unconscious* (Ithaca: Cornell University Press, 1981), Michael Levenson, *A Genealogy of Modernism: A Study of English Literary Doctrine, 1908–1922* (Cambridge University Press, 1985), and John Carlos Rowe, "James's Rhetoric of the Eye: Re-Marking the Impression," *Criticism* 24.3 (1982): pp. 233–60) – have had shaping influence on this book's reappraisal of Impressionism, and will appear often as touchstones in the chapters that follow. Other landmarks in the study of literary Impressionism include: Maria Elisabeth Kronegger, *Literary Impressionism* (New Haven: College and University Press, 1973); Ian Watt, *Conrad in the Nineteenth Century* (Berkeley: University of California Press, 1979); James Nagel, *Stephen Crane and Literary Impressionism* (Penn State University Press, 1980); Stowell, *Literary Impressionism*; Paul Armstrong, *The Challenge of Bewilderment: Understanding and Representation in James, Conrad, and Ford* (Ithaca: Cornell University Press, 1988); Julia van Gunsteren, *Katherine Mansfield*

and *Literary Impressionism* (Atlanta: Rodopi, 1990); and Todd K. Bender's *Literary Impressionism in Jean Rhys, Ford Madox Ford, Joseph Conrad, and Charlotte Brontë* (New York: Garland Publishing Inc., 1998).

9 Kronegger, *Literary Impressionism*, p. 125n.14; Stowell, *Literary Impressionism*, p. 4; Jameson, *Political Unconscious*, p. 236.

10 Herbert Howarth, "Symposium in Literary Impressionism," *Yearbook of Comparative Literature* 17 (1968): pp. 41–42.

11 Ferdinand Brunetière, "L'impressionisme dans le roman," *La revue des deux mondes* (1879), pp. 458, 456.

12 Joseph Conrad, to Stephen Crane, December 1, 1897, *Stephen Crane: Letters*, ed. R. W. Stallman and Lillian Gilkes (New York University Press, 1960), p. 154.

13 Joseph Conrad, to Ezra Pound, December 5, 1897, *The Collected Letters of Joseph Conrad*, eds. Frederick Karl and Laurence Davies (Cambridge University Press, 1983–96), vol. I, p. 416.

14 Ezra Pound, "Review in *New Freewoman* I (December 1913)," quoted in *Ford Madox Ford: The Critical Heritage*, ed. Frank MacShane (London: Routledge and Kegan Paul, 1972), pp. 55, 58; R. A. Cassell, *Ford Madox Ford: Modern Judgements* (London: Macmillan, 1972), p. 16. Other key accounts of literary Impressionism of this moment include: a two-part article in the *Spectator* for 1886, "Impressionist Descriptions" (778–80) and "Literary Impressionists" (810–12); Joseph Warren Beach, *The Twentieth Century Novel: Studies in Technique* (New York: The Century Co., 1932); and Herbert J. Muller, "Impressionism in Fiction: Prism vs. Mirror," *The American Scholar* 7 (1938): pp. 355–67.

15 Calvin Brown, "Symposium in Literary Impressionism," *Yearbook of Comparative Literature* 17 (1968): p. 59.

16 Michael Fried, "Almayer's Face: On 'Impressionism' in Conrad, Crane, and Norris," *Critical Inquiry* 17 (1990): pp. 197–98.

17 Other skeptical accounts include Eloise Knapp Hay's "Impressionism Limited," *Joseph Conrad: A Commemoration*, ed. Norman Sherry (Macmillan, 1976), pp. 54–64, and "Proust, James, Conrad, and Impressionism," *Style* 22.3 (Fall 1988): pp. 368–81. Other more positive accounts include A. N. Lytle, "Impressionism, the Ego, and the First Person," *Daedalus* 92 (1963): pp. 281–96.

18 Peter Stowell considers Impressionism the harbinger of much twentieth-century perceptual theory (see below); Elisabeth Maria Kronegger notes that Impressionism was "anticipated by Balzac in 1832" and remains the predominant style to the present day in literature (*Literary Impressionism* 30, 33); Paul Armstrong notes that "'Impressionism' covers so much ground that one might despair at discovering common properties which unite even the novelists it designates" ("The Hermeneutics of Literary Impressionism: Interpretation and Reality in James, Conrad, and Ford," *Analecta Husserliana*, ed. A. Tymieniecka (New York: D. Reidel Publishing Company, 1985), p. 477).

19 Brown, "Symposium," p. 55.
20 Chris Baldick, "Impressionism," *The Concise Oxford Dictionary of Literary Terms* (Oxford University Press, 1990), p. 108.
21 William Hazlitt, "On Poetry in General," *The Complete Works of William Hazlitt*, ed. A. R. Waller and Arnold Glover, 12 vols. (London: J. M. Dent and Sons, 1902), vol. I, p. 3.
22 Wilde, "The Critic as Artist," p. 394.
23 William Gass, "Ford's Impressionisms," *Finding a Form* (New York: A. A. Knopf, 1996), pp. 85–86.
24 Meyer Schapiro, *Impressionism*, p. 28.
25 Michael Levenson comes closest to making uncertainty definitive in this sense, and my account is everywhere indebted to his foundational account of the genealogy of Modernism. My account differs from his, however, by locating what he sees as the ambivalence *about* Impressionism *within* Impressionism. Levenson argues, for example, that "two aims – the registering of fact and the recording of consciousness, *physis* and *psyche* – have invited contradictory interpretations of Impressionism; it has been characterized as both a precise rendering of objects and an unrepentant subjectivizing . . ." (*Genealogy*, p. 36). I mean to argue that Impressionism aims to make these two aims one, and that they only devolve into two when "contradictory interpretations" on the part of the Impressionists themselves make the juncture of the two terms seem impossible.
26 See primarily Stowell, *Literary Impressionism*; Johnson "Conrad's Impressionism and Watt's 'Delayed Decoding'," *Conrad Revisited: Essays for the Eighties*, ed. Ross Murfin (University: University of Alabama Press, 1985), pp. 51–70;, and Rowe, "James's Rhetoric of the Eye."
27 M. H. Abrams, *The Mirror and the Lamp: Romantic Theory and the Critical Tradition* (Oxford University Press, 1953), p. 57.
28 Jules David Law, *The Rhetoric of Empiricism: Language and Perception from Locke to I. A. Richards* (Ithaca: Cornell University Press, 1993), p. 12.
29 For an account of the impression's early life in classical philosophical debates, see Michael Frede, "Stoics and Skeptics on Clear and Distinct Impressions," *The Skeptical Tradition*, ed. M. Burnyeat (Berkeley: University of California Press, 1983), pp. 65–94, and Martha Nussbaum, *Love's Knowledge* (Oxford University Press, 1990), pp. 263–72.
30 Frances Yates, *The Art of Memory* (University of Chicago Press, 1966), pp. 75, 124.
31 For a good discussion of the wax-impression metaphor and its legacy in classical thought Mary Carruthers, *The Book of Memory: A Study of Memory in Medieval Culture* (University of Chicago Press, 1992), pp. 21–32.
32 John Locke, *An Essay Concerning Human Understanding*, ed. Alexander Campbell, 2 vols (New York: Dover Publications, 1959), vol. I, pp. 1, 140. For the first usage, see Locke's initial statement of intention: ". . . if I should only show (as I hope to show in the following parts of this

Discourse) how men, barely by the use of their natural faculties, may
attain to the knowledge they have, without the help of innate impressions" (I: 38); for the second, see his baseline formulation of empiricist
doctrine: ". . . I conceive that ideas in the understanding are coeval
with sensation; which is such an impression or motion made in some
part of the body, as produces some perception in the understanding. It is
about these impressions made on our senses by outward objects that the
mind seems *first* to employ itself . . ." (I: 141); for more examples of the
first see I: 53, 56, 67, 82, 94, 102, 112, and II: 417; for more examples of
the second see I: 59, 140, 158, 183, 243, 298, and 308.

33 Watt, *Conrad in the Nineteenth Century*, pp. 168–80.

34 David Hume, *Treatise of Human Nature*, ed. L. A. Selby-Bigge (Oxford:
Clarendon Press, 1978), p. 1. Future references will cite this edition in
parentheses.

35 Smith describes the *Treatise* as "nothing less than a resolute reversing
. . . of the roles hitherto ascribed to reason and feeling respectively,"
*The Philosophy of David Hume: A Critical Study of Its Origins and Central
Doctrines* (London: Macmillan, 1960), p. 11.

36 Hume makes this comment retrospectively in the later *Enquiry Concerning
Human Understanding*, 2 vols., ed. L. A. Selby-Bigge (Oxford: Clarendon
Press, 1975), vol. II, pp. 12, 18.

37 R. J. Butler, "Hume's Impression," *Impressions of Empiricism*, ed. Godfrey
Vesey (London: Macmillan, 1976), pp. 135–36.

38 Norman Kemp Smith, *David Hume*, pp. 448, 84.

39 Richard Rorty notices something like this conflation in Locke: see
Philosophy and the Mirror of Nature (Princeton University Press, 1979),
pp. 143–44.

40 William Hazlitt, *Lectures on English Philosophy*, *The Complete Works of
William Hazlitt*, ed. P. P. Howe (London: Frank Cass and Co., Ltd.,
1967), vol. II, p. 152.

41 Stephen Everson, "The Difference Between Thinking and Feeling,"
David Hume: Critical Assessments, ed. Stanley Tweyman (London: Routledge, 1995), vol. I, p. 22.

42 Henri Bergson, *Time and Free Will: An Essay on the Immediate Data of
Consciousness*, trans. F. L. Pogson (London: George Allen Unwin, Ltd.,
1910), p. 131.

43 Edmund Husserl, *Cartesian Meditations: An Introduction to Phenomenology*, trans.
Dorion Cairns (Dordrecht: Kluwer Academic Publishers, 1993), p. 33.

44 Butler, "Hume's Impression," p. 131.

45 Kronegger, *Literary Impressionism*, pp. 36, 14.

46 Stowell, *Literary Impressionism*, pp. 16–17.

47 Henri Bergson, *An Introduction to Metaphysics* (1903), trans. T. E. Hulme
(New York: Macmillan and Company, 1955), pp. 23–24.

48 Edmund Husserl, *Ideas* I (1913), trans. W. R. Boyce Gibson (New York:
Collier Books, 1962), pp. 213–35.

49 William James, *The Principles of Psychology*, 2 vols. (1890; New York: Dover Publications, 1950), vol. II, p. 345.

50 Maurice Merleau-Ponty, *Phenomenology of Perception* (1962; London: Routledge, 1992), p. 148.

51 See Jacques Derrida, *Speech and Phenomena, And Other Essays on Husserl's Theory of Signs*, trans. David B. Allison (Evanston: Northwestern University Press, 1973), pp. 4–5.

52 Judith Ryan, *The Vanishing Subject: Early Psychology and Literary Modernism* (University of Chicago Press, 1991), p. 3.

53 Ryan, *Vanishing Subject*, p. 19

54 See Immanuel Kant, *Critique of Judgment*, trans. James Creed Meredith (Oxford: Clarendon Press, 1992), p. 179.

55 Walter Besant, *The Art of Fiction* (Boston: Cupples, Upshaw and Co., 1884), pp. 17–18.

56 Geoffrey Hartman, *The Unmediated Vision: An Interpretation of Wordsworth, Hopkins, Rilke, and Valery* (New Haven: Yale University Press, 1954), p. 169.

57 This particular use of the term comes from Armstrong, "Hermeneutics," pp. 488–89.

58 The chapters that follow will discuss the part modernist writing plays in the history of this pattern of association, which really begins as soon as psychology and philosophy begin (in Aristotle, in Burke) to differentiate functions of human being: see Elizabeth Spelman, "Woman as Body: Ancient and Contemporary Views," *Feminist Studies* 8.1 (Spring 1982): pp. 109–31 (which discusses, for example, Aristotle's treatment of the baser sensuality of women and slaves); and Genevieve Lloyd, *The Man of Reason: 'Male' and 'Female' in Western Philosophy* (London: Routledge, 1993); and, for modern versions of the association, the "deconstruction is a woman" debate and the association of femininity with modernity in such studies as Rita Felski, *The Gender of Modernity* (Cambridge: Harvard University Press, 1995); see also the references in subsequent chapters to "standpoint" epistemology, and to its sources in Marxism.

59 M. H. Abrams, *Natural Supernaturalism: Tradition and Revolution in Romantic Literature* (New York: W. W. Norton and Company, 1971), p. 65.

60 James Engell, *The Creative Imagination: Enlightenment to Romanticism* (Cambridge: Harvard University Press, 1981), p. 222.

61 Abrams, *Supernaturalism*, p. 13.

62 Engell, *Imagination*, p. 338.

63 S. T. Coleridge, *Biographia Litteraria; or, Biographical Sketches of My Literary Life and Opinions* (1817), ed. James Engell and W. Jackson Bate (Princeton University Press, 1983), vol. I, p. 304.

64 Engell, *Imagination*, p. 338.

65 See John Ruskin, *Modern Painters, The Library Edition of the Works of John Ruskin* (London: George Allen, 1903), vol. II, pp. 42, 47, 49.

66 Quoted in Engell, *Imagination*, p. 281.

67 Mary Wollstonecraft, *A Vindication of the Rights of Woman,* 2nd edition (1792), ed. Carol H. Poston (New York: Norton, 1988), pp. 60–61.

68 Edgar Allan Poe, "The Philosophy of Composition" (1846), *The Complete Works of Edgar Allan Poe* (New York: The Society of English and French Literature, 1902), vol. xiv, p. 194.

69 Poe, "Tale-Writing – Nathaniel Hawthorne – Twice Told Tales" (1847), *Complete Works,* vol. xiii, p. 145.

70 Poe, "Composition," p. 196; "Hawthorne," p. 152.

71 Robert D. Jacobs, *Poe: Journalist and Critic* (Baton Rouge: Louisiana State University Press, 1969), pp. 319–20.

72 William Wordsworth, "Preface to *Lyrical Ballads*" (1802), *William Wordsworth: The Poems,* ed. John O. Hayden (New Haven: Yale University Press, 1977), vol. ii, p. 878.

73 G. W. F. Hegel, *Introductory Lectures on Aesthetics,* trans. Bernard Bosanquet (1886), ed. Michael Inwood (London: Penguin, 1993), pp. 251–52.

74 T. J. Clark, *Farewell to an Idea: Episodes from a History of Modernism* (New York: Yale University Press, 1999), p. 8.

75 Jonathan Crary, *Techniques of the Observer: On Vision and Modernity in the Nineteenth Century* (Cambridge: MIT Press, 1990), pp. 3, 17.

76 Louis Menand, "Literature and Professionalism," *Discovering Modernism* (New York: Oxford University Press, 1987), pp. 99–100.

77 See Chapters Three and Five for reference to the advice Besant and Bennett give.

78 Angus Fletcher, *Allegory: The Theory of a Symbolic Mode* (Ithaca: Cornell University Press, 1964), p. 301.

79 Fletcher, *Allegory,* p. 298.

80 Paul de Man, "The Rhetoric of Temporality," *Blindness and Insight: Essays in the Rhetoric of Contemporary Criticism* (Minneapolis: University of Minnesota Press, 1983), p. 206.

81 Standard warnings against interart analogies include Alastair Fowler, "Periodization and Interart Analogies," *New Literary History* 3.3 (1972): pp. 487–509; Suzanne Langer, "Deceptive Analogies: Specious and Real Relationships Among the Arts," *Problems of Art* (New York: Scribner's, 1957), pp. 75–89; and René Wellek, "The Parallelism Between Literature and the Arts," *English Institute Annual, 1941* (New York, 1942).

82 Max Nordau, *Degeneration* (1892; Lincoln: University of Nebraska Press, 1993), p. 485.

83 Two studies that make pictorialist connections (though not to misdefine Impressionism) are Daniel R. Schwarz's *Reconfiguring Modernism: Explorations in the Relationship between Modern Art and Modern Literature* (Macmillan, 1997) and Marianna Torgovnick's *The Visual Arts, Pictorialism, and the Novel: James, Lawrence, and Woolf* (Princeton University Press, 1995). The tendency to define Impressionism as a literary pictorialism appears most strongly in Jack Stewart's "Impressionism in the Early Novels of Virginia Woolf," *Journal of Modern Literature* 9 (1982): pp. 237–66.

84 Henry James, "Parisian Festivity," *Impressionists in England*, ed. Kate Flint (London: Routledge and Kegan Paul, 1984), pp. 37–38.

85 Quoted in Stowell, *Literary Impressionism*, p. 48.

86 Kronegger, *Literary Impressionism*, p. 13; Stowell, *Literary Impressionism*, p. 6.

87 David Scott, "Writing the Arts: Aesthetics, Art Criticism, and Literary Practice," *Artistic Relations: Literature and the Visual Arts in Nineteenth-Century France*, ed. Peter Collier and Robert Lethbridge (New Haven: Yale University Press, 1994), pp. 61–75.

88 See Fry on the transitional distinction: "The Post-Impressionists," *A Roger Fry Reader*, ed. Christopher Reed (University of Chicago Press, 1996), p. 82.

89 T. E. Hulme, "A Lecture on Modern Poetry," *The Collected Writings of T. E. Hulme*, ed. Karen Csengeri (Oxford University Press, 1994), p. 53.

90 Alastair Fowler, "Periodization and Interart Analogies," *New Literary History* 3.3 (1972): p. 489. See for example Pierre Bourdieu, "The Link Between Literary and Artistic Struggles," trans. Elinor Dorday, *Artistic Relations*, ed. Collier and Lethbridge (New Haven: Yale University Press, 1994), 36, and Clement Greenberg, "Modernist Painting," *Clement Greenberg: The Collected Essays and Criticism*, ed. John O'Brian (University of Chicago Press, 1993), p. 86.

91 Comparison between the Impressionisms should therefore take its cue from W. J. T. Mitchell, whose theory of the "pictorial turn" emphasizes the way that arts differently and agonistically lay claim to experiential accuracy: see *Picture Theory: Essays on Visual and Verbal Representation* (University of Chicago Press, 1994), p. 43.

92 Wendy Steiner, *The Colors of Rhetoric: Problems in the Relation between Modern Literature and Painting* (Chicago: University of Chicago Press, 1982), p. 5.

93 Susanne Langer similarly describes the tendency of language to lead us to make inappropriate interart analogies. See "Deceptive Analogies: Specious and Real Relationships Among the Arts," *Problems of Art* (New York: Scribner's, 1957), p. 77.

94 Ian Watt, *The Rise of the Novel* (Berkeley: University of California Press, 1957), p. 62.

95 Similar observations have been made by those who want to deny that Conrad is an Impressionist. See for example Eloise Knapp Hay, "Proust, James, Conrad, and Impressionism," *Style* 22.3 (1988): pp. 370–74.

96 E. H. Gombrich, *Art and Illusion: A Study in the Psychology of Pictorial Representation* (Princeton University Press, 1989), p. 110.

97 Leonard Diepeveen, "Shifting Metaphors: Interarts Comparisons and Analogy," *Word and Image* 5.2 (1989): p. 207.

98 Jean Hagstrum, *The Sister Arts: The Tradition of Literary Pictorialism and English Poetry from Dryden to Gray* (University of Chicago Press, 1958), p. 97.

99 Steiner, *Colors*, p. 6.
100 See Gotthold Ephraim Lessing, *Laocoön: An Essay on the Limits of Painting and Poetry*, trans. Edward Allen McCormick (Baltimore: The Johns Hopkins University Press, 1984), p. 77.

2 PATER'S HOMOEROTIC IMPRESSION

1 Matthew Arnold, "On Translating Homer," *Matthew Arnold on the Classical Tradition, The Complete Prose Works of Matthew Arnold*, ed. Robert H. Super (Ann Arbor: University of Michigan Press, 1960), vol. 1, p. 174; Pater, Introduction, *The Renaissance: Studies in Art and Poetry* (1893), p. xix (future references will cite this edition in parentheses); Oscar Wilde, "The Critic as Artist," *The Artist as Critic*, ed. Richard Ellmann (University of Chicago Press, 1969), p. 369. For standard critical views of Pater's place in this progression see Harold Bloom, Introduction, *Selected Writings of Walter Pater*, ed. Harold Bloom (New York: Columbia University Press, 1974), pp. 1–2; Ian Fletcher, *Walter Pater* (London: Longman's Green, 1959), pp. 16–17; Ellmann, Introduction *The Artist as Critic: Critical Writings of Oscar Wilde* (University of Chicago Press, 1968), p. xi; and for a study of the progression as a whole see Wendell V. Harris, "Arnold, Pater, Wilde, and the Object as in Themselves They See It," *Studies in English Literature, 1500–1900* 2 (1971): pp. 733–47.
2 Harold Bloom, *Ringers in the Tower: Studies in the Romantic Tradition* (University of Chicago Press, 1971), p. 186.
3 The epithet (in which "demoralizing" means "corrupting" rather than "discouraging") comes from "Is Walter Pater Demoralizing?," *Current Literature* 50 (1911): p. 667.
4 Richard Dellamora's *Masculine Desire: The Sexual Politics of Victorian Aestheticism* (Chapel Hill: University of North Carolina Press, 1990) and his "Critical Impressionism as Anti- Phallocentric Strategy," *Pater in the 1990s*, ed. Laurel Brake and Ian Small (Greensboro: ELT Press, 1991), pp. 127–42; James Eli Adams's "Gentleman, Dandy, Priest: Manliness and Social Authority in Pater's Aetheticism," *ELH* 59.2 (1992): pp. 441–67; and Linda Dowling's *Hellenism and Homosexuality in Victorian Oxford* (Ithaca: Cornell University Press, 1994), are among the best efforts to show how Pater's sexuality conditions his thinking and writing.
5 William Hazlitt, "On Poetry in General," *The Complete Works of William Hazlitt*, ed. A. R. Waller and Arnold Glover, 12 vols. (London: J. M. Dent and Sons, 1902), vol. 1, p. 3.
6 See David Bromwich, "The Genealogy of Disinterestedness," *Raritan* 1 (1982): pp. 67, 76, 83.
7 Billie Andrew Inman, "The Intellectual Context of Walter Pater's 'Conclusion'," *Prose Studies* 4.1 (1981): p. 14; Anthony Ward, *Walter Pater: The Idea in Nature* (London: Trinity Press, 1966), p. 33.
8 See Ward, *Idea*, p. 33.

9   See Pater's essay on Coleridge for Pater's own account of Romanticism's fatal idealism, and his observations about the problems that face such idealism in an Empirical age, *Appreciations, With an Essay on Style* (1889; New York: Macmillan, 1908), p. 105.

10 Wolfgang Iser, *Walter Pater: The Aesthetic Moment*, trans. David Henry Wilson (Cambridge University Press, 1987), p. 36.

11 See Iser on the impression's indeterminacy: *The Aesthetic Moment*, 36.

12 Walter Pater, "The History of Philosophy," Unpublished manuscript, Houghton Library, Harvard University, Cambridge, MA, p. 1a. Future references will cite this manuscript in parentheses.

13 Pater also seems to find the same appealing inconsistency in Plato, in *Plato and Platonism* (1893; London, Macmillan, 1910), p. 126.

14 Pater refers to it in "The School of Giorgione" as "imaginative reason," writing that "art addresses not pure sense, still less the pure intellect, but the 'imaginative reason' through the senses" (*Renaissance* 102).

15 Immanuel Kant, *Critique of Judgment*, trans. James Creed Meredith (Oxford: Clarendon Press, 1992), 41.

16 For the most thorough account of the philosophical background to Pater's writing see Billie Andrew Inman, "Intellectual Context"; an old standard is Helen Hawthorne Young, *The Writings of Walter Pater: A Reflection of British Philosophical Opinion from 1860–1890* (Bryn Mawr, PA.: Bryn Mawr College, 1933); on the issue of the kind of philosophical synthesis at work in Pater's use of Kant and Hume see Wendell V. Harris, *The Omnipresent Debate: Empiricism and Transcendentalism in Nineteenth-Century English Prose* (De Kalb: Northern Illinois University Press, 1981); and for an excellent recent account of Pater's relation to his philosophical context see Peter Allan Dale, " 'Distractions of Spirit': Walter Pater and Modernity," *Papers on Literature and Language* 28 (1992): pp. 319–48.

17 David Hume, *Treatise of Human Nature*, ed. L. A. Selby-Bigge (Oxford: Clarendon Press, 1978), p. 269.

18 Bromwich, "Genealogy," p. 76.

19 F. C. McGrath, *The Sensible Spirit: Walter Pater and the Modernist Paradigm* (Tampa: University of South Florida Press, 1986), pp. 23–24. It is by now in fact common to place Pater at the beginning of Modernism. Two of the more influential accounts of Modernism – Levenson's *A Genealogy of Modernism: A Study of English Literary Doctrine, 1908–1922* and Perry Meisel's *The Myth of the Modern: A Study in British Literature and Criticism after 1850* (Yale University Press, 1987) – do so as well.

20 Pater, "Style," *Appreciations*, p. 7.

21 Pater, "Style," pp. 31–32.

22 Pater, *Marius the Epicurean: His Sensations and Ideas.* 2 vols. (1885; London: Macmillan, 1910), vol. II, p. 51.

23 For a more liberal account of Pater's Impressionism, and a good account of the hazards of using the term to characterize Pater's

aesthetic, see Paul Zietlow, "Pater's Impressionism Reconsidered," *ELH* 44 (1977): pp. 150–70.

24 Perry Meisel, *The Absent Father: Virginia Woolf and Walter Pater* (New Haven: Yale University Press, 1980), p. 69.

25 In this sense "collaboration" resembles Wayne Koestenbaum's theory of male literary collaboration. See *Double Talk: The Homoerotics of Male Literary Collaboration* (New York: Routledge, 1989), pp. 2–3.

26 See Michael Levey, *The Case of Walter Pater* (London: Thames and Hudson, 1978) for the full history of Pater's relationship with Shadwell.

27 For the relevant sources in Winckelmann see Billie Andrew Inman, *Walter Pater's Reading: A Bibliography of His Library Borrowings and Literary References, 1858–1873* (New York: Garland Publishing Inc., 1981), p. 108.

28 H. Montgomery Hyde, *The Trials of Oscar Wilde* (New York: Dover Publications, 1962), p. 201.

29 Dowling, *Hellenism*, p. 81.

30 Pater, "Diaphaneitè," *Imaginary Portrait*, ed. Eugene Brzenk (New York: Harper and Row, 1964), pp. 210–11 (further references will cite this edition in parentheses).

31 This theory bears some resemblance to that recently expressed by Jeffrey Wallen in "Reflections and Self-Reflections: Narcissistic or Aesthetic Criticism? (Conflicted Aesthetics and Authenticity, 1870–1900)," *Texas Studies in Literature and Language* 34 (1992): p. 302.

32 Dellamora, *Masculine Desire*, p. 58.

33 Denis Donoghue, *Walter Pater: Lover of Strange Souls* (New York: A. A. Knopf, 1995), p. 112; Dowling, *Hellenism*, p. 92.

34 William Shuter makes a similar point in "The 'Outing' of Walter Pater," *Nineteenth Century Literature* 48.4 (1994): p. 505.

35 Pater, *Greek Studies* (London: Macmillan, 1922), pp. 286–87.

36 Michael Levey sums up the negative contemporary response well in *Walter Pater*, p. 97, and Richmond Crinkley refers to W. H. Mallock's *The New Republic* to prove that it was evidence of homosexuality that riled Pater's critics, *Walter Pater: Humanist* (Lexington: University Press of Kentucky, 1970), p. 138. For the variety of interpretations of Pater's actions in this regard see Lawrence Schuetz, "The Suppressed 'Conclusion' to *The Renaissance* and Pater's Modern Image," *ELT* 17 (1974): pp. 251–58; and Ian Small, "Pater and the Suppressed 'Conclusion' to *The Renaissance*: Comment and Reply" *ELT* (1976): pp. 313–16. The best recent account of Pater's response to his critics is Matthew Potolsky's "Fear of Falling: Walter Pater's *Marius the Epicurean* as a Dangerous Influence," *ELH* 65.3 (1998): pp. 701–29, which also helpfully surveys the critical history, and offers a convincing account of the way *Marius the Epicurean* reflects the problem.

37 Pater, *Imaginary Portraits*, p. 188.

3 THE WOMAN OF GENIUS

1 Laurence Sterne, *The Life and Opinions of Tristram Shandy*, ed. Melvyn New and Joan New, 3 vols. (The University Presses of Florida, 1978), vol. I, p. 97. Future references will cite this edition in parentheses.

2 See the *Essay* II, vol. I, p. 487.

3 Ernest Tuveson, "Locke and Sterne," *Reason and Imagination: Studies in the History of Ideas, 1600–1800*, ed. J. A. Mazzeo (New York: Columbia University Press, 1962), pp. 260–61.

4 See Armstrong, *Desire and Domestic Fiction: A Political History of the Novel* (New York: Oxford, 1987); Battersby, *Gender and Genius: Towards a Feminist Aesthetic* (London: The Women's Press, 1989); Broude, *Impressionism: A Feminist Reading: The Gendering of Art, Science, and Nature in the Nineteenth Century* (New York: Rizzoli, 1991); Douglas, *The Feminization of American Culture* (New York: Random House, 1977); Felski *The Gender of Modernity* (Cambridge: Harvard University Press, 1995); Mellor, *Romanticism and Gender* (London: Routledge, 1993).

5 Helen Longino, "Feminist Standpoint Theory and the Problems of Knowledge." *Signs* 19.1 (1993): pp. 201–02.

6 See, in addition to Longino's overview account, Susan Hekman's "Truth and Method: Feminist Standpoint Theory Revisited," *Signs* 22.2 (1977): pp. 340–65, and the replies (by Nancy Hartsock, Patricia Collins, Sandra Harding, and Dorothy Smith) which follow.

7 Alfred Habegger, *Henry James and "The Woman Business"* (Cambridge University Press, 1989), p. 230; and Lyndall Gordon, *A Private Life of Henry James: Two Women and His Art* (New York: W. W. Norton and Co., 1999), which claims that James "collaborated" with women friends in lethally exploitative fashion.

8 Particularly relevant here is the "gender critique of Modernism," carried on most incisively by Rita Felski. See *The Gender of Modernity*, pp. 21, 48.

9 "Literary Impressionists" *The Spectator* 59 (1886): p. 811.

10 Irving Babbitt, *The New Laokoon* (Boston: Houghton Mifflin, 1910), p. xiii.

11 Babbitt, *Laokoon*, pp. 185, 207.

12 H. G. Wells, "Introduction," *Nocturne* by Frank Swinnerton (New York: George H. Doran Co., 1917), p. xi.

13 W. L. George, "A Painter's Literature," *English Review* 30 (1920): pp. 228, 230.

14 W. W. Frierson, *English Novel in Transition, 1885–1940* (Norman: University of Oklahoma Press, 1942), p. 216.

15 May Sinclair, *A Journal of Impressions in Belgium* (London: Macmillan, 1915), p. v.

16 Elizabeth Bowen, "Foreword," *Collected Impressions* (London: Longmans, Green and Co. Ltd., 1950), p. vi.

17 What follows here contributes to a growing body of work on James's "use" of the feminine, highlights of which include William Veeder's "Henry James and the Uses of the Feminine," (*Out of Bounds: Male Writers and Gender(ed) Criticism* (Amherst: University of Massachusetts Press, 1990); John Carlos Rowe, *The Theoretical Dimensions of Henry James* (Madison: University of Wisconsin Press, 1984); Habegger's *Henry James and the "Woman Business"*; and, most recently, Gordon's *A Private Life of Henry James.*

18 Henry James, Letter to Edmund Gosse, December 13, 1894, *Letters of Henry James*, 2 vols., ed. Percy Lubbock (New York: Charles Scribner's Sons, 1920), vol. I, p. 222.

19 Walter Besant, *The Art of Fiction* (Boston: Cupples, Upshaw and Co., 1884), pp. 17–18.

20 Henry James, "The Art of Fiction" (1884), *The Art of Criticism: Henry James on the Theory and Practice of Fiction*, ed. W. Veeder and S. Griffin (University of Chicago Press, 1986), p. 170. Emphasis added. Future references will cite this edition in parentheses.

21 Robert Louis Stevenson, "A Humble Remonstrance" (1884), *Henry James and Robert Louis Stevenson: A Record of Friendship and Criticism*, ed. Janet Adams Smith (London: Rupert Hart- Davis, 1948), p. 94.

22 Richard Ellmann, "Henry James Among the Aesthetes," *Proceedings of the British Academy* (Oxford University Press, 1984), p. 215.

23 William James, Letter to Henry James, April 13, 1868, *The Correspondence of William James*, ed. Ignas K. Skrupsklesis and Elizabeth M. Berkeley (Charlottesville: University Press of Virginia, 1992), pp. 46–47.

24 As a theory about the brothers' intellectual sharing, this observation resists the sense recently conveyed by Ross Posnock (*The Trial of Curiosity: Henry James, William James, and the Challenge of Modernity* (Oxford University Press, 1991)) that Henry led the way to modernity's innovations, and looks back instead to earlier accounts, such as Richard A. Hocks' *Henry James and Pragmatistic Thought: A Study in the Relationship between the Philosophy of William James and the Literary Art of Henry James* (Chapel Hill: University of North Carolina Press, 1974), which acknowledge the inevitably greater systematicity of William's theoretical formulations.

25 See Leon Edel, *Henry James*, 5 vols. (New York: Avon Books, 1953–72), vol. III, pp. 95–106, and the account of James's conversation with Daudet by Theodore Child (published anonymously) in "Contributor's Club," *Atlantic* LIII (May 1884): pp. 724–27.

26 Henry James, "George Eliot's Life," *Atlantic Monthly* 55.331 (1885): p. 677.

27 For a thorough account of Daudet's influence on James see Lyall H. Powers, "James's Debt to Alphonse Daudet," *Comparative Literature* 24 (1972): pp. 150–62.

28 Henry James, "Alphonse Daudet" (1883), *Partial Portraits* (1888), ed. Leon Edel (Ann Arbor: University of Michigan Press, 1970), pp. 205, 207.

29 James's lack of full enthusiasm for French Impressionism has been well explained, typically by critics who quote his 1876 review of Impressionist painting: ". . . the 'Impressionist' doctrines strike me as incompatible with the existence of first-rate talent. To embrace them you must be provided with a plentiful absence of imagination" (*The New York Herald Tribune* (May 13, 1876): p. 2, in *Impressionists in England: The Critical Reception*, ed. Kate Flint (London: Routledge and Kegan Paul, 1984), pp. 37–38). See especially Eloise Knapp Hay, "Proust, James, Conrad, and Impressionism," *Style* 22.3 (1988): pp. 368–81.

30 Besant, *The Art of Fiction*, p. 18.

31 Leo Bersani gets at the double gesture in this style of argument when he writes that James "proves the novel's connection with life by deprecating its derivation from life" ("The Jamesian Lie," *Partisan Review* 36.1 (1969): p. 54).

32 The best accounts of the Besant–James interchange are Mark Spilka's "Henry James and Walter Besant: 'The Art of Fiction' Controversy," *Towards a Poetics of Fiction*, ed. Spilka (Bloomington: Indiana University Press, 1977), pp. 190–208, and the commentary and references in Veeder and Griffin, *Henry James*.

33 Paul Armstrong's excellent account of the impression reads this dilemma as a positive, phenomenological synthesis: see *The Phenomenology of Henry James* (The University of Chapel Hill Press, 1983), p. 102.

34 Henry James, *The Princess Casamassima* (1886), *The Novels and Tales of Henry James: The New York Edition*, 26 vols. (1907–09; Scribner Reprint Editions. Fairfield: Augustus M. Kelly Publishers, 1978), vol. v, p. 82. All future references to those novels and stories by James included in *The New York Edition* will cite the edition by volume and page number in parentheses.

35 Ellmann, "Henry James," p. 219.

36 Jonathan Freedman, *Professions of Taste: Henry James, British Aestheticism, and Commodity Culture* (Stanford: Stanford University Press, 1990), pp. 148–49.

37 Henry James, "A New England Winter" (1884), *The Complete Tales of Henry James*, ed. Leon Edel (New York: J. B. Lippincott, 1963), vol. vi, p. 114.

38 James was not alone in singling out Ritchie as an exemplary Impressionist. An anonymous writer in the *Spectator* for 1886 does so as well, writing of Impressionism that "if we had to illustrate the influence of the same school of fiction again at its best, we would go to Miss Thackeray" ("Literary Impressionists," p. 810).

39 Unsigned Review in *Critic* xxxv (August 1889): pp. 754–56, quoted in *Henry James: The Critical Heritage*, ed. Roger Gard (London: Routledge and Kegan Paul, 1968), p. 196.

40 Another, perhaps surprisingly, would be George Sand, who, as Leland Person notes, "combined the capacity to live all she could with the power to make her experiences 'pay' dividends in her writing," and

therefore aroused James's envy ("Henry James, George Sand, and the Suspense of Masculinity," *PMLA* 106.3 (May 1991): p. 519).

41 Armstrong, *Desire and Domestic Fiction*, p. 9.

42 James, "George Eliot's Life," p. 668.

43 See also one last sign of James's uncertainty, in James's only other reference to literary Impressionism: "Pierre Loti" (1888), *Essays in London* (New York: Harper and Bros., 1893), pp. 153, 183, 185.

44 John Carlos Rowe, "James's Rhetoric of the Eye: Re-Marking the Impression," *Criticism* 24.3 (1982): pp. 244, 247.

45 R. P. Blackmur, *Studies in Henry James* (New York: New Directions, 1983), p. 193; Millicent Bell, *Meaning in Henry James* (Cambridge: Harvard University Press, 1991), p. 85.

46 To note the bad version of collaboration at work here is to say in different terms what critics say when they point out Osmond's effort to "aestheticize" Isabel (see for example Michael Gilmore, "The Commodity World of *Portrait of a Lady*," *New England Quarterly* 59 (1986): pp. 51–74).

47 James, "The Art of Fiction," p. 172.

48 Even a glance through the critical heritage turns up any number of such charges – William seeing a "want of blood in your stories," complaints about "perpetual analysis," the way James's art is "too subtly delicate for its purposes," and has "not *sense* enough"; James's habit of "looking at an object by reflection and under cross-lights, – of divining and comprehending instead of seeing it"; and the claim, felt by many readers but expressed colorfully by Mrs. Henry Adams who wrote to her father that James "chaws more than he bites off" (Gard, *Critical Heritage*, pp. 24, 41, 64, 73, 119, 120).

49 See Rudolph Arnheim's *Visual Thinking*, (Berkeley: University of California Press, 1969), p. 134.

50 For an excellent account of something very much like "collaboration" in *The Ambassadors* see Julie Rivkin, "The Logic of Delegation in *The Ambassadors*," *Henry James: A Collection of Critical Essays* (New Jersey: Prentice Hall Press, 1994), pp. 135–53.

51 Blackmur, "The Critical Prefaces of Henry James" (1924), *Studies in Henry James*, p. 15.

52 Henry James, Letter to Robert Louis Stevenson, December 5, 1884, in Smith, *Friendship*, p. 102.

53 Henry James, letter to H. G. Wells, *Letters*, vol. II, p. 490.

54 For relevant readings of the Prefaces see Paul Armstrong, "Reading James's Prefaces and Reading James," *Henry James's New York Edition: The Construction of Authorship*, ed. David McWhirter (Stanford University Press, 1995), p. 135, and Sharon Cameron, *Thinking in Henry James* (Chicago: University of Chicago Press, 1989), pp. 19, 77.

55 Henry James, *Notes of a Son and Brother* (1914), *Autobiography*, ed. Frederick W. Dupee (New York: Criterion Books, 1956), p. 253.

56 Thomas Hardy, *Tess of the D'Urbervilles* (1891; London: Penguin, 1978), p. 5. Future references will cite this edition in parentheses.

57 *The Life and Work of Thomas Hardy, by Thomas Hardy,* ed. Michael Millgate (Athens: University of Georgia Press, 1985), p. 192.

58 Morton Zabel, "Hardy in Defense of His Art: The Aesthetic of Incongruity," *Thomas Hardy: Critical Assessments,* ed. Graham Clarke (Helm Information, 1993), p. 386.

59 Tony Tanner, "Colour and Movement in *Tess of the D'Urbervilles,*" *Thomas Hardy: Critical Assessments,* p. 126.

60 Hardy, Preface, *Jude the Obscure* (1896; London: Penguin, 1985), pp. 39–40.

61 Hardy, *Life,* p. 406.

62 Hardy, *Life,* p. 441.

63 Hardy, *Life,* pp. 432–33.

64 Mowbray Morris, "Culture and Anarchy," *Quarterly Review* 174.348 (1892): pp. 323, 325.

65 Andrew Lang, "At the Sign of the Ship," *Longman's Magazine* xxi (November 1892): p. 102.

4 THE DISTANT LABORER

1 Marcel Proust, *In Search of Lost Time,* trans. Andreas Mayor and Terence Kilmartin, 6 vols. (New York: Modern Library, 1993), vol. VI, pp. 274–75.

2 Terry Eagleton, *The Ideology of the Aesthetic* (London: Blackwell, 1990), p. 13.

3 This is not to agree with John Spagnoli that Proust exhibits considerable sympathy for the working classes, or that such sympathy should determine our response to his writing, but rather to show how the working class enters into Proust's aesthetic itself (*The Social Attitude of Marcel Proust* (New York: Institute for French Studies, 1936)).

4 Fredric Jameson, *The Political Unconscious* (Ithaca: Cornell University Press, 1981), p. 237.

5 Joseph Conrad to Edward Garnett, March 29, 1898, *The Collected Letters of Joseph Conrad,* ed. Frederick Karl and Laurence Davies (Cambridge University Press, 1983), vol. II, p. 50. See also Conrad to Cunninghame Graham, February 16, 1898: "I *suspect* my brain to be yeast and my backbone to be cotton. And I *know* that the quality of my work is of the kind to confirm my suspicions" (*Letters* vol. II, p. 39).

6 Joseph Conrad, Preface, *The Nigger of the "Narcissus"* (1897; 1950), *Collected Edition of the Works of Joseph Conrad,* 22 vols. (London: J. M. Dent and Sons, 1946–1954), p. vii. Future references to Conrad's works will cite this collected edition in parentheses.

7 See Albert Guerard, *Conrad the Novelist* (Cambridge: Harvard University Press, 1966), pp. 91, 77, 126–7. See below for a discussion of Watt's view of Conrad's skepticism.

8 Lionel Trilling, *Sincerity and Authenticity* (Cambridge: Harvard University Press, 1971), p. 70.

9 David Goldknopf, *The Life of the Novel* (University of Chicago Press, 1972), p. 82; Ian Watt, *Conrad in the Nineteenth Century* (Berkeley: University of California Press, 1979), p. 84. The tendency has been to call Conrad's Impressionism a limited sensationism that he outgrows, or an interest in sights and surfaces that he finds he must match with some better and more serious power of literary intellection. See Eloise Knapp Hay, "Proust, James, Conrad, and Impressionism," *Style* 22.3 (1988): pp. 370, 378; Ian Watt, "Conrad's Preface to *The Nigger of the 'Narcissus*,'" *Novel* 7.2 (1979): p. 109; and Levenson, *A Genealogy of Modernism: A Study of English Literary Doctrine, 1908–1922* (Cambridge University Press, 1985), pp. 1–10.

10 Ramon Fernández, "The Art of Conrad," trans. Charles Owen, *Joseph Conrad: A Critical Symposium*, ed. Robert Stallman (Michigan State University Press, 1960), p. 8.

11 Aristotle, *Art of Rhetoric*, trans. John Henry Freese (Cambridge: Harvard University Press, 1959), vol. III, pp. 405–06.

12 Hans Vaihinger, *The Philosophy of "As If"* (London: Routledge and Kegan Paul, 1965), p. 91.

13 Elaine Scarry, "On Vivacity: The Difference between Daydreaming and Imagining-Under-Authorial-Instruction," *Representations* (Fall 1995): p. 4.

14 Watt, *Conrad in the Nineteenth Century*, p. 175.

15 Bruce Johnson makes a similar point in his critique of "delayed decoding": see "Conrad's Impressionism and Watt's 'Delayed Decoding,'" *Conrad Revisited: Essays for the Eighties*, ed. Ross Murfin (University: University of Alabama Press, 1985), pp. 53, 55, 57.

16 Michael Levenson has established the relevance of Worringer to modernist literary aesthetics, in *Genealogy*, pp. 94–95.

17 Wilhelm Worringer, *Abstraction and Empathy* (1908), trans. Michael Bullock (London: Routledge and Kegan Paul, 1953), p. 17.

18 Wollaeger discusses the "modes of consolation or shelters, which Conrad proposes in response to the potential corrosiveness of total skepticism," *Joseph Conrad and the Fictions of Skepticism* (Stanford University Press, 1990), p. 79.

19 Bernard Meyer, *Joseph Conrad: A Psychoanalytic Biography* (Princeton University Press, 1967), pp. 32, 30, 34.

20 Johnson, "Conrad's Impressionism," p. 62.

21 Watt, "Conrad's Preface," p. 110.

22 John Barrell, *The Dark Side of the Landscape: The Rural Poor in English Painting 1730–1840* (Cambridge University Press, 1980), p. 5.

23 Marianna Torgovnick, *Gone Primitive: Savage Intellects, Modern Lives* (University of Chicago Press, 1990), p. 151.

24 Avrom Fleishman, *Conrad's Politics: Community and Anarchy in the Fiction of*

Joseph Conrad (Baltimore: The Johns Hopkins University Press, 1967), p. 47.

25 Jameson, *Political Unconscious*, p. 229.

26 Zdzislaw Nadjer, ed., *Conrad's Polish Background: Letters to and from Polish Friends*, trans. Halina Carroll (Oxford University Press, 1964), p. 240, quoted in Watt, *Conrad in the Nineteenth Century*, p. 24.

27 Bruce Johnson, *Conrad's Models of Mind* (Minneapolis: University of Minnesota Press, 1971), pp. 66–67.

28 Albert Guerard, *Conrad the Novelist*, p. 32.

29 Walter de la Mare, *TLS* (August 7, 1919), p. 422, quoted in *Joseph Conrad: The Critical Heritage*, ed. Norman Sherry (London: Routledge and Kegan Paul, 1973), p. 317.

30 Conrad (to a reviewer), December 9, 1897, Karl and Davies, *Letters*, 421.

31 Donald C. Yelton, *Mimesis and Metaphor* (The Hague: Moulton, 1967), p. 158.

32 Paul Armstrong, "The Hermeneutics of Literary Impressionism: Interpretation and Reality in James, Conrad, and Ford," *Analecta Husserliana*, ed. A. Tymieniecka (New York: D. Reidel Publishing Company, 1985), pp. 484–85.

33 Worringer, *Abstraction and Empathy*, p. 6.

34 Raymond Williams, *Marxism and Literature* (Oxford University Press, 1977), pp. 132–33.

35 Levenson writes that Ford "became the acknowledged representative of Impressionism" and that "this would make him the target of the anti-Impressionist reaction" because "the Impressionist influence on pre-war literary activity was transmitted entirely through Ford's interpretation of that method" (Levenson, *Genealogy*, p. 49).

36 Ford Madox Ford, "The Function of the Arts in the Republic" (1909), *The Critical Attitude* (London: Duckworth and Company, 1911), p. 29.

37 Levenson sees different stages in Ford's Impressionism – "Impressionism as precise description, Impressionism as egoism" (Levenson, *Genealogy*, p. 115). The former constitutes a *"civic realism"* (108), which "collapses into an egoism which no longer attempts to establish shared norms of reality" (115).

38 Ford expresses these egalitarian literary politics in his "Stocktaking" essays in the *Transatlantic Review*, "Stocktaking iii" (March 1924): pp. 51–52, and "Stocktaking ii" (February 1924): p. 61.

39 Ford, "English Literature of Today" (1909–10), *The Critical Attitude*, p. 65.

40 And see Brian May for another claim that Ford's Impressionism has this kind of political unconscious: "Ford Madox Ford and the Politics of Impressionism," *Essays in Literature* 21.1 (1994): p. 83.

41 For complete account of Ford's conservatism in these years see Robert Green, *Ford Madox Ford: Prose and Politics* (Cambridge University Press, 1981), pp. 3–50.

42 Green, *Ford*, 33; Ford, "Historical Vignette," *Outlook* (July 3, 1913): p. 14.
43 For the best account of the way this kind of ambivalence works in the backgrounds of modernist fiction see Michael Tratner, *Modernism and Mass Politics: Joyce, Woolf, Eliot, Yeats* (Stanford University Press, 1995), pp. 21–47.
44 Ford, "Historical Vignette," p. 15.
45 Ford, "Stocktaking IV," *Transatlantic Review* 1.4 (April 1924): p. 168.
46 Robie Macauley, "The Good Ford," *The Kenyon Critics: Studies in Modern Literature from the Kenyon Review*, ed. John Crowe Ransom (Cleveland: The World Publishing Company, 1951), p. 151.
47 Ford, "Impressionism – Some Speculations," *Poetry* II (1913): p. 3; Ford, "Techniques," *The Southern Review* I (1935): p. 31; Ford, *The March of Literature* (New York: The Dial Press, 1938), pp. 840–41; Ford, "On Impressionism," *Poetry and Drama* II (1914): p. 174; see Levenson, *Genealogy*, pp. 105–20, for an account of the way these uncertainties boil down to conflict between civic realism and subjective egoism.
48 Ford, "On Impressionism," pp. 171, 175. Future references will cite the essay in parentheses.
49 William Gass, "Ford's Impressionisms," *Finding a Form* (New York: A. A. Knopf, 1996), pp. 85–86.
50 Gass, "Ford's Impressionisms," p. 102.
51 Gass notices something like the indecision that is Impressionism's definitive aspect: see "Ford's Impressionisms," p. 100.
52 These allegations make "On Impressionism" and Ford's nostalgic fictions party to the many anti-socialist satires that had been appearing in England since 1907. See David Smith, *Socialist Propaganda in the Twentieth-Century British Novel* (London: Macmillan, 1978), pp. 4–9, for context here, and, for standard accounts of such resistances to Fabianism and Labour politics at this moment, Paul Thompson, *Socialists, Liberals and Labour: The Struggle for London, 1885–1914* (London: Routledge and Kegan Paul, 1967) and A. M. McBriar, *Fabian Socialism and English Politics, 1884–1918* (Cambridge University Press, 1962).
53 Max Saunders argues that *Ladies* involves "temporal doubling rather than an escapist displacement" – that Ford juxtaposes modern and medieval times, to incisive critical effect. My account here emphasizes, by contrast, the perhaps more obvious escapism at work in the novel (Max Saunders, *Ford Madox Ford*, 2 vols. (Oxford University Press, 1996–97), vol. I, p. 308).
54 Ford, *Ladies Whose Bright Eyes* (1911; 1935; New York: Ecco Press, 1989), p. 9. Future references to the novel will cite this edition in parentheses.
55 For the range of readings see Samuel Hynes, "The Epistemology of *The Good Soldier*," *Ford Madox Ford: Modern Judgments*, ed. R. A. Cassell (London: Macmillan, 1972), pp. 99, 101.
56 Ford, *The Good Soldier* (London: Penguin, 1946), p. 99.
57 The relationship may also be a homoerotic one, as Bruce Bassoff

suggests in "Dipal Fantasy and Arrested Development in *The Good Soldier*," *Twentieth Century Literature* 34.1 (1988): pp. 40–48.

58 Robert Huntley, *The Alien Protagonist of Ford Madox Ford* (Chapel Hill: The University of North Carolina Press, 1970), p. 168.

5 WOOLF'S PHENOMENOLOGICAL IMPRESSION

1 Wyndham Lewis, *Men Without Art* (1933; Black Sparrow Press, 1987), p. 133.

2 See (for each respectively) Judith Ryan's reading of Woolf as "one of the last outposts of empiricist modernism," *The Vanishing Subject: Early Psychology and Literary Modernism* (University of Chicago Press, 1991), p. 190; S. P. Rosenbaum, "The Philosophical Realism of Virginia Woolf," *English Literature and British Philosophy*, ed. Rosenbaum (Chicago: University of Chicago, 1971), pp. 316–56; Bruce Johnson, "A Modernist Noesis," *Omnium Gatherum: Essays for Richard Ellmann*, ed. Susan Dick et al. (Gerards Cross: Colin Smyths, 1989), pp. 60–71, and Mark Hussey, *The Singing of the Real World: The Philosophy of Virginia Woolf's Fiction* (Columbus: Ohio University Press, 1986).

3 Virginia Woolf, *The Diary of Virginia Woolf*, ed. Anne Olivier Bell, 6 vols. (New York: Harcourt Brace Jovanovich, 1978), vol. IV p. 126.

4 Woolf, *Diary*, vol. IV, p. 145.

5 Virginia Woolf, "Modern Novels" (1919), *The Essays of Virginia Woolf*, ed. Andrew McNeillie, 4 vols. to date (New York: Harcourt Brace Jovanovich, 1986–), vol. III, p. 33. Future references to the essay will cite this edition in parentheses.

6 Andrew McNeillie's annotation in *The Essays of Virginia Woolf* attributes this line to *The Village Priest and Other Stories* by Elena Militsina and Mikhail Saltikov, trans. Beatrix L. Tollemache (London: T. Fisher Unwin, 1918), p. 34.

7 Pamela Caughie, for example, claims that Woolf's rhetoric is "performative," and that her "refusal to choose" makes her "postmodern," *Virginia Woolf and Postmodernism: Literature in Quest and Question of Itself* (Chicago: University of Illinois Press, 1991), pp. 12, 197. Bette London also notes that "the search for an answer is not her real intent," and sees Woolf's real intent as a subversion of narrative authority (*The Appropriated Voice: Narrative Authority in Conrad, Forster, and Woolf* (Ann Arbor: University of Michigan Press, 1990), p. 116).

8 Woolf, *Diary*, vol. IV, p. 161.

9 Virginia Woolf, *The Waves* (1931; New York: Harcourt Brace, 1939), pp. 276, 291.

10 Woolf, *The Waves*, pp. 130, 27, 131.

11 Virginia Woolf, *Mrs. Dalloway* (1925; New York: Harcourt Brace Jovanovich, 1989), p. 57.

12 Woolf, *Mrs. Dalloway*, p. 58.

13 Woolf, *Diary*, vol. v, p. 298; vol. iii, p. 218; vol. iv p. 161.
14 The problem of the impression might also be the point of connection between Woolf's aesthetic and her mental illness. See Thomas Caramagno on Woolf's "bipolar theory of being" in *The Flight of the Mind: Virginia Woolf's Art and Manic-Depressive Illness* (Berkeley and Los Angeles: University of California Press, 1992), pp. 2–3, 73.
15 Woolf, *Diary*, vol. iv, p. 151.
16 For a comprehensive account of this sort of ambivalence in Modernism, see Peter Nicholls' account of the "ironies of the modern" (*Modernisms: A Literary Guide* (Berkeley and Los Angeles: University of California Press, 1995), pp. 5–23).
17 Michael Tratner notes that Woolf uses Mrs. Brown, as she tended to use working-class women figures, not "as seers or poetic voices that could replace upper-class artists, but as the visible manifestation of hidden forces that could release buried voices within those artists," and Tratner then goes on to see Mrs. Brown as an example of the way "modernist artists drew inspiration from the others politically challenging the social order" (*Modernism and Mass Politics: Joyce, Woolf, Eliot, Yeats* (Stanford University Press, 1995), p. 58).
18 Virginia Woolf, "The Mark on the Wall" (1917), *The Complete Shorter Fiction of Virginia Woolf*, ed. Susan Dick (New York: Harcourt Brace Jovanovich, 1989), p. 88. Future references to the story will cite this edition in parentheses.
19 Sartre uses a tree as an example to explain Husserlian phenomenology (specifically, Husserl's theory of intentionality): "'Intentionality': A Fundamental Idea of Husserl's Phenomenology" (1939), trans. Joseph P. Fell, *Journal of the British Society for Phenomenology* 1.2 (May 1970): p. 4.
20 For a good basic account of the classic phenomenological orientation and its aims see Edmund Husserl, "Phenomenology," *Encyclopedia Brittanica* (1911), p. 700.
21 Virginia Woolf, "The Death of the Moth" (1917), *The Death of the Moth and Other Essays* (New York: Harcourt Brace Jovanovich, 1942), p. 4. Future references to the essay will cite this edition in parentheses.
22 See Forster on *The Voyage Out* in *Daily News and Leader* (April 8, 1915), quoted in Robin Majumdar and Allen McLaurin, ed., *Virginia Woolf: The Critical Heritage* (London: Routledge and Kegan Paul, 1975), p. 53.
23 Virginia Woolf, "An Unwritten Novel" (1920), *Shorter Fiction*, p. 112. Future references to the story will cite this edition in parentheses.
24 See Perry Meisel, *The Absent Father: Virginia Woolf and Walter Pater* (New Haven:Yale University Press, 1980), p. xvi; Maxwell Bodenheim, "Underneath the Paint in *Jacob's Room*," *Nation* (NY) (March 28, 1923): p. 368; and Clive Bell in Majumdar and McLaurin, *Critical Heritage*, p. 146.
25 Arnold Bennett, "Neo-Impressionism in Literature," *Books and Persons* (New York: George Doran and Company, 1917), p. 285.

26 Woolf, *Essays*, vol. II, p. 130.

27 See also Bennett's "The First Post-Impressionist Show" (1910), in *The Author's Craft and Other Critical Writings of Arnold Bennett*, ed. Samuel Hynes (Lincoln: University of Nebraska Press, 1968), p. 244, and, for this pre-history, Paul Groetsch, "A Source for Virginia Woolf's 'Mr. Bennett and Mrs. Brown'," *English Literature in Transition* 7 (1964): pp. 188–89.

28 Bennett's relevant opinions and MacCarthy's review appear reprinted as context to Woolf's response, "The Intellectual Status of Women," Appendix III, *Diary*, vol. II, p. 339.

29 Woolf, *Diary*, vol. II, p. 169.

30 Quoted in Woolf, *Diary*, vol. II, pp. 339–42.

31 Beth Rigel Daugherty describes many of these developments in her argument against Samuel Hynes's interpretation of the debate between Bennett and Woolf: "The Whole Contention Between Mr. Bennett and Mrs. Woolf, Revisited," *Virginia Woolf: Centennial Essays*, ed. Elaine K. Ginsberg and Laura Moss Gottlieb (Troy, NY: The Whitson Publishing Company, 1983), p. 269.

32 Virginia Woolf, "Mr. Bennett and Mrs. Brown" (1923), *Essays*, vol. III, p. 387.

33 Virginia Woolf, "Character in Fiction" (1924), *Essays*, vol. III, p. 421. Future references to the essay will cite this edition in parentheses.

34 See Maria DiBattista, *Virginia Woolf's Major Novels: The Fables of Anon* (New Haven: Yale University Press, 1980), p. 162; Armstrong, *Desire and Domestic Fiction: A Political History of the Novel* (New York: Oxford, 1987), p. 243; Sandra Gilbert and Susan Gubar, "Sexual Linguistics: Women's Sentence, Men's Sentencing," *No Man's Land: The Place of the Woman Writer in the Twentieth Century*, 3 vols. (New Haven: Yale University Press, 1984–), pp. 227–71; Ann Ardis, *New Women, New Novels: Feminism and Early Modernism* (New Brunswick: Rutgers University Press, 1990); Bonnie Kime Scott, *The Gender of Modernism: A Critical Anthology* (Bloomington: Indiana University Press, 1990), p. 16; and Felski, *The Gender of Modernity* (Cambridge: Harvard University Press, 1995), p. 31.

35 Jane Goldman's *The Feminist Aesthetics of Virginia Woolf: Modernism, Post-Impressionism and the Politics of the Visual* (Cambridge University Press, 1998) sees similar connections at work in Woolf's outlook.

36 Fuss of course aims to undo the difference between Essentialism and Constructionism, and to show that "essentialist" has become a derogatory charge largely as a result of misunderstandings about the definition and deployment of essence (*Essentially Speaking* (New York: Routledge, 1989), p. 3).

37 Makiko Minow-Pinkney, *Virginia Woolf and the Problem of the Subject* (Sussex: Harvester, 1987), p. 60.

38 Minow-Pinkney, *Subject*, p. 194.

39 See Julia Kristeva, *Revolution in Poetic Language*, trans. Margaret Waller (New York: Columbia University Press, 1984), p. 36.

40 Jane Marcus, *Virginia Woolf and the Languages of Patriarchy* (Bloomington: Indiana University Press, 1987), p. 13.

41 Sandra Harding, "Rethinking Standpoint Epistemology: 'What is Strong Objectivity?'" *Feminist Epistemologies*, ed. Linda Alcoff and Elizabeth Potter (London: Routledge, 1993), pp. 49–82.

42 See Samuel Hynes, "The Whole Contention Between Mr. Bennett and Mrs. Brown," *Edwardian Occasions* (London: Routledge and Kegan Paul, 1972), pp. 25–27, 37.

43 Arnold Bennett, *How to Become an Author: A Practical Guide* (London: C. Arthur Pearson, Ltd., 1903), p. 27; *Literary Taste and How to Form It* (London: The New Age Press, 1909), p. 31.

44 Virginia Woolf, "Middlebrow," *The Death of the Moth*, p. 177.

45 Mary Childers, "Virginia Woolf on the Outside Looking Down: Reflections on a Class of Women," *Modern Fiction Studies* 38.1 (1992): pp. 76–77.

46 The version of "Mr. Bennett and Mrs. Brown" that appeared in *Nation and Athenaeum* and the *New York Evening Post* in 1923 has much less to say about Mrs. Brown's social situation than the version that appeared in the *Hogarth Essays* in 1924. For proof that Woolf meant Mrs. Brown to have some specific class status – that is, that she meant the embodiment of "life" to come from a class beneath her own – we might have to look to other texts. Vernon Lee's *Miss Brown* (Blackwood, 1884), for example, says explicitly that its heroine gets her name from a father who was "a scotch mechanic" (42).

47 Woolf, "Character in Fiction," *Essays*, vol. III, p. 423.

48 Woolf, *Diary*, vol. III, p. 104.

6 THREE IMPRESSIONIST ALLEGORIES

1 Edwin Honig, *Dark Conceit: The Making of Allegory* (Providence: Brown University Press, 1959), p. 3.

2 Benjamin, Walter, *The Origin of German Tragic Drama*, trans. John Osborne (London: Verso, 1985), pp. 176, 226, 229.

3 Bernard Cowan, "Walter Benjamin's Theory of Allegory," *New German Critique* 22 (1981): p. 116.

4 Benjamin, *Tragic Drama*, p. 162.

5 Paul de Man, "The Rhetoric of Temporality," *Blindness and Insight: Essays in the Rhetoric of Contemporary Criticism* (Minneapolis: University of Minnesota Press, 1983), p. 206.

6 de Man, "Rhetoric of Temporality," p. 206.

7 Watt, *Conrad in the Nineteenth Century* (Berkeley: University of California Press, 1979), pp. 180–87.

8 For the best recent account of the different ways criticism has tried to explain the relationship between *The Renaissance* and *Marius the Epicurean*, see Matthew Potolsky's "Fear of Falling": Walter Pater's *Marius the Epicurean* as a Dangerous Influence," *ELH* 65.3 (1998): pp. 701–29.

9 Walter Pater, *Marius the Epicurean: His Sensations and Ideas.* 2 vols. (1995; London: Macmillan, 1910), vol. I, pp. 25, 33, 24.

10 James Eli Adams also notes that "in presenting Marius's skepticism as a mode of strenuous, even religious self-discipline, Pater implicitly responds to the many attacks on his *Studies in the History of the Renaissance*" ("Gentleman, Dandy, Priest: Manliness and Social Authority in Pater's Aestheticism," *ELH* 59.2 (1992): p. 441).

11 Harold Bloom, Introduction, *Selected Writings of Walter Pater,* ed. Bloom (New York: Columbia University Press, 1974), p. xviii.

12 Two major allegorical interpretations of the novel are Guerard's argument that it represents a "journey within" (Albert Guerard, *Conrad the Novelist* (Cambridge: Harvard University Press, 1966), pp. 33–48) and J. Hillis Miller's observation that it is "parabolic in form" (J. Hillis Miller, "*Heart of Darkness Revisited,*" *Conrad Revisited: Essays for the Eighties,* ed. Ross Murfin (University: University of Alabama Press, 1985), pp. 32–50).

13 Patrick Brantlinger blames Jameson for this kind of irresponsibility in his argument that interest in Impressionism as an aesthetic technique would obscure the novel's political orientations: see "*Heart of Darkness*: Anti-Imperialism, Racism, or Impressionism?" *Criticism* 27.5 (1985): pp. 374, 380.

14 See Chinua Achebe, "An Image of Africa," *The Massachusetts Review* 18.4 (Winter 1977): pp. 782–94, and a response to it, Cedric Watts, " 'A Bloody Racist': About Achebe's View of Conrad," *Yearbook of English Studies* (1983): pp. 196–209; see also C. P. Sarvan, "Racism and the *Heart of Darkness,*" *The International Fiction Review* 7 (1980): pp. 6–10, and Edward Said, "Two Visions of *Heart of Darkness*" in *Culture and Imperialism* (New York: Alfred A. Knopf, 1994), pp. 19–31.

15 Joseph Conrad, *Heart of Darkness* (1902), p. 61.

16 For another interpretation of the power in Kurtz's voice see Vincent Pecora, "*Heart of Darkness* and the Phenomenology of Voice" *ELH* 52.4 (1985): pp. 993–1015.

17 Stephen Spender described Woolf's writing in a manner that seems to pick up on the double movement of the "permeating center": Obituary, Listener (April 10, 1941), 533, quoted in *Virginia Woolf: The Critical Heritage,* ed. Robin Majumdar and Allen McLaurin (London: Routledge and Kegan Paul, 1975), p. 428.

18 Virginia Woolf, *The Letters of Virginia Woolf,* ed. Nigel Nicolson and Joanne Trautman. 6 vols (New York: Harcourt Brace Jovanovich, 1978), vol. V, p. 36.

19 See for example Maria DiBattista, *Virginia Woolf's Major Novels: The Fables of Anon* (New Haven: Yale University Press, 1980), p. 43; Makiko Minow-Pinkney, *Virginia Woolf and the Problem of the Subject* (Sussex: Harvester, 1987), p. 180; and especially Avrom Fleischman, *Virginia Woolf: A Critical Reading* (Baltimore: Johns Hopkins University Press, 1975), for its bibliography of such accounts (p. 80).

20 This life–death connection prompts Elaine Showalter to call the "survival tactics" at work here "instructive and chilling" (*A Literature of Their Own: British Women Novelists from Lessing to Brontë* (Princeton University Press, 1977), p. 247).

CONCLUSION

1 Vanessa Bell, "Lecture Given at Leighton Park School" (1925), *Sketches in Pen and Ink*, ed. Lia Giachero (London: Pimlico, 1998), p. 151.

2 I emphasize this difference despite my sense of the crucial overlap between the sisters' arts (influenced mostly by Jane Goldman's recent account in *Feminist Aesthetics of Virginia Woolf: Modernism, Post-Impressionism and the Politics of the Visual* (Cambridge University Press, 1998), pp. 137–65) in order to emphasize the way the impression leads to difference even where we otherwise find affinity.

3 See James Joyce, *Stephen Hero* (New York: New Directions, 1944), p. 188, and D. H. Lawrence, "Education of the People," *Reflections on the Death of a Porcupine*, ed. Michael Herbert, *The Works of D. H. Lawrence* (Cambridge University Press, 1988), vol. XII, p. 156 and "Why the Novel Matters," *Study of Thomas Hardy and Other Essays*, ed. Bruce Steele, *Works* (Cambridge University Press, 1988), vol. XII, pp. 193–95.

4 For an account specifically of the connections between the primitivisms of Gauguin and Conrad see Schwarz's *Reconfiguring Modernism: Explorations in the Relationship between Modern Art and Modern Literature* (New York: Macmillan, 1997), p. 79.

5 Robert Goldwater, *Primitivism in Modern Art* (1938; Cambridge: Harvard University Press, 1986), pp. 252–53.

6 Clement Greenberg, "Modernist Painting," *Clement Greenberg: The Collected Essays and Criticism*, ed. John O'Brian, 4 vols. (The University of Chicago Press, 1993), vol. IV, p. 86.

Index

Abrams, M. H., 18
abstraction, 29, 50–51, 111–13, 145, 220, 226
Achebe, Chinua, 219
Adams, James Eli, 258n.4, 273n.10
Aesthetic, the, 6, 9, 13, 55, 72–73, 90, 94, 98, 134, 243, 247
Aestheticism, 15, 66, 88
allegory, 35, 43–44, 207–10
apophasis, 81–82, 95, 114, 116
Aquinas, Thomas, 19
Ardis, Ann, 271n.34
Aristotle, 141
Armstrong, Nancy, 41–42, 99
Armstrong, Paul, 26, 252n.18, 255n.57, 263n.33
Arnheim, Rudolph, 110–11, 246
Arnold, Matthew, 50, 53, 61, 15

Babbitt, Irving, 16, 83
Barrell, John, 147–48
Bell, Millicent, 106
Bell, Vanessa, 239–40, 245, 246–47, 249
Benjamin, Walter, 207–09
Bennett, Arnold, 42, 50, 174, 194–95, 202–03
Bergson, Henri, 14, 25, 26
Berkeley, George, 59–61
Bersani, Leo, 263n.31
Besant, Walter, 31, 42, 40, 86, 90–91
Blackmur, R. P., 106
Bloom, Harold, 53, 215
Bowen, Elizabeth, 13, 84
Brantlinger, Patrick, 273n.13
Bromwich, David, 47, 55, 63
Broude, Norma, 261n.4
Brown, Calvin, 253n.19
Brunetiére, Ferdinand, 14
Butler, R. J., 22, 25

Cameron, Sharon, 264n.54
Caramagno, Thomas, 270n.14
Carruthers, Mary, 253n.31

Caughie, Pamela, 269n.7
Cézanne, Paul, 245
Chevreul, Michel–Eugéne, 47
Childers, Mary, 204
Cicero, 19
Clark, T. J., 42
Coleridge, S. T., 36–37, 38, 39, 207
collaboration, 9, 33–35
  Conrad, in, 146–50
  Ford, in, 164
  Hardy, in, 126–27
  James, Henry, in, 94–100
  Pater, in, 67–70
  prehistory of, 33–39
  Proust, in, 91, 130–32
  Woolf, in, 176–77, 187–88
Conrad, Joseph, 8, 13, 32, 33, 39, 40, 46–47, 50–51, 136–38, 138–55, 219–27, 242
  works
    Heart of Darkness, 219–27
    The Mirror of the Sea, 142
    The Nigger of the "Narcissus", 139–41, 145–50
    A Personal Record, 146
    The Rescue, 151–52
    Under Western Eyes, 142–43
Cowan, Bernard, 207
Crane, Stephen, 14
Crary, Jonathan, 42

Daudet, Alphonse, 87–90, 102–4
Daugherty, Beth Rigel, 202
de Man, Paul, 44, 207–08
Deleuze, Gilles, 250n.3
Dellamora, Richard, 71, 258n.4
Derrida, Jacques, 27–28
Diepeveen, Leonard, 51
Donoghue, Denis, 71
Dowling, Linda, 68, 71

Eagleton, Terry, 134

Eliot, George, 101–05
Ellmann, Richard, 87, 251n.6
Empiricism, 16, 20–25, 57, 62–64, 79–81, 85
energeia, 141
Engell, James, 255n.60
Epicureanism, 63
Everson, Stephen, 25

Fabianism, 163–64
Felski, Rita, 255n.58, 261n.8
Feminism, Standpoint, 81–85, 176, 200–01
feudalism, 164–69, 242
Fichte, Johann Gottlieb, 37
Fletcher, Angus, 43–44
Ford, Ford Madox, 14, 32, 33, 155–73, 219, 242
  works
    "English Literature of Today," 158–59
    The Good Soldier, 169–73
    Ladies Whose Bright Eyes, 164–69
    "On the Function of the Arts in the Republic," 155–58
    "On Impressionism," 161–64
Fowler, Alastair, 49
Frede, Michael, 253n.29
Freedman, Jonathan, 93
Fried, Michael, 14
Frierson, Norman, 83
Fry, Roger, 47–48
Fuss, Diana, 199

Garland, Hamlin, 13
Gass, William, 15, 16, 161–62
Gaugin, Paul, 246
George, W. L., 83
Gimore, Michael, 264n.46
Goethe, Johann Wolfgang von, 37–38, 58, 60
Goldman, Jane, 271n.35, 274n.2
Gombrich, E. H., 51
Goncourt, Edmond and Jules de, 46
Green, Robert, 267n.41
Greenberg, Clement, 49, 248
Guerard, Albert, 140, 150–51

Habegger, Alfred, 262n.17
Hagstrum, Jean, 52
Harding, Sandra, 200–01
Hardy, Thomas, 13, 120–29, 242
  works
    Jude the Obscure, 122
    Tess of the D'Urbervilles, 123–29
Hartley, David, 35–36
Hartman, Geoffrey, 33
Hay, Eloise Knapp, 252n.17, 266n.9
Hazlitt, William, 24, 37, 55, 57

Hegel, G. W. F., 30, 41
Heidegger, Martin, 175
Hocks, Richard, 262n.24
homosexuality, 53–55, 68–78, 215–16, 234–35
Howarth, Herbert, 252n.10
Hulme, T. E., 13, 48–49
Hume, David., 20–25, 35, 62–64, 162, 241
Husserl, Edmund, 14, 25, 26, 27–28, 175, 185
Hussey, Mark, 269n.2
Hynes, Samuel, 202

Idealism, 57, 174, 214
Imperialism, 219–20
impressions, 1–2, 6, 9, 15–17, 23–25, 49–51, 244–49
  Conrad, in, 32, 140, 143
  Ford, in, 161–62
  Hardy, in, 122
  Hume, in, 20–25
  James, Henry, in, 31, 91–92, 103–05, 113, 117–20
  Pater, in, 30–31, 56, 61–64
  Proust, in, 32, 4–6, 130–31
  Woolf, in, 32–33, 175, 197–99
impressionability, 54, 67, 86, 92, 114, 216
Impressionism, in painting, 45–52, 194–95, 244–49
Inman, Billie Andrew, 55
Iser, Wolfgang, 56

James, Henry, 10, 13, 14, 27, 31, 33–34, 42, 46–47, 49–50, 82, 85–120, 133, 176, 241–42
  works
    The Ambassadors, 114–15
    "The Art of Fiction," 90–92, 94–96
    "The Life of George Eliot," 100–05
    "A New England Winter," 93–94
    Notes of a Son and Brother, 117–20
    The Portrait of a Lady, 105–09
    What Maisie Knew, 96–98, 109–14
Jameson, Fredric, 13, 41, 136–37, 149–50
Johnson, Bruce, 150, 266n.15, 269n.2
Joyce, James, 177, 243–44

Kant, Immanuel, 29, 62
Koestenbaum, Wayne, 260n.25
Kristeva, Julia, 199, 250n.3
Kronegger, Maria Elisabeth, 13, 26, 252n.18

Lang, Andrew, 127–28
Langer, Susanne, 257n.93
Law, Jules David, 18–19
Lawrence, D. H., 243–44
Lee, Vernon, 13, 272n.46

Leroy, Louis, 12, 17
Lessing, Gotthold Ephraim, 52, 248
Levenson, Michael, 13, 83, 141, 157, 253n.25, 267n.35, 267n.37
Lewes, George Henry, 56, 100–05
Lewis, Wyndham, 174
Lloyd, Genevieve, 255n.58
Locke, John, 20, 22, 79–81, 253n.32
London, Bette, 269n.7
Longino, Helen, 82

Mallarmé, Stéphane, 46
Marcus, Jane, 199
Marxism, 41, 133–37, 149–50
materialism, 174–75, 192, 205, 214
May, Brian, 267n.40
McCarthy, Desmond, 195
McGrath, F. C., 64
mediation, 1, 17, 30–33, 243
Meisel, Perry, 67, 259n.19
Menand, Louis, 42
Merleau–Ponty, Maurice, 27, 175
Miller, J. Hillis, 273n.12
Minow–Pinkney, Makiko, 199
Mitchell, W. J. T., 246, 257n.91
Modernism, 11, 36, 40, 64–65, 66, 139, 140–41, 150, 155, 173, 178, 180, 197, 227
Monet, Claude, 12
Moore, G. E., 175
Morris, Mowbray, 123–25

Nagel, James, 251n.8
Nicholls, Peter, 270n.16
Nordau, Max, 45–46
Nussbaum, Martha, 250n.3, 253n.29

paiderastia, 68–69, 74, 141, 211
Pater, Walter, 6–7, 13, 30–31, 33, 47–48, 49–50, 53–78, 86, 210–19, 241
  works
    "Apollo in Picardy," 74–77
    "Diaphaneitè," 68–71
    "The History of Philosophy," 57–61
    Marius the Epicurean, 65, 73–74, 210–19
    The Renaissance, 61–63, 64, 65, 66–67, 73–74
    "Style," 64, 65
Pecora, Vincent, 273n.16
Phenomenology, 18, 25–29, 175–76, 179, 185–86, 197, 232
pictorialism, 4, 46
Plato, 19
Poe, Edgar Allan, 38–39
Posnock, Ross, 262n.24
Post–Impressionism, 12, 48, 194–95

Potolsky, Matthew, 260n.36, 272n.8
Pound, Ezra, 14, 247
primitivism, 40–41, 133–36, 148, 246–47
Proust, Marcel, 2–11, 32, 33, 130–38, 173
psychology, empirical, 28–29

Rewald, John, 251n.1
Richardson, Dorothy, 83
Ritchie, Anne Thackeray, 83, 95–96, 98
Rogers, John, 250n.1
Romanticism, 16, 36–41, 55–56
Rorty, Richard, 254n.39
Rosenbaum, S. P., 269n.2
Rowe, John Carlos, 13, 105
Ruskin, John, 37–38
Ryan, Judith, 28–29, 269n.2

Sand, George, 263n.40
Sartre, Jean–Paul, 27, 185
Saunders, Max, 268n.53
Scarry, Elaine, 143–44
Schapiro, Meyer, 16, 250n.1
Schelling, Friedrich, 37
Schiller, J. C. F. von, 29, 37–38
Schlegel, August and Friedrich von, 29–30
Schuetz, Lawrence, 260n.36
Schwartz, Daniel, 274n.4
Scott, David, 47
Scott, Bonnie Kime, 271n.34
Seurat, George, 245
Shadwell, Charles, 68
Shelley, P. B., 37
Shelley, Mary, 38
Showalter, Elaine, 274n.20
Sinclair, May, 13, 84
Skepticism, 19, 58, 88, 214
Small, Ian, 260n.36
Smith, Norman Kemp, 22, 23
somatophobia, 138–39, 217
Spagnoli, John, 265n.3
Spelman, Elizabeth, 255n.58
Spencer, Herbert, 55–56
Spender, Stephen, 273n.17
Spilka, Mark, 263n.32
Steiner, Wendy, 49
Sterne, Lawrence, 79–81
Stevenson, R. L. S., 86–87, 115
Stewart, Jack, 256n.83
Stoicism, 19, 217
Stowell, H. Peter, 13, 26, 252n.18
Symbolism, 37, 40, 208

Tanner, Tony, 121
Tolstoy, Leo, 158–59
Torgovnick, Marianne, 148

Tratner, Michael, 268n.43, 270n.17
Trilling, Lionel, 141
Tuveson, Ernest, 80

Vaihinger, Hans, 143
van Gunsteren, Julia, 251n.8
Veeder, William, 262n.17

Wallen, Jeffrey, 260n.31
Ward, Anthony, 55
Watt, Ian, 13, 20, 50, 144–45, 208
Wells, H. G., 83, 115
Whistler, James A. McNeill, 48
Wilde, Oscar, 13, 16, 53, 68, 77
Williams, Raymond, 156, 160
Wollaeger, Mark, 146
Wollstonecraft, Mary, 2, 38
Woolf, Virginia, 8, 10, 13, 32–33, 33–34, 42,
    46–47, 49–50, 174–206, 227–38,
    239–40, 243, 246– 47, 249
  works

"Character in Fiction," 196–99,
    204–05
"The Death of the Moth," 187–89
Jacob's Room, 193
"The Mark on the Wall," 182–7
"Middlebrow," 203–04
"Modern Novels," 177–78, 193
"Mr. Bennett and Mrs. Brown," 195–6,
    204–05
Mrs. Dalloway, 179–80, 227–38
A Room of One's Own, 201, 227–28
"An Unwritten Novel," 189–93
The Waves, 179, 201
Wordsworth, William, 37–38, 40
Worringer, Wilhelm, 145, 154, 220

Yates, Frances, 19

Zabel, Morton, 121
Zietlow, Paul, 259n.23
Zola, Émile, 47